The Challenge of Severe Mental Handicap

THE WILEY SERIES IN CLINICAL PSYCHOLOGY

Series Editors

Fraser N. Watts
MRC Applied Psychology Unit
Cambridge

J. Mark G. Williams
Department of Psychology
University College of North Wales,
Bangor

Severe Learning Disability
and Psychological Handicap
John Clements

Cognitive Psychology
and Emotional Disorders
*J. Mark, G. Williams, Fraser N. Watts,
Colin MacLeod and Andrew Mathews*

Community Care in Practice
Services for the Continuing Care Client
Edited by Anthony Lavender and Frank Holloway

Attribution Theory in
Clinical Psychology
Friedrich Försterling

Panic Disorder:
Theory, Research and Therapy
Edited by Roger Baker

Measuring Human Problems
A Practical Guide
Edited by David Peck and C.M. Shapiro

Clinical Psychology for the Child
Development, Social Learning and Behaviour
Martin Herbert

The Psychological Treatment of Insomnia
Colin A. Espie

The Challenge of Severe Mental Handicap
A Behaviour Analytic Approach
Edited by Bob Remington

Further titles in preparation

The Challenge of Severe Mental Handicap

A Behaviour Analytic Approach

Edited by

BOB REMINGTON

Reader in Psychology, Department of Psychology,
University of Southampton, UK

JOHN WILEY & SONS

Chichester · New York · Brisbane · Toronto · Singapore

Other Wiley Editorial Offices

John Wiley & Sons, Inc., 605 Third Avenue,
New York, NY 10158-0012, USA

Jacaranda Wiley Ltd, G.P.O. Box 859, Brisbane,
Queensland 4001, Australia

John Wiley & Sons (Canada) Ltd, 22 Worcester Road,
Rexdale, Ontario M9W 1L1, Canada

John Wiley & Sons (SEA) Pte Ltd, 37 Jalan Pemimpin #05-04,
Block B, Union Industrial Building, Singapore 2057

Library of Congress Cataloging-in-Publication Data:
The challenge of severe mental handicap : a behaviour analytic
    approach / edited by Bob Remington.
        p. cm. — (The Wiley series in clinical psychology)
    Includes bibliographical references.
    Includes index.
    ISBN 0-471-92503-9 (ppc.)
    1. Mentally handicapped—Rehabilitation.   2. Behavior therapy
    I. Remington, Bob.   II. Series.
        [DNLM: 1. Behavior Therapy.   2. Mental Retardation—therapy. WM
300 C437]
    RC520.2C49   199
    616.85'88—dc20
    DNLM/DLC
    for Library of Congress   90–13162
                                                                                      CIP

British Library Cataloguing in Publication Data
The Challenge of severe mental handicap
    1. Mentally handicapped persons
    I. Remington, Bob
    616.891420874

    ISBN 0-471-92503-9

Typeset in 10/12 Palatino by Photo·graphics, Honiton, Devon
Printed and bound in Great Britain by Biddles Ltd, Guildford, Surrey

Dedicated to the memory of B.F. Skinner (1904–1990), whose thinking and writing contributed so much to the development of the work described here.

Contents

List of Contributors

ALASTAIR AGER

Senior Lecturer in Psychology, Department of Psychology, PO Box 280, University of Malawi, Zomba, Malawi

WENDY K. BERG

Division of Developmental Disabilities, Department of Pediatrics, University Hospital School, University of Iowa, Iowa City, Iowa 52242, USA

DANIEL CRIMMINS

Mental Retardation Institute, Valhalla, New York, USA

RITA CURL

Department of Special Education, Utah State University, Utah, USA

ADRIA DIBENEDETTO

Department of Psychology, State University of New York at Binghamton, Binghamton, New York 13901, USA

PIETER C. DUKER

Process Research Group, Instituut voor Orthopedagogiek, University of Nijmegen, Erasmusplein 1, Postbus 9103, Nijmegen 6500 HD, The Netherlands

V. MARK DURAND

Department of Psychology, State University of New York at Albany, 1400 Washington Avenue, Albany, New York 12222, USA

IAN M. EVANS

Department of Psychology, State University of New York at Binghamton, Binghamton, New York 13901, USA

DAVID FELCE

Mental Handicap in Wales, Applied Research Unit, 55 Park Place, Cardiff CF1 3AT, UK

The late ROBERT   Department of Special Education, Peabody
GAYLORD-ROSS   College, Vanderbilt University, Nashville,
                         Tennessee 37240, USA

JULIE GOODMAN   Department of Psychology, University of
                         Southampton, Highfield, Southampton
                         SO9 5NH, UK

ROBERT S.P. JONES   Department of Psychology, University College
                         of North Wales, Bangor, Gwynedd LL37 2DG,
                         UK

KATHRYN G. KARSH   Educational Research and Services Center
                         Inc., 425 East Fisk Avenue, DeKalb, Illinois
                         60115, USA

CHRIS KIERNAN   Hester Adrian Research Centre, Manchester
                         University, Oxford Road, Manchester
                         M13 9PL, UK

HARRY A. MACKAY   Behavior Analysis Department, Eunice
                         Kennedy Shriver Center, 200 Trapelo Road,
                         Waltham, Massachusetts 02115, USA

LUANNA H. MEYER   Department of Psychology, Syracuse
                         University, Syracuse, New York, USA

CHRIS OLIVER   Research Psychologist, Department of
                         Psychology, Institute of Psychiatry, De
                         Crespigny Park, Denmark Hill, London
                         SE5 8AF.

JOE REICHLE   Department of Communication Disorders,
                         University of Minnesota, 115 Shevlin Hall,
                         164 Pillsbury Drive S.E., Minneapolis,
                         Minnesota 55455, USA

BOB REMINGTON   Department of Psychology, University of
                         Southampton, Highfield, Southampton
                         SO9 5NH, UK

ALAN C. REPP   Educational Research and Services Center
                         Inc., 425 East Fisk Avenue, DeKalb, Illinois
                         60115, USA

CHUCK SALZBERG   Department of Special Education, Utah State
                         University, Utah, USA

JOSEPH R. SCOTTI   Department of Psychology, West Virginia
                          University, Morgantown, WV 26506-6040,
                          USA

JEFF SIGAFOOS   Fred and Eleanor Schonell Special Education
                          Research Centre, University of Queensland,
                          Queensland, Australia

KEITH STOREY   Allegheny Singer Research Institute, 320 East
                          North Avenue, Pittsburg, Pennsylvania 15212-
                          9986, USA

DAVID P. WACKER   Division of Developmental Disabilities,
                          Department of Pediatrics, University Hospital
                          School, University of Iowa, Iowa City, Iowa
                          52242, USA

Series Preface

The Wiley Series in Clinical Psychology seeks to include books covering the major client groups with which clinical psychology is concerned. Severe mental handicap is undoubtedly one of these. Moreover, there is probably no other field of clinical work which has been so radically changed by the developing contributions of clinical psychologists over the last 25 years. John Clement's book on *Severe Learning Disability and Psychological Handicap*, the first book to be published in the series, provided a psychologically-grounded overview of work with severe mental handicap. The present book, edited by Bob Remington, has a more specific focus on the contribution of Behaviour Analysis.

Terminology represents a particular problem in this area of psychology. There has been a proper reluctance to use terms that refer to the people concerned in a way that may sound pejorative. However, this has led historically to repeated changes in terminology, with each new term initially appearing less pejorative than the one it replaced. The result is that it has become very difficult to choose a term that will be regarded as acceptable in its connotations and which will also be generally understood. After careful consideration, 'severe mental handicap' has been selected for the title of this book.

Though behavioural methods of intervention have undoubtedly made a major contribution in the field of mental handicap, one of the problems, as Bob Remington points out in his introductory chapter, is that the interventions used have tended to become divorced from the methodological principles from which they were originally derived. One of the unfortunate consequences of this is that reinforcement-based interventions are frequently introduced without an adequate analysis of the reinforcement contingencies already operating in the environment. This book represents, in part, an appeal for the reintegration of basic principles of functional analysis with practical behavioural interventions. This is the central theme of the first section of the book. The book then turns to a specific problem of many people with severe learning disabilities—that of communication—and presents the contribution of the behavioural approach to ways in which people with learning difficulties can supplement the normal modes of verbal communication. The final section of the book deals with the increasingly important problem of service delivery. Too often clinical psychology has found itself with powerful interventions which are not delivered with the reliability and comprehensiveness that they deserve. Increasingly, professional psychologists have had to grapple with issues of service delivery to overcome this problem.

There is much in this book that will be of interest to all those concerned with the application of methods of experimental analysis of behaviour to practical problems. The book will also appeal to the range of professions engaged in services for people with severe mental handicap. My hope is that it will strengthen the movement towards a style of behavioural intervention with these clients that has a stronger theoretical grounding, takes more notice of the actual circumstances and characteristics of the people concerned, and, hence, will be of greater practical effectiveness.

FRASER WATTS
Series Editor

Preface

It is more than twenty years since clinical psychologists working in the field of learning disability began to use the principles and methods of operant psychology. In a field that previously had been dominated by pessimism about the capabilities of people with severe mental handicap and thus about the possibilities of change, the new approach offered the dazzling prospect of effective intervention to facilitate development and growth. Behaviour analysts emphasized the central importance of learning. People with even the most profound mental handicap could acquire new skills and, if environmental contingencies could be structured carefully enough, self-limiting ways of behaving could be reduced or removed. In the last two decades, the clinical utility of this way of thinking has been strongly supported by research, and behaviourally based approaches have come to dominate the field.

The primary aim of the book is to present current research activity based on a behaviour analytic approach to the remediation of severe and profound mental handicap, and to do this in such a way as to keep practitioners abreast of current advances. It might be thought that, because the basic methods of behavioural intervention are now so well known, widely used and successful, they hardly need to be reiterated. This view, however, fails to acknowledge the major changes that have taken place in the field in recent years. Two kinds of developments have occurred. First, pure research in behaviour analysis has gradually expanded both theoretically and methodologically, and many of the ideas that have evolved are now being incorporated in applied research with people with mental handicap. These new concepts and ways of working, which take behavioural intervention far beyond the simple application of operant consequences, are strongly reflected in the contributions that follow. Secondly, there has been a growing realization that some of the more important original insights that flowed from a systematic behaviour analytic perspective have been relatively underplayed in clinical application. One such principle, central in the writing of B.F. Skinner, has been seminal in the work of many of the contributors. This is the simple but profoundly important idea of analysing the functions of current behaviour, including verbal behaviour, prior to any attempt at intervention. Despite its significance, functional analysis has been a neglected aspect of clinical work with people with severe mental handicap. The contributors to the present volume describe why such an approach is important, show how it can be achieved, and explain why it is critical to the success of behavioural interventions.

As this book was going to press, it was reported that B.F. Skinner had died, aged 86, shortly after receiving the American Psychological Association's Presidential Citation for Lifetime Contributions to Psychology. I have chosen to dedicate this book to his memory to mark the fact that, although he never worked in the field of mental handicap, his writing has contributed so greatly to its development. As he commented in one of the last articles he wrote,[1] 'If architecture is frozen music, then books are frozen verbal behavior. Writing leaves durable marks, and as readers we respond to durable stimuli.' Most of the contributions to this text are, in part at least, responses occasioned by the durable stimuli that B.F. Skinner's work created. I would like to acknowledge my debt.

I must also record the fact that Robert Gaylord-Ross, one of the most notable contributors to this volume, died suddenly in December 1990. He will be remembered warmly not only by his family, friends, and colleagues, but also by many people whom he never met—those whose work he developed through his own research and writing.

I would like to express my gratitude for the assistance that many friends, students, and colleagues have provided during the preparation of this book. Among the people that have helped and advised me, I should like particularly to mention Sue Clarke, Nina Dick, Jon Evans, Kate Foote, Tony Gale, Julie Goodman, Martin Hall, Richard Hastings, Jim Hewitt, Peter Hopkinson, Marina Remington, and John Williams.

Finally, I would like to thank Marina (again), Becky, Tom, and Lewis Remington for their support and encouragement during the time that it took to produce this book. Now I will mend the shed roof.

Bob Remington
Southampton
April 1991

---

[1] Skinner, B.F. (1989) The behavior of the listener. In S.C. Hayes (ed.), *Rule Governed Behavior: Cognition, Contingencies and Instructional Control*, Plenum Press, New York.

Chapter 1

Behaviour Analysis and Severe Mental Handicap: The Dialogue Between Research and Application

BOB REMINGTON

INTRODUCTION

As an undergraduate, in 1969, I happened across a paper by Paul R. Fuller (1949) gruesomely entitled, 'Operant conditioning of a vegetative human organism' (sic). Fuller showed that the behaviour of a young man with both physical and profound mental handicap could be shaped by operant conditioning: the behaviour in question was differentiated arm movement; the reinforcer, milk delivered directly into the man's mouth through a syringe. Fuller's study both appalled and fascinated me. Its technical precision seemed so heartless, the behaviour change achieved so pointless. And yet the man's behaviour *did* change when a reinforcement contingency was arranged, and there was the promise that 'other responses could (have been) conditioned and discriminations learned' (p. 339). If so, and if intervention had begun much earlier in his life, perhaps Fuller's 'subject' might have developed differently. Perhaps, then, the careful extrapolation of principles of reinforcement really did offer the best hope for remediation of profound or severe mental handicap. Laboratory research on operant conditioning, however distanced it was from real problems, could eventually pay applied dividends.

Reading Fuller's report did not prepare me for my first real encounter, in 1972, with a ward full of children who were non-ambulant and had profound mental handicap. That was shocking too, but for a different reason: no one was doing anything much about it. By then I had begun to read the *Journal of Applied Behavior Analysis* (*JABA*), and knew there was much that could have been done. The need for careful research, inculcated by the previous three years spent working on a PhD in operant

The Challenge of Severe Mental Handicap. Edited by Bob Remington
© 1991 John Wiley & Sons Ltd

conditioning (and reading the *Journal of the Experimental Analysis of Behavior*), seemed much less compelling than the need to act immediately, use what I already knew, do something *now*.

I recount this small piece of personal history because it was my first experience with a conflict between research and application that touches anyone who adopts a broadly behavioural approach in working with people with severe or profound mental handicap. My aim in this chapter is to highlight that conflict. First, I want to discuss the distinctive contribution of applied behaviour analysis (ABA) in this domain. I will briefly review the key dimensions of ABA, and show why the approach offers such promise as a way of producing immediate practical benefits for people with learning difficulties.

In so doing, however, I will stress the importance of maintaining an often-neglected link between the technology of intervention identified with 'behavioural' psychology (sometimes called 'behaviour modification') and the systematic analysis of behaviour from which it developed. My argument will be that behavioural intervention for people with mental handicap has been the poorer, both conceptually *and* practically, to the extent that it has ignored theoretical and empirical developments that have occurred in the experimental analysis of behaviour (EAB) over the last twenty years. In making this argument, I will try to show that, in practice, ABA has too often disregarded some of its own fundamental principles, and I will review some recent research in EAB which has major implications for ABA.

This brings me to my second aim, which is to introduce the other contributions to this volume. The authors are all active researchers, working to reduce the suffering, and enhance the functioning, of people with mental handicaps. But they are also among those who have retained a systematic behaviour analytic perspective and, by so doing, they have actively contributed to the development of the field. In the final part of this chapter I will briefly outline the organization of the book as it relates to the issues raised earlier.

BEHAVIOUR ANALYSIS AND SEVERE MENTAL HANDICAP

Skinner and the experimental analysis of behaviour

Although B.F. Skinner never worked directly in the field of mental handicap, it is difficult to overestimate his contribution to it. Skinner's experimental analysis of behaviour, and the radical behaviourist philosophy on which it was predicated, has had a pervasive effect. The central focus of Skinner's psychology is function. Thus, he defined an operant class in terms of the common environmental effect of the actions which comprise it, and not in terms of their physical topography. Further, operant behaviour is not elicited by antecedent stimuli; rather it is shaped and maintained by its consequences. The antecedent stimuli in Skinner's three-term contingency (antecedent: behaviour: consequence, or A: B: C) acquire functional control of behaviour by virtue of their presence when behaviour is reinforced.

As has frequently been pointed out (e.g., Schick, 1971), the elements in operant three-term contingencies cannot be defined independently of each other. For this reason, A: B: C analysis is primarily a descriptive tool that can be used to make tentative hypotheses about behaviour–environment interactions. For example, if self-injurious behaviour (SIB) is observed to occur frequently in a particular location and is sometimes followed by attention from a particular caregiver, one might hypothesize the location is a discriminative stimulus, and SIB an operant maintained by attention as an intermittent reinforcer. Testing the truth of such a functional analysis involves changing the contingencies and looking for correlated behavioural changes. This approach to behaviour makes for a particular kind of understanding based on demonstrable control. The proof of the interpretation is in the intervention (Hayes, Hayes and Reese, 1988).

Where intervention is not possible, a Skinnerian account of behaviour remains contextually oriented, but becomes interpretive. For example, the current behaviour of an 'aggressive' resident might be interpreted in terms of his or her history of interactions with caregivers in chronically understaffed facilities where violent behaviour was most likely to produce results. Skinner's environmentalism was evident in the importance he placed on history of reinforcement, but this did not—as some have argued—blind him to the role of genetic causation (Skinner, 1969). Rather, his focus on the present context of behaviour is simple pragmatism; the only *manipulable* causes of behaviour are those of the present (and the future). Thus, in his work on teaching, Skinner (e.g., 1968) outlined ways in which tasks could be structured so as gradually to develop competent performance. In contrast, much (but not all) of his work on reinforcement schedules showed how particular patterns of performance could be stably maintained by unchanging environmental contingencies.

One final feature of Skinner's psychology made it ripe for application to human problems. At a time when most learning theorists' attention focused on non-human animals, Skinner maintained a stubborn interest in people. Much of his writing concerned human action (e.g., Skinner, 1948, 1953, 1957), and promoted the idea that by analysing current contingencies of reinforcement and/or supplementing or modifying them it was possible to produce rapid and dramatic changes in behaviour. These claims quickly attracted empirical support. For example, in the field of mental handicap, Wolf *et al.* (1965) showed that a 9-year-old girl's classroom vomiting declined dramatically when it was no longer followed by removal from a classroom situation, thus suggesting the behaviour had been maintained by negative reinforcement through escape from task demands. In a contemporaneous study, Kerr, Meyerson and Michael (1965) showed that a shaping procedure based on the addition of a social reinforcement contingency was effective in teaching a mute 3-year-old girl to vocalize. By 1968, sufficient studies involving problems of social importance testified to the efficacy of operant analysis to merit the separate publication of a new journal (*JABA*).

Applied behaviour analysis: Strengths

In a seminal article, Baer, Wolf and Risley (1968) established seven key dimensions for the new field of ABA. I will briefly review these, using examples drawn from the field of mental handicap. First, ABA is *applied* in the sense of focusing on behaviours that are 'immediately important'. Thus, studies concerned with teaching work skills, or reducing SIB, would qualify; those concerned with reaction time or short-term memory would not. Next, Baer *et al.* stressed a *behavioural* focus: a study aimed at reducing hand stereotypies would involve a measurable change in behaviour; one increasing social competence would not (unless operational definitions of competent behaviours could be provided). The third dimension of ABA relates strongly to the second. Studies should be *technological*, in the sense of accurately describing the procedures that were used. A study reducing stereotypies using differential reinforcement of incompatible behaviour (DRI) would be suitably technological if the specifications of behavioural measurement and reinforcement schedule were sufficiently precise to facilitate replication.

A fourth dimension of ABA ensures that research is *analytic*, in the sense of showing that any claims of successful intervention are demonstrably valid. For example, in a study designed to increase the frequency of functional communication using manual signs, it would be necessary to show that improvements result from the methods used, rather than uncontrolled factors. In short, studies should have internal validity. Next, Baer *et al.* stressed the importance of *effectiveness* and *generality* in studies of ABA. These two dimensions relate to the outcome of interventions, the former highlighting the importance of clinical significance; the latter that the changes achieved should be long lasting and wide ranging. To continue the signing example, the intervention should result in clinically (rather than statistically) significant changes in functional communication skills, which should be maintained beyond the end of the study, and used in contexts remote from those in which they were initially acquired. Finally, research in ABA is based on the principles of behaviour analysis, the *conceptual system* pioneered by Skinner and his followers. For example, manual signing is a form of 'verbal behaviour' (Skinner, 1957), and intervention programmes should consider the function of signing behaviour as a central issue.

Baer *et al.*'s dimensions are more than a set of descriptors; they have also had a strongly prescriptive function in guiding the development of ABA for more than two decades. Mental handicap has been one of the foremost beneficiaries of the approach to research that they advocated, and the impact of behavioural methods on the field would have been almost unimaginable twenty years ago. The contributions in this volume all testify to that, as do many other texts originating on both sides of the Atlantic (e.g., Matson and McCartney, 1981; Yule and Carr, 1987). A glance through any issue of *JABA*, or any of several other international journals, is sufficient to convey the continuing impact of applied behaviour analytic research, both in terms of producing effective behavioural change and habilitation, and in enhancing our understanding of developmental disabilities.

Applied behaviour analysis: Potential weaknesses

Rather than review the many successes of the field, however, I want to play devil's advocate by proposing that, in some ways, progress has been disappointing. My argument will be that many behaviourally oriented researchers and practitioners in mental handicap have set more store by some of the dimensions of ABA than others, and thus distorted the development of the field in ways which have only recently been recognized. Further, this emphasis has been such that ideas that were available to Skinnerian behaviour analysts a generation ago are only now finding their way firmly into research and practice (indeed the contributors in this volume are among those who have been instrumental in bringing about that change). In the following section, I will review some of the ways in which behaviour analysis has moved on in recent years, and sketch the significance of some of the developments for the field of severe mental handicap.

The hospital scenario I outlined at the start of this chapter will be familiar to most who have worked with people with severe developmental disabilities. The behavioural deficits and excesses shown by such people are undoubtedly *applied* problems of immediate importance. Chronic passivity is demeaning and undignified; self-injury may also be life threatening. These behaviours are a legitimate focus for intervention based on ABA—which, ideally, should be *effective*. Further, such effectiveness is best demonstrated by *analytic* procedures, based on single-case experimental design methodology of the kind proposed by Baer, Wolf and Risley (1968). For example, both the ABAB and multiple baseline designs analytically demonstrate the effectiveness of an intervention (i.e., the independent variable: IV) by repeated application. In the case of ABAB designs, the IV is successively presented and removed, and the effect on a single response (dependent variable: DV) noted; with a multiple baseline design, the intervention is successively introduced to a number of different DVs. In either case, close temporal correlation between changes in the IV and DV(s) is the guarantee of internal validity.

In general, however, I would argue that the approach occasioned by this set of essentially reasonable guidelines has led to the relative neglect of another kind of analysis. As mentioned earlier, the essence of behavioural analysis is the use of careful observation to generate hypotheses about functional relationships between behaviour and its environmental context. But an intervention whose effectiveness can be substantiated by single case research methodology involves little more than recording the frequency of behaviour before, during, and after successive interventions. Early, and convincing, demonstrations of the impact of operant contingencies (e.g., Ayllon and Azrin, 1968; Lovaas, Schaeffer and Simmons, 1965) encouraged a trend towards this kind of intervention and away from functional analysis. To ensure effectiveness is achieved, the intervention should be as salient as possible, and powerful operant contingencies are more likely than not to prove effective. Indeed, the very power of the added contingencies may well overwhelm those previously responsible for the maintenance of target behaviours.

There are, however, several problems with an intervention philosophy leaning towards exploiting the raw power of motivational stimuli. First, as the 'aversives' debate has shown so clearly (see Kiernan, this volume), powerful reinforcers have a potential for abuse. Secondly, the changes repeatedly reported by published studies may show little more than that the law of effect has not yet been repealed—how many times do we need to discover that some consequences can be effective reinforcers or punishers? Moreover, because studies where behavioural change is not achieved are rarely published, the research literature is a relatively poor guide to the effectiveness of 'bolt-on' contingencies, as clinicians know from experience. Third, even successful interventions leave questions regarding the variables previously controlling target behaviours un-answered. This involves more than intellectual dissatisfaction with lack of complete understanding; the unexamined variables may reassert control, resulting in a failure to produce generalized and lasting behavioural change.

It is difficult to argue with Baer *et al.*'s insistence that work in ABA should be *behavioural*. There is scope, however, for considering how fully this has been achieved. Given the *technological* emphasis of the approach, a great deal of effort has been expended in achieving reliable recording of behaviour, and the first step in such a process is to write tight operational definitions. Thus, SIB might be defined in terms of hitting with open or closed hand, biting, scratching, and so on; social engagement as being within 1 metre of another person, smiling, eye contact and so forth. The problem arises because this inevitable focus on behavioural topography (or form) risks losing sight of the central Skinnerian concept of the operant as a *functional* unit of behaviour. If an operant class is united by a common function in terms of controlling a particular outcome, it follows that topographically unrelated behaviours may be members of the same class. For example, the behaviours of signing 'ketchup', pointing to the ketchup, and head banging on the meal table could conceivably be instances of the same verbal operant class under the functional control of ketchup as a reinforcer. The failure fully to integrate the basic operant concept into much applied research and practice has meant that concepts of functional equivalence have been relatively slow to emerge in the ABA literature (e.g., Carr, 1988). As several contributions to this volume show, however, the implications of this view are critical to the development of behavioural intervention based on functional analysis.

Viewing operants as functional units raises a number of other applied questions only rarely addressed by practice and research in ABA. Although clinical intervention may focus on particular specified behaviours (e.g., aggression, engagement in a computer-assisted learning task), such activities form only part of the behavioural repertoire of the person concerned. By 1968, when Baer *et al.*'s guidelines were proposed, it was well known that changes in the reinforcement of one specified response could produce correlated changes in other behaviours that could be performed either contemporaneously (Herrnstein, 1961), or soon afterwards (Reynolds, 1961), even though the reinforcement contingencies for these other behaviours remained constant. Despite occasional calls for the applied implications of these behavioural contrast and matching effects to be considered (e.g., Gross and Drabman, 1981; Myerson and Hale, 1984), multiple response measurement in assessing the impact of intervention is, in clinical practice, the exception rather than the rule.

Contrast and matching effects are more than theoretical curiosities. Although applied research is sparse, there is evidence for their clinical reality in mental handicap research (e.g., Carr and McDowell, 1980; Kelly and Drabman, 1977), and their existence has potentially major implications for creating interventions that are *effective* and *generalizable*. For example, the matching law (Herrnstein, 1961) implies that the impact of a particular reinforcement contingency will depend critically on the opportunities for reinforcement of other behaviours that are concurrently available. Thus, exactly the same reinforcement procedure may either be completely effective, or completely ineffective, depending on factors apparently unrelated to the target behaviour. Similarly, behavioural contrast research has shown that increasing the frequency of behaviour in one situation can result in 'compensatory' decreases in the same behaviour in temporally adjacent but different situations. An implication is that reinforcement-produced increases in classroom interaction might not generalize to the playground, instead inducing decreases in target behaviour in that setting.

All the above criticisms bear on one neglected dimension of ABA—the *conceptual system* within which it evolved. The distinctive glitter of a Skinnerian conceptual analysis has gradually been obscured by a patina of technologically-based interventions. There are several possible reasons for the trend. First, theory and research in behaviour analysis is, in many ways, subtle and complex, and therefore discouraging to hard-pressed practitioners. Basic concepts of reinforcement and punishment are, however, straightforward and, at the level of 'carrot and stick', simple to pass on (or 'give away'). There are urgent demands for proper care and habilitation for people with mental handicap, and, perhaps paradoxically, behavioural principles suggest that these might best be met by training direct care staff who are in minute-by-minute contact with them, and thus able to control important contingencies of reinforcement. But however good training packages are (e.g., McBrien and Foxen, 1981), they can do little more than introduce the most basic—and powerful—techniques of behavioural intervention. Apart from the dangers of misuse that might arise from such teaching, it can create circumstances where behavioural methods are seen as little more than the manipulation of incentives. A further reason for the 'technological drift' of ABA (Hayes, Rincover and Solnick, 1980) is that its analytic methods are powerful partly because they are essentially self-adjusting. The monitoring and evaluation processes used in single-case research designs ensure that successful outcomes can be maintained, and failures corrected.

Together, these factors have acted to produce a powerful but unimaginative behavioural technology. Thus, there has been no shortage of research reporting the success of particular interventions, but there is a shortage of more analytical work aimed at developing behaviour analysis in applied contexts. The field has expanded quickly but progressed only slowly.

THE CONTINUING NEED FOR ANALYSIS IN APPLIED BEHAVIOUR ANALYSIS

Criticisms of this kind were voiced in the 1980s (e.g., Deitz, 1978; Epling and Pierce, 1983, 1986; Hayes, Rincover and Solnick, 1980; Michael, 1980, 1985; Pierce and Epling, 1980; Poling *et al.*, 1981), and most commentators asserted that severing the link between behaviour analysis and clinical application would weaken both. In the area of mental handicap, the currently renewed interest in functional analysis, verbal behaviour, and environmental design—all topics originally discussed by Skinner—is reflected in many of the contributions to this volume. Work of this kind gets back to principles that have always been at the heart of a behaviour analytic approach, but it does not lose sight of the essential practical thrust of ABA as a way to produce significant and lasting behavioural change.

Before introducing these contributions, however, I would like to dwell briefly on some of the recent *empirical* advances in EAB that underline the continuing need for a conceptual framework. I will concentrate on one aspect of current research that is central to clinical intervention in mental handicap—the control of behaviour by contingencies of reinforcement.

Conceptualizing reinforcement: Contingency-shaped behaviour

Behaviour is shaped and maintained by its consequences. No behavioural principle could be more central than the law of effect, but even this simple idea has been subject to a range of interpretation and development. An early distinction was that the probability of behaviour could be increased or decreased by either the presentation or removal of critical events. This framing of operant principles sometimes leads to the kind of 2 × 2 matrices which appear in many pure and applied behavioural texts. Figure 1.1 is based on the terminology used by Schwartz (1989) and Kazdin (1975). Reinforcement and punishment are defined in terms of 'positive' and 'aversive' (or 'negative') events, but there is no *independent* criterion which allows one to decide how events should be categorized into types. Thinking about operant contingencies in this way brings with it several problems. First, it implies that the character of consequences is somehow independent of both the people with whom they might be employed, and the context of their use—in essence, a consensual conception of reinforcement and punishment. Herbert *et al.* (1973), working with both cognitively impaired and normal children, showed the weakness of this approach. On the basis of other studies, and probably strong intuition, they assumed that parental attention would be a 'positive' event, and designed intervention procedures to use it to reinforce 'appropriate' behaviour, while removing attention to extinguish 'deviant' behaviour. In fact, for most children the procedures had the opposite effects—attention functioned as a punisher, in the sense of reducing the probability of behaviour on which it was contingent. Referring back to Figure 1.1, it must have been 'aversive' all along! The study thus makes a point with obvious implications for the 'aversives' debate. If attention is 'aversive', in that it can function as a positive punisher, it may be psychologically distressing (as it appears to be with 'shy' children), and should presumably be proscribed. But there are many other studies, with other children and in other contexts, demonstrating that attention is reinforcing. At the heart of the problem is the fact that proscribing a treatment procedure must be based on consensual, legalistic criteria, but categorizing effective consequences depends on functional, behavioural criteria.

Figure 1.2 therefore presents functional definitions of reinforcement and punishment. It is clearly no more than a descriptive framework: behaviour leads to contingent consequences, and the subsequent probability of that behaviour may change. If upward changes are noted, the consequence is said to be a reinforcer; if downward changes occur, a punisher. The consequence is 'positive' if added (+) to produce behaviour

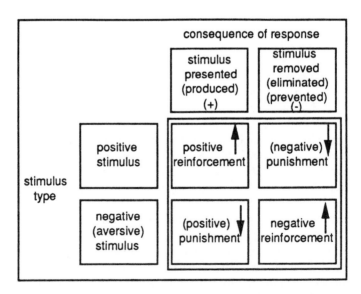

Figure 1.1 Consensual definitions of reinforcement and punishment. Upward arrows indicate observed increases in response rate; downward arrows, decreases.

change; 'negative' (−) if removed. The taxonomy is etirely *post hoc*: its merit is that it allows behaviour to be observed in its environmental context, and generates a categorization. This in turn can suggest hypotheses for functional analysis, based on a thorough understanding of the effects of varying such parameters of reinforcement or punishment as schedule, rate, amount, and delay. Moreover, Figure 1.2 carries no predictive implications. It allows reinforcers and punishers to be identified only in particular situations for particular individuals. Although it is often true that the same event has transituational reinforcing properties (i.e. is capable of reinforcing a range of behaviours in a variety of situations), there is nothing in this framework to guarantee, or even imply, that this is so.

Although the Figure 1.2 categorization is exceptionally useful (see particularly Oliver; Repp, Felce and Karsh, this volume), its disregard for independent criteria on which to decide in advance whether a given event will act as a reinforcer or punisher has long been a theoretical embarrassment. One distinctively behavioural attempt to resolve the difficulty has had major implications for conceptions of reinforcement, and thus for our understanding of behaviour in applied settings. Premack (1959, 1965) proposed that earlier conceptualizations of reinforcers were fundamentally flawed because it was behaviours, not events, that were reinforcing; events merely provided the opportunity to behave in reinforcing ways (e.g., social attention (an event) allows social interaction

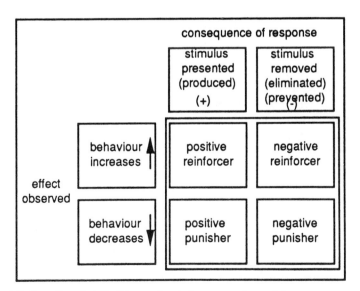

Figure 1.2 Functional definitions of reinforcers and punishers.

(a behaviour)). Premack's strategy was to use the time spent engaging in various behaviours before a reinforcement contingency was arranged as a way of predicting in advance whether that contingency would be effective. For example, a person in a residential setting might be observed to spend 60% of her morning watching TV, and 10% doing domestic tasks at the 'free behaviour point' (FBP), i.e. when there were no constraints on transitions between these activities. TV watching is a high-probability behaviour (HPB) and domestic work a low-probability behaviour (LBP). The basic 'Premack principle' proposed that access to the HPB would reinforce the LPB, so that if access to TV for, say, 30% of the time was permitted only when, say, 50% of time had been used in domestic tasks, the latter would increase in frequency—a reinforcement effect. This example is obviously simplified, but there is substantial evidence that contingencies based on the Premack principle are effective in changing the behaviour of people with mental handicap (e.g. Allen and Iwata, 1980; Konarski et al., 1982).

Premack's argument has several important implications for any intervention based on reinforcement principles. First, assessment of the relative frequencies of HPB and LPB must be entirely contextually determined. The resident's FBP distribution of activities might change completely from morning to afternoon, or in the morning if others were present. Thus, reinforcement is strongly contextual in character. Premack and others have demonstrated this by showing that the reinforcement relation is reversible, depending on the context in which it is imposed (i.e. what Michael (1982) has called the 'establishing operation', and Wahler and Fox (1981) the 'setting event'). Continuing the example, the same person sated with TV viewing but deprived of physical activity (say, by a period of illness) might well spend more time at the FBP doing domestic work than viewing. If so, the opportunity to work should reinforce TV watching. There is yet a further reason not to expect reinforcers to be transituational. The Premack principle defines one behaviour as reinforcing only with respect to another. Thus, a behaviour of intermediate probability would reinforce one of lower, but not one of higher, probability. In clinical practice, attempts are made to find highly preferred activities, but this limit on the generality of reinforcers should not be overlooked.

Another implication of Premack's position is the blurring of distinctions between positive and negative reinforcement. Is the contingency described in the residential example above based on the provision of TV (positive reinforcement) or the removal of domestic work (negative reinforcement)? All that is important is the transition between LPB and HPB, and the fact that the opportunity to make it is dependent on the occurrence of more than the baseline rate of LPB. Thus, the operant contingency is best seen as a *constraint* on the preferred distribution of activities identified at the FBP. Again, the implications for the 'aversives' debate are worth considering. Positive reinforcement techniques are usually regarded as non-aversive in that they involve the delivery of events that we might, consensually, agree are 'rewarding' or 'positive'. On Premack's view, however, the use of reinforcement must, explicitly or implicitly, involve creating a situation that constrains the optimal distribution of activities a person would have chosen—and 'constraint' does not sound quite so appealing as 'reward'.

The power of this argument is underlined by Rachlin *et al.*'s (1981) maximization theory. Essentially, Rachlin *et al.* argue that there are no differences whatsoever between reinforcement and punishment contingencies save for the order in which constrained behaviours are permitted to occur on a schedule arranged by experimenter or clinician. To continue the earlier example, it would be possible to punish TV watching by ensuring that if, say, 30% of time was spent viewing, the person would subsequently be required to spend 50% of her time in domestic work. The 'package' of time spent viewing and working is identical to that used above to illustrate a Premackian reinforcement contingency, with viewing occupying less, and working more, time than the FBP. The only difference is that in a reinforcement contingency the HPB is permitted to occur contingent on LPB, while a punishment contingency demands the occurrence of an LPB contingent on an HPB (see, for example, Holburn and Dougher (1986) for a clinical application to challenging behaviour). In summary, it is possible to see 'non-aversive' reinforcement procedures and 'aversive' punishment procedures as identical in terms of the constraints that they impose on behaviour.

The idea that a scheduled contingency forces a person to choose some 'package' of activities raises interesting questions not at first obvious in Premack's approach. Any limitation of the distribution of behaviour at the FBP creates a state of *response deprivation* (Timberlake and Allison, 1974). For example, if the preferred package of activities at the FBP includes *some* LPB, it implies *a little* LPB is better than *no* LPB. If so, there might be circumstances under which the LPB could reinforce the HPB, in addition to those already discussed in which the HPB can reinforce the LPB. Konarski and his colleagues, working with people with mental handicap, have demonstrated that both LPBs and HPBs will act as reinforcers provided that the schedule arrangement produces response deprivation (Konarski, 1987; Konarski, Crowell and Duggan, 1985). In the now-familiar example, some domestic work is preferred to none at all. Thus, if a suitably constraining contingency were arranged, the resident would spend more time viewing than at the FBP to earn back the preferred (small) amount of worktime. Because the FBP represents the optimal package of activities, current conceptions of schedule control (e.g., Rachlin *et al.*, 1981; Timberlake, 1980) interpret operant behaviour as an attempt to return to the equilibrium of the FBP, i.e. to get as close to that optimum as the schedule constraint allows.

This is a far cry from the simple conception that we began with. Yet its implications for functional analysis in clinical settings are quite immediate. Imposing a schedule of reinforcement is adding a constraint on behaviour, but many such constraints are already present. Given this, the purpose of observing behaviour–environment interactions in the natural settings is to understand their nature, prior to an intervention that may either modify them, remove them, or impose others. The principal message here is that understanding the ways in which operant contingencies affect behaviour, even under controlled conditions, may involve relatively sophisticated conceptualization. If so, thinking at least as sophisticated will be needed to interpret the complexities of behaviour–environment interactions in the real world.

Recent research on the concept of response deprivation makes this point very clearly. In the examples used so far, I have assumed that a behavioural repertoire consists of two behaviours—the HPB and LPB. But this assumption is clearly untenable: a person's behaviour in home or work situations will involve any of a large number of activities. Aeschleman and Williams (1989) evaluated the impact of operant contingencies based on response deprivation in a classroom for children with mental handicap. Three activities (e.g., electronic game, colouring, writing) were available without restriction at the FBP, and a contingency was subsequently introduced to constrain transitions between two of them while leaving the third freely available. When the remaining (freely available) response had a low baseline probability, contingencies defined by the response deprivation hypothesis produced a consistent reinforcement effect, but that effect was markedly attenuated when the third response was highly probable at the FBP.

One implication of this study is that the behavioural repertoire of an individual with learning difficulties is best conceptualized as a behavioural system of elements that interact in complex ways. Unconstrained, these behaviours occur according to the demands of the person's motivational system, but when constraints are imposed changes may arise not only in the reinforced and reinforcing behaviours but possibly also in many other aspects of the repertoire. Until recently, such changes have attracted little serious attention by clinicians and researchers, save for the long-term interest in the 'side effects' of punishment (e.g., Skinner, 1953; Newsom, Favell and Rincover, 1983). It has now been acknowledged that reinforcement can have similar 'side effects' (Balsam and Bondy, 1983). As the above discussion implies, however, the connotation of 'side effects' does not sufficiently indicate the nature of the change in thinking that is needed. Both punishment and reinforcement contingencies impose constraints on a behavioural system, and the system's adjustments, whether intended or unintended, are all part and parcel of the effect of the contingency.

At present, theoretical accounts of the nature of changes induced by constraint are sketchy. However, in recent years behaviour analysis has started to use principles drawn from microeconomics to guide experimentation and theory development (e.g., Hursh, 1984). One important development is the suggestion that when particular behaviours are constrained by contingencies there may be correlated changes in other behaviours that function either as substitutes or complements to the restricted behaviour (see, for example, Green and Striefel, 1988). For example, if access to TV viewing is restricted, self-stimulatory behaviour may increase—not because it has previously been reinforced with access to TV but because it provides a substitute source of visual stimulation. Changes in complementary behaviour may be seen when, for example, a restriction on the opportunities to smoke leads to correlated decreases in coffee drinking.

Conceptualizing reinforcement: Rule-governed behaviour

All of the conceptions of reinforcement discussed so far have demonstrated promise in application with people with mental handicap, but all derived originally from research by psychologists interested in animal behaviour. There is nothing very new in that: successful extrapolation of this kind has always been a hallmark of behaviour analysis. However, in recent years, behaviour analytic research has focused directly on human behaviour, and laboratory-based work has begun to chart distinctive differences between humans and other animals in terms of the ways in which their behaviour is affected by operant contingencies. One central distinction, initially proposed by Skinner (1969), that has received increasing experimental support is that animal behaviour is *contingency shaped*, but that human behaviour can be *rule-governed*. Contingency-shaped behaviour is under the *direct* control of schedules of operant reinforcement or punishment of the kind discussed above. Thus, the operant behaviour of non-human animals, infants, and non-verbal people must be seen as contingency-shaped. However, as infants acquire language they develop the capacity to respond indirectly to contingencies of reinforcement, initially through instruction from others, but later through self-instruction. Operant behaviour that is mediated by verbal behaviour in this way is said to be rule-governed. There is a growing body of evidence that, with the development of functional language skills, children's behaviour comes under the control of verbally formulated rules (e.g., Bentall, Lowe and Beasty, 1985). Moreover, the behaviour of normal human adults is often rule-governed (e.g., Lowe and Horne, 1985), and the formulation of rules may, under particular circumstances, render such behaviour insensitive to the *immediate* consequences that are central to the acquisition and maintenance of contingency-shaped behaviour (Cerrutti, 1989).

It is unclear at present what the implications of this rapidly developing line of research will be for intervention with people with mental handicap, but several foci are likely to emerge. First, to the extent that clients have functional language skills, the impact of contingencies may be indirect, depending on the relations between instructions (or self-instructions), and the consequences that are provided for behaviour change. Secondly, the effect of an intervention that creates functional language skills must produce major changes in the functioning of people with mental handicap. Apart from simply enhancing efficient control over their environments, verbal behaviour opens a gateway to a completely different mode of relating to experience. Third, the behaviour of people who work as caregivers, teachers or clinical psychologists is often likely to be rule-governed. It may prove important to understand the ways in which interactions with clients may be mediated either through external instruction (e.g., the behaviour required of care staff) or self-instruction (e.g., the belief that 'all SIB is a way of getting attention'). This way of thinking about staff behaviour may lead to more effective intervention procedures based on a better understanding of the functions of training.

To conclude, the importance of these new behaviour analytic conceptions for successful remediation of mental handicap is only now beginning to be recognized. Certainly, the principles discussed have not yet found their way into routine clinical application. There is a yawning gap between what we know of how operant behaviour is controlled, and how we attempt to control it to achieve habilitation and remediation. Bridging that gap demands halting the drift towards the scattergun technology of the intervention package, and returning to the more sophisticated concepts and principles of behavioural analysis. A technology needs its science.

A BRIEF INTRODUCTION TO THE BOOK

The contributions which follow this chapter provide some current attempts to bridge the gap between analysis and intervention. The central focus of the first section of the book is functional analysis and intervention for challenging behaviours. A single principle underlies all of these contributions: behaviour has its functions. To the extent that these functions are in some sense valid goals of the individuals displaying them, alternative, constructional, more effective (i.e., less damaging to self and others) means of achieving the same goals should be substituted (Goldiamond, 1974).

Jones begins by reviewing work published over the past twenty years to evaluate the effectiveness of differential reinforcement-based interventions as an alternative to 'aversive' methods of behaviour reduction. He attributes the mixed outcomes of this body of research to the failure to pay sufficient attention to behavioural function, and suggests that the role of instructional variables on the outcome of interventions, although currently unanalysed, may be central. Berg and Wacker review procedures for identifying effective consequences that can be used in such differential reinforcement procedures, based on criteria of preference, function, and Premackian probability differential. Like Jones, Berg and Wacker discuss the danger of intervening without prior functional analysis, but describe ways in which differential reinforcement and functional analysis methods can be combined. Durand and Crimmins exhaustively review the range of methods of assessing behavioural functions, and describe how analysis can lead to intervention which is both effective and sustainable. This theme is echoed by Oliver, who closely analyses the strengths and weaknesses of one important method of functional analysis—the use of analogue methodology. Analogue and other behaviour analysis methods rely heavily on a technology capable of recording the complex relationships between myriad behavioural and environmental events, and Repp, Felce and Karsh describe a microcomputer system that performs this kind of sophisticated analysis. They also describe a new taxonomy developed to categorize behaviour–environment interactions, and they show how this form of descriptive analysis can lead to effective intervention. Scotti, Evans, Meyer and DiBenedetto show that intervention designed to change one behaviour may produce changes throughout the behavioural system. They therefore argue that it is essential to consider how the complete behavioural repertoire is structured, and present a number of theoretical analyses. Sophisticated data acquisition and analysis procedures of the kind possible using Repp et al.'s programs are essential to understand the nature of these interactions.

Together, the above chapters describe the current state of the art of functional analysis. One important theme to have emerged from many such analyses is that some forms of maladaptive behaviour may serve a social control, or communicative, function. For this reason, and for many others, a great deal of recent research has been concerned with improving the communicative skills of people with mental handicap through speech, sign, or symbolic language systems. The chapters in Section 2 (Behavioural Approaches to Communication and Language) explore some ways in which language and symbolic functions have been approached by applied behaviour analysts. Duker and Remington and Reichle, Sigafoos and Remington review the utility of gestural and symbol-based communication systems (respectively). Both contributions consider the nature of the systems, the characteristics of clients for whom they would be suitable, and the functional characteristics of communication. Their discussion of functionality is firmly grounded in Skinner's (1957) account of verbal behaviour, and both raise a number of issues about the spontaneity and appropriateness of sign or symbol use which has been taught by behavioural methods. This theme is taken up by Goodman and Remington, who discuss the transfer of use of manual signs between requesting (manding) to labelling (tacting) functions, and consider its implications for spontaneous communication. Their account of transfer is based on concepts which have been developed in the study of stimulus equivalence, the topic of Mackay's chapter. Equivalence research has been at the forefront of recent laboratory analyses of human operant behaviour for both theoretical and practical reasons. Theoretically, equivalence once again underlines the importance of context in behaviour analysis, by showing that the stimulus control of operant behaviour can itself be subject to higher levels of contextual control. Practically, equivalence offers a behavioural analysis of semantic relations, and thus opens the way for interventions aimed at teaching elementary verbal skills to people with mental handicap.

Together, the chapters in Section 2 concentrate on behavioural approaches to the effective teaching of skills with enormous functional relevance. The final section of the book focuses on the relationship between behaviour analytic approaches and service delivery for people with mental handicap. Repp and Karsh show how a Task Demonstration Model (TDM) using laboratory-developed discrimination training procedures, including procedures involved in teaching equivalence, can be applied in real world contexts to produce rapid and effective learning. The contributions by Felce and Gaylord-Ross, Salzberg, Curl and Storey both describe behaviour analytic projects designed to bring about normalized living in the community for people with mental handicap. Felce details how constructional principles (Goldiamond, 1974) were used to set up and evaluate a successful housing service in the UK. Gaylord-Ross and his associates describe how integration into working environments in the US is being achieved, both in terms of teaching the necessary work skills and establishing the social–behavioural networks that can support community living. The changes that both of these contributions describe fit intimately with the ecology of the community, and are thus sustainable. Ager codifies a set of general principles based on behaviour analytic concepts that can be used to audit any intervention with respect to its long-term sustainability, and to prescribe changes that are likely to increase the probability of successful maintenance.

Despite these, and the many other accounts of the successful use of behavioural means to achieve the goals of normalization, there is sometimes a damaging and quite unnecessary antipathy towards ABA by proponents of community integration (see Emerson and McGill, 1989, for an informative discussion). In the final chapter, Kiernan reflects on the historical roots of this disharmony and reviews some of the current conflicts in the area. He concludes by pointing to ways in which a behaviour analytic approach, suitably tied to the conceptual framework on which it was originally based, can move the process of normalization forward. Every chapter in this volume has been written with the aim of making a direct, positive contribution to that process.

Address for correspondence

Bob Remington, Department of Psychology, University of Southampton, Highfield, Southampton SO9 5NH, UK.

REFERENCES

Aeschleman, S.R. and Williams, M.L. (1989) A test of the response deprivation hypothesis in a multiple-response context. *American Journal on Mental Retardation*, **93**, 345–353.
Allen, L.D. and Iwata, B. (1980) Reinforcing exercise maintenance using existing high-rate activities. *Behavior Modification*, **4**, 337–354.
Ayllon, T. and Azrin, N.H. (1968) *The Token Economy*, Appleton–Century–Crofts, New York.
Baer, D.M., Wolf, M.M. and Risley, T.R. (1968) Current dimensions of applied behavior analysis. *Journal of Applied Behavior Analysis*, **1**, 91–97.
Balsam, P.D. and Bondy, A.S. (1983) The negative side effects of reward. *Journal of Applied Behavior Analysis*, **16**, 283–296.
Bentall, R.P., Lowe, C.F. and Beasty, A. (1985) The role of verbal behavior in human learning. II. Developmental differences. *Journal of the Experimental Analysis of Behavior*, **43**, 165–181.
Carr, E.G. (1988) Functional equivalence as a mechanism of response generalization. In R.H. Horner, G. Dunlap and R.L. Koegel (eds), *Generalization and Maintenance: Life-Style Changes in Applied Settings*, Brooks, Baltimore.
Carr, E.G. and McDowell, J.J. (1980) Social control of self-injurious behavior of organic etiology. *Behavior Therapy*, **11**, 402–409.

Cerrutti, D.T. (1989) Discrimination theory of rule-governed behavior. *Journal of the Experimental Analysis of Behavior*, **51**, 259–276.

Deitz, S.M. (1978) Current status of applied behavior analysis: Science versus technology. *American Psychologist*, **33**, 805–814.

Emerson, E. and McGill, P. (1989) Normalization and applied behaviour analysis: Values and technology in services for people with learning difficulties. *Behavioural Psychotherapy*, **17**, 101–117.

Epling, W.F. and Pierce, W.D. (1983) Applied behavior analysis: New directions from the laboratory. *Behavior Analyst*, **6**, 27–37.

Epling, W.F. and Pierce, W.D. (1986) The basic importance of applied behavior analysis. *Behavior Analyst* **9**, 89–99.

Fuller, P.R. (1949) Operant conditioning of a vegetative human organism. *American Journal of Psychology*, **62**, 587–590. Reprinted in L. Ullmann and L. Kranser (eds), *Case Studies in Behavior Modification*, Holt, Rinehart and Winston, New York.

Goldiamond, I. (1974) Towards a constructional approach to social problems. *Behaviorism*, **2**, 1–84.

Green, G. and Striefel, S. (1988) Response restriction and substitution with autistic children. *Journal of the Experimental Analysis of Behavior*, **50**, 21–32.

Gross, A.M. and Drabman, R.S. (1981) Behavioral contrast and behavior therapy. *Behavior Therapy*, **12**, 231–246.

Hayes, S.C., Hayes, L.J. and Reese, H.W. (1988) Finding the philosophical core: A review of Stephen C. Pepper's world hypotheses: A study in evidence. *Journal of the Experimental Analysis of Behavior*, **50**, 97–111.

Hayes, S.C., Rincover, A. and Solnick, J.V. (1980) The technical drift of applied behavior analysis. *Journal of Applied Behavior Analysis*, **13**, 275–285.

Herbert, E.W., Pinkston, E.M., Hayden, M.L., Sajwaj, T.E., Pinkston, S., Cordua, G. and Jackson, C. (1973) Adverse effects of differential parental attention. *Journal of Applied Behavior Analysis*, **6**, 15–30.

Herrnstein, R.J. (1961) Relative and absolute strength of a response as a function of frequency of reinforcement. *Journal of the Experimental Analysis of Behavior*, **4**, 267–272.

Holburn, C.S. and Dougher, M.J. (1986) Effects of response satiation procedures in the treatment of aerophagia. *American Journal of Mental Deficiency*, **91**, 72–77.

Hursh, S. (1984) Behavioral economics. *Journal of the Experimental Analysis of Behavior*, **42**, 435–452.

Kazdin, A.E. (1975) *Behavior Modification in Applied Settings*, Dorsey Press, Homewood, Illinois.

Kelly, J.A. and Drabman, R.S. (1977) Generalizing response suppression of self-injurious behavior through an overcorrection punishment procedure: A case study. *Behavior Therapy*, **8**, 468–472.

Kerr, N., Meyerson, L. and Michael, J. (1965) A procedure for shaping vocalizations in a mute child. In L. Ullmann and L. Krasner (eds), *Case Studies in Behavior Modification*, Holt, Rinehart and Winston, New York.

Konarski, E.A. (1987) Effects of response deprivation on the instrumental performance of mentally retarded persons. *American Journal of Mental Deficiency*, **91**, 537–542.

Konarski, E.A., Crowell, C.R. and Duggan, L.M. (1985) The use of response deprivation to increase the academic performance of EMR students. *Applied Research in Mental Retardation*, **6**, 15–31.

Konarski, E.A., Crowell, C.R., Johnson, M.R. and Whitman, T.L. (1982) Response deprivation, reinforcement and instrumental academic performance in an EMR classroom. *Behavior Therapy*, **13**, 94–102.

Lovaas, I.O., Schaeffer, B. and Simmons, J.Q. (1965) Building social behavior in autistic children by use of electric shock. *Journal of Experimental Research in Personality*, **1**, 99–109.

Lowe, C.F. and Horne, P. (1985) On the generality of behavioural principles: Human choice and the matching law. In C.F. Lowe, D.E. Blackman and C.M. Bradshaw (eds), *Behaviour Analysis and Contemporary Psychology*, LEA, London.

Matson, J.L. and McCartney, J.R. (1981) *Handbook of Behavior Modification With The Mentally Retarded*, Plenum Press, New York.

McBrien, J. and Foxen, T. (1981) *Training Staff in Behavioural Methods*. University of Manchester Press, Manchester.

Michael, J. (1980) Flight from behavior analysis. *Behavior Analyst*, **3**, 1–22.

Michael, J. (1982) Distinguishing between discriminative and motivational functions of stimuli. *Journal of the Experimental Analysis of Behavior*, **37**, 149–155.

Michael, J. (1985) Fundamental research and behaviour modification. In C.F. Lowe, D.E. Blackman and C.M. Bradshaw (eds), *Behaviour Analysis and Contemporary Psychology*, LEA, London.

Myerson, J. and Hale, S. (1984) Practical applications of the matching law. *Journal of Applied Behavior Analysis*, **17**, 367–380.

Newsom, C., Favell, J.E. and Rincover, A. (1983) Side effects of punishment. In S. Axelrod and J. Apsche (eds), *The Effects of Punishment on Human Behavior*, Academic Press, New York.

Pierce, W.D. and Epling, W.F. (1980) Whatever happened to analysis in applied behavior analysis? *Behavior Analyst*, **3**, 1–9.

Poling, A., Picker, M., Grossett, D., Hall-Johnson, E. and Holbrook, M. (1981) The schism between experimental and applied behavior analysis: Is it real and who cares? *Behavior Analyst*, **4**, 93–102.

Premack, D. (1959) Towards empirical behavior laws. I: Positive reinforcement. *Psychological Review*, **66**, 219–233.

Premack, D. (1965) Reinforcement theory. In D. Levine (ed.), *Nebraska Symposium on Motivation*, University of Nebraska Press, Lincoln.

Rachlin, H., Battalio, R., Kagel, J. and Green, L. (1981) Maximization theory in behavioral psychology. *Behavior and Brain Sciences*, **4**, 371–417.

Reynolds, G.S. (1961) Behavioral contrast. *Journal of Experimental Analysis of Behavior*, **4**, 57–71.

Schick, K. (1971) Operants. *Journal of the Experimental Analysis of Behavior*, **15**, 413–423.

Schwartz, B. (1989) *The Psychology of Learning And Behavior*, Norton, New York.

Skinner, B.F. (1948) *Walden II*, Macmillan, New York.

Skinner, B.F. (1953) *Science and Human Behavior*, Macmillan, New York.

Skinner, B.F. (1957) *Verbal Behavior*, Appleton–Century–Crofts, New York.

Skinner, B.F. (1968) *The Technology of Teaching*, Appleton–Century–Crofts, New York.

Skinner, B.F. (1969) *Contingencies of Reinforcement*, Appleton–Century–Crofts, New York.

Timberlake, W. (1980) A molar equilibrium theory of learned performance. In G.H. Bower (ed.), *Psychology of Learning and Motivation* (Vol. 14), Academic Press, New York.

Timberlake, W. and Allison, J. (1974) Response deprivation: An empirical approach to instrumental performance. *Psychological Review*, **81**, 146–164.

Wahler, R.G. and Fox, J.J. (1981) Setting events in applied behavior analysis: Toward a conceptual and methodological expansion. *Journal of Applied Behavior Analysis*, **14**, 327–338.

Wolf, M.M., Birnbrauer, J.S., Williams, T. and Lawler, J. (1965) A note on apparent extinction of the vomiting behavior of a retarded child. In L. Ullmann and L. Kranser (eds), *Case Studies in Behavior Modification*, Holt, Rinehart and Winston, New York.

Yule, W. and Carr, J. (1987) *Behaviour Modification for People with Mental Handicaps* (2nd edn), Croom Helm, London.

Section 1

Functional Analysis and Intervention for Challenging Behaviours

Chapter 2

The Assessment and Evaluation of Reinforcers for Individuals with Severe Mental Handicap

WENDY K. BERG AND DAVID P. WACKER

INTRODUCTION

Individuals who are diagnosed as severely/profoundly mentally handicapped represent an extremely heterogeneous group of people who are frequently characterized by both excess (e.g., self-injury, stereotypy) and deficit (e.g., lack of independent responding) behaviors both within individuals and across groups (Wacker, Steege and Berg, 1990). The heterogeneity of the people included within this group is evidenced by the diversity in the descriptive summaries of persons who participated as subjects in the research that we will discuss in this chapter. The participants in these investigations were all persons diagnosed with severe handicaps, from those who were nonverbal, nonambulatory, had seizure disorders, cerebral palsy, sensory impairments, and who were completely dependent in all basic self-care tasks, to those who were ambulatory, had no sensory or motor impairments, and routinely performed multiple functional skills.

The diversity among individuals labeled severely/profoundly handicapped prevents the application of uniform or generic program goals and strategies. Instead, each individual's idiosyncratic set of strengths and weaknesses must be considered and addressed in the development of habilitative programming. An integral part of this programming is the identification of stimuli that serve to reinforce and strengthen the occurrence of the target behaviors (Repp, Barton and Brulle, 1983).

As discussed by Repp, Barton and Brulle (1983), in order for a stimulus to serve as a reinforcer for a desired response, a functional relationship must exist between the presentation of that stimulus and the occurrence

The Challenge of Severe Mental Handicap. Edited by Bob Remington
© 1991 John Wiley & Sons Ltd

of the target response. In other words, a reinforcer is a stimulus which, when presented contingently upon the occurrence of a behavior, increases the likelihood that the behavior will occur again. Stimuli that serve as reinforcers for an individual may include tangible items such as favorite foods or toys, preferred activities, different levels of social attention, sensory experiences, or the termination of (or escape from) nonpreferred stimuli. Stimuli that reinforce one behavior may not reinforce other behaviors for the same individual, and what reinforces a behavior in one context may not reinforce the same behavior under different circumstances. Perhaps the most important point to consider is that a reinforcer cannot be identified apart from the behavior it affects.

Providing positive or negative reinforcement contingent on desired behavior is, of course, the basis of operant conditioning programs. All treatments that focus on increasing the frequency of a behavior, shaping a new behavior, or replacing an undesired behavior with a more appropriate or acceptable behavior are based on the provision of reinforcers as a consequence to the desired behavior. Unfortunately, our ability to reliably identify stimuli that are reinforcing to persons with severe handicaps is frequently limited. As a result, the ability of persons with severe/profound mental handicap to benefit from educational programming as demonstrated in the display of meaningful behavioral outcomes is often debated. At the center of this controversy is the issue of whether stimuli that function reliably as reinforcers can be identified for all persons with severe/profound mental handicap.

We will review a variety of procedures developed to identify reinforcing stimuli for persons with severe mental handicap and discuss them in terms of their implications for educational programming. Each of the investigations examined in this chapter represents an approach to the identification of reinforcers for persons with severe/profound mental handicap that is based on individual assessment and programming. Although the procedures we consider are similar in their focus upon the individual rather than upon the group, they are very different in terms of the methods and behavioral observations they use in the identification and selection of reinforcing stimuli.

The procedures we present are categorized into two groups: those that increase low-rate behaviors for the identification of reinforcing stimuli and those that rely on high-rate behavior to identify reinforcers. The first category of procedures focuses on the identification of preferred stimuli, and the subsequent effect of such stimuli on the occurrence of low-frequency adaptive behaviors. These procedures include systematic assessment of preferred stimuli to identify reinforcers (Green et al., 1988; Pace et al., 1985), the use of small but apparently controlled motor responses to identify reinforcers (Wacker et al., 1985, Wacker et al., 1988), and identification of preferred stimuli in a choice-making situation (Parsons and Reid, 1990).

The second category of procedures uses high-frequency aberrant behaviors to identify and select reinforcing stimuli. The procedures we discuss within this section include the use of functional assessment and analysis procedures (Carr and Durand, 1985; Durand *et al.*, 1989; Iwata *et al.*, 1982; Northup *et al.*, 1989; Steege *et al.*, 1989), as well as the use of the opportunity to engage in aberrant behavior as a reinforcer (Charlop, Kurtz and Casey, 1990; Lovaas, Newsom and Hickman, 1987; Rincover and Newsom, 1985). With each of these procedures, the focus is on either the identification of consequences that currently maintain high-frequency behavior or the identification of high-frequency behavior that can be used as a reinforcer for low-frequency behavior within a Premack paradigm (Premack, 1959).

IDENTIFYING REINFORCERS FOR LOW-RATE BEHAVIORS

One of the common difficulties encountered in attempting to identify reinforcing stimuli for persons with profound handicaps is identifying operant behavior. Typically, these individuals have very limited response repertoires including minimal, if any, engagement in formal communication systems such as speech or manual signs. In many cases, their motor movements are poorly controlled due to extreme muscular rigidity or flaccidity and are frequently accompanied by involuntary activity. As a result, it is difficult not only to identify an appropriate response that is within the person's repertoire, but also to discriminate between voluntary and involuntary movements. In addition to the presence of motoric and sensory limitations, frequent fluctuations in health and medication status further inhibit our ability to identify 'independent' movement; the occurrence of behaviors that appear to be purposeful is frequently minimal. Three distinct procedures have been developed to identify reinforcing stimuli that use infrequent but apparently controlled behaviors.

Assessment of preferred stimuli

One approach to the identification of reinforcers has been to identify stimuli that the person 'prefers' and then to present those stimuli contingently upon performance of a designated response. If the contingent presentation of a stimulus results in increased performance by the person, then a reinforcer has been identified.

Such procedures are typically conducted in two phases: an assessment phase in which the preferred stimuli are identified, and a validation phase in which the effectiveness of the stimulus as a reinforcer is evaluated. Within the assessment phase, a variety of stimuli are presented for brief intervals, typically 5–10 seconds, and the participant's reaction to each stimulus is evaluated. By observing differences in the participant's reactions across stimuli, one may be able to identify preferred and nonpreferred stimuli. Stimuli identified as preferred are subsequently presented contingent on a selected response during the validation phase. If the frequency of the response increases, a positive reinforcer has been identified.

Pace *et al.* (1985) used a stimulus assessment procedure to identify reinforcers for six children with profound mental handicap. Sixteen items that varied in the type of sensation provided (e.g., visual, olfactory, gustatory, tactile, or social) were selected as the stimulus pool. Each stimulus was presented to the child for a 5-second interval and remained available for an additional 5 seconds if the child made an approach response to the stimulus. Approach responses were defined as movements of the hand or body toward the stimulus that occurred within 5 seconds of its appearance. Ten probes were conducted for each stimulus. By recording the frequency with which a child approached the different stimuli, the investigators were able to determine varying degrees of preference across stimuli.

One difficulty in assessing a child's preferences among various stimuli in this way is determining if the child's failure to make an approach response is due to a lack of preference or a lack of familiarity with the stimulus. To ensure that the children were familiar with the stimuli evaluated during the assessment condition, Pace *et al.* (1985) used a stimulus sampling procedure. This procedure was conducted for the first presentation of a stimulus within a session and consisted of providing the stimulus to the child for 5 seconds following a non-occurrence of approach behavior. The stimulus sample consisted of providing the child with a small taste of the food stimuli or activation and brief presentation of the remaining stimuli. A second probe with the stimulus was conducted following the stimulus sampling.

The children assessed in the Pace *et al.* (1985) investigation each approached at least one of the stimuli on 80% or more of the trials, demonstrating that they differentiated between the stimuli and appeared to prefer certain stimuli over others. To determine the effectiveness of the preferred stimuli as reinforcers for target behavior, Pace *et al.* conducted a validation phase of the experiment in which one or two stimuli previously identified as preferred and one or two stimuli identified as nonpreferred were presented contingently upon the occurrence of prespecified behaviors. A child was asked to perform a specific behavior, and a demonstration of the behavior was provided. During a baseline condition, the experimenter requested and modeled the target behavior, but no consequences were delivered contingent upon performance of the target response. Following the baseline period, the request and demonstration were again provided to the child, and either one of the preferred stimuli (stimuli approached on 80% or more trials) or one of the nonpreferred stimuli (stimuli approached on less than 50% of the trials) was presented contingent on the target behavior. An ABC design was used with the B and C phases corresponding to either preferred or nonpreferred stimulus presentation. The order of treatments was counterbalanced across subjects.

The results of the validation phase indicated that for five of the six children only the preferred stimuli served as reinforcers (increased responding) for the target behaviors. For the sixth child, however, the nonpreferred stimulus increased responding as effectively as the preferred stimulus. A second nonpreferred stimulus was therefore substituted and responding decreased. The results of the Pace *et al.* investigation thus demonstrated that preferred stimuli could be identified for each child and that these preferred stimuli subsequently served as positive reinforcers within a training situation.

In a subsequent investigation, Green *et al.* (1988) further developed the work of Pace and his colleagues by applying the reinforcer assessment procedures to persons with multiple handicaps (profound mental handicap accompanied by sensory, seizure, or motor disorders). Green *et al.* followed the procedures outlined by Pace *et al.*, except that 12 stimuli were included within the preference assessment rather than 16, and the repertoire of responses identified as approach behaviors indicating preference was expanded to include positive facial expressions and vocalizations in addition to the hand and body movements used by Pace *et al.* Green *et al.* also identified and recorded what they labeled avoidance responses, which included negative vocalizations, turning away from the stimulus, or pushing the stimulus away. To ensure that the lack of an approach response reflected a lack of preference rather than a lack of familiarity, Green *et al.* (1988) included a primer condition. The primer condition occurred at the beginning of each assessment condition and included a 5-second presentation of the stimulus in which the participant was prompted to touch, taste, observe or otherwise interact with the stimulus prior to the implementation of the assessment trials.

As with the Pace *et al.* (1985) investigation, Green and her colleagues evaluated the effectiveness with which stimuli identified as preferred would function as reinforcers for performance of targeted behaviors. These procedures resulted in the identification of effective positive reinforcers for five of seven participants. In addition, Green *et al.* (1988) compared the results of the stimulus preference assessment to stimulus rankings obtained through a staff opinion survey in which direct care workers rated each individual's preference for selected stimuli. This comparison was significant because care givers did *not* reliably predict which stimuli from a defined set would be preferred by participants. The results of the Green *et al.* investigation indicated that the systematic preference assessment procedure developed by Pace *et al.* could be applied to persons with profound multiple handicaps and that the preference assessment procedure was more accurate than the judgment of direct caregivers.

In both sets of investigations, behaviors were identified as representing approach responses, and measures of the occurrence or non-occurrence of these approach responses in the presence of selected stimuli were used to determine whether each stimulus was a preferred or nonpreferred item. Once selected, preferred and nonpreferred stimuli were presented contingently on the occurrence of a desired behavior in a training situation to compare the reinforcing value of the two sets of stimuli. The behaviors for this latter condition were selected from adaptive behaviors (e.g., establishing eye contact with the therapist) which the participants demonstrated at low rates prior to the implementation of the assessment procedure (Pace *et al.*, 1985), or responses that indicated increased levels of independence (e.g., client responds to a less restrictive prompt in a graduated prompt hierarchy) in performing a target response or increased speed in completing a target task (Green *et al.*, 1988). In both investigations, this phase provided a validation component in which the reinforcing effects of the preferred stimuli were evaluated directly. Thus, Pace *et al.*'s and Green *et al.*'s studies provided for a very comprehensive evaluation of positive reinforcers.

Directly increasing existing response repertoires

Wacker *et al.* (1985, 1988) pursued a different approach to the identification of positive reinforcers for persons with profound multiple handicaps. Whereas Pace *et al.* (1985) and Green *et al.* (1988) first identified preferred stimuli and then presented those stimuli contingently upon the demonstration of target behaviors, Wacker and his colleagues conducted a more direct reinforcer preference assessment by presenting various stimuli contingently upon the occurrence of a targeted behavior and recording which stimuli resulted in increased occurrence of behavior.

In both Wacker *et al.* investigations, adolescents classified as profoundly/multiply handicapped were observed within their classroom settings to identify adaptive motor responses that the students emitted independently but on an infrequent or inconsistent basis. The targeted behaviors included lifting one's head into an upright position, raising one's arm, and reaching. Once a target behavior was identified for each student, a microswitch (Burkhart, 1982) was placed on or near the student in such a way that it would be activated when the student made the target response. For example, mercury switches were used for those students with target behaviors of head or arm lifting. The mercury switch was attached to either the student's head with a hair band (for head lifting) or his or her arm with an elastic arm band (for arm raising). The switch was positioned on the band in such a way that it was engaged whenever the student moved his or her head or arm to the upright position. For students with a target behavior of reaching, a pressure-activated switch was placed on the student's lap (or lap tray) within the desired range of movement. When the student reached out and pressed the switch, an electrical circuit was completed and the switch engaged.

The reinforcer assessment procedure began with a baseline condition in which the microswitch was in place and attached to a cassette tape player containing a blank tape. At the beginning of each 20-minute session, the student was verbally and then physically prompted to engage in the desired response. This prompt sequence was repeated every 5 minutes if the student did not emit the desired behavior. Each time the student independently emitted the desired behavior, the tape player counter was activated and remained in motion as long as the microswitch was engaged. Baseline sessions were conducted to determine the student's duration of performing the target behavior in the presence of the microswitch but when no other stimuli were presented. These baseline levels of responding provided a necessary base rate of switch activation for comparing the impact of the battery-operated toys and devices on the student's behavior during the reinforcer assessment phase.

The reinforcer assessment phase was conducted similarly to baseline, except that the microswitches were connected to a battery-operated toy or appliance that the teacher had recommended as having potential as a reinforcer for that student. At least two items were assessed for each student within an alternating treatments design (Barlow and Hayes, 1979). Only one item was made available for each 20-minute session, with five sessions conducted for each item in a counterbalanced order. By comparing the student's frequency and duration of switch activation across conditions and battery-activated items, reinforcers were identified for each student.

All items selected for assessment were considered to be likely reinforcers for that student, based on the teachers' informal observations of the student's reaction to these items prior to the investigation. However, the results of the reinforcer assessment phase indicated that some of the items might, instead, have been aversive to the student. For example, one student operated the microswitch on several sessions during the baseline condition and on every session when a game was provided contingent on switch activation during the first reinforcer assessment phase of the investigation. However, when taped music was provided for switch activation during the same reinforcer assessment phase, the student activated the switch on only one session (see Figure 2.1). Based on these results, not only was the game an effective reinforcer for the target behavior, but taped music suppressed or punished the target behavior in comparison to the student's baseline levels of switch activation. Similar results occurred with two games during a second reinforcer assessment phase. These results support the suggestions of Fehr *et al.* (1979) that students with profound mental handicap may be inadvertently provided with aversive stimuli if caretakers rely on informal observations rather than systematic evaluations in which the student is provided with the means to control the presentation of the stimuli in question.

In both investigations conducted by Wacker and his colleagues, preferences between stimuli were identified by increases in selected motor responses. In addition to the identification of preferred stimuli that might serve as reinforcers for other target behaviors, the procedures

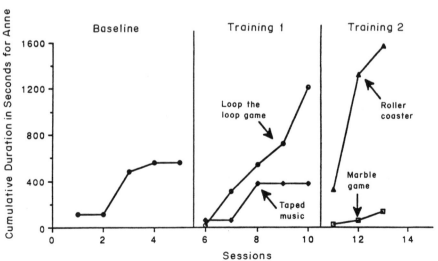

Figure 2.1 Cumulative duration of lifting response for Anne. (Reproduced by permission.)

used also resulted in the identification of operant behavior that could be incorporated into other programming goals. In the Wacker et al. (1988) investigation, the same motor responses that were used to identify toy reinforcers were subsequently used to activate taped messages requesting social attention from the classroom teacher. The same baseline and assessment procedures used in the 1985 investigation were used to determine the reinforcing value of social attention. Within one of the reinforcer assessment conditions, the student's production of the target response activated a pre-taped message that repeatedly stated the teacher's name and resulted in the teacher approaching the student and providing verbal and tactile attention. In the second condition, the target behavior resulted in the activation of the pre-taped message only. The second condition was included to control for the effects the sound of the teacher's name may have had on the student's responding.

The results of the assessment indicated not only that the students were able to discriminate between the trials when social attention was provided and when it was not, but also that seven of the nine students clearly preferred the social attention condition, indicating that they were responsive to the caretakers in their environment. The results of one student, who preferred the name-only condition as opposed to social attention, further demonstrated that individual preferences between consequences cannot be adequately identified in the absence of systematic assessments.

The pre-taped messages activated by the occurrence of the target behaviors provided the students with an appropriate means to gain teacher attention. Subsequently, these same behaviors were used to operate pre-taped messages that indicated preferred activities in community settings such as a shopping mall (Wacker et al., 1988). The series of experiments conducted by Wacker and his colleagues demonstrated that when provided with the appropriate materials, persons with profound mental handicap can indicate their preferences among available stimuli in a manner that is clearly understood by others, thus providing a direct measure of the reinforcing value of various stimuli.

Preference in choice situations

Parsons and Reid (1990) reported an alternative procedure to allow adults with profound mental handicap to directly indicate their preferences between available stimuli. As with the investigations conducted by Wacker and his colleagues, Parsons and Reid identified a behavior (food consumption) that could be controlled by the subjects to directly indicate their preferences in a manner that was clearly understood by others. In this investigation, food or drink items were presented in pairwise comparisons to five adults who were allowed to select and consume one of the items. The food and drink items were paired to represent items that were typically available at the subjects' meals and to reflect choice-making opportunities that would be encountered by a nonhandicapped person (e.g., black coffee versus coffee with cream). Each set of paired items was presented to the subject across ten sessions; each session consisted of one demonstration trial and five assessment or choice-making trials. Through repeated presentations of the paired items, the investigators demonstrated that every subject showed stable preferences between the available items. In a second experiment, Parsons and Reid demonstrated the applicability of the choice-making routine to the clients' regular meal-time setting by training direct care staff to offer the clients choices among the selected food and drink items. The clients behaved similarly with the direct care staff in the meal-time setting as they had for the investigators in the experimental setting, thus demonstrating the usefulness of the choice-making model in the clients' routine setting.

Although all of the investigations discussed in this section measured increases in the occurrence of low-frequency adaptive behaviors to identify reinforcers, two distinct approaches were used based on the way in which potential reinforcers were selected. Pace et al. (1985) and Green et al. (1988) selected stimuli that varied in terms of the sensory or social stimulation provided. Preferred and nonpreferred stimuli were identified by differences in the frequency of approach behaviors demonstrated toward each stimulus. Wacker et al. (1985, 1988) and Parsons and Reid (1990) evaluated preferences between items that had been suggested by teachers or direct care staff as potential reinforcers for each student. Reinforcers were then identified through direct observation of activation or consumption. Thus, in the former approach, preferred stimuli were first identified and then shown to be reinforcing with a different behavior, whereas the second approach directly increased an existing behavior.

However, one limitation of both approaches is the relatively small number of stimuli included within the assessment conditions. Although the procedures resulted in the identification of stimuli that served as reinforcers for selected responses, one cannot assume that the assessment resulted in the identification of a stimulus that could serve as a reinforcer for more complex responses or that would demonstrate durability over long periods of time.

IDENTIFYING REINFORCERS THROUGH HIGH-RATE BEHAVIOR

As mentioned previously, many individuals who are severely/profoundly handicapped, in addition to having obvious behavioral deficits, also display high-frequency behavior that interferes with task performance. Historically, the most common approach to treatment was to suppress these behaviors. Thus, rather than to attempt to identify how the behaviors were maintained, or to consider if at least some of them (e.g., stereotypy) might function as reinforcers, the goal was simply to reduce the inappropriate behaviors. A problem with this approach is that even when it is successful the client is still frequently unresponsive to the environment, requiring that a reinforcer assessment be conducted prior to beginning to construct a more appropriate behavioral repertoire.

Recently, two very distinct approaches to reinforcer assessment have been developed that offer a radically different approach: observing the occurrence of high-frequency behavior with the aim of identifying contingent reinforcers, or actually using these behaviors as reinforcers for shaping other behavior.

Functional analysis of behavior

It has been a common procedure to evaluate high-frequency behavior in terms of form (response topography) rather than function (the reinforcement gained from the behavior). However, recent work in self-injury and aggression has indicated that our approach should be just the opposite; function is more important than form if we are to analyze and treat these behaviors (Carr, 1988). This approach to assessment, termed a functional analysis of behavior (Iwata et al., 1982), seeks to identify the function served by the behavior, or, more precisely, to identify the variables maintaining behavior. Four classes of maintaining variables have been identified consistently in the literature (Carr and Durand, 1985; Iwata et al., 1982): (a) social attention (positive reinforcement), (b) tangible (positive reinforcement), (c) escape (negative reinforcement), and (d) sensory (automatic reinforcement). A more extensive discussion of functional analysis is provided by Oliver in Chapter 5.

The maintaining contingency for high-frequency behavior is often identified through a series of analog assessments, such that the target behavior is consequated by a specific class of reinforcement. Thus, the individual is provided with social attention, a tangible item, or brief escape contingent upon the occurrence of the target behavior. When we evaluate patterns of behavior within and across these potential maintaining conditions, positive or negative reinforcers can frequently be isolated. As a control condition, a free play, differential reinforcement of other behaviors, or an 'alone' condition is also utilized. If behavior occurs uniformly across all conditions, including the control condition, or if it occurs only or primarily within the 'alone' condition, the possibility that externally presented consequences are not controlling behavior must be considered; hence, the notion of automatic reinforcement (Cowdery, Iwata and Pace, 1990).

Functional analyses of behavior can be used to assess reinforcers for individuals who display high rates of aberrant behavior (Durand et al., 1989; Northup et al., 1989). For example, Northup et al. (1989) demonstrated that the results of a functional analysis can be used to increase appropriate behavior as well as to decrease inappropriate behavior. Northup et al. first conducted a functional analysis of aberrant behavior (in this case, aggressive behavior) to identify the maintaining condition.

This assessment was novel in that it was conducted as part of a single 90-minute outclinic evaluation. Each of the four clients' aggressive behavior was initially evaluated in single 10-minute sessions (one session per condition) that included alone, social disapproval (attention), tangible, or escape conditions. This initial assessment phase, which was conducted to determine if aggressive behavior occurred more frequently during one condition than during any other, in fact showed that there was no consistent pattern across clients. However, in each case, a condition that supported high frequencies of aggression was identified.

Following the initial assessment phase, Northup et al. conducted what they termed a 'contingency reversal procedure' whereby the variables maintaining aggressive behavior were differentially applied to an appropriate behavior, which, for each client, was a signed or verbal mand ('please'). Three conditions, each lasting about 10 minutes, were then conducted using a multi-element design (Hersen and Barlow, 1976). In the first condition, the client was told or shown to sign or say 'Please' and provided with a model from the therapist. Both prompted and independent displays of the mand resulted in the presentation of the reinforcer identified through the initial assessment. For two clients, a brief (10–15 seconds) break from task was provided, for one client social attention was provided, and for the fourth client a play item was provided. Aggressive behavior was ignored. In every case, a substantial increase in manding occurred and a concomitant decrease in aggression also occurred. This was followed by the second (control) condition, in which the consequence was again provided for aggressive behavior and manding was ignored. In all cases, aggressive behavior again occurred at a high frequency, and manding decreased. In the third and final condition, manding was again reinforced, and the effects observed in the first session were replicated.

For all four clients, the maintaining contingency (positive or negative reinforcement) for aggressive behavior also functioned as a reinforcer for appropriate behavior, directly demonstrating that reinforcers identified for aberrant behavior can have utility for shaping appropriate behavior. In addition, the use of a multi-element design, with rapidly changing reversals across conditions, was apparently adequate for evaluation. Thus, even within the limited context of an outclinic evaluation, the variables maintaining inappropriate behavior were identified and used to shape more appropriate responses. However, the brief duration of assessment needs to be interpreted with caution, as it is not known if the brief version of functional analysis used in the Northup *et al.* investigation is consistent with the longer versions used in virtually all other investigations.

It is also possible, and in many cases desirable, to combine the results of functional analysis with a direct assessment of reinforcer preferences. It is important to remember that functional analyses simply provide the class of reinforcers (positive, negative, or automatic reinforcement) maintaining behavior. Determining the specific members of that class for a given client may require additional assessment. Variability within the identified class of reinforcers is very probable, and we cannot assume, for example, that behavior that is maintained by social attention from person A will continue when social attention is provided by person B. Similarly, escape from one task situation may function as negative reinforcement, but escape from other tasks or even from variations of the original task may *not* be reinforcing. Thus, it may be necessary to combine functional analysis with direct assessment of reinforcer preferences. Steege *et al.* (1989) accomplished this by combining the direct assessment methodology developed by Pace *et al.* (1985) with the functional analysis procedures described by Carr and Durand (1985).

Steege *et al.*, working on an inpatient unit, began their assessment of a child's self-injurious behavior by conducting a functional analysis. As the child engaged in self-injury, positive reinforcement (attention and tangibles) and negative reinforcement (brief escape from task) were provided in a counterbalanced order across days within an alternating treatments design. Very few occurrences of self-injury occurred when the child was provided with positive reinforcement or when left alone. However, in one case, substantial self-injury appeared to be maintained by negative reinforcement. One treatment option might have been escape extinction, in which self-injury is ignored and the task continues (Iwata *et al.*, 1990). Cooperative responding is reinforced with brief breaks (10–30 seconds); thus, negative reinforcement is provided contingently for appropriate rather than for aberrant behavior.

A different option was selected by Steege *et al.* (1989), which illustrates how functional analysis and reinforcer assessment technologies can be linked to form an intervention package. Local educational staff were called and asked to identify what they considered to be preferred activities for the child. These activities, which included contact with a variety of tangible and edible items, were presented to the child using a procedure similar to that employed by Pace et al. (1985). The child's approach behaviors were recorded, and activities or items approached at least 80% of the time were defined as reinforcers.

The results of both the functional analysis and the reinforcer identification assessment were used to develop a treatment package. Cooperative behavior on demanding tasks resulted in brief breaks (negative reinforcement), and, during these breaks, the child had access to previously identified positive reinforcers. A multiple baseline design across demanding tasks showed that the treatment package resulted in immediate reduction of self-injury, and long-term follow-up showed that the treatment effects were durable over time. The combined use of negative and positive reinforcement was possible because of the separate assessments conducted.

Given that, at least in some cases, appropriate and aberrant behavior are members of the same operant class (Carr, 1988), then functional analysis procedures might be used as a direct assessment of reinforcers for appropriate behavior. Rather than focusing on aberrant behavior during assessment, we might instead provide the same analog conditions contingently for appropriate behavior and thus directly identify positive and negative reinforcers. As an example, in our outclinic evaluations, we have sometimes conducted a functional analysis entirely with appropriate mand behavior. The initial assessment conditions (alone, tangible, social attention, and escape) are set up to provide positive or negative reinforcement *only* for appropriate manding (e.g., signing), and aberrant behavior is ignored. Assessment is conducted to identify if appropriate manding increases in one condition relative to the others. This initial assessment is then followed by a replication phase, in which the best (most appropriate manding) and worst (least appropriate manding) conditions are repeated within a reversal design to further replicate the initial assessment results. We have found this approach to be especially useful with very severe aberrant behavior and with clients who display low-frequency but high-intensity aberrant behavior. If, as we believe, aberrant behavior and appropriate mand behavior are in the same response class (Carr, 1988), then a direct assessment of appropriate mand behavior should be useful to identify reinforcers for aberrant behavior. The advantage of this approach, of course, is that a differential reinforcement of appropriate behaviors treatment is directly derived from assessment. However, the relationship between aberrant behavior and appropriate mand behavior needs continued, long-term evaluation.

Use of aberrant behavior as reinforcers

When functional analysis procedures reveal no distinct pattern of behavior, or when aberrant behavior occurs during only alone conditions, behavior may be maintained by automatic reinforcement. This outcome of assessment is problematic because it is frequently difficult to make use of the results to build a treatment plan. In many cases, the target behavior involves stereotypy, and an obvious concern is how we use automatic reinforcement for programming other, more appropriate behavior. Several researchers (e.g., Lovaas, Newsom and Hickman, 1987; Rincover and Newsom, 1985) have documented the perceptual characteristics of stereotypic behaviors, and evaluated the effects of sensory reinforcement in maintaining these behaviors (e.g., to augment or reduce sensory stimulation). Others (Durand and Carr, 1987; Steege and Wacker, 1989) have evaluated whether the display of stereotypic behavior is actually maintained by extrinsic reinforcers; that is, the behaviors are socially mediated. Durand and Carr (1987) reported that stereotypic behaviors can serve an escape function; while the individuals are engaging in aberrant behavior, they are avoiding or escaping other individuals and tasks in their environment. Thus, the behavior is maintained by negative reinforcement.

Given this possibility, we recently developed what we termed an 'automatic assessment protocol' (Wacker et al., 1990) to more directly evaluate positive and negative reinforcement related to stereotypic responding. If results from typical functional analysis conditions (alone, tangible, attention, and escape) suggest that the aberrant behavior is in fact maintained by automatic reinforcement, the following assessment protocol is used. Sensory stimuli (tactile, auditory, visual, etc.) are presented in a counterbalanced order. In some conditions, aberrant behavior results in increased stimulation (positive reinforcement) whereas in other conditions aberrant behavior results in decreased stimulation (negative reinforcement). By evaluating patterns of behavior across these conditions, we can often identify both replacement stimuli (i.e., when provided, aberrant behavior decreases) and can help to determine if the behavior functions to augment or reduce existing stimulation. If, as reported by Steege and Wacker (1989), the behavior serves to augment existing sensory stimulation, then increased sensory stimulation can be used as a reinforcer for task performance. If behavior serves to reduce ongoing stimulation (i.e., blocks out sensory stimuli), then reduced stimulation can be used to negatively reinforce task performance.

A relatively innovative approach to using behaviors maintained by automatic reinforcement as reinforcers for more appropriate behavior was recently reported by Charlop, Kurtz and Casey (1990) (also see Foxx and Dufrense, 1984). Charlop and co-workers conducted a series of experiments over a five-year period with autistic children who displayed a variety of stereotypic, echolalic, and perseverative behavior. An extensive baseline condition was initially conducted where appropriate and aberrant behaviors were recorded over a long period of time while the children completed ongoing educational tasks. The baseline data were used to establish criterion levels against which the results of intervention were compared. Using a hypothesis testing approach (Repp, Felce and Barton, 1988), the investigators inferred that aberrant behavior was maintained by automatic reinforcement (behavior occurred consistently across situations, but a functional analysis was not conducted). For all children, the opportunity to perform these 'inappropriate' behaviors was then used as a positive reinforcer for task completion. An alternating treatments design was used to compare their effects with those of food reinforcers. Thus, when the children participated appropriately on a designated task, they were given the opportunity, and sometimes prompted, to engage briefly in the stereotypic behavior or were provided with a food reinforcer. In the majority of cases reported, the stereotypic behavior functioned as a positive reinforcer and was more effective than food as a reinforcer. Of equal importance, minimal or no negative side effects occurred; generalization probes revealed that the children did not increase their frequency of stereotypic behavior at other times or in other settings. These results suggest that mildly aberrant behavior (e.g., aberrant behavior that is not harmful) can be used as a reinforcer for more appropriate behavior; instead of suppressing these high-rate behaviors entirely, one can instead use the behaviors as reinforcers without apparent negative side effects.

The approach used by Charlop, Kurtz and Casey (1990) provides a very different direction for treatment than we discussed previously. If behavior is maintained by automatic reinforcement, then it may be more beneficial to schedule the occurrence of reinforcement at more appropriate times (during breaks from tasks rather than during task completion) than to attempt to suppress it entirely. We consider this to be an innovative approach because the behavior used as the reinforcer is typically defined as being inappropriate and as having no functional value. If Charlop, Kurtz and Casey's (1990) findings can be replicated, these behaviors may indeed have functional value as positive reinforcers.

SUMMARY AND CONCLUSIONS

In this chapter, we considered several distinct methods for identifying reinforcers based on an operant technology. All of the participants discussed were diagnosed as severely handicapped, with the majority functioning within the profound range of mental retardation. It is critical that reinforcers be identified for severely handicapped persons if programming is to be effective (Repp, Barton and Brulle, 1983). An obvious question, then, is: can reinforcers be identified for everyone? Put another way, is an operant approach possible for even the most profoundly handicapped persons? We strongly believe that it is, but also believe that we must continue to both expand and refine an aspect of our technology that has been poorly developed—behavioral assessment. Our approaches to treatment have far exceeded our approaches to assessment, such that we have numerous treatment options and very few assessment options. This is ironic given that our ability to provide treatment ultimately depends upon our ability to identify effective reinforcers.

To refine and expand our assessment options, we must, in our view, resist the use of indirect measures of assessment, such as reinforcer surveys, surveys of maintaining conditions, and staff reports. As exemplified by Green et al. (1988), the relation between staff reports and direct observation is questionable at best, and we know of no survey that is as valid as direct assessment. The obvious question, then, is whether there is a place for indirect measures. We believe that there is, but only as a way of augmenting, not replacing, direct assessment. Reinforcer surveys or questionnaires of client behavior can frequently provide a rational basis for formulating hypotheses. If, for example, a teacher checklist indicates that aberrant behavior only occurs during demanding activities, then a functional analysis might directly compare demand versus no demand conditions. The possible benefit of this approach is that the direct assessment can be more efficient if hypotheses are first generated about maintaining conditions (cf. chapter 5). A second way that indirect measures might be used is to assess the acceptability, or social validity (Reimers, Wacker and Koeppl, 1987), of the recommended intervention. If a teacher or parent does not view the use of a particular reinforcer to be acceptable, there is a reduced probability that the reinforcer will be used consistently. Assessing the acceptability of a recommended reinforcer may improve both the integrity with which the reinforcer is used and the long-term maintenance (continued use of treatment) of the recommended program. That said, we also believe that the literature reviewed in this chapter offers several guidelines for direct assessment.

First, as best exemplified by the research of Parsons and Reid (1990) and Steege et al. (1989), some training is almost certainly needed during assessment. We cannot expect individuals with long histories of being unresponsive, with minimal response repertoires and restricted motoric topographies, to respond immediately to reinforcing stimuli. Parsons and Reid (1990), Steege et al. (1989), and Wacker et al. (1988) provided physical prompting during assessment. Until individuals have actually made contact with potential reinforcers, we cannot expect their behavior to be influenced by any contingencies in which they are involved. Moreover, simply exposing a person to long periods of noncontingent sensory stimuli is unlikely to be useful and may be counterproductive. There is a great deal of evidence that prolonged exposure to noncontingency can decrease the likelihood of future operant behavior (Seligman, 1975). Brinker and Lewis (1982) have proposed that a 'learned helplessness' effect of this kind may occur when profoundly handicapped individuals are deprived of control of sensorimotor stimulation. Exposing severely handicapped children to long periods of sensory stimuli may have an opposite effect from what was intended; independent displays of behavior may decrease over time.

Second, we must begin to incorporate the use of negative reinforcement (Iwata, 1987) more fully into our assessment practices. Unfortunately, a strikingly large number of individuals can be shown to engage in high frequencies of aberrant behavior maintained by negative reinforcement contingencies (Iwata et al., 1990; Steege et al., 1989). This is not ideal, but is, nevertheless, an accurate description of the present situation. Moreover, as Steege et al. showed, if we can initially increase the occurrence of adaptive responding through negative reinforcement, then we can perhaps begin to use additional positive reinforcers to maintain the gains. The key, we believe, is first to increase adaptive responding. This does not mean, however, that we should artificially increase the aversiveness of the educational or residential setting to increase the probability of escape responding. Instead, we should directly measure whether escape responding is already occurring, and if so, then use negative reinforcement to shape desired behavior.

Third, we must follow the lead of Carr and Durand (1985) and Iwata et al. (1982) and begin to analyze the function of high-rate behavior rather than its form. Numerous investigators have reported the utility of this approach, and studies that compared treatments based on functional analyses to treatments based on literature reviews have further demonstrated the benefits of this approach (Durand et al., 1989; Repp, Felce and Barton, 1988). If we avoid simply suppressing unwanted behavior, but instead assess that behavior using methods such as those of Northup et al. (1989), then we may be able to identify reinforcers.

Finally, the research by Charlop, Kurtz and Casey (1990) provided what for us was a completely novel approach: the use of high-rate behavior as the reinforcer. In at least some cases, this may provide us with a means to shape more desirable behavior that can hopefully be reinforced through more conventional positive reinforcers.

At the very least, we believe that a number of very creative approaches have been reported recently for both deficit and excess behavior. There is every reason to believe that these approaches will provide a strong basis for developing a much more refined and expanded operant assessment technology for assessing individuals with severe handicaps.

Address for correspondence

Wendy K. Berg, Division of Developmental Disabilities, Department of Pediatrics, University Hospital School, University of Iowa, Iowa City, Iowa 52242, USA.

REFERENCES

Barlow, D. and Hayes, S. (1979) Alternating treatments design: One strategy for comparing the effects of two treatments on a single subject. *Journal of Applied Behavior Analysis*, **12**, 199–210.

Brinker, R.P. and Lewis, M. (1982) Making the world work with microcomputers: A learning prosthesis for handicapped infants. *Exceptional Children*, **49**, 162–170.

Burkhart, L. (1982) *More Homemade Battery Powered Toys and Educational Devices for Severely Handicapped Children*, Burkhart, Millville, Pennsylvania.

Carr, E. (1988) Functional equivalence as a mechanism of response generalization. In R. Horner, R. Koegel and G. Dunlap (eds), *Generalization and Maintenance: Life Style Changes in Applied Settings*, Brookes, Baltimore.

Carr, E. and Durand, V.M. (1985) Reducing behavior problems through functional communication training. *Journal of Applied Behavior Analysis*, **18**, 111–126.

Charlop, M., Kurtz, P. and Casey, F. (1990) Motivating autistic children: Using aberrant behaviors as reinforcers. *Journal of Applied Behavior Analysis*, **23**, 163–181.

Cowdery, G., Iwata, B. and Pace, G. (1990) Effects and side effects of DRO as treatment for self-injurious behavior. *Journal of Applied Behavior Analysis*, **23**, 487–503.

Durand, V.M. and Carr, E. (1987) Social influences on 'self-stimulatory behavior': Analysis and treatment application. *Journal of Applied Behavior Analysis*, **20**, 119–132.

Durand, V.M., Crimmins, D., Caulfield, M. and Taylor, J. (1989) Reinforcer assessment I: Using problem behavior to select reinforcers. *Journal of the Association for Persons with Severe Handicaps*, **14**, 113–126.

Fehr, M., Wacker, D., Trezise, J., Lennon, R. and Meyerson, L. (1979) Visual, auditory, and vibratory stimulation as reinforcers for profoundly retarded children. *Rehabilitation Psychology*, **26**, 201–209.

Foxx, R. and Dufrense, D. (1984) 'Harry': The use of physical restraint as a reinforcer, timeout from restraint, and fading restraint in treating a self-injurious man. *Analysis and Intervention in Developmental Disabilities*, **4**, 1–13.

Green, C., Reid, D., White, L., Halford, R., Brittain, D. and Gardner, S. (1988) Identifying reinforcers for persons with profound handicaps: Staff opinion versus systematic assessment of preferences. *Journal of Applied Behavior Analysis*, **21**, 31–43.

Hersen, M. and Barlow, D. (1976) *Single Case Experimental Designs: Strategies for Studying Behavior Change*, Pergamon Press, New York.

Iwata, B. (1987) Negative reinforcement in applied behavior analysis: An emerging technology. *Journal of Applied Behavior Analysis*, **20**, 361–378.

Iwata, B., Dorsey, M., Slifer, K., Bauman, K. and Richman, G. (1982) Toward a functional analysis of self-injury. *Analysis and Intervention in Developmental Disabilities*, **2**, 3–20.

Iwata, B., Pace, G., Kalsher, M., Cowdery, G. and Cataldo, M. (1990) Experimental analysis and extinction of self-injurious escape behavior. *Journal of Applied Behavior Analysis*, **23**, 11–27.

Lovaas, O., Newsom, C. and Hickman, C. (1987) Self-stimulatory behavior and perceptual reinforcement. *Journal of Applied Behavior Analysis*, **20**, 45–68.

Northup, J., Wacker, D., Steege, M., Cigrand, K., Sasso, G. and Cook, J. (1989) *Outpatient Evaluation of Self-injurious and Aggressive Behavior Using Functional Analysis*, Association for Behavior Analysis, Milwaukee, Wisconsin.

Pace, G., Ivancic, M., Edwards, G., Iwata, B. and Page, T. (1985) Assessment of stimulus preferences and reinforcer values with profoundly retarded individuals. *Journal of Applied Behavior Analysis*, **18**, 249–255.

Parsons, M. and Reid, D. (1990) Assessing food preferences among persons with profound mental retardation: Providing opportunities to make choices. *Journal of Applied Behavior Analysis*, **23**, 183–195.

Premack, D. (1959) Toward empirical behavior laws: I. Positive reinforcement. *Science*, **136**, 255–257.

Reimers, T., Wacker, D. and Koeppl, G. (1987) Acceptability of behavioral interventions: A review of the literature. *School Psychology Review*, **16**, 212–227.

Repp, A., Barton, L. and Brulle, A. (1983) A comparison of two procedures for programming the differential reinforcement of other behaviors. *Journal of Applied Behavior Analysis*, **16**, 435–445.

Repp, A., Felce, D. and Barton, L. (1988) Basing the treatment of stereotypic and self-injurious behaviors on hypotheses of their causes. *Journal of Applied Behavior Analysis*, **21**, 281–289.

Rincover, A. and Newsom, C. (1985) The relative motivational properties of sensory and edible reinforcers in teaching autistic children. *Journal of Applied Behavior Analysis*, **18**, 237–248.

Seligman, M. (1975) *Helplessness: On Depression, Development, and Death*, W.H. Freeman, San Francisco.

Steege, M. and Wacker, D. (1989) Use of behavioral assessment and functional communication training in the treatment of self-injury and stereotypy in individuals with severe, multiple handicaps. In V.M. Durand (chair), *Reinforcement Redux: Motivation and Persons with Severe Handicaps*, Association for Behavior Analysis, Milwaukee, Wisconsin.

Steege, M., Wacker, D., Berg, W., Cigrand, K. and Cooper, L. (1989) The use of behavioral assessment to prescribe and evaluate treatments for severely handicapped children. *Journal of Applied Behavior Analysis*, **22**, 23–33.

Wacker, D., Berg, W., Wiggins, B., Muldoon, M. and Cavanaugh, J. (1985) Evaluation of reinforcer preferences for profoundly handicapped students. *Journal of Applied Behavior Analysis*, **18**, 173–178.

Wacker, D., Wiggins, B., Fowler, M. and Berg, W. (1988) Training students with profound or multiple handicaps to make requests via microswitches. *Journal of Applied Behavior Analysis*, **21**, 331–343.

Wacker, D., Steege, M. and Berg, W. (1990) Best practices in assessment and intervention with persons who have severe/profound handicaps. In A. Thomas and J. Grimes (eds), *Best Practices in School Psychology—II*, National Association of School Psychologists, Washington, DC.

Wacker, D., Northup, J., Sasso, G., Steege, M., Cigrand, K. and Cook, J. (1990) *Outclinic Evaluation of Automatic Reinforcement with Profoundly Mentally Retarded Individuals*, Association for Behavior Analysis, Nashville.

Chapter 3

Reducing Inappropriate Behaviour Using Non-aversive Procedures: Evaluating Differential Reinforcement Schedules

ROBERT S.P. JONES

INTRODUCTION

Although prevalence figures show wide variation, it is clear that a significant minority of people with severe mental handicap engage in some form of behaviour which can be regarded as inappropriate (Cipani, 1989; Emerson, *et al.*, 1987; Gorman-Smith and Matson, 1985; LaGrow and Repp, 1984; Lennox *et al.* 1988; Matson and Taras, 1989). An analysis of the relevant literature reveals that the most frequently encountered inappropriate behaviours have been aggression, self-injury and stereotyped behaviours (c.f. Matson and Taras, 1989).

A number of literature reviews have shown that over the last two decades the most popular interventions used to reduce inappropriate behaviour have involved the administration of aversive punishment procedures (Matson and DiLorenzo, 1984). In the field of behaviour analysis, punishment has been defined in terms of a functional relationship between a behaviour and the environment. Thus, punishment refers to a reduction in the future probability of a behaviour resulting from providing a consequence for that behaviour (Azrin and Holz, 1966). It has proven more difficult to define accurately what constitutes an *aversive* procedure due to an inability to gauge the subjective feelings of the recipient of the aversive stimulation. It is perhaps easier to define an aversive procedure on the basis of the intentions of the therapist. Thus for the purposes of this review, aversive procedures involve *the intentional use of physical or emotional pain to reduce inappropriate behaviour.*

The Challenge of Severe Mental Handicap. Edited by Bob Remington
© 1991 John Wiley & Sons Ltd

Although the use of such procedures to control behaviour is not new, recent years have seen an intense debate concerning the use of aversives and this debate has focused on ethical, moral, legal and philosophical aspects of using pain-inducing stimuli to reduce behaviour. To a lesser extent, the debate has focused on the ability of different procedures to reduce inappropriate behaviour. In the wider context, some parents and professionals have argued that aversive treatments should not under any circumstances be used with people with mental handicap. In the USA such groups include the influential Association for Persons with Severe Handicaps (TASH) and the Association for Retarded Citizens (ARC). Some states uniformly ban the use of aversive treatments while others impose severe restrictions on their use. It seems clear that the debate on the use of aversives has led to changes in the treatment of people with mental handicap. In recent years aversive treatments have become less common and more 'humane' treatments have increased. In particular, one set of procedures based on the reinforcement of other behaviours and known as differential reinforcement has become increasingly popular.

One side effect of the aversives debate is that the professional who looks to the literature to guide clinical practice is faced with a plethora of arguments for and against the use of certain procedures. For example O'Brien (1981), reviewing the literature on the treatment of 'self-stimulatory' behaviour, concluded that in many cases the use of differential reinforcement procedures could produce such minimal results that 'treatment procedures (e.g., punishment) for directly decreasing self-stimulatory behaviours should be strongly considered' (p. 126). On the other hand, in a more comprehensive review of reductive procedures, Lennox et al. (1988) suggested that reinforcement procedures were successful in 62% of the studies where they are applied to treat self-injurious behaviour, 64% of the studies on aggression, 66% of the studies of disruption and destruction, 79% of the studies on stereotypy and 88% of the studies on inappropriate social behaviour. In an oft-cited book on alternatives to punishment LaVigna and Donnellan (1986) suggest that the literature in the field 'overwhelmingly' suggests that differential reinforcement techniques represent 'a viable alternative to punishment' (p. 61).

It is of considerable importance to evaluate such claims objectively. Without detailed scientific evidence to support non-aversive interventions, the aversives debate runs the danger of degenerating into confusing sloganeering and emotional campaigning (see Kiernan, this volume). Of more concern, if initial claims for treatment effectiveness are made prematurely, the search for more effective non-aversive techniques will be delayed and practitioners may slowly drift back to the increasing use of aversive procedures in the absence of effective alternatives.

This chapter critically evaluates the evidence for and against the use of differential reinforcement in relation to the four most popular schedules of reinforcement. These are the differential reinforcement of other behaviour (DRO), the differential reinforcement of alternative behaviour (DRA), the differential reinforcement of incompatible behaviour (DRI) and the differential reinforcement of low rates of responding (DRL). What these schedules have in common is that they do *not* programme consequences for inappropriate behaviour but for alternatives to it. Table 3.1 presents the definitions of the four schedules together with the variations contained within each.

REVIEWS OF DIFFERENTIAL REINFORCEMENT SCHEDULES

The differential reinforcement of other behaviour schedule

The DRO schedule is defined as reinforcement for engaging in any unspecified response (or responses) other than the target behaviour for a specified period of time (Reynolds, 1961). DRO has proven to be a popular schedule particularly with applied researchers in the field of mental handicap. A number of reviews of the use of DRO procedures are available (e.g., Lennox *et al.*, 1988; Poling and Ryan, 1982).

Although the essence of the DRO schedule involves the presentation of a reinforcer contingent on the absence of the inappropriate behaviour for a specified time period, there are a number of variations which satisfy the criteria for the definition of DRO. The first of these is termed *reset-interval DRO*. This is probably the most frequently reported variant and requires that a response-free interval is timed from the moment the inappropriate behaviour ceases. The interval is reset when the behaviour has terminated rather than when it begins. For example, if the inappropriate behaviour is hand-biting and the specified interval is 10 seconds, the client would be presented with a reinforcer at the end of every 10-second period in which hand-biting did not occur. If an incident of hand-biting did occur, however, the reinforcer would be postponed and a new 10-second interval would begin from the moment that the hand-biting ceased. The presentation of a reinforcer is thus indefinitely postponed until such time as the inappropriate behaviour is not displayed during the preset interval.

A second variation is termed *fixed-interval DRO*, and here reinforcement is also provided at the end of each interval if the inappropriate behaviour does not occur. The difference is that if the inappropriate behaviour occurs, a new interval is not timed from the moment the inappropriate

Table 3.1 Definitions of differential reinforcement schedules

Name of Schedule	Definition	Variations
Differential reinforcement of other behaviour (DRO)	The presentation of a reinforcer contingent on the absence of an inappropriate behaviour for a specified time period	Whole-interval DRO Reset-Interval DRO Fixed-Interval DRO Escalating DRO Variable DRO Momentary DRO
Differential reinforcement of alternative behaviour (DRA)	The presentation of a reinforcer contingent on the occurrence of an appropriate behaviour which is an alternative to the behaviour selected for reduction	None
Differential reinforcement of incompatible behaviour (DRI)	The presentation of a reinforcer contingent on the performance of an appropriate behaviour which is physically incompatible with the behaviour selected for reduction	None
Differential reinforcement of low-rate behaviour (DRL)	The presentation of a reinforcer contingent upon the occurrence of an inappropriate behaviour if the behaviour occurs at a sufficiently low rate	Spaced-responding DRL Full-session DRL Interval DRL

behaviour ceases. Rather, reinforcement is simply not provided at the end of that particular interval. To use the same example of hand-biting, reinforcement would be presented at the end of each 10-second interval in which no hand-biting occurs. If an incident of hand-biting were to occur, however, the interval would not be reset, no reinforcement would be provided at the end of the 10-second interval, and a new interval would begin.

A third variation, termed *escalating DRO*, involves the gradual increase of the interval size as a function of reinforcement delivery. In escalating interval DRO, if the specificed interval (e.g., 10 seconds) passes without the inappropriate behaviour occurring and reinforcement is delivered, the next interval would be increased by a certain amount (e.g. to 15 seconds). If the inappropriate behaviour does occur, however, the next interval would remain at 10 seconds.

A fourth variation is termed *variable DRO* and involves varying the response-free interval from trial to trial. In fixed-interval DRO, the interval (e.g., 10 seconds) remains the same from trial to trial. A variable DRO of 10 seconds would mean that, on average, a reinforcer follows every 10 seconds of behaviour omission. These time intervals might be 2, 5, 7, 12, 14, and 20 seconds programmed to occur in random sequence. A final variant of DRO has been termed *momentary DRO,* and in this procedure reinforcement is provided if the behaviour is not occurring at a particular moment of observation. Momentary DRO is arranged in a different manner from the previously mentioned variations. In all of these the behaviour is observed for the whole of the specified interval. Thus, all of these variations could be classed as whole-interval DRO schedules. The relationship between momentary and whole-interval DRO is analogous to the relationship between momentary and whole-interval time sampling (e.g., Powell *et al.,* 1977). In whole-interval DRO, reinforcement is provided if the inappropriate behaviour has not occured for the whole of a specifed interval (e.g., 10 seconds). In momentary DRO reinforcement is provided if the behaviour is not occurring at the moment between two intervals (e.g., at the moment of transition from one 10-second interval to the next). As with momentary time sampling, the moment of observation would be signalled, often by an auditory tone or similar electronic mechanism.

A close analysis of the literature suggests that evidence for the effectiveness of DRO is inconclusive. Some studies show DRO to be effective when used alone, others show it to be effective only when used in combination with other response reduction procedures, and yet others report DRO to be ineffective or even to increase the target behaviour. Many studies reported in the literature do not specify which variant of DRO has been used, and some studies do not present sufficient procedural information to allow a categorization to be made. For this reason the following discussion relates to DRO procedures in general and will not specify which variant is being discussed.

There are many recent examples where DRO has been reported as being effective when used alone. These include the reduction of stereotypy (Haring *et al.,* 1986), aggression (Redmon, 1987), inappropriate masturbation (Foxx *et al.,* 1986) and self-injurious behaviour (Luiselli, 1986). In comparison studies, Luiselli (1986) found DRO to be superior to medication in reducing the self-injurious behaviour of two children with severe mental handicap, and Christensen and Sanders (1987) using a group study found DRO and a habit reversal procedure to be equally effective in reducing thumb-sucking in pre-school children.

More frequently, studies report the use of DRO in combination with other procedures, and one of the major strengths of the schedule lies in its ability to combine with a host of other treatments. Peterson and Peterson (1968) successfully used DRO to reduce the self-destructive behaviour of a client with mental handicap, but found its effectiveness was enhanced with time out (see also Bostow and Bailey, 1969). Repp and Deitz (1974) found reductions in the aggressive and self-injurious behaviours of four children with mental handicap when DRO was used in combination with either mild verbal punishment, brief time out, or response cost. More recently, Matson and Keys (1990) found that combining DRO with mild punishment procedures (verbal reprimands, response interruption and movement suppression time out) was more effective than DRO alone.

Less frequently, but perhaps more importantly, there have been a growing number of studies in which DRO has been shown to be ineffective. Occasionally, this lack of effectiveness has been cited as a reason to use another procedure in combination with DRO (e.g., Sissons et al., 1988), including using additional aversive treatments such as electric shock (e.g., Foxx, Bittle and Faw, 1989). Interestingly, some studies have been published which report contradictory results to the initial positive findings. Thus, DRO has been reported to be ineffective when used alone in the treatment of self-injury (Scotti, Evans and Murphy, 1988), stereotypy (Jones and Baker, 1988a) and aggression (Friman et al., 1986). Earlier studies also reported similar results (Dorsey et al., 1980; Tarpley and Schroeder, 1979; Tierney, McGuire and Walton, 1979).

Of still more concern are the small but growing number of studies in which the DRO procedure has been reported as leading to an increase in the target behaviour. Recently, such results have been reported by Friman et al. (1986) and by Jones and Baker (1988a), but earlier studies had also reported similar findings (Foxx and Azrin, 1973; Harris and Wolchik, 1979).

What can be concluded from this short review is that overall pronouncements as to the effectiveness of DRO cannot as yet be reliably made with any degree of confidence. The evidence for treatment effectiveness is contradictory and confusing. The most important question therefore does not concern the overall effectiveness of the schedule but rather the reasons for the mixed success reported in the literature. As will be seen, reviews of other differential reinforcement schedules reveal similar findings.

The differential reinforcement of alternative behaviour schedule

The DRA schedule is one in which reinforcement is provided contingent on the occurrence of a specified appropriate behaviour which is an alternative to the behaviour selected for reduction. It is possible for the appropriate behaviour and the inappropriate behaviour to be displayed at the same time (topographical compatibility) and it is this topographical compatibility which differentiates DRA from the more popular DRI schedule. If a client was engaged in hand-flapping, for example, reinforcement could be provided for kicking a football (DRA). Under a DRI schedule, however, the appropriate behaviour would have to be incompatible with the hand-flapping (e.g., painting or keyboard work). Although some reviewers do not distinguish between DRA and DRI (e.g., LaVigna and Donnellan, 1986, use the term Alt-R as a combined label), these schedules contain specific and different schedule parameters and should be regarded separately. For example, Young and Wincze (1974) directly compared the effects of DRA and DRI on the self-injurious behaviour (SIB) of a female adult diagnosed as profoundly handicapped. Using a multiple baseline, within-subject design, the authors showed that the mere presence of an opportunity to engage in an alternative behaviour, for which reinforcement was programmed, was not sufficient in itself to reduce self-injurious behaviour. Although the same reinforcers (ice cream and social praise) were available under both schedule conditions, the DRI schedule effected a superior reduction in SIB. This study suggested that the degree of incompatibility of the target response was the key variable.

As with DRO, reports of the outcome of using DRA have been mixed. Some studies report that DRA when used alone can reduce inappropriate behaviours (e.g., Schneider, Ross and Drubin, 1979). Others have reported DRA to have mixed effects (e.g., Johnson et al., 1982), and some reports suggest that DRA is only effective when used in combination with other procedures such as brief physical restraint (e.g., Saloviita, 1988), time out (e.g., Ralph, 1987) and a 'mild slap' (e.g., Cavalier and Ferretti, 1980). In general, however, DRA has not proven to be a popular reinforcement procedure and most authors appear to have chosen an alternative behaviour which was incompatible with the target response and implemented a DRI schedule. DRI has obvious advantages over DRA in that with DRA the inappropriate behaviour could still occur even though the appropriate behaviour may increase.

The differential reinforcement of incompatible behaviour schedule

Like DRA, DRI is a procedure which has its origins in the clinical rather than in the research field. The rationale for using a DRI procedure is that increasing the targeted appropriate behaviour should lead to a contingent decrease in the frequency of the inappropriate behaviour if the appropriate behaviour occurs often enough (see Jones and Baker, 1990, for a detailed review).

A number of recent examples show DRI to be successful in a wide variety of contexts. These include stereotypy (Jones and Baker, 1988a; Jones, Baker and Murphy, 1988), SIB (Azrin et al., 1988; Underwood et al., 1989), hand mouthing (McClure et al., 1986), pica (Smith, 1987), and aggression (Swerissen and Carruthers, 1987; Friman et al., 1986).

As with DRO, some of these studies reported success using DRI alone (e.g., Jones and Baker, 1988a 1988b; Smith, 1987; Wolery, Kirk and Gast, 1985), while others found DRI to be successful only when used in combination with other procedures (e.g., McGreevy and Arthur, 1987; Neufeld and Fantuzzo, 1987; Underwood et al., 1989). In the study comparing DRA with DRI mentioned earlier, for example, although DRI proved to be superior to DRA in reducing SIB, it was not until DRI was combined with contingent electric shock that all classes of SIB were reduced (Young and Wincze, 1974).

Thus, once again, no general recommendations can be made as to whether DRI should be used in combination with other procedures or whether it can safely be used alone. Clearly a host of factors related to the individual client and the type of behaviour measured will influence the success of the intervention. Similarly, despite the findings of the studies outlined above where DRI was shown to be successful, there have been a smaller number of studies in which DRI was used without apparent success (Bird et al., 1989; Borreson, 1980; Denny, 1980; Luiselli et al., 1977). Once again, as with DRO, there is not enough unequivocal information concerning the effectiveness of this schedule to be dogmatic concerning its use. As with DRO, therefore, the most important question does not concern whether the schedule can be regarded as successful but rather concerns the reasons for the mixed success reported in the literature.

The differential reinforcement of low-rate behaviour schedule

In 1957, Ferster and Skinner published *Schedules of Reinforcement*, which detailed the many types of schedule which could be programmed to control operant behaviour. One schedule consistently produced very low rates of responding and accordingly was named the differential reinforcement of low rates of behaviour schedule, or DRL. This schedule provides reinforcement for a response only if it occurs at a sufficiently low rate. Based on the laboratory procedures described by Ferster and Skinner, Deitz (1977) described three types of DRL schedules: spaced responding DRL, interval DRL, and full-session DRL.

Spaced responding DRL

This schedule requires the delivery of reinforcement, contingent on the occurrence of a specified behaviour that is separated from its previous occurrence by a minimum amount of time. This interval is known as the inter-response time (IRT). Thus a reinforcer is delivered following a target response only if that response occurs after a specified interval of time has elapsed since the last response (Kramer and Rilling, 1970).

Once the behaviour meets the IRT requirement, it is possible to further reduce the response rate by differentially reinforcing progressively longer IRTs, thus achieving lower rates of the inappropriate behaviour (Deitz, 1977). The length of the IRT is usually determined by the rate of responding exhibited by the client in a baseline observation phase. Spaced responding DRL has been used frequently in laboratory settings (see Kramer and Rilling, 1970, for a review), but comparatively little has been published on applied usage (but see Deitz, 1977; Favell, McGimsey and Jones, 1980). One of the major drawbacks with this method is the ethical difficulty that the unwanted behaviour continues to be reinforced, albeit at a low rate.

Full-session DRL

Deitz (1977) also suggested a second method which could be applied in programming DRL, which involved delivering a reinforcer at the end of the session if the number of responses in a specified period of time is less than, or equal to, a prescribed limit. For example, if baseline observations showed that a client engages in an average of five incidences of swearing during a one-hour teaching session, the reinforcer could be delivered at the end if the client swears four times or less during the teaching session. No effort is made to reinforce spaced responding because the schedule is intended instead to produce a low rate of responding across the entire session. Once behavioural control has been established, it is possible to reduce the DRL parameter (e.g., to three responses), thus further lowering the average rate of responding.

Deitz (1977) called this full-session DRL, and it is this method which is found in most applied studies investigating DRL (e.g., Barrish, Saunders and Wolf, 1969; Deitz and Repp, 1973; Hall *et al.*, 1971; Schmidt and Ulrich, 1969). An advantage with this method is that because the reinforcer is delivered at the end of the session, this avoids directly reinforcing the inappropriate behaviour.

Interval DRL

Deitz (1977) also suggested a third type of DRL schedule, which he named interval DRL. This is similar to spaced responding in that both reduce the rates of responding by separating responses by some amount of time. Interval DRL, however, requires that, instead of specifying a particular IRT criterion for a response to be reinforced, the *average* number of responses made by the client is used to determine reinforcer delivery. The length of the interval is determined by baseline responding, the experimenter calculating the base rate and setting the interval to a value equal to or slightly less than the average interval found between responses in the baseline.

For example, if a subject emits a targeted behaviour, such as shouting out in class, an average of five times in every 15-minute period this equates to approximately one shout every three minutes. If the DRL interval is thus set at 3 minutes, and the DRL limit per interval is set at one, this means that the subject is permitted to shout once in any given interval without comment from the teacher. Should the rest of the interval pass without further instances of the behaviour, then the client will receive a reinforcer. If, however, the client should shout a second time within the interval, then a new interval is begun and no reinforcer is delivered. Once the behaviour is under control of the schedule, increasing the interval but holding the DRL limit constant can reduce the rate of responding further. Thus, changing the interval from 3 minutes to 4 minutes, and keeping the DRL limit at one, will, when established, mean that an average of less than four instances of target behaviour will now occur in any 15-minute interval, and so on. Although Deitz (1977) used this method in an applied setting to demonstrate its effectiveness, it is not as frequently employed in clinical contexts as full-session DRL.

In summarizing the research on DRL three difficulties arise. Firstly, compared with the other three schedules mentioned previously only a small number of research studies using humans have been carried out with this schedule. Of these studies, only a tiny minority were carried out with people with severe mental handicap and there is consequently only a small number of studies available from which to draw conclusions concerning the effectiveness of the schedule. Secondly, most of the applied work with DRL has used the modified procedures outlined by Deitz and Repp (1973, 1974) and by Deitz (1977) which, as has been mentioned, utilizes different schedule criteria to that first proposed by Ferster and Skinner (1957). Thus, whether or not a DRL 'schedule' can be regarded as a single entity is open to debate. It could be argued, for instance, that interval DRL has more in common with DRO than with full-session DRL. Thirdly, of the studies reported using DRL, the majority were carried out with verbally able clients. As will be discussed later, the verbal ability of the client may be a key variable in explaining the effectiveness of a reinforcement schedule in exercising efficient control of behaviour. This may be particularly true with a schedule as complex as DRL. Thus, once again, there are insufficient data available to draw firm conclusions about the applicability of DRL to clients with severe mental handicap.

CRITIQUE OF RESEARCH USING REINFORCEMENT SCHEDULES

Less than a decade ago, it was common to see differential reinforcement-based schedules hailed as the way forward in the treatment of inappropriate behaviour and the main approach to take in avoiding the use of aversive interventions. Even in situations where punishment procedures were deemed appropriate, ethical guidelines often specified the concurrent use of reinforcement procedures (e.g., Favell et al., 1982). It would seem from a close analysis of the literature that such optimism is scarcely justified today. In summarizing the findings from reviewing the literature on the reinforcement schedules, what seems clear is that the results are more variable than might be expected from a superficial examination of textbooks or individual review articles. In general, although many studies report success using reinforcement procedures, other studies have been unsuccessful. On rare occasions, reinforcement procedures have actually led to an increase in the inappropriate behaviour. Further, it is likely that many studies showing a lack of success may not be reported due to a probable publication bias against unsuccessful interventions (Westland, 1978). The remainder of this chapter argues that it is therefore misguided to try to make firm prescriptive statements about particular intervention procedures. The key tasks are to account for the variable results and to examine ways of optimizing the probability of success.

In attempting to account for these variable results a number of factors will be examined. These are reinforcement, functional analysis, baseline data, verbal behaviour, and ease of implementation.

Reinforcer potency

It seems clear that similar response-contingent stimuli can have different functions for different individuals. Thus, the same stimulus can function as a reinforcer or a punisher depending on the circumstances. For example, contingent restraint has been used as a *punisher* for stereotyped behaviour (e.g., Bitgood *et al.*, 1980; Reid, Tombaugh and Heuvel, 1981) and as a *reinforcer* for increasing periods of time without self-injury (e.g., Favell, McGimsey and Jones, 1978). It is therefore inappropriate to label a stimulus as a reinforcer in the absence of further evidence. Social praise, for example, is frequently referred to as social reinforcement even in situations where the praise has no reinforcing properties (Brophy, 1981; Cullen, 1983). For a reinforcement schedule to maintain control over responding there must be an initial identification of reinforcers stronger than those maintaining the inappropriate behaviour. Although this appears almost a truism, it is remarkable how many studies appear to give little consideration to issues of reinforcer potency. Edibles and social praise are often assumed to function as reinforcers with little, if any, systematic attempt to test their reinforcing properties. As Repp, Barton and Brulle (1983) point out, many studies on reinforcement schedules 'may have demonstrated the extent to which some researchers are poor or unlucky at the task of selecting reinforcers, rather than the extent to which some schedules are ineffective' (p. 444). At the simplest level, an explanation for the lack of success of some of the studies mentioned earlier could simply be due to the fact that the stimuli scheduled as reinforcers were not, in fact, reinforcing or were not powerful enough reinforcers to compete with the reinforcement which was maintaining the inappropriate behaviour (see Berg and Wacker, this volume).

Functional analysis

In addition to the difficulties with reinforcer potency, the reasons for the failure of an imposed reinforcement schedule to control inappropriate behaviour may be traced to a lack of analysis of the existing relationships between the behaviour and its consequences. There is considerable recent evidence to suggest that an intervention based on an assessment of the function of inappropriate behaviour shows a high probability of success if that intervention addresses the identified functions (see Durand and Crimmins; and Oliver, this volume). It is rare, however, to find a detailed analysis of the function of behaviour reported in the literature on differential reinforcement. For example, Lennox *et al.* (1988), reviewing the decelerative literature for five years from 1981 to 1985, found that in 64% of all treatment studies no form of functional analysis was used. Of the remaining studies, 17% obtained staff reports, 18% made some reference to an A: B: C type analysis and only 6% undertook a more sophisticated analysis such as analogue assessment (Iwata *et al.*, 1982; Parrish *et al.*, 1985; Repp, Felce and Barton, 1988; Sturmey *et al.*, 1988). It is quite possible that without an awareness of the functions of the behaviour (e.g., attention-seeking, self-stimulation, task avoidance), the scheduling of even a potent reinforcer may have little effect in the long term unless the client can obtain an alternative way of fulfilling these functions.

To illustrate with a hypothetical example, a client might be observed to engage in hand-biting and this behaviour targeted for reduction. A functional analysis is not carried out but baseline observations show that the hand-biting is frequently consequated with attention which is known to function as a powerful social reinforcer. A DRO procedure could be implemented whereby staff spend time helping the client with some academic work, thus providing social attention contingent on a period of absence from hand-biting. If the function of the inappropriate behaviour is to obtain social reinforcement then the procedure should be successful and a paper may be published suggesting that a DRO procedure can be successful when used alone to reduce the SIB (hand-biting). To modify the scenario slightly, however, the hand-biting observed might also have served a task-avoidance function. If this function was not assessed before the DRO procedure was instigated, it is likely that the inappropriate behaviour would remain constant or even increase due to an increase in task demands which occurred as staff attempted to provide social attention in the context of academic work. Here the paper would show that DRO is ineffective when used alone and, in fact, can even lead to an increase in the inappropriate behaviour. Such a finding might be used to justify the implementation of a more restrictive or punitive treatment to reduce the SIB.

The central point here is that to use the findings of such hypothetical research papers to assess whether or not DRO is an effective reductive procedure would clearly be inappropriate. The implications for the assessment of the literature on differential reinforcement reviewed earlier are clear, and point to a further possible explanation for the inconsistent findings reported for these procedures.

Baseline data

Even if a sophisticated functional analysis is not undertaken it is important that procedures are not implemented in an arbitrary manner but are based on data obtained from a careful observation of the client during baseline conditions. The choice of schedule parameters should be determined by baseline data in all instances but this is perhaps of most importance in scheduling DRO and DRL procedures. With DRL, the programming of the initial DRL value should be based on baseline values of IRTs or, in the case of full-session DRL, numbers of responses. This relationship between baseline data and schedule programming is an important consideration in the application of DRL because it is difficult to see how the schedule contingencies could contact the behaviour in the absence of such programming.

It is with DRO, however, that the greatest variation occurs. There is no universally accepted standard for setting the DRO interval but many researchers adhere to the principle of setting the initial DRO interval slightly shorter than the average baseline IRT.

Once again, however, it seems that although appropriate suggestions for the correct use of DRO have been in the literature for many years (e.g., Repp and Deitz, 1979), some studies report inappropriate schedule procedures. Borreson (1980), for example, states that a DRO 5-minute programme was ineffective in reducing the self-injurious biting of a 22-year-old client with profound mental handicap. However, Borreson's data show that in a 6-hour day the client produced in excess of 2000 incidents of SIB, i.e. one hit approximately every 10 seconds. It is not surprising therefore that a DRO 5-minute interval was unsuccessful! After further attempts at a less restrictive alternative, SIB was successfully reduced using an aversive (forced running) procedure. The central point here is that the Borreson study does not constitute an adequate evaluation of the effectiveness of DRO in applied settings. There may be a considerable number of other studies which report failure using differential reinforcement schedules where a change in the procedure could have led to success. Most studies simply do not report sufficient procedural detail to determine how DRO intervals were calculated. Once again a possible explanation for the mixed results reported in the literature is suggested.

Verbal behaviour

More than fifty years ago, Skinner had indicated that whether or not one can extrapolate operant principles from animals to humans is a question that can only be resolved by systematic experimental investigation of both human and animal operant behaviour (Skinner, 1938). What is clear from a host of studies conducted since then is that considerable differences exist in the schedule performance of animals and humans. In particular, human responding on schedules of reinforcement frequently bears little resemblance to the documented performance of animal subjects. Recent research has focused on the role of verbal stimuli in determining performance (cf. Hayes *et al.*, 1986). These differences include patterns of schedule performance and particularly a marked insensitivity to changes in schedule conditions. For example, in a series of experiments, Lowe and his colleagues (Bentall and Lowe, 1987; Bentall, Lowe and Beasty, 1985; Lowe, Beasty and Bentall, 1983) have investigated the role of verbal behaviour in human operant behaviour. They showed that, with respect to patterns of responding and schedule sensitivity, infants under 12 months responded in animal-like ways on a fixed-interval schedule (i.e., producing a scalloped pattern of responses, typical of animal responding). Adult humans produce behavioural patterns distinctly different from those of animals. Subsequent experiments examined the performance of children at different levels of verbal ability, aged between 2 and 9 years, and found that children aged 5 years and over exhibited patterns of behaviour similar to those found in human adults (i.e., high- and low-rate response patterns), while the performance of the younger children differed from both the infant pattern of responding of the earlier experiment and that of the older children although it contained elements of both. Lowe interprets these findings as implying that younger children were in a state of change in performance which related to their acquisition of language ability. They had considerable language ability but were not capable of formulating the kinds of verbal descriptions of the contingencies, and rules to guide responding, that were produced by the older children. Instead, the apparently unsystematic and varied verbalizations of this group were accompanied by varied and irregular response patterning (Bentall, Lowe and Beasty, 1985, p. 178). These findings suggest that the ability to describe the contingencies of reinforcement verbally will exert a powerful influence over a client's performance on reinforcement schedules.

Despite these findings, however, workers in the field of mental handicap have largely ignored the influence of verbal behaviour and have continued to schedule reinforcement using procedures directly adapted from work with animal subjects. An underlying assumption behind this practice is that people with mental handicap represent a homogeneous group and therefore that they can be treated in a similar manner. Clearly, however, any large group of such people will include individuals who have differing verbal abilities. It is likely, therefore, that the responses of these individuals to particular interventions will differ on the basis of their ability to formulate and use verbal rules describing schedule contingencies. Despite the obvious relevance of Lowe's work, as yet there have been few applications to people with mental handicap. Although differences in clients' ability to formulate verbal rules may account for some of the mixed results reported in the literature, once again the majority of studies provide insufficient information to enable firm conclusions to be drawn.

If future research confirms the importance of verbal behaviour in the programming of reinforcement schedules, then it is likely that this would lead to more careful matching of schedule parameters and client characteristics. By tailoring an intervention programme to both the needs and the abilities of the client, it should more often be possible to produce effective interventions that will both last over time and generalize to novel settings (Stokes and Baer, 1977).

In situations where clients have only limited verbal ability, it may be possible to improve schedule performance by making the rules relating to the schedule contingency more explicit, or expressing them in simpler terms or indeed by teaching these subjects to formulate and use their own verbal rules (e.g., Bentall and Lowe, 1987). This should also aid retention of the newly learned behaviour, and thus positively influence maintenance and generalization.

Ease of implementation

The implementation of differential reinforcement procedures is costly in terms of staff time and energy (see Felce; and Ager, this volume). At minimum, the use of the schedules described previously requires the undivided attention of at least one staff member working full time for the duration of the programme. Where more sophisticated analyses are required (e.g., reliability measures, analogue assessments, concurrent schedule presentation), one staff member is seldom enough.

Many studies of the efficacy of reinforcement procedures have taken place in well-staffed and highly controlled settings more reminiscent of experimental laboratories than the busy, noisy, understaffed environments in which many people with mental handicaps work and live. Yet it is these everyday environments which will provide the acid test for the effectiveness of reinforcement procedures. Poling and Ryan (1982), for example, stated that 'a response-suppression procedure such as DRO that requires intensive and prolonged effort is of limited worth in many applied settings, where staff time is at a premium' (p. 15).

A number of studies have suggested that procedures which work well in laboratory settings fail to show consistent results in applied situations because of difficulties in implementing the schedules. For example, Tierney, McGuire and Walton (1979), in a comparison study between a DRO schedule and a variable time (VT) schedule, reported abandoning the use of DRO due to the difficulty that staff reported in programming the schedule. In their first experiment they had used a resetting DRO 20-second procedure timed with a stopwatch. 'The degree of vigilance required by this schedule was considerable, and without exception each staff member reported difficulty in concentrating to the required standard' (p. 178). In a second experiment a reinforcer was administered on a noncontingent, VT 10-minute schedule. The actual durations varied from 1 to 19 minutes and the staff were supplied with a list of duration times and a simple kitchen timer. The authors found that the VT procedure resulted in significant reductions in the stereotyped body-rocking of five profoundly handicapped female clients. A major factor in the comparative success of the VT procedure appears to have been the relative ease with which it could be programmed by the nursing staff. In the study by Jones and Baker (1988b) on the effects of DRI on SIB mentioned previously, nursing staff had to abandon precise measurements with an electronic timer in order to continue to implement the DRI procedure. Similarly, Saloviita (1988) also found staff unwilling or unable to carry out intervention procedures using a DRA procedure combined with physical restraint. 'The regular staff were not able to organize the necessary supervision of Paul, nor . . . to efficiently carry out the reinforcement programme' (p. 61).

Woods and Cullen (1983) make the point that our analysis of staff reinforcers can at times be naive, and that staff behaviour is more often negatively reinforced by senior staff than positively reinforced by the gradual but often barely perceptible changes in the client's behaviour. The influence of staff behaviour is a vital but often ignored variable in the successful implementation of a differential reinforcement procedure. When considering the difficulties in implementing reinforcement schedules, the influence of staff behaviour on the variable results reported earlier cannot be ruled out.

CONCLUSIONS

Undoubtedly there are other aspects to the choice of intervention procedure besides its therapeutic efficacy (LaVigna and Donnellan, 1986; McGee et al., 1987). These aspects include ethical, moral and humanitarian decisions as well as legal and professional guidelines and codes of practice. All these considerations will affect the choice of intervention for any one client. It can be argued, however, that demonstrated therapeutic efficacy should be the most important consideration guiding this decision (O'Brien, 1989). On the basis of demonstrated efficacy alone, more work is required before differential reinforcement can be regarded as the treatment of first choice. This work might, for example, involve the use of differential reinforcement procedures under ideal conditions across a variety of behaviours and situations. These ideal conditions would involve adequate staff provision and would include the systematic assessment of stimuli scheduled as reinforcers, the selection of the reinforcement conditions on the basis of baseline data, and a functional analysis of the relationship between the behaviour and its scheduled consequences.

An analysis of the successes and failures of these 'ideal' procedures could then be undertaken to determine the overall efficacy of differential reinforcement in the reduction of inappropriate behaviour. Until such studies are carried out, however, we must remain open minded in our evaluation of the reductive power of these procedures.

In the meantime, what can be concluded from this review is that overall pronouncements as to the effectiveness of differential reinforcement procedures cannot as yet be reliably made with any degree of confidence. The evidence for treatment effectiveness is contradictory and confusing. On the basis of our current level of awareness, it simply does not make sense to try to make statements as to the overall utility of differential reinforcement as an alternative to more aversive procedures. On the basis of existing published work a therapist would have no way of knowing the probability of a particular reinforcement schedule reducing a client's inappropriate behaviour. The message from the literature is clear. Although the differential reinforcement schedule *might* be successful in reducing the inappropriate behaviour, it might alternatively have no effect, and it might possibly even make the behaviour worse.

Address for correspondence

Robert S.P. Jones, Department of Psychology, University College of North Wales, Bangor, Gwynedd LL57 2DG, UK.

REFERENCES

Azrin, N.H., and Holz, W.C. (1966) Punishement. In W.K. Honig (ed.), *Operant behavior: Areas of research and application* (pp. 380–447), Appleton–Century–Crofts, New York.

Azrin, N.H., Besalel, V.A., Jamner, J.P. and Caputo, J.N. (1988) Comparative study of behavioral methods of treating self-injury. *Behavioral Residential Treatment*, 3, 119–152.

Barrish, H.H., Saunders, M. and Wolf, M.M. (1969) Good behaviour game: Effects of individual contingencies for group consequences on disruptive behaviour in a classroom. *Journal of Applied Behavior Analysis*, **2**, 119–124.

Bentall, R.P. and Lowe, C.F. (1987) The role of verbal behavior in human learning: III. Instructional effects in children. *Journal of the Experimental Analysis of Behavior*, **47**, 177–190.

Bentall, R.P., Lowe, C.F. and Beasty, A. (1985) The role of verbal behavior in human learning: II. Developmental differences. *Journal of the Experimental Analysis of Behavior*, **43**, 165–181.

Bird, F., Dores, P.A., Moniz, D. and Robinson, J. (1989) Reducing severe aggressive and self-injurious behaviors with functiional communication training. *American Journal on Mental Retardation*, **94**, 37–48.

Bitgood, S.C., Crowe, M.J., Suarez, Y. and Peters, R.D. (1980) Immobilization: Effects and side effects of stereotyped behavior in children. *Behavior Modification*, **4**, 187–208.

Borreson, P.M. (1980) The elimination of a self-injurious avoidance response through a forced running consequence. *Mental Retardation*, **18**, 73–77.

Bostow, D.E. and Bailey, J.B. (1969) Modification of severe disruptive behavior using brief time out and reinforcement procedures. *Journal of Applied Behavior Analysis*, **2**, 31–37.

Brophy, J. (1981) Teacher praise: A functional analysis. *Review of Educational Research*, **51**, 5–32.

Catania, A.C. (ed.) (1968) *Contemporary Research in Operant Behavior*, Scott Foresman, Glenview, Illinois.

Cavalier, A.R. and Ferretti, R.P. (1980) Stereotyped behaviour, alternative behaviour and collerateral effects: A comparison of four intervention procedures. *Journal of Mental Deficiency Research*, **24**, 219–229.

Christensen, A.P. and Saunders, M.R. (1987) Habit reversal and differential reinforcement of other behavior in the treatment of thumb-sucking: An analysis of generalization and side-effects. *Journal of Child Psychology and Psychiatry and Allied Disciplines*, **28**, 281–295.

Cipani, E. (ed.) (1989) *The Treatment of Severe Behavior Disorders*, American Association on Mental Retardation, Washington, DC.

Cullen, C. (1983) Implications of functional analysis. *British Journal of Clinical Psychology*, **22**, 137–138.

Denny, M. (1980) Reducing self-stimulatory behavior of mentally retarded persons by alternative positive practice. *American Journal of Mental Deficiency*, **84**, 610–615.

Deitz, S.M. (1977) An analysis of programming DRL schedules in educational settings. *Behaviour Research and Therapy*, **15**, 103–111.

Deitz, S.M. and Repp, A.C. (1973) Decreasing classroom misbehavior through the use of DRL schedules of reinforcement. *Journal of Applied Behavior Analysis*, **6**, 457–463.

Deitz, S.M. and Repp, A.C. (1974) Differentially reinforcing low rates of misbehavior with normal elementary school children. *Journal of Applied Behavior Analysis*, **7**, 622.

Dorsey, M.F., Iwata, B.A., Ong, P. and McSween, T.E. (1980) Treatment of self-injurious behavior using a water mist: Initial response suppression and generalization. *Journal of Applied Behavior Analysis*, **13**, 343–353.

Emerson, E., Barrett, S., Bell, C., Cummings, R., McCool, C., Toogood, A. and Mansell, J. (1987) *Developing Services for People With Severe Learning Difficulties and Challenging Behaviours*, Institute of Social and Applied Psychology, University of Kent at Canterbury.

Favell, J.E., McGimsey, J.F. and Jones, M.L. (1978) The use of physical restraint in the treatment of self-injury and as positive reinforcement. *Journal of Applied Behavior Analysis*, **11**, 225–241.

Favell, J.E., McGimsey, J.F. and Jones, M.L. (1980) Rapid eating in the retarded: Reduction by nonaversive procedures. *Behavior Modification*, **4**, 481–492.

Favell, J.E., Azrin, N.H., Baumeister, A.A., Carr, E.G., Dorsey, M.F., Forehand, R., Foxx, R.M., Lovaas, O.I., Rincover, A., Risley, T.R., Romanczyk, R.G., Russo, D.C., Schroeder, S.R. and Solnick, J.V. (1982) The treatment of self-injurious behavior (AABT task force report). *Behavior Therapy*, **13**, 529–544.

Ferster, C.B. and Skinner, B.F. (1957) *Schedules of Reinforcement*, Appleton–Century–Crofts, New York.

Foxx, R.M. and Azrin, N.H. (1973) The elimination of autistic self-stimulatory behavior by overcorrection. *Journal of Applied Behavior Analysis*, **6**, 1–14.

Foxx, R.M., Bittle, R.G. and Faw, G.D. (1989) A maintenance strategy for discontinuing aversive procedures: A 52-month follow-up of the treatment of aggression. *American Journal on Mental Retardation*, **94**, 27–36.

Foxx, R.M., McMorrow, M.J., Fenlon, S. and Bittle, R.G. (1986) The reductive effects of reinforcement procedures on the genital stimulation and stereotypy of a mentally retarded adolescent male. *Analysis and Intervention in Developmental Disabilities*, **6**, 239–248.

Friman, P.C., Barnard, J.D., Altman, K. and Wolf, M.M. (1986) Parent and teacher use of DRO and DRI to reduce aggressive behavior. *Analysis and Intervention in Developmental Disabilities*, **6**, 319–330.

Gorman-Smith, D. and Matson, J.L. (1985) A review of treatment research for self-injurious and stereotyped responding. *Journal of Mental Deficiency Research*, **29**, 295–308.

Hall, R.V., Williard, D., Goldsmith, S., Emerson, M., Owen, M., Davis, F. and Porcia, E. (1971) The teacher as observer and experimenter in the modification of disputing and talking-out behaviors. *Journal of Applied Behavior Analysis*, **4**, 141–149.

Haring, T.G., Breen, C.G., Pitts-Conway, V. and Gaylord-Ross, R. (1986) Use of differential reinforcement of other behavior during dyadic instruction to reduce stereotyped behavior of autistic students. *American Journal of Mental Deficiency*, **90**, 694–702.

Harris, S.L. and Wolchik, S.A. (1979) Suppression of self-stimulation: Three alternative strategies. *Journal of Applied Behavior Analysis*, **12**, 185–198.

Hayes, S.C., Brownstein, A.J., Hass, J.R. and Greenway, D.E. (1986) Instructions, multiple schedules and extinction: Distinguishing rule-governed from schedule-controlled behavior. *Journal of the Experimental Analysis of Behavior*, **46**, 137–147.

Iwata, B.A., Dorsey, M.F., Slifer, K.J., Bauman, K.E. and Richman, G.S. (1982) Towards a functional analysis of self-injury. *Analysis and Intervention in Developmental Disabilities*, **2**, 3–20.

Johnson, W.L., Baumeister, A.A., Penland, M.J. and Inwald, C. (1982) Experimental analysis of self-injurious, stereotypic, and collateral behavior of retarded persons: Effects of overcorrection and reinforcement of alternative responding. *Analysis and Intervention in Developmental Disabilities*, **2**, 41–66.

Jones, R.S.P. and Baker, L.J.V. (1988a) Reducing stereotyped behaviour using differential reinforcement: A comparison of DRO and DRI schedules. *Mental Handicap*, **16**, 171–174.

Jones, R.S.P. and Baker, L.J.V. (1988b) The differential reinforcement of incompatible responses in the reduction of self-injurious behaviour: A pilot study. *Behavioural Psychotherapy*, **16**, 323–328.

Jones, R.S.P. and Baker, L.J.V. (1990) Differential reinforcement and challenging behaviour: A critical analysis of the DRI schedule. *Behavioural Psychotherapy*, **18**, 35–47.

Jones, R.S.P., Baker, L.J.V. and Murphy, M. (1988) Reducing stereotyped behaviour: The maintenance effects of a DRO reinforcement procedure. *Journal of Practical Approaches to Developmental Handicap*, **12**, 24–30.

Kramer, T.J. and Rilling, M. (1970) Differential reinforcement of low rates: A selective critique. *Psychological Bulletin*, **74**, 225–254.

LaGrow, S.J. and Repp, A.C. (1984) Stereotypic responding: A review of intervention research. *American Journal of Mental Deficiency*, **88**, 595–609.

LaVigna, G.W. and Donnellan, A.M. (1986) *Alternatives to Punishment: Solving Behavior Problems with Non-Aversive Strategies*. Irvington, New York.

Lennox, D.B., Miltenberger, R.G., Spengler, P. and Erfanian, N. (1988) Decelerative treatment practices with persons who have mental retardation: A review of five years of the literature. *American Journal on Mental Retardation*, **92**, 492–501.

Lowe, C.F., Beasty, A. and Bentall, R.P. (1983) The role of verbal behaviour in human learning: infant performance on fixed-interval schedules. *Journal of the Experimental Analysis of Behavior*, **39**, 157–164.

Luiselli, J.K. (1986) Behavior analysis of pharmacological and contingency management interventions for self-injury. *Journal of Behavior Therapy and Experimental Psychiatry*, **17**, 275–284.

Luiselli, J.K., Helfen, C.S., Pemberton, B.W. and Reisman, J. (1977) The elimination of a child's in-class masturbation by overcorrection and reinforcement. *Journal of Behavior Therapy and Experimental Psychiatry*, **8**, 201–204.

Matson, J.L. and DiLorenzo, T.M. (1984) *Punishment and its Alternatives*, Springer, New York.

Matson, J.L. and Keys, J.B. (1990) A comparison of movement suppression time out and DRO with two self-injurious and aggressive mentally retarded adults. *Research in Developmental Disabilities*, **11**, 111–120.

Matson, J.L. and Taras, M.E. (1989) A 20 year review of punishment and alternative methods to treat problem behaviors in developmentally delayed persons. *Research in Developmental Disabilities*, **10**, 85–104.

McClure, J.T., Moss, R.A., McPeters, J.W. and Kirkpatrick, M.A. (1986) Reduction of hand mouthing by a boy with profound mental retardation. *Mental Retardation*, **24**, 219–222.

McGee, J.J., Menolascino, F.J., Hobbs, D.C. and Menousek, P.E. (1987) *Gentle Teaching: A Non-aversive Approach to Helping Persons With Mental Retardation*, Human Sciences Press, New York.

McGreevy, P. and Arthur, M. (1987) Effective behavioral treatment of self-biting by a child with Lesch–Nyhan syndrome. *Analysis and Intervention in Developmental Disabilities*, **29**, 536–540.

Neufeld, A. and Fantuzzo, J.W. (1987) Treatment of severe self-injurious behavior by the mentally retarded using the bubble helmet and differential reinforcement procedures. *Journal of Behavior Therapy and Experimental Psychiatry*, **18**, 127–136.

O'Brien, F. (1981) Treating self-stimulatory behavior. In J.L. Matson and J.R. McCartney (eds.), *Handbook of Behavior Modification with the Mentally Retarded*, Plenum Press, New York.

O'Brien, F. (1989) Punishment for people with developmental disabilities. In E. Cipani (ed.), *The Treatment of Severe Behavior Disorders*, American Association on Mental Retardation, Washington, DC.

Parrish, J.M., Iwata, B.A., Dorsey, M.F., Bunck, T.J. and Slifer, K.J. (1985) Behavior analysis, program development, and transfer of control in the treatment of self-injury. *Journal of Behavior Therapy and Experimental Psychiatry*, 16, 159–168.

Peterson, R.F. and Peterson, L.R. (1968) The use of positive reinforcement in the control of self-destructive behavior in a retarded boy. *Journal of Experimental Child Psychiatry*, 6, 351–360.

Poling, A. and Ryan, C. (1982) Differential-reinforcement of other behavior schedules. *Behaviour Modification*, 6, 3–21.

Powell, J., Martindale, B., Kulp, S., Martindale, A. and Bauman, R. (1977) Taking a closer look: Time sampling and measurement error. *Journal of Applied Behavior Analysis*, 10, 325–332.

Ralph, A. (1987) Utilising family resources to manage tantrum behaviour: A home-based single-subject study. *Behaviour Change*, 4, 30–35.

Redmon, W.K. (1987) Reduction of physical attacks through differential reinforcement of other behavior. *Journal of Child and Adolescent Psychotherapy*, 2, 107–111.

Reid, J.G., Tombaugh, T.N. and Heuvel, K.V. (1981) Application of contingent physical restraint to suppress stereotyped body rocking of profoundly mentally retarded persons. *American Journal of Mental Deficiency*, 86, 78–85.

Repp, A.C. and Deitz, D.E.D. (1979) Reinforcement-based reductive procedures: Training and monitoring performance of institutional staff. *Mental Retardation*, 17, 221–226.

Repp, A.C. and Deitz, S.M. (1974) Reducing aggressive and self-injurious behavior of institutionalized retarded children through reinforcement of other behaviors. *Journal of Applied Behavior Analysis*, 7, 313–325.

Repp, A.C., Barton, L.E. and Brulle, A.R. (1983) A comparison of two procedures for programming the differential reinforcement of other behaviors. *Journal of Applied Behavior Analysis*, 16, 435–445.

Repp, A.C., Felce, D. and Barton, L.E. (1988) Basing the treatment of stereotypic and self-injurious behaviors on hypotheses of their causes. *Journal of Applied Behavior Analysis*, 21, 281–289.

Reynolds, G.S. (1961) Behavioral contrast. *Journal of the Experimental Analysis of Behavior*, 4, 57–71.

Saloviita, T. (1988) Elimination of self-injurious behaviour by brief physical restraint and DRA. *Scandinavian Journal of Behavior Therapy*, 17, 55–63.

Schmidt, G.W. and Ulrich, R.E. (1969) Effects of group contingent events upon classroom noise. *Journal of Applied Behavior Analysis*, 2, 171–179.

Schneider, H.C., Ross, J.S.G. and Drubin, W.J. (1979) Practical alternative for the treatment of tantrum and self-injurious behavior. *Journal of Behavior Therapy and Experimental Psychiatry*, 10, 73–75.

Scotti, J.R., Evans, I.M. and Murphy, R.T. (1988, September) *Differential Effects of Brief Response Interruption: Three Case Studies*. Paper presented at the Third World Congress on Behaviour Therapy, Edinburgh, UK.

Skinner, B.F. (1938) *The Behavior of Organisms: An Experimental Analysis*, Appleton–Century–Crofts, New York.

Sissons, L.A., Van Hasselt, V.B., Hersen, M. and Aurand, J.C. (1988) Tripartite behavioral intervention to reduce stereotypic and disruptive behaviors in young multihandicapped children. *Behavior Therapy*, 19, 503–526.

Smith, M.D. (1987) Treatment of pica in an adult disabled by autism by differential reinforcement of incompatible behavior. *Journal of Behavior Therapy and Experimental Psychiatry*, **18**, 285–288.

Stokes, T.F. and Baer, D.M. (1977) An implicit technology of generalisation. *Journal of Applied Behavior Analysis*, **10**, 349–367.

Sturmey, P., Carlsen, A., Crisp, A.G. and Newton, J.T. (1988) A functional analysis of multiple aberrant responses: A refinement and extension of Iwata *et al.'s* (1982) methodology. *Journal of Mental Deficiency Research*, **32**, 31–46.

Swerissen, H. and Carruthers, J. (1987) The use of a physical restraint procedure to reduce a severely intellectually disabled child's tantrums. *Behavior Change*, **4**, 34–38.

Tarpley, H.D. and Schroeder, S.R. (1979) Comparison of DRO and DRI on rate of suppression of self-injurious behavior. *American Journal of Mental Deficiency*, **84**, 188–194.

Tierney, I.R., McGuire, R.J. and Walton, H.J. (1979) Reduction of stereotyped body-rocking using variable reinforcement: Practical and theoretical implications. *Journal of Mental Deficiency Research*, **23**, 175–185.

Topping, J.S. and Crowe, J.T. (1974) Comparison of three response elimination procedures following FI and VI reinforcement training in humans. *Bulletin of the Psychonomic Society*, **3**, 49–52.

Underwood, L.A., Figueroa, R.G., Thyer, B.A. and Nzeocha, A. (1989) Interruption and DRI in the treatment of self-injurious behavior among mentally retarded and autistic self-restrainers. *Behavior Modification*, **13**, 471–481.

Westland, G. (1978) *Current Crises of Psychology*, Heinemann, London.

Whitman, T.L., Sciback, J.W. and Reid, D.H. (1983) *Behavior Modification with the Severely and Profoundly Retarded*, Academic Press, New York.

Wolery, M., Kirk, K. and Gast, D.L. (1985) Stereotypic behavior as a reinforcer: Effects and side effects. *Journal of Autism and Developmental Disorders*, **15**, 149–161.

Woods, P.A. and Cullen, C. (1983) Determinants of staff behaviour in long-term care. *Behavioural Psychotherapy*, **11**, 4–17.

Woods, P.A. and Lowe, C.F. (1986) Verbal self-regulation of inappropriate behaviour with mentally handicapped adults. In J.M. Berg (ed.), *Science and Service in Mental Retardation*, Methuen, London.

Young, J.A. and Wincze, J.P. (1974) The effects of the reinforcement of compatible and incompatible behaviors on the self-injurious and related behaviors of a profoundly retarded female adult. *Behavior Therapy*, **5**, 614–623.

Chapter 4

Teaching Functionally Equivalent Responses as an Intervention for Challenging Behavior

V. Mark Durand and Daniel Crimmins

INTRODUCTION

Understanding and managing challenging behavior continues to be a priority among persons who interact with individuals displaying severe developmental disabilities. Behaviors such as aggression, self-injury, and tantrums are often among the most cited obstacles in attempting to place persons with handicaps in community settings (Eyman and Borthwick, 1980; Eyman and Call, 1977; Jacobson, 1982). Additionally, such behaviors can pose a physical threat to these individuals and those that work with them, and almost always impede educational and habilitation efforts. Problematic behaviour compounds the already difficult task of improving the lives of persons with severe mental handicap.

The goal of this chapter is to discuss one general strategy for reducing severe challenging behavior that is consistent with a positive, constructional approach to intervention (Goldiamond, 1974). This strategy, teaching functionally equivalent responses, involves the analysis of the function of the problem behavior (e.g., attention-getting) and the teaching of a more appropriate form that serves the same function (e.g., verbal requests for attention) (Durand, 1990). A number of recent investigations of this approach to intervention have been published and suggest that it may be an effective and non-aversive method for reducing even the most severe forms of problem behavior.

The Challenge of Severe Mental Handicap. Edited by Bob Remington
© 1991 John Wiley & Sons Ltd

The empirical approach

Past efforts at designing interventions for behavior problems have emphasized an empirical approach. This approach relies on the use of a variety of procedures in a trial-and-error manner until one or more of these procedures effectively reduces the problem behavior. And, although this tactic in intervention design has led to documented reductions in the problem behavior of many individuals, it is clear that the generalization and maintenance of such results have been limited (Durand and Carr, 1989). Rarely have significant reductions in severe challenging behavior been documented across important persons and settings, and over long periods of time. In addition, there remain many individuals who have not benefited from such an approach (Meyer and Evans, 1989). This lack of meaningful success in reducing challenging behavior has precipitated a re-evaluation of the trial-and-error to approach to selecting interventions.

The prescriptive approach

More recently, workers in this field have begun to incorporate information about the variables maintaining problem behavior into decisions regarding intervention. In contrast to the empirical approach, contemporary efforts emphasize a prescriptive approach to intervention design. The prescriptive approach combines the assessment of the function(s) of problem behavior with the design of interventions that address these functions. Therefore, what becomes of major interest to the clinician/ educator is not what this person is doing (e.g., aggression or self-injury) but rather, why this person is doing it (e.g., to elicit attention or to avoid unpleasant tasks). The prescriptive approach has led logically to a number of new and innovative interventions for problematic behavior (Durand and Carr, 1989).

What follows is a description of assessment procedures and a review of the evidence for the effectiveness of teaching functionally equivalent responses as an intervention. Assessment will be discussed in some detail because of the significance of this information for designing interventions. Following this discussion on assessment, research on teaching functionally equivalent responses will be reviewed.

ASSESSING THE FUNCTION OF PROBLEM BEHAVIOR

Almost every writer on the subject of severe behavior problems has warned clinicians, educators, and other service providers that, prior to implementing any intervention, an effort should be made to assess for the variables controlling these behaviors. Attempting a functional analysis has been seen as important because intervention may be unsuccessful if the variables maintaining the targeted behavior are not identified and the learner is not provided with an alternative means of obtaining these reinforcers. Until recently, however, there have been few specific guidelines for conducting a functional analysis (Voeltz, *et al.*, 1983).

What follows is a review of the assessment methods currently being used to collect information on the variables maintaining problem behavior (for a more complete discussion, see Durand, 1990). Table 4.1 lists these methods, and summarizes the advantages and disadvantages of each approach. It is important to note here that *no single assessment methodology is recommended*. It is always best if converging information about these variables can be obtained. In other words if, for example, direct 'naturalistic' observations about a behavior reveal the same information as a rating scale, then we would have more confidence in that information. All forms of assessment include sources of error (including direct observation). Therefore, we never can be completely certain of the variables maintaining problem behavior. Yet, our hypotheses are better if two or more methods agree. Readers interested in more detailed information should refer to more extensive discussion on this topic elsewhere (e.g., Anastasi, 1958; Cronbach *et al.*, 1972; Haynes and Horn, 1982; Nelson and Hayes, 1986).

Clinical intuition

Perhaps the most common method of assessing the variables maintaining problem behavior is *guessing*. Guessing (or clinical intuition) typically involves unsystematic hypothesizing about the relative influence of numerous variables presumably maintaining a student's problem behavior. Our data suggest that guessing, even by teachers with extensive histories with their students, is not predictive of how these students will later behave (Durand and Crimmins, 1988).

Clinical intuition is mentioned here as a caveat. It *is* important to get information from those who know the students best. And historical information (e.g., how they misbehaved in the past and under what circumstances) is also invaluable. However, because more formal methods of collecting this information exist (some of which have demonstrated

Table 4.1 Assessment methods

Procedure	Example	Advantages	Disadvantages
Clinical intuition		Possibility of sampling a wide range of stimuli Ease of Use	Lacks demonstrated reliability and validity No specific guidelines to assist identifying stimuli Restrospective reporting of events
Structured interviews	Bailey and Pyles (1989) O'Neill et al. (1989)	Possibility of sampling a wide range of stimuli Ease of use Specific guidelines to assist in identifying stimuli	Retrospective reporting of events Lack reliability and validity
Rating scales	Durand and Crimmins (1988) Wieseler et al. (1985)	Ease of use Some have demonstrated reliability and validity Specific guidelines to assist in identifying stimuli	Some scales lack demonstrated reliability and validity Retrospective reporting of events
Record reviews	Crimmins and Durand (in press)	Can assess history of successes and failures Ease of use	Sample of stimuli limited to history of assessment and intervention and to thoroughness of documentation Lack reliability and validity No specific guidelines to assist in identifying stimuli Retrospective reporting of events

Table 4.1 Continued

Procedure	Example	Advantages	Disadvantages
Informal observations	Repp *et al.* (1988)	Possibility of sampling a wide range of stimuli Ease of use	Lack reliability and validity No specific guidelines to assist in identifying stimuli
Logs/incident reports	Evans and Meyer (1985)	Ease of use Some provide guidelines to assist in identifying stimuli Concurrent reporting of events	Lack reliability and validity Sample of stimuli assessed guided by form used and training of staff
Scatter plot	Touchette *et al.* (1985)	Ease of use Can point to schedule and activity-related influences Concurrent reporting of events	Limited guidelines for assessing stimuli Limited validity data
Formal observations	Bijou *et al.* (1968) Evans and Meyer (1985)	Ease of use Possibility of sampling a wide range of stimuli Concurrent reporting of events	Limited guidelines for assessing stimuli Lack reliability and validity
Analog assessments	Durand and Crimmins (1988) Iwata *et al.* (1982)	Possibility of sampling a wide range of stimuli Concurrent reporting of events Experimental demonstration of influence	Difficult to conduct in some settings Can be time consuming and labor intensive Limited use with life-threatening behavior

reliability and validity), it is recommended that those involved with the decision-making process look to these other, more valid methods, for assessing behavior problems.

Structured interviews

One method that has recently been proposed as an additional method for assessing past instances of behavior problems is the use of structured interviews (e.g., Bailey and Pyles, 1989; O'Neill *et al.*, 1989). For example, the interview described by O'Neill and colleagues involves questioning teachers, parents, and/or other concerned persons about the nature of the behavior problem(s) and possible controlling variables. Questions include ones concerning the respective roles of such influences as medication, sleep, eating routines, and daily activities on the behaviors of interest. This approach has advantages over less formal questioning because of the structured nature of the questions. Because a variety of influences are surveyed each time and with each individual, important influences are less likely to be overlooked.

An important limitation of the proposed structured interviews that is common to most of the assessment strategies reviewed here is that there is no demonstrated reliability or validity. For example, would the same answers and conclusions be made if two individuals were interviewed separately (e.g., a teacher and an aide)? Will the conclusions made from the interview predict how the student will behave later (e.g., scream if a toy is taken away)? Such interviews *may* be reliable and valid, but to date there have been no such demonstrations. Therefore, persons using such interviews should be cautious about the conclusions drawn from them. Again, one safeguard is to use *multiple* forms of assessment to strengthen the inferences made about why a student is misbehaving.

Rating scales

More recently rating scales have been developed that attempt to address the issue of the function of problem behaviors. In an effort to provide an alternative assessment method, several authors have developed rating scales (e.g., Donnellan *et al.*, 1984; Durand and Crimmins, 1988; Schuler *et al.*, 1984; Wieseler *et al.*, 1985). These scales are designed to be completed by care-givers, and ask questions about the variables that may be maintaining problematic behavior. The scales vary in terms of ease of use and the degree to which the findings can lead to the development of an intervention plan. Described here will be the Motivation Assessment

Scale (Durand, 1990; Durand and Crimmins, 1988), because it is currently the only scale of this kind with demonstrated reliability and validity. Because the MAS has been used in several studies which have taught functionally equivalent responses and has been integral in developing plans with functional communication training, its use will be discussed below.

The Motivation Assessment Scale

The Motivation Assessment Scale (MAS) was developed over a period of several years with the help of numerous teachers, parents, and service providers of persons with autism and other developmental disabilities. During the years in which the MAS was developed, numerous questions were added and deleted from the scale. Questions and wordings were tested until it became clear that persons involved in the care of individuals with developmental disabilities could, through the scale, adequately report how these individuals would behave in situations such as difficult tasks, unstructured settings, being denied reinforcers, and in settings with reduced adult attention. The resulting scale is a 16-item questionnaire that assesses the functional significance of behavior along the dimensions of sensory, escape/avoidance, social attention, and tangible rewards. For example, one of the questions from the 'escape' category is 'Does the behavior occur following a request to perform a difficult task?' One question that is designed to assess 'social attention' as an influence is 'Does the behavior occur whenever you stop attending to this person?' One 'tangible' question is 'Does the behavior stop occurring shortly after you give this person the toy, food, or activity he or she has requested?' One sensory question is 'Would the behavior occur continuously, over and over, if this person was left alone for long periods of time (for example, several hours)?'

Research on the Motivation Assessment Scale

Durand and Crimmins (1988) describe the first data on reliability and validity for the MAS. The reliability study was conducted with the teachers of 50 students with developmental disabilities who exhibited self-injurious behavior. Interrater reliability (i.e., data from the student's teacher and assistant teacher) was measured by Pearson correlation coefficients, and ranged from 0.80 to 0.95. Test–retest reliability (i.e., data from the teachers' MAS responses 30 days apart) was also measured by Pearson correlation coefficients, and ranged from 0.89 to 0.98. These data suggest that the MAS is a reliable instrument. Two raters can generally agree on the variables maintaining a student's problem behavior, and this rating remains stable over time.

The validity study compared teacher's ratings on the MAS with data on eight students' behaviors in a variety of analog assessment conditions. All of the rating on the MASs and all of the analog conditions were conducted anonymously. Neither the teachers filling out the scales nor the experimenters running the assessment sessions knew of the other's results. These data support the validity of the MAS, because the teachers' ratings on the scale predicted how the students would behave in analog settings (i.e., with reduced attention, difficult tasks, with the withdrawal of tangibles, and in unstructured settings).

A number of other studies have employed the MAS to assess the variables maintaining problem behavior. For example, the MAS has been used to assess behaviors such as aggression, tantrums, and severe self-injury, with that information resulting in the design of successful interventions (e.g., Bird et al., 1989; Durand and Carr, in press; Durand and Kishi, 1987; Hall, Laitinen and Mozzoni, 1985). The MAS was used in one study to assess the variables maintaining dangerous climbing (Swahn, 1988). In addition, we have recently used the scale to select reinforcers (Durand et al., 1989). Although additional research on the scale is necessary, the MAS may provide one additional method of assessing the variables maintaining challenging behavior.

Review of available records

An additional method of assessing severe behavior problems is the review of available records. A variety of routine records are maintained by most programs, which may be of some help in assessment. Daily logs, for example, are kept in many residential programs and may serve as a source of informal information about the relationship between specific incidents and locations, staffing patterns or times of the day. They, unfortunately, rarely report information in a standardized format so that consistent themes are sometimes difficult to determine because of the different reporting styles of multiple recorders.

One source of data that captures the seriousness of a behavior is official incident reports (e.g., Berkman and Meyer, 1988; Meyer and Evans, 1989). These documents usually follow a standard format and are submitted to a supervisor or organizational committee for review. They are useful because the occasions when they are completed are defined by organizational policies—usually in the case of injury or significant property destruction. Information presented contains a description of the incident and the circumstances surrounding it. Because their use is prescribed, they can serve as a relatively unbiased source of information. Their usefulness is, however, limited to relatively severe behaviors with serious outcomes.

Reviewing existing records can be helpful to some degree in assessing severe problem behaviors. These records are likely to convey a sense of the history and context for a behavior. Existing records are not typically directed toward the assessment of the function of a problem behavior. Thus, their utility is in identifying other considerations that may be influencing the individual.

Informal observation

First efforts at assessment of a behavior often focus on informal observation and discussion of the problem with caregivers in an effort to develop initial hypotheses about the function of a problem behavior. The initial observation would minimally consist of some period of time in one or more environments where the behavior is likely to occur. It would also include an examination of the appropriateness of the individual's overall plan of activities and the environment. These methods may lead to a preliminary formulation of how the behavior might be maintained in the context of an interaction between the individual's capabilities, the types of interactions between that person and caregivers or peers, and qualities of the environment.

There are limits on the utility of informal observation in developing intervention recommendations for individuals. This procedure is potentially subject to bias from a number of sources that suggest caution as the best course of action. It is, however, potentially useful in making a number of suggestions about the environment in which the behavior is occurring, and can help in generating a variety of hypotheses to be assessed through other, more valid, means.

Formal observations

Direct observation of behavior is perhaps the most common means of collecting information about maintaining variables (see Table 4.1) in preparation for developing a behavior plan. These observations are typically carried out by persons in the environment with the individual with the behavior problem. Formal observations are, therefore, less prone to problems with reactivity noted in the section on informal observation. They are potentially limited in their usefulness by the degree of compliance with the observation procedure by the caregivers. Because observation procedures require time to carry out, they compete with

other responsibilities of caregivers and are subject to sampling biases
that only very salient events are recorded or that observations are reliably
performed on 'not busy days'.

Within this general category of procedures, the direct observation of
antecedents and consequences (Bijou, Peterson and Ault, 1968) is most
often used. Meyer and Evans (1989), for example, describe a formalized
procedure (ABC charts) for recording each instance of a behavior (e.g.,
hand-biting), its antecedent (e.g., teacher presented new task), and the
consequence (e.g., teacher walked away). Another example of this
approach is provided by Groden (1989), who describes a detailed
behavioral report that requests that a target behavior, immediate and
distant antecedents, and different classes of consequences be specified
for each occurrence of a behavior. These observation methods presume
that over time a pattern will emerge that reveals the relationship between
the behavior and either a specific or general class of antecedents and/or
consequences. As mentioned before, these methods do require relatively
good compliance by care staff in terms of accuracy and completeness of
the information to provide a full record of the behavior and its possible
controlling variables. Again, information from ABC charts can be helpful,
especially if used in combination with other forms of assessment.

Scatter plot

An alternative direct observation procedure that is somewhat easier to
complete is described by Touchette and colleagues (Touchette, MacDonald
and Langer, 1985). These authors suggest the use of a data collection
procedure called a 'scatter plot' that provides general information
concerning the distribution of incidents of a problem behavior across
the day. The procedure is somewhat easier to complete because it requires
only a categorization of the number of incidents (e.g., none, one to three,
four or more) during a unit time (e.g., one half hour) rather than an
absolute count and documentation of each incident. Further analysis of
times of the day during which behaviors are particularly likely allows
for the assessment of potential maintaining variables correlated with that
time of day. For example, if the scatter plot shows that a behavior occurs
during a one-hour period from noon to 1 p.m., the follow-up analysis
would focus on events unique to that time period—perhaps environmental
conditions in the cafeteria, the opportunities for using time following
lunch, etc. Identified variables can be manipulated to determine their
effect on the behavior. Touchette and his colleagues provide some initial
reliability and validity data for this method (Touchette, MacDonald and
Langer, 1985).

Setting event checklist

The previously described devices are designed to assess influences that are discrete and relatively close in time with the targeted behavior. Other influences, called *setting events*, are more complex conditions that occur concurrent with problem behaviors or are more distant in time (Bijou and Baer, 1961; Wahler and Fox, 1981). One of the few devices specifically designed to assess setting events has been developed by Gardner *et al.* (1986). The questions from this instrument assess the influences of such factors as previous negative interactions, medication changes, or illness on behavior problems. Again, the checklist is unique in its attempt to assess more global influences on behavior problems. Several studies have been conducted with the instrument, and results suggest that the information it provides can improve the reliability of assessment for behaviors such as aggression (Gardner *et al.*, 1986; Gardner, Karan and Cole, 1984).

Analog assessment

A set of procedures that do offer guidelines on methods of identifying specific variables for consideration are described as analog assessments. These assessments involve the manipulation of various antecedents and consequences that are presumed to be important and observing their effect on an individual's problem behavior (see Chapter 5). Carr and Durand (1985) and Iwata *et al.* (1982) provide examples of this type of work. Carr and Durand (1985) observed that low levels of adult attention and high task demands were correlated with high rates of problem behavior in four children with developmental disabilities. Providing the children with alternative verbal responses based on the assessment findings (functional communication training) resulted in significant reductions in aggression, self-injury, and tantrums. Thus, knowledge of the role of these variables was predictive of intervention outcome.

Although constructing analog situations in order to observe changes in problem behavior may be a valid way of assessing maintaining variables, the approach has several drawbacks. First, several highly trained staff are usually employed in these studies, necessitating extra personnel. Second, assessments can take several days, weeks, or even months, and the delay may be unacceptable in certain crisis situations. Third, there are times when the problem behavior is so dangerous that no instances of the behavior can be tolerated. Derivations from these procedures can be helpful but often face the same obstacles as direct observation procedures mentioned previously—that guidelines on identifying relevant variables for assessment are not widely available.

Summary

As mentioned previously, there is no *one* correct way to assess the variables maintaining problem behavior. There will always be trade-offs between the amount of effort employed in conducting these assessments, and the quality of information received. Less formal methods can be advantageous in generating hypotheses. However, these hypotheses should always be confirmed by information collected from more formal assessment methods. Again, our rule of thumb has been to use two or more formal assessment methods, preferably ones with some data available on reliability and validity.

TEACHING FUNCTIONALLY EQUIVALENT RESPONSES

As was described previously, teaching functionally equivalent responses involves both the assessment of the function of the problem behavior and the teaching of a more appropriate form that serves the same function (e.g., verbal requests for attention). This type of intervention has been applied to severe forms of self-injurious behavior and aggression, as well as less dangerous behaviors including stereotyped behavior and psychotic speech. This emerging body of work is reviewed below.

Dangerous behavior

A number of studies have been conducted that demonstrate the value of this procedure in reducing severe behavior problems (e.g., Carr and Durand, 1985; Durand, 1984; Durand and Carr, in press; Durand and Kishi, 1987; Horner and Budd, 1985; Smith 1985; Smith and Coleman, 1986). In one example, Durand and Kishi (1987) assessed the function of the severe behavior problems of five adults with multiple handicaps (deaf and blind and severe/profound retardation) through the use of a rating scale (the MAS—Durand and Crimmins, 1988). Based on this information (i.e., that these behaviors were maintained by escape, social attention, and their tangible consequences), these individuals were taught to nonverbally communicate requests that were equivalent to the assessed functions of their behavior problems (e.g., requests for assistance, requests for attention, and requests for tangibles). This intervention (referred to as functional communication training) resulted in significant improvements in their problematic behavior (severe self-injury and aggression).

In a similar study, Smith (1985) treated one 18-year-old male with autism who presumably engaged in aggression to obtain tangible reinforcers (i.e., food) (no formal assessment of the function of his aggression was performed in this study). Teaching him to request favorite foods resulted in dramatic improvements in the number of his aggressive episodes.

Bird *et al.* (1989) have recently documented the successful use of teaching functionally equivalent responses with two adult males with extensive histories of severe aggression and self-injury. The MAS was used in this study to assess the function of these challenging behaviors. Improvements were observed in problematic behavior as well as work productivity and the use of spontaneous communication, and these results were maintained over six months following intervention. Hunt, Alwell and Goetz (1988) observed similar improvements in their high school-aged students following conversation skill training.

Wacker, Steege and colleagues (Steege *et al.*, 1990; Wacker *et al.*, 1990; see also Berg and Wacker, this volume) have conducted a series of studies that further support the use of teaching functionally equivalent responses as an intervention for severe challenging behavior. In one study (Wacker *et al.*, 1990), they identified two children who exhibited severe self-injury (hand-biting) and aggression (slapping and biting peers and staff). For one student they both taught a functionally equivalent response (signing for a break from work) and added a response-contingent time out contingency (sitting at a table alone), and with a second student teaching a functionally equivalent response (signs for 'break', 'please', and 'eat') was combined with response-contingent graduated guidance (hand-over-hand guidance to pick up a toy). The results of this approach were that the students were exhibiting no or few occurrences of the challenging behaviors after intervention.

In the second study (Steege *et al.*, 1990), two children with severe disabilities were taught to press a microswitch that activated a pre-recorded message of 'stop'. Because their self-injurious behavior (hand and arm-biting) was assessed to be maintained by escape from tasks, they were taught a means of requesting a brief end to their tasks. Again, this intervention resulted in significant reductions in their self-injurious behaviors.

In a related study, Favell, McGimsey and Schell (1982) worked with individuals engaging in self-injurious behavior maintained by sensory consequences. Participants were taught to manipulate toys that provided equivalent sensory input, with the result that self-injurious behavior was substantially reduced. Providing these individuals with a more appropriate way of obtaining their preferred reinforcers (i.e., through toy play rather than through self-injury) resulted in clinically significant reductions in their dangerous behaviors. Teaching functionally equivalent alternative behaviors is an intervention strategy that holds much promise for the treatment of the more severe behavior problems.

Stereotyped behavior

A number of studies have reported that teaching toy play can lead to reduced levels of stereotyped behavior (e.g., Azrin, Kaplan and Foxx, 1973; Eason, White and Newsom, 1982; Favell, 1973). However, a limitation of these studies is that there is no pre-intervention assessment of the function of the stereotyped behavior exhibited by the participants. Thus, it is not clear that stereotyped behaviors in fact functioned to gain access to specific sensory input, or that the types of toys these individuals were taught to play with provided alternative access to this sensory input. Research needs to be conducted that first uses an assessment methodology to determine the sensory function of stereotypic behaviors, and second, demonstrates that teaching participants to manipulate objects providing alternative sensory consequences will reduce stereotyped motor behavior. One example of this type of research (Rincover et al., 1979) demonstrated that for three of four students with autism, significant reductions in stereotyped behavior were observed during toy play that matched the function of their behavior. Additional work in this area is recommended to validate this type of treatment.

Some individuals appear to engage in stereotyped motor behavior for social reasons. For these individuals, then, functionally equivalent responses would include behavior that elicits specific social reactions by others (as opposed to producing specific sensory feedback). Following this reasoning, Durand and Carr (1987) assessed that the rocking and hand-flapping of four individuals were maintained by escape from unpleasant situations. Using this information, participants were taught assistance-seeking responses (e.g., saying the phrase, 'Help me') during difficult tasks. This treatment resulted in significant reductions in stereotyped motor behavior for all four individuals. This finding has recently been replicated in a study by Wacker et al. (1990). In summary, although relatively few studies have so far examined the efficacy of teaching functionally equivalent behavior as a treatment for stereotyped motor responses, the approach warrants further investigation, particularly given its non-aversive and constructive nature.

Psychotic speech

Durand and Crimmins (1987) applied the logic of teaching functionally equivalent behaviors, effectively applied with dangerous and stereotyped motor behavior, to the treatment of psychotic speech. They found that the peculiar speech (phrases such as 'Parachute now' and 'Fried eggs on your head') of one male with autism appeared to be maintained by its ability to remove him from unpleasant situations. Therefore, he was taught to say 'Help me' when faced with a difficult situation, in an effort to reduce the unpleasantness of such things as academic tasks. Teaching him this functionally equivalent response (i.e., saying 'Help me', which elicited trainer prompts which, in turn, presumably reduced the aversiveness of the training situation) resulted in significant reductions in psychotic speech at implementation and at a six-month follow-up. This socially mediated peculiar speech pattern was effectively treated by teaching an alternative assistance-seeking response.

Carr and Kemp (1989) targeted 'autistic leading' as a communication disorder in four children with autism. Autistic leading was defined as a nonverbal form of requesting in which the child takes an adult by the wrist, leads him or her to a desired object, and then places the adult's hand on the object. They found that by teaching the children to point to what they wanted, autistic leading was eliminated. Pointing, which was functionally equivalent to autistic leading, served to replace this behavior. Similar results have been observed with echolalic speech among persons with autism (e.g., Schreibman and Carr, 1978). No equivalent research has been conducted on hallucinatory or delusional speech, although social functions have been hypothesized to play a part in the maintenance of these responses as well (Layng and Andronis, 1984).

CONCLUSIONS

The studies just reviewed suggest that significant improvements in the lives of persons with severe disabilities can be achieved through teaching functionally equivalent responses as a method of intervention for problem behavior. The introduction of any new technique should be viewed with caution, along with the initially optimistic results. However, given the replication of these results in a variety of settings and with a variety of research/clinical groups, there is room for optimism.

Role of functional equivalence

Cumulative data across several studies have demonstrated that these interventions are successful because functionally equivalent responses are taught that replace the challenging behavior. Investigations using control conditions such as teaching alternatives that elicit stimuli *not* assessed to be maintaining the challenging behavior (e.g., Carr and Durand, 1985; Durand and Crimmins, 1987) and studies that controlled for independent variable manipulations such as adult attention and task demands (e.g., Durand and Carr, 1987) have shown that behavior reductions cannot be attributed to such mechanisms as physical incompatibility or stimulus control. A study by Durand and Carr (in press) lends additional support to the functional equivalence explanation for the success of this intervention. Sequential observational data on one student's problem and communicative behavior indicated that when his teacher did not respond to his trained requests (he was taught to say 'I don't understand' in response to questions that he could not answer), he stopped using the request, and began to hit himself. When his articulation was improved with additional training, and his teacher began to appropriately respond to his requests, he again used the request and significantly reduced his self-injury. Again, these findings support the hypothesis that these interventions are successful when a response is taught to the student which serves the same function as his or her challenging behavior, and the environment responds in the desired manner.

Implications for consequences

In several of the studies just reviewed (e.g., Carr and Durand, 1985; Durand and Carr, 1987, in press), there were no specific consequences for problem behaviors. The interventions involved teaching an alternative response, and caregivers (whenever possible) responded to instances of challenging behavior as if it were not occurring. The use of ignoring as the only consequence was derived directly from the functional equivalence hypothesis. If these problem behaviors serve a purpose in the student's environment, then not only do we want to provide the student with an alternative, but we also want to let the student know that the problem behavior no longer has an effect on the environment. It is important to note here that response-independent consequences are only used in combination with teaching functionally equivalent behaviors. Using this intervention strategy alone could lead to a number of undesired effects (e.g., increases in other inappropriate behaviors, 'learned helplessness').

A major reason why intervention occurs in this manner is that we do not know why any particular student engages in any individual behavior at any specific point in time. As reviewed above, the field has made progress in determining why a student might, in general, be engaging in certain behaviors under certain conditions. It may be possible, for example, to determine that screaming and hand-biting in group settings *probably* serves to get attention in many cases. However, at any one time, there is no way to know why a student just screamed or just bit his arm. Because it is difficult if not impossible to evaluate the variables controlling each instance of a behavior, there is an effort not to try. We attempt to limit speculation about why each episode occurred. Instead, it is recommended not to let any particular consequence follow the behavior (e.g., more attention or less attention).

Although this strategy seems to contradict traditional behavioral teaching approaches, it is consistent with classic learning models of behavior. For example, researchers in the area of Pavlovian conditioning have used what is called a 'truly random' control group to obtain a behavioral baseline against which the effects of conditioning could be compared (Prokasy, 1965; Rescorla, 1967). Prior to this work, researchers compared the effects on a subject's conditioned responding (e.g., salivation) of pairing a conditioned stimulus (CS) (e.g., a light) and an unconditioned stimulus (UCS) (e.g., food delivery) (i.e., the light means food is coming), with a control condition in which the CS (light) was never paired with the UCS (food) (i.e., they never occur together). The *intention* of this control was to create a condition in which no learning of the relation between light and food could occur. What Prokasy and Rescorla pointed out was that in fact this latter condition did lead to learning and what is learned is that, in the present example, the light signals a period of time when no food is coming. In their truly random control, Prokasy and Rescorla set up a situation where the light and the food were presented randomly. Sometimes the food was presented before the light, sometimes after, and sometimes concurrently. The message here is that the light and the food are independent. When they are presented randomly, having the light on tells you nothing about the food.

Similarly, work in operant psychology has introduced a procedure known as response-independent reinforcer delivery (Catania, 1984). Here, known reinforcers are presented randomly, sometimes at the same time as a particular response, and sometimes not. In a manner similar to the truly random control condition for classical conditioning, response-independent reinforcers are occasionally used in research with animals to assess the effects of terminating contingencies (Boakes, 1973; Rescorla and Skucy, 1969). Responding in a certain way results in no predictable reaction from the environment.

This is relevant for the present discussion because what these studies were trying to accomplish were response-independent consequences for problem behavior. The goal was to let the student know that behavior problems will not affect others in any predictable way. It is important to note here that educators, parents and professionals often relate that they are already doing this. They explain that their typical response to a behavior problem is to ignore it. But are they really not responding?

The recommendation for *response-independent consequences* can be viewed as true ignoring. In other words, if one is to act as if the problem behavior is not occurring at all, then the consequence would involve no change in the environment or anyone else's behavior, with any changes being independent of the behavior problem itself. We have found that specifying ignoring in this way (i.e., pointing out that there are times when you might follow the behavior problem with a presumed reinforcer) makes it clear to those interacting with the student that 'ignoring does not mean turning and walking away' (Durand, 1990).

Speed of reduction

Several of the studies using this intervention approach based on functional equivalence reported rapid reductions in the challenging behaviors (e.g., Bird *et al.*, 1989; Durand and Carr, in press; Wacker *et al.*, 1990). In each instance, problem behaviors were reported to be significantly reduced immediately following the teaching of the functionally equivalent response. In most cases this reduction occurred within a few days of the initial intervention effort. It is important to note this rapid reduction when using non-aversive intervention strategies, because the failure to observe quick reductions has often been reported as a limitation of positive intervention efforts. Arguments for using more restrictive or intrusive procedures sometimes involve the need to obtain the quick elimination of the problem behavior. The research just reported undermines this argument by showing that equally rapid results can be obtained using a functional equivalence strategy.

There are several possible explanations for the rapid reductions observed in the studies just described. One view is that teaching an alternative, but functionally equivalent response provides the student with a choice. The choice becomes one of obtaining a desired goal (e.g., escape from work) by either inappropriate (e.g., hand-biting) or appropriate (e.g., signing for a break from work) means. If the training situation is constructed such that the appropriate response is more *efficient* in obtaining the goal than the inappropriate response, the student should quickly choose to obtain the goal with the new response. For example, if hand-biting resulted in removing the student from work about 50% of the time, but signing 'break' resulted in ending work 100% of the time, then it seems obvious that the student would select using the sign over the hand-biting. Extinction bursts (i.e., increases in behaviors following the removal of reinforcement) should not occur because the student still has a way of obtaining the reinforcers. The new response *replaces* the challenging behavior.

Generalization and maintenance

One criticism of aversive consequence-based interventions (e.g., timeout, contingent electric shock) has been that although they can often reduce the frequency of problem behavior initially, their effects are often temporary and/or limited to the intervention agent and setting in which intervention is conducted (e.g., Guess *et al.*, 1987; Meyer and Evans, 1986; Murphy and Wilson, 1981). Research on teaching functionally equivalent responses has begun to address issues of generalization and maintenance.

One study illustrates the advantages of this intervention approach. Durand and Carr (in press) identified three boys who were reported to be extremely disruptive (e.g., they engaged in highly frequent self-injury, aggression, and tantrums) in their classroom. Assessments conducted with these students included analog assessments as well as administrations of the MAS to their teacher. Functional communication training involved teaching all three boys to request assistance and, additionally, the third boy was also taught to request teacher attention appropriately. Extensive observational data collected in their classroom indicated that this intervention resulted in substantial improvements in their behavior.

Follow-up observations of the students in their new classrooms the following year indicated that two of the three students continued to use the phrases taught to them, and they continued to engage in few problem behaviors. One student required additional work to articulate the trained phrase so that his new teacher could understand it. Following this training, improvement in his problem behavior was again observed. A subsequent follow-up the next school year showed all three boys maintaining their improvements.

A second study was conducted to further assess generalization (Durand, 1984). Twelve students were selected for participation because they exhibited frequent problem behavior (e.g., aggression, self-injury, disruption), and because they were assessed to be engaging in these behaviors for adult attention. Functional communication training was compared with the most widely used intervention for presumed attention-getting behavior, timeout from positive reinforcement. One group of six students received timeout (i.e., teacher stopped interacting with the student and turned away) when they exhibited an instance of problem behavior, and a second group of six students was taught to appropriately elicit adult attention (i.e., through the use of a phrase such as, 'Am I doing good work?'). Initial intervention for both groups was successful in significantly reducing their behavior problems.

Prior to intervention, each student was placed with a teacher who was naive to the interventions, and monitored the students' behavior. This was repeated following the students' participation in either the timeout intervention or functional communication training. It was found that the timeout group resumed their disruptive behavior with the naive teacher despite their improvements in the previous intervention sessions. However, the group who received functional communication training did not resume their disruptive behavior with the naive teacher. It appears that this latter group 'took their intervention with them'. In other words, this group continued to appropriately request attention and, *without specific training*, the naive teachers provided it. By providing this attention for their verbal requests, these naive teachers unknowingly reinforced a functionally equivalent response and thereby reduced disruptive behavior. In contrast, when the students in the timeout group were disruptive, the naive teacher frequently provided some form of reinforcement because he or she had not been instructed on how to respond to problem behavior, thus ensuring its continued presence.

The advantage of functional communication training (or teaching functionally equivalent responses in general) may lie in its ability to be successful without specific training of others. As the previous studies indicated, without detailed instruction and practice teachers will not carry out timeout procedures effectively with every student who is disruptive. Because this very specific intervention needs to be taught to everyone who may come in contact with the student, persons unfamiliar with the student or his or her program may inadvertently reinforce (thereby maintaining) instances of problem behavior. On the other hand, the previous studies did not have to teach teachers to respond to a verbal request for attention. When the students said, 'Am I doing good work?' the teachers attended to them without instruction or prompts. The verbal requests allowed students to enter this 'natural community of reinforcement' thereby maintaining their verbal requests and at the same time the reductions in their problem behaviors (Ager, this volume; Baer and Wolf, 1970).

SUMMARY

The studies just reviewed suggest that significant improvements in the lives of persons with severe disabilities can be achieved through teaching functionally equivalent responses as a method of intervention for problem behavior. Given the replication of these results in a variety of settings and with a variety of research/clinical groups, there is room for optimism. As noted above, one of the advantages of this method of intervention may lie not only in its ability to initially reduce problem behavior, but also in its ability to facilitate generalization and maintenance of treatment gains (Durand, 1987; Horner and Billingsley, 1988). Because our technology for teaching adaptive responses that generalize and maintain well over time is quite advanced when compared to our behavior reduction technology, this should allow us to provide more lasting and durable interventions (Stokes and Baer, 1977). Successful generalization and maintenance of functionally equivalent responses should, in turn, lead to generalization and maintenance of reductions in problem behavior.

Address for correspondence

V. Mark Durand, Department of Psychology, State University of New York at Albany, 1400 Washington Avenue, Albany, New York 12222, USA.

REFERENCES

Anastasi, A. (1958) *Differential Psychology* (3rd edn), Macmillan, New York.

Azrin, N.H., Kaplan, S.J. and Foxx, R.M. (1973) Autism reversal: Eliminating stereotypic self-stimulation of retarded individuals. *American Journal of Mental Deficiency*, **78**, 241–248.

Baer, D.M. and Wolf, M.M. (1970) The entry into natural communities of reinforcement. In R. Ulrich, T. Stachnik and J. Mabry (eds), *Control of Human Behavior: From Cure to Prevention* (pp. 319–324), Scott, Foresman, Glenview, Illinois.

Bailey, J.S. and Pyles, D.A.M. (1989) Behavioral diagnostics. In E.Cipani (ed.), *The Treatment of Severe Behavior Disorders*, American Association on Mental Retardation, Washington, DC.

Berkman, K.A. and Meyer, L.H. (1988) Alternative strategies and multiple outcomes in the remediation of severe self-injury: Going 'all out' nonaversively. *Journal of the Association for Persons with Severe Handicaps*, **13**, 76–86.

Bijou, S.W. and Baer, D.M. (1961) *Child Development: A Systematic and Empirical Theory*, Appleton–Century–Crofts, New York.

Bijou, S.W., Peterson, R.F. and Ault, M.H. (1968) A method to integrate descriptive and experimental field studies at the level of data and empirical concepts. *Journal of Applied Behavior Analysis*, **1**, 175–191.

Bird, F., Dores, P.A., Moniz, D. and Robinson, J. (1989) Reducing severe aggressive and self-injurious behaviors with functional communication training: Direct, collateral and generalized results. *American Journal of Mental Retardation*, **94**, 37–48.

Boakes, R.A. (1973) Response decrements produced by extinction and by response-independent reinforcement. *Journal of the Experimental Analysis of Behavior*, **19**, 293–302.

Carr, E.G. and Durand, V.M. (1985) Reducing behavior problems through functional communication training. *Journal of Applied Behavior Analysis*, **18**, 111–126.

Carr, E.G. and Kemp, D.C. (1989) Functional equivalence of autistic leading and communicative pointing: Analysis and treatment. *Journal of Autism and Developmental Disorders*, **19**, 561–578.

Catania, A.C. (1984) *Learning.* (2nd edn), Prentice-Hall, New Jersey.

Crimmins, D.B. and Durand, V.M. (in press) Assessment and evaluation. In I.M. Evans and B. Warren (eds), *Positive Approaches to Behavior Change,* Office of Mental Retardation and Developmental Disabilities, Albany, New York.

Cronbach, L.J., Gleser, G., Nanda, H. and Rajaratnam, N. (1972) *The Dependability of Behavioral Measurements: Theory of Generalizability for Scores and Profiles,* Wiley, New York.

Donnellan, A.M., Mirenda, P.L., Mesaros, R.A. and Fassbender, L.L. (1984) Analyzing the communicative functions of aberrant behavior. *Journal of the Association for Persons with Severe Handicaps*, **9**, 201–212.

Durand, V.M. (1984) Attention-getting problem behavior: Analysis and intervention. Unpublished doctoral dissertation, SUNY, Stony Brook.

Durand, V.M. (1987) 'Look Homeward Angel': A call to return to our (functional) roots. *Behavior Analysis*, **10**, 299–302.

Durand, V.M. (1990) *Severe Behavior Problems: A Functional Communication Approach.* Guilford Press, New York.

Durand, V.M. and Carr, E.G. (in press) Functional communication training to reduce challenging behavior: Maintenance and application in new settings. *Journal of Applied Behavior Analysis.*

Durand, V.M. and Carr, E.G. (1987) Social influences on 'self-stimulatory' behavior: Analysis and treatment application. *Journal of Applied Behavior Analysis*, **20**, 119–132.

Durand, V.M. and Carr, E.G. (1989) Operant learning methods with chronic schizophrenia and autism: Aberrant behavior. In J.L. Matson (ed.), *Chronic Schizophrenia and Adult Autism: Issues on Diagnosis, Assessment, and Psychological Treatment*, Springer, New York.

Durand, V.M. and Crimmins, D.B. (1987) Assessment and treatment of psychotic speech in an autistic child. *Journal of Autism and Developmental Disorders*, **17**, 17–28.

Durand, V.M. and Crimmins, D.B. (1988) Identifying the variables maintaining self-injurious behavior. *Journal of Autism and Developmental Disorders*, **18**, 99–117.

Durand, V.M. and Kishi, G. (1987) Reducing severe behavior problems among persons with dual sensory impairments: An evaluation of a technical assistance model. *Journal of the Association for Persons with Severe Handicaps*, **12**, 2–10.

Durand, V.M., Crimmins, D.B., Caulfield, M. and Taylor, J. (1989) Reinforcer assessment I: Using problem behavior to select reinforcers. *Journal of the Association for Persons with Severe Handicaps*, **14**, 113–126.

Eason, L.J., White, M.J. and Newsom, C. (1982) Generalized reduction of self-stimulatory behavior: An effect of teaching appropriate play to autistic children. *Analysis and Intervention in Developmental Disabilities*, **2**, 157–169.

Evans, I.M. and Meyer, L.H. (1985) *An Educative Approach to Behavior Problems*, Brookes, Baltimore.

Eyman, R.K. and Borthwick, S.A. (1980) Patterns of care for mentally retarded persons. *Mental Retardation*, **18**, 63–66.

Eyman, R.K. and Call, T. (1977) Maladaptive behavior and community placement of mentally retarded persons. *American Journal of Mental Deficiency*, **82**, 137–144.

Favell, J.E. (1973) Reduction of stereotypes by reinforcement of toy play. *Mental Retardation*, **11**, 21–23.

Favell, J.E., McGimsey, J.F. and Schell, R.M. (1982) Treatment of self-injury by providing alternate sensory activities. *Analysis and Intervention in Developmental Disabilities*, **2**, 83–104.

Gardner, W.I., Karan, O.C. and Cole, C.L. (1984) Assessment of setting events influencing functional capacities of mentally retarded adults with behavior difficulties, In A.S. Halpern and M.J. Fuhrer (eds); *Functional Assessment in Rehabilitation* (pp. 171–185), Brookes, Baltimore.

Gardner, W.I., Cole, C.L., Davidson, D.P. and Karan, O.C. (1986) Reducing aggression in individuals with developmental disabilities: An expanded stimulus control, assessment, and intervention model. *Education and Training in Mental Retardation*, **21**, 3–12.

Goldiamond, I. (1974) Toward a constructional approach to social problems. *Behaviorism*, **2**, 1–84.

Groden, G. (1989) A guide for conducting a comprehensive behavioral analysis of a target behavior. *Journal of Behavior Therapy and Experimental Psychiatry*, **20**, 37–49.

Guess, D., Helmstetter, E., Turnbull, H.R. III and Knowlton, S., (1987) *Use of Aversive Procedures with Persons who Are Disabled: A Historical Review and Critical Analysis, TASH Monograph Series, No. 2*, Association for Persons with Severe Handicaps, Seattle.

Hall, T., Laitinen, R. and Mozzoni, M. (1985, May) *The Reduction of Aggression through Student-directed Choice of Demand/No Demand Settings*. Paper presented at the annual meeting of the Association for Behavior Analysis, Columbus.

Haynes, S.N. and Horn, W.F. (1982) Reactivity in behavioral observations: A methodological and conceptual critique. *Behavior Assessment*, **4**, 369–385.

Horner, R.H. and Billingsley, F. (1988) The effect of competing behavior on the generalization and maintenance of adaptive behavior in applied settings. In R.H. Horner, G. Dunlap and R.L. Koegel (eds), *Generalization and Maintenance: Life-style Changes in Applied Settings*, (pp. 197–220), Brookes, Baltimore.

Horner, R.H. and Budd, C.M. (1985) Acquisition of manual sign use: Collateral reduction of maladaptive behavior, and factors limiting generalization. *Education and Training in Mental Retardation*, **20**, 39–47.

Hunt, P., Alwell, M. and Goetz, L. (1988) Acquisition of conversation skills and the reduction of inappropriate social interaction behaviors. *Journal of the Association for Persons with Severe Handicaps*, **13**, 20–27.

Iwata, B.A., Dorsey, M.F., Slifer, K.J., Bauman, K.E. and Richman, G.S. (1982) Toward a functional analysis of self-injury. *Analysis and Intervention in Developmental Disabilities*, **2**, 3–20.

Jacobson, J.W. (1982) Problem behavior and psychiatric impairment within a developmentally disabled population I: Behavior frequency. *Applied Research in Mental Retardation*, **3**, 121–139.

Laying, T.V.J. and Andronis, P.T. (1984) Toward a functional analysis of delusional speech and hallucinatory behavior. *Behavior Analyst*, **7**, 139–156.

Meyer, L.H. and Evans, I.M. (1986) Modification of excess behavior: An adaptive and functional approach for educational and community contexts. In R.H. Horner, L.H. Meyer and H.D. Fredericks (eds), *Education of Learners with Severe Handicaps: Exemplary Service Strategies*, (pp. 315–350), Brookes, Baltimore.

Meyer, L.H. and Evans, I.M. (1989) *Nonaversive Intervention for Behavior Problems: A Manual for Home and Community*, Brookes, Baltimore.

Murphy, G.H. and Wilson, B. (1981) Long-term outcome of contingent shock treatment for self-injurious behavior. In P. Mittler (ed.), *Frontiers of Knowledge in Mental Retardation*, (pp. 303–311), IASSMD, London.

Nelson, R.O. and Hayes, S.C. (eds) (1986) *Conceptual Foundations of Behavioral Assessment*, Guilford, New York.

O'Neill, R.E., Horner, R.H., Albin, R.W., Storey, K. and Sprague, J.R. (1989) *Functional Analysis: A Practical Assessment Guide*, Research and Training Center on Community-Referenced Nonaversive Behavior Management, University of Oregon.

Prokasy, W.F. (1965) Classical eyelid conditioning: Experimenter operations, task demands, and response shaping. In W.F. Prokasy (ed.) *Classical Conditioning: A Symposium*, (pp. 208–225), Appleton–Century–Crofts, New York.

Rescorla, R.A. (1967) Pavlovian conditioning and its proper control procedures. *Psychological Review*, **74**, 71–80.

Rescorla, R.A. and Skucy, J.C. (1969) Effect of response-independent reinforcers during extinction. *Journal of Comparative and Physiological Psychology*, **67**, 381–389.

Rincover, A., Cook, R., Peoples, A. and Packard, D. (1979) Sensory extinction and sensory reinforcement principles for programming multiple adaptive behavior change. *Journal of Applied Behavior Analysis*, **12**, 221–233.

Schreibman, L. and Carr, E.G. (1978) Elimination of echolalic responding to questions through the training of a generalized verbal response. *Journal of Applied Behavior Analysis*, **11**, 453–463.

Schuler, A.L., Peck, C.A., Tomlinson, C. and Theimer, R.K. (1984) Assessment. In C.A. Peck, A.L. Schuler, C. Tomlinson, R.K. Theimer, T. Haring and M.I. Semmel (eds), *The Social Competence Curriculum Project: A Guide to Instructional Programming for Social and Communicative Interactions*, (pp. 22–106), University of California–Santa Barbara Special Education Research Institute, Santa Barbara.

Smith, M.D. (1985) Managing the aggressive and self-injurious behavior of adults disabled by autism. *Journal of the Association for Persons with Severe Handicaps*, **10**, 228–232.

Smith, M.D. and Coleman, D. (1986) Managing the behavior of adults with autism in the job setting. *Journal of Autism and Developmental Disorders*, **16**, 145–154.

Steege, M.W., Wacker, D.P., Cigrand, K.C., Berg, W.K., Novak, C.G., Reimers, T.M., Sasso, G.M. and DeRaad, A. (1990). Use of negative reinforcement in the treatment of self-injurious behavior. *Journal of Applied Behavior Analysis*, **23**, 459–467.

Stokes, T.F. and Baer, D.M. (1977) An implicit technology of generalization. *Journal of Applied Behavior Analysis*, **10**, 349–367.

Swahn, O. (1988) Effect of parent-administered interruption on excessive climbing in a 2-year-old developmentally disabled girl. *Scandinavian Journal of Behaviour Therapy*, **17**, 17–24.

Touchette, P.E., MacDonald, R.F. and Langer, S.N. (1985) A scatter plot for identifying stimulus control of problem behavior. *Journal of Applied Behavior Analysis*, **18**, 343–351.

Voeltz, L.M., Evans, I.M., Derer, K.R. and Hanashiro, R. (1983) Targeting excess behavior for change: A clinical decision model for selecting priority goals in educational contexts. *Child and Family Behavior Therapy*, **5**, 17–35.

Wacker, D.P., Steege, M.W., Northup, J., Sasso, G., Berg, W., Reimers, T., Cooper, L., Cigrand, K. and Donn, L. (1990). A component analysis of functional communication training across three topographies of severe behavior problems. *Journal of Applied Behavior Analysis*, **23**, 417–429.

Wahler, R.G. and Fox, J.J. (1981) Setting events in applied behavior analysis: Toward a conceptual and methodological expansion. *Journal of Applied Behavior Analysis*, **14**, 327–338.

Wieseler, N.A., Hanson, R.H., Chamberlain, T.P. and Thompson, T. (1985) Functional taxonomy of stereotypic and self-injurious behavior. *Mental Retardation*, **23**, 230–234.

Chapter 5

The Application of Analogue Methodology to the Functional Analysis of Challenging Behaviour

CHRIS OLIVER

INTRODUCTION

The last decade of research into interventions for challenging behaviour has been characterized by a growing awareness that technique-orientated behaviour modification has become increasingly divorced from many facets of applied behaviour analysis, and thus from its roots, the experimental analysis of behaviour (Michael, 1985). Intervention research has long been dominated by a paradigm based on manipulating independent variables within a self-corrective system, with the hallmark of increasingly elaborate single-case designs almost exclusively demonstrating the law of effect. These studies commonly lack an analysis of the variables which maintain or influence challenging behaviour—the basis to applied behaviour *analysis*—and concentrate only on decreasing its occurrence (Lundervold and Bourland, 1988; Repp *et al.*, 1990). As a result, this single aspect of applied behaviour analysis has almost become synonymous with 'the behavioural approach'. One consequence of the concentrated effort on decreasing challenging behaviours is that there are few indicators of how intervention efficacy is related to the initial determinants of such behaviour (Oliver and Head, 1990). There is little doubt that research demonstrating behaviour modification yielded effective interventions has made a major contribution to the amelioration of challenging behaviour. However, the links between behaviour modification and applied behaviour analytic principles have become increasingly weak.

Recently a return to understanding the determinants of challenging behaviour has been advocated, primarily in order to relate interventions

The Challenge of Severe Mental Handicap. Edited by Bob Remington
© 1991 John Wiley & Sons Ltd

in a meaningful way to the determinants of the behaviour (Carr and Durand, 1985a; Durand and Crimmins, Chapter 4 this volume). Consequently, functional analysis has become re-established as an important area for basic research and application in clinical practice. Although the term 'functional analysis' is generally accepted, it is important to note the two meanings it may have. It may be used to refer to a description of the functional relationship that exists between a behaviour and events in a mathematical sense, or to refer to an assessment of the function the behaviour may have for an individual in terms of its 'purpose'. The latter use of the term has gained popularity, but in order to ascribe function to a behaviour in terms of 'purpose' it is necessary to evaluate its relationship with other events systematically, most commonly via examining the operant three-term contingency A: B: C (antecedent: behaviour: consequences). The term 'functional analysis' is therefore perhaps best used to denote this complete procedure.

Alongside the rediscovery of functional analysis, there has been a necessary conceptual shift from considering the form a behaviour takes to its function. If two behaviours which differ in form (e.g., self-injury and aggression) vary in the same way in response to the same environmental contingencies, they are functionally more alike than two behaviours similar in form but which vary in different ways in response to the same environmental contingencies. This development has major implications for how interventions are selected, and has been supported by the application of functional analysis to a variety of challenging behaviours (Carr and Durand, 1985a).

Challenging behaviour can be categorized as potentially achieving either negative reinforcement functions (e.g., by contingent escape from or avoidance of aversive stimuli such as instructional settings or social interactions), or positive reinforcement functions (e.g., by contingent procurement of appetitive stimuli such as attention, stimulation, tangible items). Initially, self-stimulation was seen as a separate function (Carr, 1977) but this was later subsumed under the positive reinforcement hypothesis because the maintenance of such behaviour could be described as positive reinforcement by sensory stimulation. Recently it has been suggested that the term 'automatic reinforcement' is more technically correct because it is unclear whether the reinforcement is positive or negative in nature (Iwata et al., 1990). These functions have been demonstrated for challenging behaviour in studies of stimulus control (Carr, Newsom and Binkoff, 1976; Durand, 1982; Murphy and Oliver, 1987), the manipulation of reinforcers (Anderson, Dancis and Alpert, 1978; Carr and McDowell, 1980), and the covariation of challenging behaviours with other behaviours which have functional similarity (Carr and Durand, 1985b; Durand and Crimmins, Chapter 4 this volume). The conclusion to be drawn from these studies is that the primary determinant of challenging behaviour is its functional relationship with environmental events. The role of functional analysis is therefore to determine the function(s) a behaviour may have whilst essentially disregarding its other qualities (e.g., form, rate, intensity) except insofar as they may provide clues to function.

With the recognition of the potential irrelevance of the form of a behaviour and the increased emphasis on evaluating the determinants of challenging behaviour, the technology of functional analysis is beginning to be reassessed and with it the problems of methodology and interpretation resurrected. The commonly accepted maxim of conducting a functional analysis prior to intervening has been found wanting in terms of practical methodology. There are many guidelines on how to interview and observe, but few demonstrations of the reliability and validity of such methodology for the functional assessment of severe challenging behaviour.

Recent interest in the technology of functional analysis has culminated in the advent of analogue methodology as an alternative or adjunct to direct observation in natural settings. Defining this methodology is problematic because the term 'analogue' is generally used to refer to the process of modelling the natural environment. But the assessment and analysis techniques actually used in analogue methodology more commonly involve systematic manipulation of potential aversive and discriminative stimuli and/or putative reinforcers while observing challenging behaviour in order to discover which of the potential functions outlined above is operative. This approach therefore contrasts with direct evaluation of the three-term contingency using purely observational methods to uncover naturally occurring functional relationships. The latter type of empirical investigation observes the effect of a natural fluctuation in an independent variable on a dependent variable, rather than actively manipulating an independent variable to observe the effect on a dependent variable.

Analogue methodology can overcome some of the problems associated with traditional observational analyses of severe challenging behaviour but, as with any method of assessment, it is open to misinterpretation. It is therefore important to evaluate its strengths and weaknesses in order to appreciate the role it can play in a functional analysis. To do this, it is necessary to consider the potential problems associated with other methods of functional analysis, the historical and theoretical basis of analogue methodology, and the current applications of the various techniques. These issues are considered in the next section.

FUNCTIONAL ANALYSIS BY THE ASSESSMENT OF NATURALLY
OCCURRING EVENTS

Commonly, the functional analysis of challenging behaviour is conducted
by attempting to elucidate the naturally occurring sequence of events
which surround challenging behaviour. This approach has therefore
sought to identify the three-term A: B: C contingency by structured
questionnaires or interviews with caregivers, direct natural observations,
or recording sequences of events on A: B: C charts (see, Murphy, 1987).
Although these methods have long been claimed to yield important
information on function, neither their reliability nor validity is well
established and there is little guidance on how to interpret the resultant
data.

While some guidelines exist for conducting clinical interviews and
undoubtedly aid decision making, there is little evidence from the
literature that they have made an impact in terms of determining the
nature of interventions for severe challenging behaviour (Oliver and
Head, 1990). In the broader research literature, there are a number of
examples where questionnaires and interviews are employed in survey
studies of self-injurious behaviour (SIB), many of which clearly originate
from the 'short screening sequence' proposed by Carr (1977). Wieseler et
al. (1985) employed a six-item questionnaire similar to Carr's in order to
determine the most common consequence to SIB and stereotypies,
and Hauck (1985) similarly developed a 77-item questionnaire which
considered antecedents, consequences, and what the author described as
'plausible implications'. Both these studies, however, use somewhat
limited methods of validation, either by selecting only participants with
particular questionnaire results for the validation study, or by validating
the conclusions against a subjective opinion. A further example of this
approach is Donnellan et al.'s (1984) checklist, which essentially lists
challenging behaviours and possible functions. Again, however, there
are no data on reliability and validity.

Interviews to assess motivation in survey studies have been employed
by Maurice and Trudel (1982), Bruhl et al. (1982) and Griffin et al. (1984)
but each of these studies presents only limited information on the content
of the interviews or the validity of the conclusions. Whilst these methods
may be useful in applied settings, their status as empirical functional
analyses of challenging behaviour is uncertain: the clinician is left with
little more than broad guidelines that can be derived from the operant
approach.

Direct natural observations may be seen as a more objective method
of establishing functional relationships, but again the literature on the
application of this method to severe challenging behaviour is limited.

Maurice and Trudel (1982) conducted such observations of 36 people who self-injured using a 10-second interval recording procedure. After observing each person for a mean of 3.5 hours, they reported that self-injurious behaviour was seen in a mean of 13.4% of intervals. For each interval in which self-injury occurred there was a mean of only 0.24 observable antecedent events and 0.25 subsequent events. Similarly Edelson, Taubman and Lovaas (1983) observed 20 people described as 'frequently' engaging in self-injury using 15-second partial interval recording. The authors report no positive reinforcement relationship between staff presence and self-injury, but clearer relationships between self-injury and demands, denials and punishment.

These research-based examples of commonly used clinical methods of functional analysis serve to demonstrate the difficulties faced by clinicians when confronted with the task of assessing severe challenging behaviour. First, there is little evaluation of these methods in terms of the predictive validity of the assessment—arguably the only reason for conducting a functional analysis. Secondly, various sources of error may be associated with these methods and may confound interpretation of their results. Structured interviews inevitably involve secondhand information yielding obvious limitations due to selective recall and interpretation. Direct natural observations with A: B: C recording may overcome this problem, but the procedure still shares some of the problems of structured interviews.

One of these problems is highlighted by the findings of Maurice and Trudel (1982) and Edelson, Taubman and Lovaas (1983). This is the seemingly low temporal association between antecedents and behaviour, and behaviour and consequences. The immediate conclusion one is tempted to draw from this finding is that the behaviour is functionally *un*related to environmental events. There are, however, alternative explanations for these data. The first is that the behaviour could be maintained on a very lean, intermittent schedule of reinforcement from social events, such as attention, and that although temporal contiguity of behaviour and social consequences occurs only infrequently, a contingency nevertheless exists. Taking the data at face value may therefore lead to an error of overlooking a function that exists. The second possible interpretation is that the antecedents and consequences occur but are simply not observed because they are too subtle or evanescent (e.g., the positive reinforcing effect of a small movement toward the participant by someone who has previously reinforced challenging behaviour; the negative reinforcing effect of temporarily—but not completely—removing an aversive stimulus). A different problem associated with these methods is that the reported antecedents and consequences may be temporally but not functionally related. For example, someone who shows SIB may be reprimanded following almost every individual occurrence, but this does not necessarily mean that the SIB is maintained by the positive reinforcer of attention; the SIB may be self-stimulatory (automatically reinforced) and the attention incidental. This problem would lead to an error of commission where a function is incorrectly ascribed to the behaviour. Finally, in the natural environment, antecedents known by caregivers to occasion challenging behaviour (e.g., demands or social isolation) may deliberately not be allowed to occur to avoid the occurrence of challenging behaviour. If so, some functions of the behaviour are simply not evaluated because the conditions which give rise to its occurrence never arise during the observation period (Oliver et al., 1988).

To summarize, there are several problems inherent in the evaluation of naturally occurring contingencies. These problems can lead both to failing to observe a functional relationship which is actually operative, and to falsely concluding there is a relationship where none in fact exists. In addition, difficulties in using naturalistic observation methods may be particularly acute in the case of evaluating severe challenging behaviour which—if dangerous and frequent—distorts opportunities for controlled observation. For these reasons, observation in more controlled settings may aid clinical decision-making. Such controlled observation is provided by analogue methodology.

FUNCTIONAL ANALYSIS USING ANALOGUE METHODOLOGY

The development of analogue methodology has been influenced by a number of factors other than the problems with the methods outlined above. Initially, controlled settings which allowed manipulation of environmental stimuli were used to demonstrate the operant nature of challenging behaviours and thus the relevance of applied behaviour analysis. Commonly these studies evaluated only a single function (usually either reinforcement by attention or escape from demands) rather than all possible functions, and thus would now be seen as incomplete in terms of a functional analysis. Nevertheless, with the recent revitalization of an analytical approach, these early demonstrations have provided the basis for more comprehensive batteries of settings and conditions which explore the various functions challenging behaviour may have. It is worth reviewing the methodology of these early demonstrations because they illustrate the various ways in which the fundamental tenet of analogue methodology, that of controlled hypothesis testing, can be applied.

Analogue methodology, by definition, is not a direct method of functional analysis. Consequently, its power to assess functional relationships lies in the evaluation of the corollaries of the negative and positive reinforcement hypotheses. It could be argued that the only completely sufficient test of either hypothesis would involve removing the putatively effective contingency (an extinction procedure) and observing whether the challenging behaviour eventually ceases. Such a test is obviously not feasible for high-rate, intense challenging behaviour with its attendant danger of injury to the individual and to others. Secondly, to employ extinction a putative reinforcer needs to be identified and this is the very reason that assessment is carried out. For these reasons, analogue methodology adopts the indirect tactic of focusing on the corollaries of the negative and positive reinforcement hypotheses to assess whether behaviour occurs in a way which would be predicted from either hypothesis under given conditions.

Research evaluating the positive reinforcement hypothesis

One corollary of the positive reinforcement hypothesis is that challenging behaviour should occur at a higher rate when the positive reinforcement is made contingent on the behaviour than in a 'control' condition. A number of studies have shown increases in self-injury when attention is artificially made contingent on responding. Some of the first operant studies of self-injury (Lovaas et al., 1965; Lovaas and Simmons, 1969) demonstrated this effect with continuous reinforcement and with some variable schedules. Other studies report similar high rates under conditions of contingent attention in comparison to differential reinforcement of other behaviour (DRO: see Jones, this volume) (Miron, 1971; Peterson and Peterson, 1968), extinction (Carr and McDowell, 1980), and noncontingent attention and timeout (Anderson, Dancis and Alpert, 1978). The last two studies also demonstrated a positive reinforcement effect even though, initially, the aetiology of self-injury was organic.

In terms of functional analysis, these studies are somewhat problematic because it could be argued that they demonstrate only that contingent attention is sufficient as a reinforcer of challenging behaviour, and not that it normally maintains the behaviour. Indeed, such an approach runs the risk that the behaviour under study may attain a function it did not previously have. Against this, however, the subsequent interventions in three of the studies validated the conclusions drawn from assessment (Anderson, Dancis and Alpert, 1978; Carr and McDowell, 1980; Miron, 1971).

A second corollary of the positive reinforcement hypothesis is that the challenging behaviour should occur at *lower* rates when the positive reinforcement is made unconditionally available than when it is either contingently available or not available. A number of studies have demonstrated such an effect (Anderson, Dancis and Alpert, 1978; Murphy and Oliver, 1987; Singh, 1976). The Murphy and Oliver study, for example, reported a lower rate of SIB in a continuous social contact condition (i.e. 1 : 1 unconditional attention) with a no social contact condition (essentially a brief extinction paradigm with the discriminative stimulus for attention present). This continuous attention procedure has some advantages over demonstrations based on contingent attention. The challenging behaviour is not artificially reinforced so the risk of its becoming attention maintained is minimal. A variation on this theme was used by Meyerson, Kerr and Michael (1967), who presented sensory stimulation in a noncontingent fashion, and compared this to periods of no stimulation. The higher rate of SIB in the latter condition suggested that SIB was normally maintained by response-contingent sensory stimulation which was reinforcing.

To summarize, these studies suggest how the positive reinforcement (attention and stimulation) hypothesis may be tested in a controlled fashion by the presentation of the presumed reinforcer contingent on responding, the noncontingent presentation of the presumed reinforcer, and the presentation of the discriminative stimulus for presumed reinforcement during a period where the reinforcer is withheld (extinction procedure).

Research evaluating the negative reinforcement hypothesis

The negative reinforcement hypothesis that challenging behaviour is maintained by escape from aversive stimuli has predominantly been explored via the corollary that it would be expected to occur at a higher rate when a putative aversive stimulus is present than when it is absent. Most demonstrations of this corollary employ instructional settings or demands as aversive stimuli.

Carr, Newsom and Binkoff (1976) demonstrated a negative reinforcement effect of verbal instructional demands on self-injury, in comparison to conditions involving neutral statements and free time. Furthermore, they explored two other corollaries of the hypothesis. The first was that the self-injurious behaviour should decrease when a safety signal is present (i.e., a stimulus associated with the termination of the aversive stimulus). The second was that the behaviour should show a characteristic gradual increase in rate following presentation of the aversive stimulus when its termination was programmed on fixed interval schedule. In both cases, results supported the conclusion that the behaviour was maintained by escape from instructional demands. More recently, Carr, Newsom and Binkoff (1980) reported a comparable analysis of aggressive behaviour, thus illustrating the irrelevance of the form of the behaviour to its function.

A similar demonstration of the main corollary of the negative reinforcement hypothesis, that behaviour should occur at comparatively high rates when aversive stimuli are present, has been provided by Gaylord-Ross (1982), who demonstrated that increased task difficulty evoked higher rates of challenging behaviour than easier tasks. Romanczyk, Colletti and Plotkin (1980) have further shown that relative, rather than absolute, task difficulty is influential, and Russo, Cataldo and Cushing (1981) that higher rates of challenging behaviour occur when the demand rate is higher.

In assessing the negative reinforcement of challenging behaviour, it is not always possible to determine the precise nature of 'the demand' (see also Iwata *et al.*, 1990). For example, a person might be reinforced by escape from aspects of the task itself (e.g., forming manual signs), the teacher's behaviour (e.g., the use of correction procedures), or the entire situation (e.g., the classroom). The stimuli which occasion escape might be either discriminative stimuli, or establishing stimuli (Michael, 1982). Essentially, establishing stimuli set the occasion for escape to be reinforcing, whereas discriminative stimuli are events which have been correlated with reinforcement of escape responses (see also Goodman and Remington, this volume). For example, the classroom situation itself may have an establishing stimulus function in that it makes escape reinforcing, but challenging behaviour may in fact be reinforced only when it occurs during a teaching episode, which thus acquires a discriminative stimulus function. This distinction is not merely academic. Presentation of a discriminative stimulus in the absence of an establishing operation would not be expected to occasion negatively reinforced behaviour, because the conditions which establish the potency of the reinforcer are absent. Similarly, presentation of an establishing stimulus might not occasion escape behaviour which is normally under the control of an additional, discriminative stimulus.

All the studies discussed above have assumed that a given behaviour may have only a single function. In questioning this assumption, Durand (1982) has made an important contribution to the development of analogue methodology. By separately manipulating both level of stimulation and the degree of task difficulty, Durand demonstrated that SIB could serve two functions in a single individual, with different topographies of SIB serving each function ('hits' were maintained by automatic reinforcement whilst 'flicks' were maintained by escape). This development revealed the complexity of function that may exist in challenging behaviour, and indicated the potential of combining analogue conditions.

Research evaluating both positive and negative reinforcement hypotheses

The influential demonstrations of a functional relationship between challenging behaviour and other environmental events reviewed above had the advantage of being well controlled and uncomplicated in comparison to other methods of functional analysis. It is likely, however, that in each case the decision to test a given hypothesis was determined by prior knowledge of an individual's behaviour derived from informal observations or interviews. Consequently, not all potential determinants were assessed in each study. For a complete assessment by analogue conditions in the absence of other information, therefore, it was necessary to combine various conditions to test the various hypotheses.

The first study of this type by Iwata *et al.* (1982) is worth considering in detail as it demonstrates the rationale behind this method of functional analysis. Four analogue conditions were designed to test three operant hypotheses, i.e. that SIB could be maintained by positive reinforcement from either attention or automatic reinforcement (sensory stimulation), or by negative reinforcement from the termination of demands. The conditions were:

- *Social disapproval*: Play materials were available to a participant, and mild reprimands plus brief physical contact were contingent on SIB.
- *Academic demands*: 'Apparently difficult tasks', never spontaneously completed, were presented to a participant using a least-to-most prompting procedure. Task completion, whether achieved independently or not, was followed by 'social praise'. The experimenter turned away for 30 seconds contingent on the occurrence of SIB.
- *Alone*: The participant was left alone in the room without play materials.
- *Unstructured play*: Both the experimenter and play materials were present. The participant was given 'social praise' and brief physical contact if there was no SIB for 30 seconds (DRO 30 seconds).

Each condition lasted 15 minutes, the order of conditions was randomly determined, and conditions were repeated until the data were stable.

Iwata *et al.* proposed that a high rate of SIB in the 'social disapproval' condition would indicate that it was normally maintained by positive reinforcement from attention; a high rate in the 'academic demands' condition would indicate that the SIB is normally maintained by the termination of such demands; and a high rate in the 'alone' condition that it is maintained by the resultant sensory stimulation. The final condition, 'unstructured play', essentially acted as a control for the other conditions.

From the resultant data, Iwata and colleagues argued that, for four people they observed, the SIB was maintained by automatic reinforcement; for two individuals it was maintained by the termination of demands, and for one other by positive reinforcement from attention. For a further two people the pattern of responding was 'undifferentiated' across conditions (although one individual's SIB was also considered to be maintained by automatic reinforcement). The authors suggested that this undifferentiated pattern may have occurred because the people concerned could not discriminate between the conditions, because other variables not manipulated in the experiment were maintaining the SIB, or because their behaviour served all three functions.

In concluding, Iwata *et al.* noted three major problems associated with their procedures. First, there was the possibility that high rates of behaviour, particularly in the 'academic demands' and the 'social disapproval' conditions, may have been artifactual. The assessment procedure itself may have led to either positive or negative reinforcement of the SIB rather than merely providing the discriminative or aversive stimuli normally associated with its occurrence. However, they further argued that if this was the case then an increase in rate of SIB would be apparent across sessions, and this outcome occurred only for one person whose responding was undifferentiated in terms of function. Second, and associated with the first point, is the possibility that a high rate of SIB in the 'alone' condition may not necessarily be indicative of a sensory reinforcement function but may instead reflect responding characteristic of the early stages of an extinction burst (i.e., extinction following removal of attentional reinforcement). Finally, the authors acknowledged that the analysis was incomplete because they did not subsequently validate their conclusions by modifying the reinforcement contingencies identified by the assessment (e.g., by extinguishing SIB associated with demands by preventing escape).

In addition to the authors' caveats, there are a number of other points worth raising. First, the test for positive reinforcement by attention may yield false negatives because the discriminative stimulus for attention (the experimenter) may have no previous history of reinforcing an individual's SIB. Although the presence of any other person *may* be sufficient, there are findings to suggest this is a relevant variable (Anderson, Dancis and Alpert, 1978). Secondly, high rates of responding in the 'academic demands' condition is interpreted as indicative of maintenance by the termination of the demand. However, it is equally plausible that the aversive stimulus is not necessarily the demand but simply the proximity of the experimenter, and SIB is in fact maintained by the termination of social interaction. Recently, Iwata *et al.* (1990) have acknowledged this point, but argued that it is unimportant because the general contingency of escape-motivated SIB is the most pertinent implication. A final point is that Iwata *et al.* (1982) did not measure independent variables: this would have allowed the influence of the conditions to be more fully evaluated (e.g., by correlating the rate of demands with the rate of SIB).

Carr and Durand (1985b) developed a different methodology for analogue assessment, although sharing some of the principles pioneered by Iwata *et al.* (1982). Carr and Durand used three conditions to assess whether challenging behaviour was maintained by attention from others or escape from difficult tasks. They involved:

- Undivided adult attention whilst the individual was required to carry out an easy task.
- Reduced adult attention whilst the individual was required to carry out an easy task.
- Undivided adult attention whilst the individual was required to carry out a difficult task.

These conditions allowed Carr and Durand to assess the effects of level of the noncontingent presentation of reinforcement, and thus test the attention hypothesis (easy task: undivided versus reduced adult attention). They could also assess the effects of presentation of the aversive stimulus (undivided attention: difficult versus easy tasks). Both manipulations were controlled for by the undivided attention, easy task condition. Their design thus focused on the social contingencies for challenging behaviour—there was no test for maintenance by automatic reinforcement.

The independent variables of task difficulty and level of adult attention were operationally defined and monitored. Higher rates of challenging behaviour in the second condition listed above compared to the first would be indicative of maintenance by adult attention, whilst a higher rate of challenging behaviour in the third condition than in the first would indicate maintenance by escape from difficult tasks. Of the four participants assessed, the challenging behaviour of two appeared to be maintained by escape from demands, another's by adult attention, and the fourth's behaviour appeared to be maintained by both kinds of consequences.

Iwata *et al.* (1982) and Carr and Durand's (1985b) studies have inspired much subsequent work that has focused on different aspects of the application and methodology of analogue-based functional analysis. Three such aspects were specifically addressed by Carr and Durand (1985b).

The first is that of 'validity', the issue of whether an intervention based on functional analysis by analogue methodology would be effective. Carr and Durand validated their assessments by showing that verbal requests ('mands': see Goodman and Remington, this volume) which served an identical function to that identified as maintaining the challenging behaviour effectively reduced it. The second—related—issue is whether the efficacy of an intervention based on functional analysis is greater than that of an intervention which is not. Carr and Durand demonstrated that, in terms of reducing the challenging behaviour, teaching a functionally *non*-equivalent request was less effective than an equivalent request. The final issue illustrated by the Carr and Durand study is that the form of the challenging behaviour was irrelevant in terms of selecting the intervention. Their four participants showed aggression, SIB, tantrums, oppositional behaviour, and stripping, but these were all unrelated to the nature or effectiveness of the interventions.

The issue of validity in terms of efficacy of interventions derived from analogue-based functional analysis has been further explored in a number of studies. Using methodology similar to that used by Carr and Durand (1985b), Durand and Crimmins (1987) and Durand and Carr (1987) taught functionally equivalent communicative responses to reduce escape-motivated rocking, hand-flapping, and 'psychotic speech'. Furthermore, in both studies additional validation was obtained by evaluating the effects of a 10-second 'timeout' contingent on the challenging behaviour in difficult demand conditions. In these conditions, timeout resulted, predictably, in higher rates of the target behaviours compared to a condition in which an easy task was presented with undivided adult attention.

A number of other studies have successfully employed Iwata *et al.*'s (1982) methodology, or variants on it, to demonstrate the efficacy of interventions derived from analogue-based functional analysis. For example, Mace *et al.* (1986) used a timeout intervention with a person whose aggression and disruption was maintained by attention from others, and DRO plus extinction for another individual whose behaviour had the same function. Steege *et al.* (1989) positively reinforced compliance to reduce SIB which was maintained by an escape function, and differentially reinforced alternative behaviour (DRA: see Jones, this volume) where SIB functioned in a self-stimulatory manner. Finally Iwata *et al.* (1990) intervened with seven individuals whose SIB was maintained by escape from aversive settings. For five of them, escape extinction was successful; for another it was effective when combined with 'guidance' (i.e., physical prompting back to task) and response blocking; for the final person escape extinction worked when combined with DRO.

A further aspect of the research-based development of analogue procedures is the adaptation and refinement of conditions in order to explore more specific hypotheses for given individuals. Examples of this are apparent in Mace et al.'s (1986) study, which used a variation of Iwata et al.'s (1982) social disapproval condition: three or four adults (including a parent) were present in the room in order to model the family's home setting. Family members were also used by Slifer et al. (1986) in a study of escape maintained aggression. Day et al. (1988) presented tangible reinforcers, rather than social attention, contingent on SIB, and Steege et al. (1989) conducted an assessment of one individual in two relevant settings (the classroom and toilet). This study also included a condition in which objects were removed from the participant when he attempted to play with them. This was done to test this hypothesis concerning the role of tangibles in maintaining challenging behaviour that had been suggested by the parents. Finally Iwata et al. (1990) included a 'medical' condition to assess one person whose SIB was thought to be motivated by escape from medical examinations rather than general instructional demands.

Two further examples of variations in analogue conditions addressing the negative reinforcement hypothesis have been described by Murphy and Oliver (1987). For one individual, a continuous social interaction condition evoked higher rates of SIB than control conditions, suggesting that the behaviour was maintained by escape from interaction per se, rather than any instructional demands. A second person produced high rates of aggression when the social interaction condition comprised just sitting and talking. Lower rates of aggression occurred when the same type of interaction occurred while the person was walking, or sitting engaged in a demanding instructional task. These demonstrations show the diversity of forms that an aversive stimulus can take, and thus emphasize how difficult it may be to arrange the conditions necessary for a complete functional analysis.

The use of analogue conditions as a method of functional analysis in clinical practice is problematic because of the time, resources and expertise needed to arrange the conditions and analyse the resultant data. Durand and Crimmins (1988, and Chapter 4 this volume) have directly addressed this problem for SIB by designing a questionnaire (the Motivation Assessment Scale: MAS) and using analogue conditions to validate it. The MAS may therefore be used in applied settings as a method of functional analysis. The analogue conditions employed were an adaptation of those used in the Carr and Durand (1985b) study, and assess the maintenance of SIB by positive reinforcement (through attention or tangible events), negative reinforcement through escape from instructional settings, or sensory stimulation. The questionnaire ratings in this study were very highly correlated with the analogue data, suggesting the MAS is a valid instrument for predicting behaviour in the analogue conditions employed.

This development was important and timely in that it has contributed a comparatively straightforward and validated instrument to support functional analysis in clinical contexts. It has, however, been argued that questionnaires are insufficient in the demonstration of a functional relationship because they do not use the methods of empirical functional analysis to verify cause and effect relationships (Iwata *et al.*, 1990). Nevertheless, the MAS is certainly preferable to anecdotal information by virtue of its reliability and validity. Its use in applied settings has been demonstrated (Bird *et al.*, 1989; Durand and Kishi, 1987) and it is likely to prove a useful instrument for research purposes.

To summarize the argument to this point, there have been a number of applications and developments of analogue methodology which are contributing directly to the understanding and thus the amelioration of challenging behaviour. The variety of analogue conditions now becoming evident in the research literature marks an important development by demonstrating that this methodology can be sensitive to the extreme diversity of forms that the aversive, discriminative, and reinforcing stimuli may take. Such flexibility is consistent with a behaviour analytic perspective which emphasizes the importance of individual differences. Perhaps the most important contribution of analogue methodology is that it offers an empirical method of demonstrating cause and effect relationships using comparatively practical procedures.

CONCLUSIONS

There is an evident trend in the literature on challenging behaviour: the notion of intervening with techniques of 'proven' efficacy is being replaced by the principle of elucidating the functional relationship between target behaviour and its determinants prior to selecting an intervention. Analogue procedures have played a significant role in this development by contributing to the methodology of functional analysis. When challenging behaviour is occurring at a high rate, naturalistic A: B: C analysis can be problematic. Analogue methodology overcomes these problems by allowing systematic analysis of the influence of potential determinants in a controlled fashion. For example, this methodology can ensure evaluation of the role of aversive stimuli, such as demands which may normally not be made by others because they are thought to occasion challenging behaviour. There is also the opportunity to evaluate positive reinforcers which act on a very lean intermittent schedule in the normal environment and may thus be difficult to identify with A: B: C analysis. Equally, the potential effect of different reinforcers can be assessed. These benefits are not without cost: analogue conditions require expertise, time, and physical resources. However, given that baseline observations of the target behaviour are an essential prerequisite to intervention, there is much to be said for carrying them out in analogue settings and thus gaining the benefits of controlled functional analysis.

The issue of whether such a methodology is valid in terms of predicting the efficacy of a given intervention is beginning to be addressed (Carr and Durand, 1985b), but a demonstration of the efficacy of a single intervention based on a functional analysis is an insufficient test: the question of whether *any* randomly selected intervention would be successful is unanswered. Questions of effectiveness, particularly relative effectiveness, are not merely academic, because alternatives which are relevant to clinical practice are already in use. For example, rather than using a functional analysis, Repp, Felce and Barton (1988) assessed the effect of two interventions delivered in parallel in different settings using an alternating treatments design. Each treatment was based on the hypothesized maintaining variables (i.e., positive reinforcement, negative reinforcement and automatic reinforcement), the more successful intervention identified, and subsequently applied to both settings. It could be argued that the time spent on a functional analysis by analogue conditions is better spent implementing interventions in this way.

A second question surrounding the utility of analogue conditions is the relevance of necessarily artificial analogue conditions to the contingencies operating in the natural environment. In a preliminary study, Oliver et al. (1988) reported only poor agreement between the outcomes of functional assessment of SIB using analogue conditions, direct natural observations, and clinical interviews. One possible reason for this is that, for some people, aversive stimuli (i.e., demands) do not occur in the natural environment—thus their role could not be evaluated. Another stems from two erroneous assumptions underlying the use of natural observations: temporal contiguity between behavioural and environmental events may not imply a contingent relationship; a contingent relationship may have no functional significance. A final reason for the disagreements may be that the maintaining reinforcers or aversive stimuli which operate in the natural environment were not considered in the particular set of analogue conditions employed.

An evaluation of the relationship between functions ascribed to behaviour on the basis of analogue studies, and those ascribed from natural observations, is clearly warranted because it has implications for how, or whether, analogue conditions should be employed. For example, in some studies reviewed above (e.g., Iwata *et al.*, 1990; Murphy and

Oliver, 1987) the aversive stimulus whose function was evaluated was quite specific (cf. an instructional demand). Given this, it is debatable whether analogues are truly useful because it may be necessary to assess challenging behaviour in a seemingly endless number of conditions in order to ascribe function accurately. Moreover, analogues may be seen as unnecessary because the final intervention could have been based directly on the information that led to the arrangement of the analogue condition (cf. Repp, Felce and Barton, 1988). For example, the 'medical' condition employed by Iwata *et al.* (1990) was used because the authors thought this was relevant for this participant. Although analogue assessment confirmed this hypothesis, it was presumably initially suspected for other reasons. The analogue stage could have been omitted.

This discussion leads to an interesting point. On the one hand, applied behaviour analysis suggests that a functional analysis should provide a detailed empirical account of the necessary and sufficient conditions for the occurrence of behavioural events. On the other hand, there is now a tendency toward a classification of the behaviour via its mode of reinforcement (i.e., positive or negative). At present, the difference seems to be one of emphasis: Iwata *et al.* (1990) suggest classifying behaviour by the general contingency first, and then assessing the potential range of effective stimuli, while Durand and Crimmins (1988) seek to distinguish between classes of positive reinforcement (e.g., tangible and social) in the first instance. In any event, it would seem important to avoid a rigid classification system which does not recognize the potential for variability in function both between individuals, and within individuals over time. An example of such rigidity in most functional analysis studies is the exclusive consideration of instructional demands as the only aversive stimuli, and social attention (and stimulation) as the only source of positive reinforcement. The examples given above of the diversity of forms positive and negative reinforcers can take is sufficient to advocate further exploration in this area. Furthermore, it is essential to avoid replacing the sterile classification of challenging behaviour by form with a narrow and equally sterile 'functional' classification system of escape-from-demands and reinforcement-by-attention.

This point relates to the use of analogue conditions in clinical practice. The approach can clearly be beneficial in offering a methodology which aids decision-making and intervention selection, but there is no one set of conditions as such which will be useful in all instances. The risk is that one variant of the methodology will be rigidly applied as 'the method of assessment'. Analogue methodology is better employed as a way of systematically testing hypotheses generated from other sources which then require further evaluation. The nature of the conditions must therefore be dependent on the hypotheses for a given individual—to do otherwise would be as ludicrous as using a WAIS to assess incontinence!

A further role for analogue methodology in clinical practice may be the detailed examination of the elements of, for example, aversive stimuli. By grading components of such stimuli which occasion challenging behaviour on a hierarchy, it may be possible to introduce more aversive components gradually, in combination with differential reinforcement procedures, as a method of intervention (see Gaylord-Ross, 1982; Iwata *et al.*, 1990; Murphy and Oliver, 1987). Such an approach may avoid the difficulties created by high rates of behaviour occurring during escape extinction procedures.

More generally, research into analogue methodology has laid to rest classification of challenging behaviour by form, and revitalized the role of applied behaviour analysis in behaviour modification. It has also enhanced understanding of challenging behaviour, regardless of the implications for interventions. The methodology may make it possible to address the potential contribution of other factors to challenging behaviour in a meaningful way. In severe SIB, for example, theories of neurotransmitter disturbance are demanding increasing attention as controlled studies of particular psychopharmacological interventions demonstrate the role of endogenous opioids as determinants (see Oliver and Head, 1990). If this organic substrate has a causal role for some individuals, it would be expected that, for them, SIB should be less sensitive to environmental control. Analogue methodology may offer a controlled way of determining the degree of environmental control of SIB, thus allowing the organic hypothesis to be tested. Another possible avenue for research concerns the session to session variability in challenging behaviour in the same analogue conditions. One may speculate on the determinants of such variability in terms of the influence of events between sessions, and the effect of prior conditions. However, there may also be broad setting events such as fatigue, hunger, or physical discomfort which interact with immediate events to influence the challenging behaviour. Analogue methodology offers a way of exploring the role of setting events in a controlled way.

In conclusion, analogue methodology has gained a place amongst techniques for the applied behaviour analysis of challenging behaviour by virtue of its empirical nature, its basis in the experimental analysis of behaviour, and its contribution to understanding and amelioration. It could be argued that its use is essential, given the problems of analysing the three-term contingency in the natural environment. With the recent application of microcomputers to collecting and analysing behavioural data, however, it is now possible to return to the study of the three-term contingency and its interactions with other determinants without the limitations imposed by time-sampling and onerous data management by hand (Repp and Felce, 1990; Repp, Felce and Karsh, this volume). Such a development promises much in the way of complex analysis of the determinants of challenging behaviour and, consequently, major increases in understanding. The combination of this development and the application of analogue methodology to the study of challenging behaviour should ease the reconciliation of behaviour modification with applied behaviour analysis.

Address for correspondence

Chris Oliver, Hilda Lewis House, Bethlem Royal Hospital, 579 Wickham Road, Shirley, Croydon CR0 8DR, UK.

REFERENCES

Anderson, L.T., Dancis, J. and Alpert, M. (1978) Behavioral contingencies and self-mutilation in Lesch–Nyhan disease. *Journal of Consulting and Clinical Psychology*, **46**, 529–536.

Bird, F., Dores, P.A., Moniz, D. and Robinson, J. (1989) Reducing severe aggressive and self-injurious behaviors with functional communication training. *American Journal on Mental Retardation*, **94**, 37–48.

Bruhl, H.H., Fielding, L., Joyce, M., Peters, W. and Wieseler, N. (1982) Thirty month demonstration project for treatment of self-injurious behavior in severely retarded individuals. In J.H. Hollis and C.E. Meyers (eds), *Life Threatening Behavior: Analysis and Intervention* (pp. 191–275), American Association of Mental Deficiency, Washington, DC.

Carr, E.G. (1977) The motivation of self-injurious behavior: A review of some hypotheses. *Psychological Bulletin*, **84**, 800–816.

Carr, E.G. and Durand, V.M. (1985a) The social-communicative basis of severe behavior problems in children. In S. Reiss and R. Bootzin (eds), *Theoretical Issues in Behavior Therapy* (pp. 219–254), Academic Press, New York.

Carr, E.G. and Durand, V.M. (1985b) Reducing behavior problems through functional communication training. *Journal of Applied Behavior Analysis*, **18**, 111–126.

Carr, E.G. and McDowell, J.J. (1980) Social control of self-injurious behavior of organic etiology. *Behavior Therapy*, **11**, 402–409.

Carr, E.G., Newsom, C.D. and Binkoff, J.A. (1976) Stimulus control of self-destructive behavior in a psychotic child. *Journal of Abnormal Child Psychology*, **4**, 139–153.

Carr, E.G., Newsom, C.D. and Binkoff, J.A. (1980) Escape as a factor in the aggressive behavior of two retarded children. *Journal of Applied Behavior Analysis*, **13**, 101–117.

Day, R.M., Rea, J.A., Schussler, N.G., Larsen, S.E. and Johnson, W.L. (1988) A functionally based approach to the treatment of self-injurious behavior. *Behavior Modification*, **12**, 565–589.

Donnellan, A.M., Mirenda, P.L., Mesaros, R.A. and Fassbender, L.L. (1984)

Analyzing the communicative functions of aberrant behavior. *Journal of the Association for Persons with Severe Handicaps*, **9**, 201–212.

Durand, V.M. (1982) Analysis and intervention of self-injurious behavior. *Journal of the Association of the Severely Handicapped*, **7**, 44–53.

Durand, V.M. and Carr, E.G. (1987) Social influences on 'self stimulatory' behavior: Analysis and treatment application. *Journal of Applied Behavior Analysis*, **20**, 119–132.

Durand, V.M. and Crimmins, D.B. (1987) Assessment and treatment of psychotic speech in an autistic child. *Journal of Autism and Developmental Disorders*, **17**, 17–28.

Durand, V.M. and Crimmins, D.B. (1988) Identifying the variables maintaining self-injurious behavior. *Journal of Autism and Developmental Disorders*, **18**, 99–117.

Durand, V.M. and Kishi, G. (1987) Reducing severe behavior problems among people with dual sensory impairments: An evaluation of a technical assistance model. *Journal of the Association of Persons with Severe Handicaps*, **12**, 2–10.

Edelson, S.M., Taubman, M.T. and Lovaas, O.I. (1983) Some social contexts of self-destructive behavior. *Journal of Abnormal Child Psychology*, **11**, 299–312.

Gaylord-Ross, R.J. (1982) Curricula considerations in treating behavior problems of severely handicapped students. In K.D. Gadow and I. Bialer (eds), *Advances in Learning and Behavioral Disabilities* (Vol. 1, pp. 193–224), JAI Press, Greenwich.

Griffin, J.C., Williams, D.E., Stark, M.T., Altmeyer, B.K. and Mason, M. (1984) Self-injurious behavior: A state-wide prevalence survey, assessment of severe cases, and follow-up of aversive programs. In J.C. Griffin, M.T. Stark, D.E. Williams, B.K. Altmeyer and H.K. Griffin (eds), *Advances in the Treatment of Self Injurious Behavior* (pp. 1–26), Planning Council for Developmental Disabilities, Texas.

Hauck, F. (1985) Development of a behavior-analytic questionnaire precising four functions of self-injurious behavior in the mentally retarded. *International Journal of Rehabilitation Research*, **8**, 350–352.

Iwata, B.A., Dorsey, M.F., Slifer, K.J., Bauman, K.E. and Richman, G.S. (1982) Toward a functional analysis of self-injury. *Analysis and Intervention in Developmental Disabilities*, **2**, 3–20.

Iwata, B.A., Pace, G.M., Kalsher, M.J., Cowdery, G.E. and Cataldo, M.F. (1990) Experimental analysis and extinction of self-injurious escape behavior. *Journal of Applied Behavior Analysis*, **23**, 11–27.

Lovaas, I. and Simmons, J.Q. (1969) Manipulation of self-destructive behavior in three retarded children. *Journal of Applied Behavior Analysis*, **2**, 143–157.

Lovaas, O.I., Freitag, G., Gold, V.J. and Kassorla, I.C. (1965) Experimental studies in childhood schizophrenia: Analysis of self-destructive behavior. *Journal of Experimental Child Psychology*, **2**, 67–84.

Lundervold, D. and Bourland, G. (1988) Quantitative analysis of treatment of aggression, self-injury, and property destruction. *Behavior Modification*, **12**, 590–617.

Mace, F.C., Page, T.J., Ivancic, M.T. and O'Brien, S. (1986) Effectiveness of brief time-out with and without contingent delay: A comparative analysis. *Journal of Applied Behavior Analysis*, **19**, 79–86.

Maurice, P. and Trudel, G. (1982) Self-injurious behavior: Prevalence and relationship to environmental events. In J. Hollis and C.E. Meyers (eds), *Life Threatening Behavior: Analysis and Intervention* (pp. 81–104), American Association of Mental Deficiency, Washington, DC.

Meyerson, L., Kerr, N. and Michael, J.L. (1967) Behavior modification in rehabilitation. In S. Bijou and D. Baer (eds), *Child Development: Readings in Experimental Analysis* (pp. 214–239), Appleton–Century–Crofts, New York.

Michael, J. (1982) Distinguishing between discriminative and motivational functions of stimuli. *Journal of the Experimental Analysis of Behavior*, **37**, 149–155.

Michael, J. (1985) Fundamental research and behaviour modification. In C.F. Lowe, M. Richelle, D.E. Blackman and C.M. Bradshaw (eds), *Behaviour Analysis and Contemporary Psychology* (pp. 159–164), Lawrence Erlbaum Associates, London.

Miron, N.B. (1971) Behavior modification in the treatment of self-injurious behavior in institutionalized retardates. *Bulletin of Suicidology*, **8**, 64–69.

Murphy, G. (1987) Direct observation as an assessment tool in functional analysis and treatment. In J. Hogg and N.V. Raynes (eds), *Assessment in Mental Handicap: A Guide to Assessment Practices, Tests and Checklists* (pp. 190–238), Croom Helm, London.

Murphy, G.H. and Oliver, C. (1987) Decreasing undesirable behaviours. In W. Yule and J. Carr (eds), *Behaviour Modification for People with Mental Handicaps* (2nd ed, pp. 102–142), Croom Helm, London.

Oliver, C. and Head, D. (1990) Self-injurious behaviour in people with learning disabilities: Determinants and interventions. *International Review of Psychiatry*, **2**, 99–114.

Oliver, C., Crayton, L., Murphy, G., Burgess, A., Clements, J. and Corbett, J.A. (1988) *The Functional Analysis of Self-injurious Behaviour: A Comparison of Methods*. Paper presented at the Behaviour Therapy World Congress, Edinburgh.

Peterson, R.F. and Peterson, L.R. (1968) The use of positive reinforcement in the control of self-destructive behavior in a retarded boy. *Journal of Experimental Child Psychology*, **6**, 351–360.

Repp, A.C. and Felce, D. (1990) A microcomputer system used for evaluative and experimental behavioural research in mental handicap. *Mental Handicap Research*, **3**, 21–32.

Repp, A.C., Felce, D. and Barton, L.E. (1988) Basing the treatment of stereotypic and self-injurious behaviors on hypotheses of their causes. *Journal of Applied Behavior Analysis*, **21**, 281–289.

Repp, A.C., Singh, N.N., Olinger, E. and Olson, D.R. (1990) The use of functional analysis to test causes of self-injurious behavior: Rationale, current status and future directions. *Journal of Mental Deficiency Research*, **34**, 95–105.

Romanczyk, R.G., Colletti, G. and Plotkin, R. (1980) Punishment of self-injurious behavior: Issues of behavior analysis, generalization and the right to treatment. *Child Behavior Therapy*, **2**, 37–54.

Russo, D.C., Cataldo, M.F. and Cushing, P.J. (1981) Compliance training and behavioral covariation in the treatment of multiple behavior problems. *Journal of Applied Behavior Analysis*, **14**, 209–222.

Singh, N. (1976) Psychological treatment of self-injury. *New Zealand Medical Journal*, **84**, 484–486.

Slifer, K.J., Ivancic, M.T., Parrish, J.M., Page, T.J. and Burgio, L.D. (1986) Assessment and treatment of multiple behavior problems exhibited by a profoundly retarded adolescent. *Journal of Behavior Therapy and Experimental Psychiatry*, **17**, 203–213.

Steege, M.W., Wacker, D.P., Berg, W.K., Cigrand, K.K. and Cooper, L.J. (1989) The use of behavioral assessment to prescribe and evaluate treatments for

severely handicapped children. *Journal of Applied Behavior Analysis*, **22**, 23–33.
Wieseler, N.A., Hanson, R.H., Chamberlain, T.P. and Thompson, T. (1985)
Functional taxonomy of stereotypic and self-injurious behavior. *Mental Retardation*, **23**, 230–234.

Chapter 6

The Use of a Portable Microcomputer in the Functional Analysis of Maladaptive Behaviour[1]

ALAN C. REPP, DAVID FELCE AND
KATHRYN G. KARSH

INTRODUCTION

The treatment of maladaptive behaviour has been a primary focus for many of us involved in working with people with severe mental handicap, from parents to service providers to researchers. The problem is a very real one, with estimates from recent studies suggesting that between 14% and 38% of people with severe mental handicap may engage in aggressive and destructive behaviours, between 6% and 40% may engage in self-injurious behaviour, and between 40% and 60% may engage in stereotypic behaviour at rates high enough to be regarded as problematic (Borthwick, Meyers and Eyman, 1981; Corbett and Campbell, 1981; Jacobson, 1982; Oliver, Murphy and Corbett, 1987; Repp and Barton, 1980).

As a result of their prevalence, considerable research has been directed toward the treatment of various maladaptive behaviours. Some of this work has been reviewed in papers which focus on either behaviour types or treatment procedures. Reviews categorized by behaviour include stereotypy (LaGrow and Repp, 1984), self-injury (Romanczyk, 1986; Repp et al., 1990), rumination (Starin and Fuqua, 1987), and pica (Paisey and Whitney, 1989). Treatments have been based on both punishment (Cataldo, 1989; Matson and DiLorenzo, 1984; Matson and Taras, 1989),

[1] This research was supported in part by a grant (H023C00092) from the Office of Special Education and Rehabilitation Services of the US Department of Education.

and reinforcement procedures (Carr *et al.*, 1989; O'Brien and Repp, 1990, in press).

In many instances, the treatment of these various behaviour problems has been successful, but in others it has not. This finding, evident in all reviews, is intriguing to us. We do not believe that there is an inherent variation in the effectiveness of treatment, that is, that some failures occurring among the successes are simply the result of a random process. Instead, we believe that failures occur because the science of treating behaviour problems has not advanced to the point where we can isolate and thus eliminate the factors which lead to it.

The problem, then, is to determine why most of us fail at times to effect sufficient behaviour change. The approach we have taken is at first glance a deceptively simple one; it is to determine why the behaviour is occurring and then to match treatment to the reason identified (Repp, Felce and Barton, 1988; Repp *et al.*, 1990). Currently, we are attempting to build a model that will identify the reasons for the behaviour problems of some individuals, and the purpose of this chapter is to present this model.

THE NATURE OF MALADAPTIVE BEHAVIOUR

The basis of our approach is the development of a taxonomy that allows us to analyse behaviour in the context of its environment. Before presenting this taxonomy, however, we would like to discuss the terms *environmentally dependent* and *environmentally independent*—terms that are central to the operation of this taxonomy. By environmentally independent, we mean those behaviours whose rate, duration, intensity, or topography are unaffected by changes in the environment surrounding the individual. An example of this classification would be the self-injurious behaviour (SIB) usually found in persons with Lesch–Nyhan syndrome or congenital sensory neuropathy, and sometimes found with persons with deLange's syndrome or dysautonomia. The Lesch–Nyhan case is a particularly good example as the biochemical basis for this disorder has been established, and this has led directly to an effective, pharmacological intervention. Specifically, Nyhan (1989) has shown that 5-hydroxytryptophan and carbidopa produce complete, although short-term, remission in SIB for this group.

Conversely, by environmentally dependent, we mean those behaviours whose rate, duration, intensity, or topography are dependent upon the environmental context. In the terminology of applied behaviour analysis, determination of the role of the environment would require an assessment of the relationship of behaviour to its antecedents and consequences. If behaviours can be clearly shown to be a function of the present environment or a previously experienced environment, then they are environmentally dependent, and treatment can be based upon the results of the baseline assessment. If behaviour cannot be shown to be a function of the environment, it *may* be environmentally independent and better treated through pharmacological means. The caveat is necessary because there is an obvious problem with 'proving' the negative. If behaviour is not shown to be a function of the environment, the finding *may* be due to our choosing the wrong environmental variables to study.

At present, we are guided by the hypothesis that the number of people who can be helped can be increased by assessing their environment, by determining which behaviours are environmentally dependent, and by basing treatment on those findings. We are currently involved in testing this proposition, and to do this we must consider three factors: the nature of hypotheses concerning the causes of severe behaviour problems; the development of a taxonomy describing the relationship between behaviour and the environment; and the creation of a method of data collection and analysis to support the taxonomy. These three elements will be briefly explained in the remainder of this chapter.

Hypothesized causes of severe behaviour problems

Baumeister (1989) has suggested seven possible aetiologies for severe behaviour problems. These are:

- A 'neural oscillator' that regulates the behaviour.
- A developmental stage through which most of us move quite quickly but at which some people with mental handicap or autism are delayed.
- Biological or neurochemical imbalances.
- Stages related to psychodynamic theory.
- An attempt to control arousal levels.
- An alternative means of communication.
- Behaviour which has been strengthened by operant conditioning.

From our viewpoint, maladaptive behaviour attributed to the neural oscillator, biological/neurochemical, developmental, and psychodynamic hypotheses may be best treated as environmentally independent behaviours, while maladaptive behaviour explained in terms of arousal control, communication, or conditioning hypotheses may best be treated as environmentally dependent behaviour. We will therefore focus on these latter hypotheses.

The *arousal theory* suggests that individuals seek a relatively even level of environmental stimulation. This means that when under-aroused we increase our activity levels possibly by engaging in maladaptive behaviour such as stereotypy or self-injury (Guess and Carr, 1990). Conversely, when overstimulated, arousal can be decreased by engaging in a repetitive form of behaviour which effectively blocks the complexity of environmental input (Cataldo and Harris, 1982).

The *communication theory* (Carr, 1985; Donnellan *et al.*, 1984) suggests that severe maladaptive behaviours may function as an elementary nonverbal means of communication. Such behaviours may serve to gain positive reinforcement, as in the gaining of attention or food, or alternatively may serve an escape or avoidance function, as in terminating a demand. The communication theory is actually a subset of the *conditioning theory* which states that some maladaptive behaviours are either positively reinforced (e.g., by attention) or negatively reinforced (e.g., by escape from difficult tasks). Arousal theory can also be subsumed as a variant of conditioning theory if it is assumed that the changes in arousal achieved by maladaptive behaviour relate to intrinsic perceptual reinforcers (cf. Lovaas, Newsom and Hickman, 1987).

These three theories thus have large areas of overlap, in that all focus on the relationship between maladaptive behaviour and the environment. By conceptualizing maladaptive behaviour as environmentally dependent, they raise the possibility that behaviour can be treated by careful analysis and manipulation of the environment. From our perspective, the task is to identify which theory provides the most satisfactory explanation of the particular behaviour problem we are observing and then to base a treatment programme on that theoretical interpretation. An essential feature of this approach is that different individuals may exhibit similar maladaptive behaviours for different functional reasons.

A taxonomy for enviornmentally dependent behaviours

The purpose of the taxonomy is to describe a functional relationship between behaviour and the environment. Surprisingly, although the basic tenet of behavioural psychology is that some behaviours are a function of their antecedents or consequences, the functional analysis of behaviour in applied settings has only recently assumed a place of central importance. At present, there are three popular ways of conducting such an analysis. One is through *indirect assessment*, in which staff are asked to recall the circumstances in which behaviour has occurred (e.g., the Motivation Assessment Scale of Durand and Crimmins, 1988; see also Durand and Crimmins, this volume). Another is through *analogue*

Table 6.1 A taxonomy of setting events that increase (R$^+$) or decrease (R$^-$) behaviour

Temporal relation to target behaviour	Environment					
	Background condition		Short-term event		Stimulus–response interaction	
Distant	R$^+$	R$^-$	R$^+$	R$^-$	R$^+$	R$^-$
Proximate	R$^+$	R$^-$	R$^+$	R$^-$	R$^+$	R$^-$
Concurrent	R$^+$	R$^-$	R$^+$	R$^-$	R$^+$	R$^-$

assessment, in which conditions related to arousal, positive reinforcement, or negative reinforcement are briefly presented to the client in a clinical setting while the maladaptive behaviours are measured (e.g., Iwata *et al.*, 1982; see also Oliver, this volume). Treatment in the natural setting is then based on the functional relationship revealed in the analogue setting. A third procedure is *naturalistic assessment*, in which conditions during a baseline phase of observation are analysed to determine their relationship to maladaptive behaviour. These same conditions are then manipulated during the treatment component.

We have used naturalistic assessment clinically for many years, and have recently demonstrated its efficacy experimentally (Repp, Felce and Barton, 1988). However, until recently, we did not attempt to analyse data within the framework provided by a formal taxonomy of behaviour–environment relationships. Such a taxonomy appears in Tables 6.1 and 6.2, which correspond to antecedent events and to subsequent events respectively. Our current work is an attempt to categorize observations into the cells of the taxonomy, to use this categorization to determine which of the three theories of maladaptive behaviour (arousal, positive reinforcement, and negative reinforcement) gives the best interpretation in a particular case, and to base treatment on the results of the assessment (Repp and Deitz, 1990).

Table 6.2 A taxonomy of subsequent events contingent on response emission or omission and which increase (R$^+$) or decrease (R$^-$) a target behaviour

Consequence contingent on response emission or omission	Stimulus presented as consequence		Stimulus removed as consequence	
Response emission	R$^+$	R$^-$	R$^+$	R$^-$
Response omission	R$^+$	R$^-$	R$^+$	R$^-$

There are two parts to the taxonomy. Table 6.1 categorizes antecedent events by type and by temporal relationship to behaviour. The types are *background conditions,* or relatively static elements of the environment (e.g., a type of curriculum, a workshop setting, a room of a residence); *short-term events* (e.g., the appearance of a caregiver); and *stimulus–response interactions* (e.g., an instructional stimulus which is followed by a failed attempt to do what was asked); all of which can occasion the target behaviour. The temporal relationship of these antecedent events to the target behaviour is categorized as *distant* (more than 1 minute); *proximate* (10–60 seconds); or *concurrent* (occurring within 10 seconds). These two dimensions of the taxonomy—type and temporal relationship—form a matrix of categories into which data about relations between antecedents and target behaviour can be sorted to assess whether a structural or functional relationship exists. Such a relationship might result in the behavioural response of concern increasing (R^+) or decreasing (R^-).

For example, we might analyse the rates or durations of various adaptive and maladaptive behaviours according to prevailing background conditions. One set of relevant background conditions could be temporally distant, such as the quality of sleep a person had during the previous night. Another set could be proximate, such as the nature of the activity that has just ended. Yet a third set could be concurrent, such as the number of staff and clients in the room at the time. Similarly, short-term events which can influence behaviour could be either distant, proximate or concurrent. For example, criticism may have a delayed or immediate effect on a person's behaviour. The same is true for stimulus–response interactions. Consider a person who looks out of the window while the teacher gives instructions at the beginning of a class assignment. This stimulus–response interaction may affect the person's behaviour immediately or at some time in the future.

The second part of the taxonomy relates subsequent events to behaviour, also along two dimensions, and it is represented in Table 6.2. One dimension describes whether a consequence is *presented* (e.g., praise) or *removed* (e.g., loss of an opportunity to do something). The second describes whether the relationship is based upon response *emission* or response *omission* (the occurrence or non-occurrence of the target behaviour). Reading from left to right, the top line of the table (response emission) describes processes of positive reinforcement, positive punishment, negative reinforcement and negative punishment (timeout or response cost). The bottom line (response omission) describes differential punishment of other behaviour (causing the target behaviour to increase), differential reinforcement of other behaviour (causing it to decrease), differential negative punishment of omission (causing behaviour to increase), and differential negative reinforcement of omission (causing behaviour to decrease). Again, data are collected and analysed to determine whether there is a relationship between any cell of the matrix and the rate or duration of the target behaviour. In the next section, we will describe the methods for collecting and analysing these data.

DATA COLLECTION AND ANALYSIS

Data for the taxonomy can be collected in several ways. One indirect method uses a rating scale for staff to recall the relationship between the environment and behaviour. Another more direct method requires staff to note the occurrence of behaviour under certain conditions (e.g., O'Neill et al., 1990; Touchette, MacDonald, and Langer, 1985). A third uses a continuous monitoring procedure in which antecedent events, subsequent events, and behaviours are observed and recorded over a number of sessions (e.g., Repp et al., in press).

The continuous observation procedure provides the most detailed information, and it lends itself ideally to a computer-driven data collection system developed and now routinely used in the US and UK (Repp and Felce, 1990; Repp et al., 1989a, 1989b). This system was originally designed to examine the behaviour of people with mental handicap in residential environments (see Felce, this volume). More recently, however, we have extended our methods considerably to study maladaptive behaviour and its relationship to the environment. In this section, we will briefly discuss the hardware and software that we have developed.

Data collection: Hardware

Programs have been written for the highly portable Epson HX-20 computer and for all portable MS–DOS laptop computers. The machines have a built-in timer, accurate to 1 second, which is used to indicate the second at which any behavioural or environmental event begins or ends. Each of 45 keys on the keyboard can be assigned as a data collection category. The Epson HX-20 is now difficult to purchase although it is not yet obsolete, but laptop MS–DOS computers as lightweight as HX-20 are becoming more common. Simple analysis of the rate and duration of each coded event can be produced directly by the HX-20. However, more complex data analysis procedures, such as lag analyses, must be done by transferring data to a larger desktop computer. All data analysis programs can be run on the MS–DOS laptop computers, although they are sometimes faster on a desktop PC.

Data collection: Software

The software consists of a suite of programs including *Collector, Reliability, Edit, Bout/Interbout, Event Lag* and *Time Lag*. The functions of these programs are outlined below, and the relationship between their output and the taxonomy is explained below.

Collector is the recording program, and it has been designed to format data for the taxonomy. Forty-five keys can be assigned codes indicating background conditions, short-term events, target behaviours, or stimulus consequences of behaviours (i.e., the presentation or removal of stimulus events). Thus, the antecedents, behaviours, and consequences referred to in Tables 6.1 and 6.2 can all be coded (stimulus–response interactions are scored by pressing the relevant combination of event and behaviour keys).

At the beginning of a session, the observer records identifying information (e.g., observer, subject, location), and then answers the following questions, which determine how data are subsequently scored:

- Which codes are to be used for discrete events? For these, the observer presses a key only once. The computer automatically records the time of the key depression and ascribes a duration of 1 second to each occurrence.
- Which codes are to be used for events with extended durations? For these, the observer presses a key to indicate the onset of the event, and presses it again to mark its termination. The computer records the starting and ending times and calculates the duration of each occurrence.
- Which codes form mutually exclusive sets?
- Is the subsession timer facility to be used? If so, the computer sounds a tone after a chosen interval (e.g., 5 minutes). This enables an experimenter to observe one member of a group for some time, then move to another member, and so forth.
- Are data to be compiled separately under conditions? If so, the observer collects data in the normal fashion, but subdivides the session according to changing environmental conditions. The observer presses a particular key signal a change in conditions and the computer then expects to receive a code to denote which condition was in effect. This is entered and the observer resumes data collection. The computer then sorts the data separately under each condition. This option allows the experimenter to record data in a way which can be sorted automatically according to different background conditions, thereby filling some of the cells of the taxonomy in Table 6.1.

After the relevant options have been selected, the observer begins the session by pressing the TAB key to activate the computer's timer. Both discrete and extended duration events are recorded by pressing the appropriate keys. The observer ends the session by pressing TAB, and can decide whether or not to print the data that have been encoded. The initial printout consists of two tables. The first shows the sequence in which each event code was recorded and the second at which it began and ended. The second table prints summary data for each coded event, including its number of occurrences, its rate (occurrences per minute), its total duration in seconds, and the percentage of the session for which it occurred. Following the print routine, or should the observer decide not to print the results of the session immediately, the data are written to cassette or disk. The data can later be read using a program called *Retrieve* and a printout obtained.

When the *Conditions* option has been chosen, these two output tables are printed separately for each condition coded. For example, if we were interested in the amount of stereotypy and self-injury under demand (i.e., task) conditions, we could define two conditions, *demand* and *no demand*, choose the *Conditions* option and ascribe a code to each condition. We would then record data on stereotypy and self-injury using keys assigned to behavioural codes, interrupting the sequence of recording each time the conditions changed to label the condition with its code. The computer would sort and print all summary data under these two conditions. In addition, we could later perform analyses such as lag sequential analysis separately for the two conditions of demand and no demand (see below).

In addition to the *Collector* program just described, the data collection suite includes the *Reliability* program. This uses two routines, the first of which addresses event data (i.e., as number of occurrences or rate) and interprets reliability to mean that two observers recorded an event at *approximately* the same time. Two separate sets of observations, recorded independently, are fed into the PC running *Reliability*. Each observer's record is read by the program, which then asks the experimenter to define 'approximately' in units of 1 second (i.e., 1, 2, 3). The program then judges whether both observers recorded an event as having started (or stopped) within the number of seconds tolerance that the experimenter has chosen. On this basis, the number of agreements and disagreements for the initiation and termination of each of the codes is calculated. The second *Reliability* routine is for duration data, and uses a different calculation. As data are analysed in terms of the number of seconds each event occurred, a reliability statistic is directly related to seconds of agreement. The computer scans each observer's record and calculates the seconds of agreement on occurrence, the seconds of agreement on non-occurrence, and the seconds of disagreement for each event code. Inter-observer agreement percentages are then calculated for occurrence, non-occurrence, and whole session reliability for each code in the traditional manner (Hartmann, 1975).

Data analysis

Several programs have been written either for data analysis or as a precursor to it. The first is the *Edit* program, which allows the experimenter to modify the data set before analysis is begun. Options include correcting a data entry error (e.g., if the observer recalled striking the wrong key at a particular moment), assigning mutually exclusive sets, creating an exhaustive data set, or assigning combinations. While the first three can be important, the last is the most relevant here.

The *Combinations* option allows the observer to combine separate codes from several keys and assign them a new code not used during data collection. The value of this option can be illustrated by a study we are currently conducting of the predictive validity of several of the cells of the taxonomy presented in Tables 6.1 and 6.2 (Repp, Karsh and Lenz, 1991). One part of the study examines the relationship between concurrent conditions and the adaptive and maladaptive behaviours of 12 persons with developmental disabilities. The concurrent conditions were par-titioned by the *Conditions* option of the *Collector* program, and the rates and durations of six separate adaptive behaviours, six stereotypic behaviours, and four self-injurious or aggressive behaviours were recorded. The *Combinations* option was then used to group the six adaptive behaviours into one class which we labelled *adaptive*. Similarly, the ten stereotypic, self-injurious, or aggressive behaviours were grouped into another class labelled *maladaptive*. To achieve this, the experimenter only had to assign the six adaptive behaviour codes one new code and the ten maladaptive behaviour codes another. This operation required a few seconds, after which the program made the adjusted calculations on the combined codes.

Another program, *Bout/Interbout*, plots a frequency distribution of the bout lengths (i.e., durations of episodes) and interbout lengths (i.e., durations of the intervals between episodes) for each coded event. The observer chooses a bin length such as 5 seconds, and the computer separately counts the frequencies of bouts and interbouts for 20 bins of the chosen length (e.g., 1–5-second, 6–10-second, 11–15-second bins, etc.). This is a useful analysis for evaluating the possible homeostatic nature of particular behaviours. For some subjects, we have found that almost all the episodes fall into two contiguous bins (e.g., the 6–10-second and

11–15 second bins) indicating very regular behaviour with respect to time. For others, however, we have found the occurrences of behaviour widely distributed across a number of bins, indicating irregular and unpredictable patterns of behaviour across time.

The next step in analysis is to go beyond looking at particular events, and begin to identify patterns, or relationships, between events. These might include the relationship between behavioural and environmental events (e.g., self-injury and staff attention), environmental and behavioural events (e.g., task demand and self-injury), and between behavioural events (e.g., eating and self-injury). These relationships can be uncovered by the techniques of lag sequential analysis. There are two types of such analyses—event-based lag and time-based lag—for which we have written programs. The *Event Lag* program is used to investigate the order of events to determine whether one event is more likely to follow another than its overall occurrence would predict. For example, we might wish to examine the relationship between an antecedent event (e.g., A) and a behaviour (e.g., B). The *Event Lag* program calculates and compares the conditional probability that the behaviour will occur given that the antecedent A has occurred (i.e., the probability of B|A), and the unconditional probability of the behaviour (i.e., the probability of B under all conditions). A relationship is revealed when these are significantly different.

The experimenter has a number of options for specifying the *Event Lag*. The lag may be taken from the point of onset or offset of the antecedent event. Similarly, it may search for the beginning or ending of the target behaviour. There is also an option for restricting the analysis only to when a particular condition is in effect. Finally, the experimenter specifies how many lags should be calculated. Lags may be conceptualized as follows: (a) lag 0—A and B occur simultaneously; (b) lag 1—B follows A immediately; (c) lag 2—B occurs after another event (e.g., R) has intervened between it and A (as in A→ R→B), and so on for as many lags as desired.

The event lag analysis progresses independent of time; that is, a lag 1 may be scored whether the target followed the antecedent by a second or a minute. The *Time Lag* program, however, is based on time. Here, a second-by-second analysis of the relationship between an antecedent and a target behaviour (or a target behaviour and consequence) is made. With a time lag analysis, the experimenter decides whether the lag should begin with the onset or offset of the antecedent (or behaviour) and relate to the onset or termination of the behaviour (or consequence). The experimenter also sets the lag size in seconds (several different lags can be performed), and this parameter is analogous to the number of lags in the event lag analysis. The conceptual and statistical analyses involved in lag analysis have been explained in more detail by Karsh, Repp and Ludewig (1989).

DATA ANALYSIS AND THE TAXONOMY

The programs just explained allow the basic analyses necessary for using the taxonomies in Tables 6.1 and 6.2. In Table 6.1, the environment was categorized in terms of background conditions, short-term events, or stimulus–response interactions. The codes used in the *Collector* program allow the experimenter to categorize the environment in these three ways. The temporal relationships (distant, proximate, or concurrent) can also be established by the computer although distant conditions, events, or interactions may be more easily analysed through traditional direct report procedures. Lag analysis, whether based on events or time, can clearly be used to analyse proximate or concurrent relationships between the environment and behaviour. For example, Repp *et al.* (1989b) present data on the relationship between stereotypy and conditions of task demand for two individuals. Demands had no effect on the stereotypic behaviour of one person as the conditional probability of stereotypy given demand was not significantly different from the unconditional probability of stereotypy. This was true across lags ranging from 1 second to 10 seconds. Further, the conditional probability of stereotypic behaviour given demand was not significantly different from the conditional probability of stereotypy given no demand. For the other person, however, demands suppressed stereotypy across the ten lag sizes calculated. The conditional probability of stereotypy given demand was significantly less than the unconditional probability of stereotypy. The conditional probability of stereotypy given no demand was significantly greater than the unconditional probability of stereotypy.

The second part of the taxonomy described in Table 6.2 concerned the relationship between behaviour and its consequences; specifically, whether events were removed or presented following the occurrence of behaviour. Such relationships can also be addressed through lag sequential analysis. An event analysis would reveal what amounts to a schedule of reinforcement (or punishment) while a time-based analysis would indicate the immediacy of the contingency. For example, in order to look at the relationship between resident behaviour and staff attention, Felce *et al.* (1987) calculated the probability of residents receiving staff attention given that they were engaged in either appropriate or maladaptive behaviour.

Hypothesis-driven interventions

As noted earlier, the seven aetiologies of maladaptive behaviour proposed by Baumeister (1989) may be related to environmentally independent and environmentally dependent behaviours. Three of the aetiological hypotheses—stimulation, positive reinforcement, and negative reinforcement—have been used to account for environmentally dependent behaviours. Our current work involves basing our intervention on the most likely hypothesis suggested by the lag sequential analysis.

Background conditions, short-term events, stimulus–response interactions, and subsequent events may influence a target behaviour through a variety of processes. For example, background conditions may influence behaviour through negative reinforcement (e.g., a person behaves in a certain way to escape from a hot, noisy room), positive reinforcement (e.g., because formal classroom lessons have become discriminative for the availability of attention, attention-seeking behaviour regularly occurs in class but rarely in the playground), or through stimulation (e.g., a person left alone on a ward behaves in a certain way to increase arousal). Both short-term antecedent events and stimulus–response interactions may act as triggers to behaviour which is maintained by its consequences, either in terms of subsequent events presented (positive reinforcement) or removed (negative reinforcement). Some examples of hypothesis-driven interventions follow.

Stimulus-based interventions

The analysis of behaviour under various background conditions is relevant to theories about level of stimulation. Here the computer can provide behaviour summaries for whatever conditions the investigator chooses to specify. Some may typically be associated with low stimulation and some with particularly high stimulation. If the data show that maladaptive behaviour occurs primarily under concurrent or proximate conditions of low stimulation (no activity, no demand, 'free time') but not when activity is structured, then programs that increase levels of stimulation should prove successful. These may include increased opportunities for interaction with the environment (Horner, 1980; Repp and Karsh, 1990), exercise (Kern et al., 1982), or other programs that differentially reinforce incompatible or alternative behaviours (Repp, 1983).

Positive reinforcement-based interventions

The traditional (antecedent: behaviour: consequence) analysis suggesting a positive reinforcement process pinpoints, firstly, the relationship between a state of deprivation and the behaviour and, secondly, the relationship between the behaviour and a subsequent event. Lag sequential analysis can investigate the conditional probability of a subsequent event following a behaviour. If the data suggest that the maladaptive behaviour occurs because it produces a consequence hypothesized to function as a positive reinforcer, a number of treatment options are available. One involves differential reinforcement procedures (e.g., differential reinforcement of other behaviour (DRO), low rates of responding (DRL), incompatible behaviour (DRI), and alternative behaviour (DRA): see Jones, this volume; O'Brien and Repp, 1990; in press). Another treatment option involves skill acquisition training. Many of our clients do not have the skills to garner reinforcement in adaptive ways. We can, however, teach a broad range of vocational, leisure, domestic, educational, and community skills that will allow the individual to access these reinforcers (e.g., see Gaylord-Ross *et al.,* and Repp and Karsh, this volume).

The key to all these interventions is the power of the reinforcer used. Traditionally, behaviour therapists use as reinforcers consequences that have face validity. More recently, methods for assessing the reinforcing properties of stimuli have been developed that attempt to predict the power of a reinforcer before it is used in treatment (e.g., Berg and Wacker, this volume; Mason *et al.,* 1989; Pace *et al.,* 1985). While these procedures are often useful, another approach is available. The functional communication model (Carr, 1985; Donnellan *et al.,* 1984) suggests that some maladaptive behaviour is communicative in nature. If so, our objective is to teach the individual how to access the *same* consequence through what society views as adaptive, appropriate responding. This procedure, termed more generically functional equivalence training (Carr, Robinson and Palumbo, 1990), is one in which the individual is taught that the reinforcer can be assessed *more efficiently* through adaptive means while the maladaptive behaviour is placed under extinction. An important component of this procedure is the theme of efficiency. Access is made less effortful, behaviour is put on a richer schedule of reinforcement, primed, and so forth (see Durand and Crimmins, this volume).

For us, the key to using these interventions appropriately is that the taxonomy and the recording technology we have developed can produce a very clear specification of the relationship between maladaptive behaviour and its consequences. In fact, the event lag analysis indicates the probability that a behaviour will be followed by a particular consequence, which is tantamount to the schedule of reinforcement experienced by the subject. With this information, the therapist can ensure that more adaptive behaviour is reinforced using the same consequence but on a richer schedule.

Negative reinforcement-based interventions

The inference that a behaviour is motivated by negative reinforcement is drawn from an observed association between the behaviour and particular antecedent conditions which cease following its occurrence. Again, lag sequential analysis can compute the conditional probabilities of the behaviour's occurring given a defined antecedent, and of that antecedent's terminating given the onset of behaviour. If the data show that the maladaptive behaviour is reinforced by terminating a condition or short-term event, then a treatment based on a negative reinforcement paradigm can be implemented. One option involves functional equivalence training in which an appropriate avoidance or escape behaviour is taught (e.g., the person is taught to say 'help', or to raise a hand) and substituted for the maladaptive behaviour (Horner, 1990). Other procedures may involve altering the aversive nature of the conditions or events which occasion escape behaviour. One option is to make tasks easier by employing errorless learning strategies (Repp and Karsh, 1990; Weeks and Gaylord-Ross, 1981). Another is to intersperse stimuli associated with low rates of maladaptive behaviour among activities associated with high rates. This could involve a task variation procedure, particularly where difficult tasks are interspersed among easier ones (Carr, Newsom and Binkoff, 1976; Winterling, Dunlap and O'Neill, 1987). Another possibility is to modify the nature of tasks which are associated with high rates of maladaptive behaviour and are repetitive, nonfunctional and boring (Green et al., 1986; Meyer and Evans, 1986).

CONCLUSION

The basis of applied behaviour analysis is an understanding of the interaction of the environment and behaviour. In many ways, this field has been immensely successful, and we do not mean to imply that it has not. However we believe that more success in the area of reducing maladaptive behaviour would be achieved by basing treatment procedures on hypotheses of the maintaining conditions of that behaviour rather than by simply applying reinforcing or punishing consequences regardless of the factors maintaining behaviour. The best way, perhaps, of meeting this objective is through a functional analysis of the environment–behaviour interaction.

The approach we have advocated here is based on a continuous monitoring of behaviour as it occurs in natural settings. We believe that it holds promise precisely because it focuses on the context in which behaviour typically occurs, and identifies what features of that context should be manipulated. We have started to evaluate the taxonomy and data collection procedure described above as an independent variable by testing whether it can predict successful and unsuccessful treatments. Hopefully, the approach can be added to the indirect and analogue assessment procedures as a technique for improving our ability to ameliorate severe behaviour problems.

Address for correspondence

Alan C. Repp, Educational Research and Services Center Inc., 425 East Fisk Avenue, DeKalb, Illinois 60115, USA.

REFERENCES

Baumeiser, A.A. (1989) *Etiologies of Self-injurious and Destructive Behavior*, Proceedings of the Consensus Conference on the Treatment of Severe Behavior Problems and Developmental Disabilities, National Institutes of Health, Bethesda, Maryland.

Borthwick, S.A., Meyers, C.E. and Eyman, R.K. (1981) Comparative adaptive and maladaptive behavior of mentally retarded clients of five residential settings in three western states. In R.H. Bruininks, C.E. Meyers, B.B. Sigford and K.C. Lakin (eds), *Deinstitutionalization and Community Adjustment of Mentally Retarded People*, American Association of Mental Deficiency, Washington, DC.

Carr, E.G. (1985) Behavioural approaches to language and communication. In E. Schopler and G. Mesibov (eds), *Current Issues in Autism: Volume 3. Communication Problems in Autism*, Plenum, New York.

Carr, E.G., Newsom, C.D. and Binkoff, J.A. (1976) Stimulus control of self-destructive behavior in a psychotic child. *Journal of Abnormal Child Psychology*, 4, 139–153.

Carr, E.G., Robinson, S. and Palumbo, R.W. (1990) The wrong issue: Aversive vs. nonaversive treatment. The right issue: Functional vs. nonfunctional treatment. In A.C. Repp and N.N. Singh (eds), *Perspectives on the Use of Nonaversive and Aversive Interventions with Persons with Developmental Disabilities*, Sycamore Publishing Co., Sycamore, Illinois.

Carr, E.G., Taylor, J.C., Carlson, J.S. and Robinson, S. (1989) *Reinforcement and Stimulus-based Treatments for Severe Behavior Problems in Developmental Disabilities*, Proceedings of the Consensus Conference on the Treatment of

Severe Behavior Problems and Developmental Disabilities, National Institutes of Health, Bethesda, Maryland.

Cataldo, M.F. (1989) *The Effects of Punishment and Other Behavior Reducing Procedures on Destructive Behaviors of Persons with Developmental Disabilities*, Proceedings of the Consensus Conference on the Treatment of Severe Behavior Problems and Developmental Disabilities, National Institutes of Health, Bethesda, Maryland.

Cataldo, M.F. and Harris, J. (1982) The biological basis for self-injury in the mentally retarded. *Analysis and Intervention in Developmental Disabilities*, **2**, 21–39.

Corbett, J.A. and Campbell, H.J. (1981) Causes of self-injurious behavior. In P. Mittler (ed.), *Frontiers of Knowledge in Mental Retardation: Volume 2. Biomedical Aspects*. University Park Press, Baltimore.

Donnellan, A.M., Mirenda, P.L., Mesaros, R.A. and Fassbender, L.L. (1984) Analyzing the communicative functions of aberrant behavior. *Journal of the Association for Persons with Severe Handicaps*, **3**, 201–212.

Durand, V.M. and Crimmins, D.B. (1988) Identifying the variables maintaining self-injurious behavior. *Journal of Autism and Developmental Disorders*, **18**, 99–117.

Felce, D., Saxby, H., deKock, U., Repp, A., Ager, A. and Blunden, R. (1987) To what do attending adults respond?: A replication. *American Journal of Mental Deficiency*, **91**, 496–504.

Green, C.W., Canipe, V.S., Way, P.J. and Reid, D.H. (1986) Improving the functional utility and effectiveness of classroom services for students with profound multiple handicaps. *Journal of the Association for Persons with Severe Handicaps*, **11**, 162–170.

Guess, D. and Carr, E. (1990) Conceptual model for the emergence and maintenance of stereotyped and self-injurious behavior among persons with disabilities. Paper submitted for publication.

Hartmann, D.P. (1975) Considerations in the choice of interobserver reliability estimates. *Journal of Applied Behavior Analysis*, **10**, 103–116.

Horner, R.D. (1980) The effects of an environmental 'enrichment' program on the behavior of institutionalized profoundly retarded clients. *Journal of Applied Behavior Analysis*, **13**, 473–491.

Horner, R.H. (1990) *Functional Analysis of Maladaptive Behavior*. Paper presented at the Educational Research and Services Center, DeKalb, Illinois.

Iwata, B.A., Dorsey, M.F., Slifer, K.J., Bauman, K.E. and Richman, G.S. (1982) Toward a functional analysis of self-injury. *Analysis and Intervention in Developmental Disabilities*, **2**, 3–20.

Jacobson, J.W. (1982) Problem behavior and psychiatric impairment within a developmentally disabled population: I: Behavior frequency. *Applied Research in Mental Retardation*, **3**, 121–139.

Karsh, K.G., Repp, A.C. and Ludewig, D. (1989) *PCS: Portable Computer Systems for Observational Research*, Communitech International, DeKalb, Illinois.

Kern, L., Koegel, R.L., Dyer, K., Blew, P.A. and Fenton, L.R. (1982) The effects of physical exercise on self-stimulation behavior and appropriate responding in autistic children. *Journal of Autism and Developmental Disorders*, **12**, 399–419.

LaGrow, J. and Repp, A.C. (1984) Stereotypic responding: A review of intervention research. *American Journal of Mental Deficiency*, **88**, 595–609.

Lovaas, O.I., Newsom, C. and Hickman, C. (1987) Self-stimulatory behavior and perceptual reinforcement; *Journal of Applied Behavior Analysis*, **20**, 45–68.

Mason, S.A., McGee, G.G., Farmer-Dougan, V. and Risley, T. (1989) A practical strategy for ongoing reinforcer assessment. *Journal of Applied Behavior Analysis*, **22**, 171–179.

Matson, J.L. and DiLorenzo, T.M. (1984) *Punishment and its Alternatives: New Perspectives for Behavior Modification*, Springer, New York.

Matson, J.L. and Taras, M.E. (1989) A 20-year review of punishment procedures and alternative methods to treat problem behaviors in developmentally disabled persons. *Research in Developmental Disabilities*, **10**, 85–104.

Meyer, L.H. and Evans, I.M. (1986) Modification of excess behavior: An adaptive and functional approach for educational and community contexts. In R.H. Horner, L.H. Meyer and H.D.B. Fredericks (eds), *Education of Learners with Severe Handicaps: Exemplary Service Strategies*, Brookes, Baltimore.

Nyhan, W.L. (1989) *Biological Etiology of Destructive Behaviors*, Proceedings of the Consensus Conference on the Treatment of Severe Behavior Problems and Developmental Disabilities, National Institutes of Health, Bethesda.

O'Brien, S. and Repp, A.C. (1990) Reinforcement-based reductive procedures: A 20-year review of their use with persons with severe handicaps. *Journal of the Association for Persons with Severe Handicaps*, **15**, 148–159.

O'Brien, S. and Repp, A.C. (in press) A review of 30 years of research on the use of differential reinforcement to reduce inappropriate responding. *Behavior Modification*.

Oliver, C., Murphy, G.H. and Corbett, J.A. (1987) Self-injurious behavior in people with mental handicap: A total population study. *Journal of Mental Deficiency Research*, **31**, 147–162.

O'Neill, R.E., Horner, R.H., Albin, R.W., Storey, K. and Sprague, J.R. (1990) *Functional Analysis: A Practical Assessment Guide*. Sycamore Publishing Co., Sycamore, Illinois.

Pace, G.M., Ivancic, M.T., Edwards, G.L., Iwata, B.A. and Page, T.J. (1985) Assessment of stimulus preference and reinforcer value with profoundly retarded individuals. *Journal of Applied Behavior Analysis*, **19**, 249–255.

Paisey, T.J.H. and Whitney, R.B. (1989) A long-term case study of analysis, response suppression, and treatment maintenance involving life-threatening pica. *Behavior Research and Treatment*, **4**, 191–211.

Repp, A.C. (1983) *Teaching the Mentally Retarded*, Prentice-Hall, Englewood Cliffs, New Jersey.

Repp, A.C. and Barton, L.E. (1980) Naturalistic observations of retarded persons: A comparison of licensure decisions and behavioral observations. *Journal of Applied Behavior Analysis*, **13**, 333–341.

Repp, A.C. and Deitz, D.E.D. (1990) An ecobehavioral taxonomy for stereotypic responding. In S. Schroeder (ed.), *Ecobehavioral Analysis and Developmental Disabilities: The Twenty-first Century*, Springer-Verlag, New York.

Repp, A.C. and Felce, D. (1990) A microcomputer system used for evaluative and experimental behavioural research in mental handicap. *Mental Handicap Research*, **3**, 21–32.

Repp, A.C. and Karsh, K.G. (1990) An ecobehavioral analysis of the effects of the Task Demonstration Model on the adaptive and maladaptive behaviors of persons with developmental disabilities. Paper submitted for publication.

Repp, A.C., Felce, D. and Barton, L.E. (1988) Basing the treatment of stereotypic and self-abusive behaviors on hypotheses of their causes. *Journal of Applied Behavior Analysis*, **21**, 281–289.

Repp, A.C., Karsh, K.G. and Lenz, M.W. (1990) Hypothesis-derived interventions for stereotypic and self-injurious behaviors of persons with developmental disabilities: An ecobehavioral analysis. Paper submitted for publication.

Repp, A.C., Harman, M.L., Felce, D., Van Acker, R. and Karsh, K.G. (1989a) Conducting behavioral assessments on computer-collected data. *Behavioral Assessment*, **11**, 249–268.

Repp, A.C., Karsh, K.G., Van Acker, R., Felce, D. and Harman, M. (1989b) A computer-based system for collecting and analyzing observational data. *Journal of Special Education Technology*, **9**, 207–217.

Repp, A.C., Singh, N.N., Olinger, E. and Olson, D.R. (1990) A review of the use of functional analyses to test causes of self-injurious behavior: Rationale, current status, and future directions. *Journal of Mental Deficiency Research*, **34**, 95–105.

Repp, A.C., Singh, N.N., Deitz, D.E.D. and Karsh, K.G. (in press). Ecobehavioral analysis of stereotypic and adaptive behaviors: Activity as a setting event. *Journal of Mental Deficiency Research*.

Romanczyk, R.G. (1986) Self-injurious behavior: Conceptualization, assessment, and treatment: In K. Gadow (ed.), *Advances in Learning and Behavioral Disabilities*, Greenwich, Connecticut.

Starin, S.P. and Fuqua, R.W. (1987) Rumination and vomiting in the developmentally disabled: A critical review of the behavioral, medical and psychiatric treatment research. *Research in Developmental Disabilities*, **8**, 575–605.

Touchette, P.E., MacDonald, R.F. and Langer, S.N. (1985) A scatter plot for identifying stimulus control of problem behavior. *Journal of Applied Behavior Analysis*, **18**, 343–351.

Weeks, M. and Gaylord-Ross, R. (1981) Task difficulty and aberrant behavior in severely handicapped students. *Journal of Applied Behavior Analysis*, **14**, 449–463.

Winterling, V., Dunlap, G. and O'Neill, R.E. (1987) The influence of task variation on the aberrant behaviors of autistic students. *Education and Treatment of Children*, **10**, 105–119.

Chapter 7

Individual Repertoires as Behavioral Systems: Implications for Program Design and Evaluation[1]

JOSEPH R. SCOTTI, IAN M. EVANS,
LUANNA H. MEYER AND ADRIA DIBENEDETTO

INTRODUCTION

In the past few years there has been considerable interest in expanding the modus operandi of applied behavior analysis for individuals with severe disabilities. There has been concern over the emphasis on isolated, discrete target behaviors, that was so characteristic of the early applications of conditioning principles. There has been growing dissatisfaction with piecemeal measures of outcome (Voeltz and Evans, 1983). New insights have emerged from the increasing recognition that individuals' responses are elements of complex repertoires or systems (e.g., Marston, 1979). The purpose of this chapter is to explore the implications of this perspective for improving the design and evaluation of behavioral interventions for persons with severe mental handicap.

Understanding the natural organization of complex repertoires seems particularly important when considering the application of behavior analysis to the habilitation of persons with significant skill deficits. Historically, people with severe mental handicap have been regarded primarily as a clinical population. Meyer (1991) maintains that this status has so pervaded professional thinking that the importance of quality daily lifestyles has been neglected in the quest to provide services.

[1] This chapter is based on one of the same title presented in I.M. Evans (Chair), Behavior therapy and meaningful life changes for individuals with severe disabilities, a symposium conducted at the World Congress on Behavior Therapy, Edinburgh, Scotland, September, 1988.

Artificial environments designed to cope with repertoires more restricted than those considered 'normal' have further impeded appreciation of the commonalities in behavioral repertoires between typical and atypical individuals (Evans and Scotti, 1989).

We will begin our discussion of these issues by examining the history of the behavioral repertoire problem within basic learning theory. Next we will summarize the major theoretical models that have been proposed to account for the relationships that exist between responses. Some clinical examples are then introduced, followed by a general discussion of the implications for clinical practice. Recognizing the systemic nature of individual response repertoires has particular implications for assessment, which will be discussed briefly. The final section will examine the general significance for program design and the evaluation of outcome.

HISTORICAL BACKGROUND

In the analysis of behavior there are few truisms more obvious than the fact that behavior consists of a complex stream within which elements are defined and abstracted by the human observer. Personality theorists argue that humans are inherent trait theorists, characterizing predictable behavior in others by means of trait descriptors (e.g., Nisbett, 1980). Yet we are equally prone to represent elaborate behavioral sequences as functional molar units. In response to the question 'What are you doing?' we have learned summary descriptors, for example, 'making lunch'. Such labels are neither too general, such as 'surviving', nor too specific, such as 'cutting bread into slices'. However, as Thompson and Lubinski (1986) point out, these functional units are made up of infinite configurations of kinetic motion. Thus, the units originally selected for measurement in behavioral research were somewhat arbitrary and these conventions had a major impact on applied behavior analysis.

Experimental investigations of learning phenomena required simplified paradigms in which easily measured, discrete responses could be studied. Some of the original responses selected were essentially historical accidents. Pavlov selected salivation because of his interest in the physiology of digestion. Skinner chanced upon the lever manipulandum because the materials were lying around (Skinner, 1956), and the short, discrete, repetitive nature of the lever press profoundly influenced the development of operant theory. Skinner (1938) soon recognized that the operant response actually represented a set of events, because the animal would not reproduce the exact pattern of movement each time. Instead, a class of behavioral events, including some irrelevant elements, would evolve, with their common function tying these events together (cf. Johnston and Pennypacker, 1980; Sidman, 1960).

It has become widely accepted that the nature or form of the behavior serving as the dependent variable limits the generality of behavioral laws. Nevertheless, the experimental analysis of behavior has managed to accommodate species-specific effects and the peculiarities of individual response systems without abandoning the basic laboratory paradigms. In applied behavior analysis, however, response selection is more complex, since social relevance is an essential criterion. Traditionally, applied behavior analysis has generalized somewhat literally from the laboratory to the clinical setting. Early behavioral clinicians relied extensively on repetitive responses whose rate could be easily recorded. This suited the simple pragmatism of behavior modification, but has had a stultifying effect on subsequent advances (see Kiernan, this volume). Even the research designs have remained those of the single-subject (Barlow and Hersen, 1984; Kazdin, 1978, 1982), limiting dependent variables to individual, discrete behaviors (Evans and Meyer, 1987).

Multiple response methodologies

Within basic learning theory, however, limitations to the investigation of isolated behavior units had been recognized, and various concepts had emerged to deal with the relationship between the response selected for investigation and the total repertoire of the organism. One such concept was that of the chain or sequence of movements within the response class. Another was that responses were arranged in hierarchies of probability, such that blocking one would result in the occurrence of a substitute. Staats and Staats (1963) elucidated this concept of response hierarchies as they apply to daily life and to language. A related organizational principle was derived from logical analysis, like the notion that the probability of one response is a function of the probability of all the other responses in the repertoire (Rachlin, 1982).

Ferster and Skinner (1957) moved the experimental focus beyond the single operant in their analysis of concurrent operants, which they defined as 'two or more responses, of different topography, capable of being executed with little mutual interference at the same time or in rapid alternation' (p. 724). As Catania (1966) pointed out, an organism's alternatives are not simply the choice between responding or not, but rather selecting which of many possible operants will be emitted. A new complexity was recognized, since it became obvious that 'concurrent operants behave differently together from the way in which each operant behaves in isolation' (Catania, 1966, p. 214).

The analysis of concurrent behaviors in the natural environment, however, has been challenging, because methodological difficulties in measuring reponse relationships arise from the most basic questions of response definition. Consider, for example, a child who rocks, screams and hits his head, all at the same time. Observers can recognize each of these elements independently, and with electronic data-logging equipment record their independent durations (see Repp, Felce and Karsh, this volume). But should these elements be extracted, or should a more molar event, possibly labelled as 'having a tantrum', be recorded instead? Independent recording to establish whether elements follow different courses might be an objective way of making such distinctions, but with two provisos. One is that there are other behavioral elements, perhaps less salient, that were not extracted from the pattern (for instance, the child's tendency to clench his right fist while hitting the side of his face with his left hand). Should all these additional elements then be analyzed for their separable existence? The other proviso is that whether behaviors 'co-occur' or 'rapidly alternate' depends on the window of time within which they are observed. A very short time interval (e.g., 1 second) would suggest that rocking and screaming do co-occur, whereas head-hitting sometimes accompanies these behavioral events and sometimes does not. A longer interval (say, 10 seconds) might indicate that all three behaviors co-occur, and a yet longer window suggests that another response (e.g., throwing objects) is also part of the pattern, but physically unable to occur at the same moment as head-hitting. These complexities have been discussed by Voeltz and Evans (1982), and the problems are not insurmountable. The crucial point is that methodological questions regarding response definition have a very significant impact on the kinds of relationships that can be inferred.

To summarize the argument thus far, we can see that in research on basic learning principles, discrete, repetitive responses were isolated from the complex stream of behavior largely for methodological convenience. Applied behavior analysis inherited this tendency to focus on individual, piecemeal behaviors as the dependent variable for studies of clinical intervention. It is being increasingly recognized that the nature of responses and their relationships with other responses must be considered in the analysis of behavior. This seems to be particularly important in applied behavior analysis, where even the initial definition of the behaviors to be observed and recorded will influence the response interrelationships that may be deduced.

THEORETICAL MODELS OF RESPONSE RELATIONSHIPS

The labels we use to impose structure upon behavior can significantly affect our understanding. The labelling of a collection of more molecular response elements determines boundaries for inclusion and exclusion of topographically dissimilar behavioral events. Thus, units for the analysis of behavior can dictate opportunities to observe structure and restrict discovery of novel relationships within repertoires. In this section we will survey some of the descriptive constructs used for defining relationships and mention some of the concepts that explain response relationships and organization.

Behavioral constructs

Descriptively, the most neutral organizational principle is that of a behavioral cluster (Evans and Meyer, 1985), referring to a number of separable responses that typically occur simultaneously or closely together in time. Physical compatibility of the behaviors is a major factor. Most behaviors cannot literally co-occur: assembling a circuit board cannot be performed while biting one's fingers, although they may occur in rapid alternation and co-relate, such that self-biting never occurs during coffee breaks, but does occur during work periods. When clusters are observed, questions arise as to their inherent organization. Because the elements are artificially extracted by the observer, they may equally well be seen as components of a larger, more complex unit, just as crying and screaming may be elements of a tantrum.

One organizational principle for an observed cluster of behaviors is that they are all based on one common foundation behavior, or keystone, to use Wahler's (1975) term. For example, watching a football match might be the keystone behavior for the cluster of drinking, social interaction, and aggression. In this example, the keystone behavior sets the occasion (provides the opportunity) for the rest of the cluster, but it is not a strict prerequisite. The concept has considerable value for the design of behavioral interventions, since it suggests they might be non-direct and that the target for change could well be some earlier, more accessible response.

Behaviors that co-occur and have more intrinsic relationship may be part of a closely interacting system of biological connections. This is often the case with emotional behavior, such as increases in heart rate and blood pressure that accompany the overt act of physical aggression. Although these elements are independently measurable, they are not necessarily at comparable levels of a causal relationship: autonomic events, for instance, typically enable an overt act. Because such events co-occur or are physically interdependent, it does not mean that they are inseparable under some circumstances (Cone, 1979; Evans, 1986). For instance, even if a person's heart rate may be elevated, he or she can learn not to strike out physically when angry.

While clusters of autonomic and motor responses can have a functional relationship to each other, clusters of motor responses might be related because of their common function. By definition, the operant is a class of somewhat different physical actions, unified by their effect on the environment. In other words, the function of the activity gives a unitary structure to otherwise discrete events. The renewed emphasis upon the function of inappropriate or excess behaviors has encouraged behavior therapists to look for alternative, more acceptable behaviors to perform the same function for a client. In principle, this means that a negative behavior such as a self-injurious head-hit and a positive behavior such as signing 'stop', although topographically very different, could be viewed as members of a common response class, if they both succeed in terminating an undesirable event for the individual. To persist as a common response class, different behaviors must be equally effective. Thus it would be important in treatment design to recognize that the appropriate alternative should be taught as a replacement skill, but that the undesirable behavior's effectiveness must also be reduced (Evans, 1989; Durand and Crimmins, this volume).

Another major organizing principle for response units is that of the behavioral chain in which one response provides the discriminative stimulus for the next reponse. Proprioceptive feedback has long been hypothesized as the primary mechanism for such linkages, but the products of the behavior may also function discriminately. Thus, head-hitting may result in arm-holding restraint by a caregiver, which in turn becomes the discriminative stimulus for screaming and kicking.

Responses such as self-injury and aggression might alternatively be organized in a hierarchical relationship. During the individual's learning history, different responses will have been effective in achieving common reinforcing outcomes. These responses continue to exist in the repertoire but have a lower probability of occurrence, since social contingencies ensure that more acceptable behaviors are reinforced. If a higher probability behavior is prevented or thwarted in some way, then previously learned but lower probability responses will emerge as alternatives. The probability of any behavior will be affected by additional factors such as practice, opportunity, ease of production, or subtle variation in levels of secondary reinforcers.

Personality and syndrome constructs

In addition to these conceptual models in learning theory, there are two constructs from personality theory that reflect recognition of behavioral organization and which potentially provide some explanatory power for the response relationships observed in persons with severe handicaps. Trait and syndrome are constructs that have been used to explain consistencies in individual repertoires, usually reflecting constancy in behavior across situation. Of the two, a trait is more specific to the individual. If we say someone is aggressive, we are referring to a set of person-specific behaviors. Aggressiveness in one individual might mean frequently hitting and kicking others, while in another person it means being verbally abusive. Syndromes, on the other hand, suggest a cluster of responses that are highly similar across individuals. A child described as having a 'conduct disorder' is expected to display a cluster of rule-violating behaviors such as aggression, stealing, and noncompliance, that are different from the cluster of fearful, shy, and withdrawn behaviors said to characterize children labeled anxious. In the case of syndromes that refer specifically to severe mental handicap, the co-occurring features are usually organic physical features; however, behavioral clusters are often identified as well, such as in autism, Lesch–Nyhan syndrome, and Rett syndrome. In the next section an example will be given of a girl with Rett syndrome who demonstrated that the characteristic behaviors of the syndrome were interrelated in quite complex ways.

As Skinner (1953) noted, traits are reducible to inventories of behavior each with strengths (probabilities) relative to the remainder of the repertoire. It is only because people vary from moment to moment and from one another that trait names become useful. Behaviors that are common to all members of a species are not well described by trait labels (Staats and Staats, 1963). Traits (as behavioral clusters) are assumed to be consistent within a person across multiple situations. Yet, cross-situational correlations among behaviors are quite low (Mischel, 1968; Wahler and Fox, 1982). While this may be partially a measurement problem (Cone, 1979; Mischel and Peake, 1983) personality theorists accept situational effects. Current personality theories and assessment strategies emphasize the interactional nature of persons and situations (Bem, 1983; Endler, 1983; McReynolds, 1979).

Lubinski and Thompson (1986) proposed a behavioral method for enumerating traits. Over an extended period an individual would be observed during all waking hours. The vast number of actions recorded would be organized into response classes based on similarity of controlling variables. The logical end result would be the arrangement of a hierarchy of responses and their relative probabilities. These authors asserted that certain clusters would easily be described by traditional trait labels. One problem noted is that responses associated with infrequently occurring situations would not be observed and thus not properly represented. This echoes the comments made by Kazdin (1982) in regard to a behavioral understanding of symptom substitution. It has been assumed that elimination of one behavior (the symptom) provides the opportunity for less probable behaviors within the same response class to be emitted. The decision that this substitute symptom and the original symptom are from the same hierarchy is *a posteriori* and of questionable validity. It is based on an inability to observe infrequent responses prior to treatment, occasioning the mistaken assumption that they did not previously occur and must then be a result of treatment.

When considering syndromes, therefore, it would be helpful to have a better understanding of how the responses within an individual repertoire are organized. In conduct disorder, for instance, is the observed cluster best conceptualized as an operant class of different forms of the same behavior (e.g., aggression is composed of hitting, kicking, and stealing), a by-product of some more fundamental deficit (e.g., lack of empathy leads to both hitting and stealing), or a causal chain (e.g., hitting leading to peer rejection, leading to isolate behavior, leading to stealing)? Nevertheless, descriptive terms such as trait and syndrome are useful in accounting for other phenomena, such as side effects, symptom substitution, and collateral effects. These phenomena have often been reported in the behavioral literature (Voeltz and Evans, 1982). Their occurrence (whether positive or negative) is almost always unplanned, and they are usually explained by perfunctory reference to response class (see Evans *et al.*, 1988). In the next section we will provide some examples from our own clinical work that illustrate the explanatory advantage of employing formal response organization concepts.

CLINICAL EXAMPLES

Excess behaviors

An example of a more detailed analysis of the response relationships within syndrome-characteristic behavior has been provided by Evans and Voeltz (1982). We reported an analysis of the behaviors of a 6-year-old girl, Kathy, with Rett syndrome. During baseline measurement, highly trained observers coded the following behaviors: body-rocking (both sitting and standing), jerky movement, hand-clapping, finger-flicking, crying, shriek/scream, blowing, vocalization (supra-glottal and babbling), facial grimace, staring/gazing, teeth-grinding, temper tantrum, rubbing eyes and face, and mouthing body parts. Two of these behaviors, hand-wringing and blowing, are characteristic of Rett syndrome, and interest therefore focused on how they were interrelated with other excess behaviors in Kathy's repertoire. We found large variations in the frequency of all excess behaviors across different situations; for instance, free play conditions yielded higher percentages of all excess behaviors. During one-to-one instruction, the teacher interfered with hand-wringing by pushing Kathy's hands apart, which resulted in an increase in finger-flicking with one hand and crying. A factor analysis revealed that the hand and finger behaviors were associated with periods of rocking and distant stare. An intervention designed to reduce her finger/hand mannerisms resulted in an *increase* in the blowing and vocalization pattern, which both increased under demand conditions and decreased during the course of the intervention. Although consistent patterns of excess behavior were not found over a three-year period, the two behaviors most characteristic of the syndrome actually represent two different clusters, with a reciprocal relationship to each other. Further, the occurrence of these two clusters related lawfully to environmental and social conditions, even though their origin is undoubtedly to be found in the organic conditions underlying the syndrome.

Pokrzywinski, Scotti and Hetz (1982) reported an intervention for a hand-mouthing stereotypy with a woman diagnosed as profoundly mentally handicapped. Figure 7.1 shows that the simple provision of leisure activities (hand-held leisure materials) was sufficient to decrease hand-mouthing to near zero levels.

One might suggest that hand-mouthing and object manipulation were within the same response class, both having a stimulatory function, but with object manipulation being the more probable response. Alternatively, provision of leisure materials might have set the occasion for a response cluster of which object manipulation was a member, but hand-mouthing was not. Finally, the responses may simply have been topographically incompatible. The session duration may not have allowed adequate time to show a possible alternation between the responses.

Understanding which of these relationships applies can provide useful direction for intervention efforts. Meyer *et al.* (1985) introduced training in leisure activities and reported that two different kinds of excess behavior showed quite different relationships to appropriate play. Self-stimulation with the leisure materials was positively related to appropriate play and to a measure of interest in the materials. Stereotypic behavior not involving the materials was negatively related to these same behaviors. Clinically, then, knowledge of these relationships could facilitate the training of skills that are both appropriate and reflect client preference.

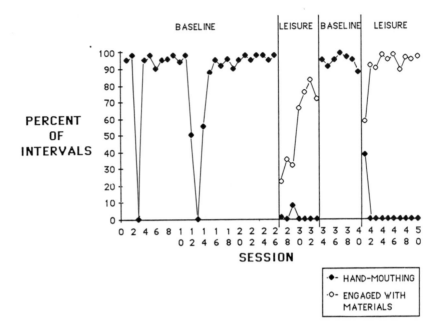

Figure 7.1 The effect of the provision of leisure activities on the hand-mouthing behaviour of a woman with profound mental handicap. (Reproduced by permission from Pokrzywinski *et al.*, 1982.)

Certain response interrelationships can result in unintended negative side effects, so that a 'cost–benefit' analysis is needed whenever behavior change is attempted (Voeltz *et al.*, 1983). For example, Scotti, Evans and Murphy (1988) found that an intervention which decreased hand-mouthing was associated with an increase in hand-wringing. In a related study, the same authors demonstrated another interaction between intervention and response patterning. Two adults with severe mental handicaps were treated by means of a brief interruption procedure that was made contingent upon self-injurious behavior (hitting head with hand, hand-biting) and self-stimulatory behavior (hand-waving, hand-mouthing, body-rocking). For both individuals, self-injury and self-stimulation performed with the hands was significantly reduced in frequency, but stimulatory body-rocking did not respond to the intervention. The putative function of body-rocking, hand-waving, and hand-mouthing is self-stimulation, yet the treatment effect differentiated between response topographies that were all thought to serve this function. One could conclude that two response classes were revealed. Alternatively, the findings could indicate a response hierarchy in which both hand mannerisms and body-rocking served the same function, but the latter was the stronger response.

Positive behaviors

Response organization concepts also suggest practical clinical approaches to teaching new skills and building positive behavioral repertoires. A result of the simplistic extension of the operant paradigm has been the tendency to break more complex skill sequences into their motor components. Traditional task analysis represents this approach. From an instructional point of view, task analysis has had some advantages in teaching behaviors to individuals with severe mental handicaps. However, the implicit organizational principles are simply those of response chaining. An alternative conceptualization, the 'routine', introduced by Neel and his colleagues (Neel and Billingsley, 1989), is very similar to what McFall (1982) has called an activity: an entire set of behaviors that have a clear purpose. In many ways routines are really the operants of everyday life, such as washing the dishes or getting to work. The concept of the routine differs from that of the motor task as it includes all the elements of a complex activity, may include a variety of adaptations and alternative forms, and is not restricted to a listing of topographically defined responses.

Evans *et al.* (1987) have developed an assessment procedure to evaluate severely handicapped learners' mastery of the routines they need to perform competently in normalized environments. The precise form of the routine, as long as it is age appropriate, socially acceptable, and safe, is of lesser importance. Thus it would not matter whether clients bought groceries using augmentative communication or simply selecting their own items in a supermarket, as long as they came out of the shop having paid for the items they wanted. Competence should then be evaluated on the basis of complete routines, however simple their form (cf. Felce, this volume).

If completed routines are hypothesized to be the basic building blocks of effective performance, a response systems perspective must specify the organization of their constituent elements. Evans and his colleagues (1987) have proposed a model that attempts to identify the components necessary to perform a routine. Some of these—the core—are the physical steps required to carry out the task, as would typically be identified in a task analysis. But others are equally necessary: the executive functions, such as initiating the activity, preparing the materials, monitoring quality on an ongoing basis, and solving problems.

Teaching effective routines could enhance a client's total repertoire through the influence both of new skills acquired and improvement in instructional atmosphere. Weld and Evans (1990) provided an illustration of the former effect. They found that those mentally handicapped clients who were able to solve problems within two practical skill routines exhibited the fewest number of inappropriate excess behaviors. An example of the influence of instructional procedures is a single-case study of a boy with profound mental handicap reported by Evans and Voeltz (1982). We observed decreases in excess behavior (running off, going limp, screaming) as a result of revising his curriculum and teaching him routines using a whole rather than part-based method of instruction. There were also marked positive changes in teacher affect. In traditional behavior modification teacher affect and instructional style have been viewed as confounds to be avoided. However, they may well represent systems-change 'ripple effects' that can be lawfully produced by the careful prioritization of treatment goals (Evans and Meyer, 1985). Thus, organizational principles refer to deficits in repertoires just as much as they do to the covariation of responses. In the next two sections we will discuss the major implications of these response relationships for conceptualizing treatment and assessment.

CLINICAL IMPLICATIONS OF RESPONSE COVARIATION

What generalizations can be made about response relationships? Are we likely to find comparable patterns of responding across individuals, as would be implied by trait and syndrome concepts? Or should we be looking for common principles of response organization that generate an infinite variation of individual patterns, lawful for the individual but, like snowflakes, quite different across individuals? Kazdin (1982) and Wahler and Fox (1982) have suggested that behavioral covariation over situations be investigated to determine if clusters of responses are stable despite different contexts. These authors anticipated that the behaviors within a cluster would interrelate in predictable ways regardless of the situation. This in turn should permit better prediction of which indirect interventions will be most effective for changing a given cluster with positive collateral effects.

Intervention with indirect target behaviors

Wahler's work provides some of the better illustrations of the practicality of an indirect approach. Wahler *et al.* (1970) demonstrated response covariation between a child's oppositional behavior and his stuttering. Successful deceleration of oppositional behavior (the target response) resulted in a concomitant decrease in stuttering (the untreated behavior). It was clear that there was a relationship between these two responses, although its precise nature could not be determined. Methodologically, the question is whether some new response replaced the decreased target behavior and, if so, whether that response caused the collateral behavior change. Wahler (1975) was subsequently able to identify covarying response clusters of problematic and appropriate behaviors for two boys. He showed that contingency management of one response had effects (both positive and negative) on the other responses in that cluster. Although a response class phenomenon was hypothesized, supporting evidence such as common environmental determinants was not forthcoming. In another study (see Wahler and Fox, 1982) one group of appropriate and problem behaviors was identified for each of four boys. The excess behaviors and the desirable behaviors were negatively correlated. Reinforcing the appropriate behavior resulted in the collateral effect of a decrease in the non-treated problem behavior. This is an excellent practical demonstration of how one might indirectly treat excess behaviors that have been previously shown to covary with other appropriate behaviors.

Collateral effects

Wahler has succeeded in demonstrating that the response interrelationships frequently observed in applied behavior analysis can be used to augment treatment. In the past, intervention studies have identified these forms of response covariation only as unintended side effects, and thus failed to capitalize on their therapeutic possibilities. Usually, a cursory analysis of these 'unplanned' changes attributes them to some principle of response organization; for example, Schefft and Lehr (1985) referred to all collateral effects as 'adjunctive' behavior. Rarely are systematic data collected to document collateral effects, and still rarer are studies that analyze response covariation prior to treatment.

The behavioral literature on the treatment of individuals diagnosed as mentally handicapped or autistic is replete with examples of unintended collateral effects. Lichstein and Schreibman (1976) reviewed studies of the side effects of punishment using electric shock. In such analyses there is already a confound between the unintended effects resulting directly from the procedure (e.g., behaviors elicited by punishment) and those that might be an indirect result of the re-organization of behaviors within the client's repertoire. In any event, their analysis revealed both negative and positive side effects, as well as the virtual absence of data beyond the impressionistic level. Newsom, Favell and Rincover (1983) conducted a subsequent, more extensive, review covering all forms of punishment applied to persons with handicaps: the data were still exclusively anecdotal. They were able to classify the types of unintended effects seen; however, they too had to call for a more empirical treatment of the topic.

Voeltz and Evans (1982) and Evans et al. (1988) reviewed the child behavior therapy treatment literature for evidence of response relationships and rated the level of evidence for concurrent behavior changes. Although the number of studies reporting collateral effects increased over the period between the two reviews, the level of empirical evidence remained weak, being primarily informal report. They suggested that treatment designs be adapted for monitoring covarying behaviors in order to allow the investigation of collateral changes. Examples of how this might be done can be found in Johnson et al. (1982) and in Meyer et al. (1985).

IMPLICATIONS FOR ASSESSMENT METHODOLOGY

While the treatment literature suggests a trend towards growing awareness of response relationships (e.g., Schroeder and MacLean, 1987), the level of sophistication in analysis and use of the resulting information has not shown a comparable growth. Perhaps there is a need for further maturation of practical, informative assessment methods that are explicitly designed to expose response relationships. A problem with simply observing response covariation is that this provides no information about causal mechanisms. Cook, Dintzer and Mark (1980) point out that over sufficiently long time intervals, causal propositions can be tested by means of concomitant time series analyses. But to discern causal relationships this way requires lengthy time periods and a great many observations. Neither of these conditions is particularly practical for treatment research, far less routine clinical work.

The clinical experiment

Since causality is generally inferred from the temporal order of events, observations of multiple behaviors in real time allows for sequential and lag analyses to be conducted, based on conditional probabilities. For example, if tooth-grinding and leg-swinging regularly precede screaming and head-hitting, this would be evidence of a causal response chain with major implications for treatment: ecologically, we might be able to deflect a tantrum before it reached serious proportions; or, if teaching adaptive alternatives, the sequential analysis helps determine the moment at which the client could be prompted to use a communication skill.

The most convincing demonstration of causal relationships is through the experimental manipulation of independent variables, in this case a *behavior* that is thought to have an important causal role. Treatment of a target behavior that results in predicted collateral change is the best way to confirm hypothesized response relationships. But because interventions should be designed on the basis of such hypotheses, procedures are needed to allow manipulation of response frequencies prior to the full implementation of treatment. For instance, it is often possible to prevent a particular behavior from occurring by physically limiting the client's opportunity to respond. As a functional analysis represents the search for conditions that will increase or decrease the probability of a response, its logic is almost identical to the traditional reversal design demonstrating that an intervention controls the target behavior. The only reason functional analyses are not conceptualized as treatment is because of an implicit but unwarranted assumption that the assessment manipulations are not ones that can be used in treatment.

If the functional analysis represents a good way of investigating the influence of a target behavior within a response repertoire, a functional analysis of *multiple* responses becomes theoretically possible. Treatment decisions could then take into account the functions of the behaviors of interest as well as their tendency to covary. Two procedures that partially accomplish this task have been developed, but not yet explicitly combined (Iwata *et al.*, 1982; and Johnson *et al.*, 1982). Iwata *et al.* (1982) described 'an operant methodology to assess functional relationships between self-injury and specific environmental events' (p. 3). Their proposed events are four analog situations, each designed to test certain hypothetical controlling variables (see also Oliver, this volume). Johnson *et al.* (1982) described a multiple baseline design to assess the impact of treatment on the targeted negative behaviors, as well as on collateral behaviors. Their procedure allowed precise assessment of response covariation under varying treatment phases, but did not attempt to assess the original functions of the responses.

We suggest combining these two procedures into one methodology that will allow treatment decisions to be based upon functional relationships and response organization. Such a procedure was partially performed by Durand (1982). He assessed two self-injurious responses under various levels of task demand, and found that both covaried as a function of demand levels. Subsequently, an overcorrection treatment, selected as a result of the initial assessment, was implemented and reduced the frequencies of both responses to near zero levels. Concurrent assessment revealed increases in social play as self-injury decreased. While Durand's analysis moves in the direction we are suggesting, it did not allow for a functional analysis of the social play behavior. Moreover, the covariation of play and self-injury was not assessed within the same experimental session. Consequently, we cannot tell whether the response relationships caused a concurrent decrease in self-injury as a function of efforts to increase play.

Another valuable illustration of combining a structured functional analysis with multiple response measurement has been provided by Sturmey *et al.* (1988). Up to six different excess behaviors in each of three adults with profound mental handicap were recorded in four situations (Social Disapproval, Academic Demand, Unstructured Leisure Time, and Alone). All six behaviors showed highest rates during the Alone condition, but different topographies were differentially influenced by the four conditions. The decrease in excess behaviors in any one condition was most influenced by the degree to which that condition permitted the emergence of appropriate behaviors. These two examples demonstrate the promise of including within the functional analysis both negative and positive behaviors in the client's repertoire, thereby reducing the ambiguity created by appropriate but unrecorded behaviors occurring in each situation.

To illustrate this, imagine a client whose inappropriate self-injury, and appropriate initiation of physical contact, were positively correlated in demand situations, with self-injury the more probable of the two. If another inappropriate behavior, stereotypic body-rocking, correlated negatively with free-play conditions, an efficient strategy to decrease rocking might involve expanding the individual's access to alternative leisure skills. With the positively covarying pair, however, reinforcing physical contact could increase both desirable and undesirable behaviors. We might therefore introduce contingent brief interruption for the self-injury, while reinforcing alternative behavior and perhaps teaching more elaborate social/communicative competencies (see Durand and Crimmins, this volume). But if body-rocking and self-injury both occur in high-demand situations, replacement skills may not be appropriate. Instead we should reduce the demands of the task or increase its natural reinforcing value. Techniques such as errorless learning (Terrace, 1963), interspersing easy trials (Winterling, Dunlap and O'Neill, 1987), and/or re-evaluating the importance of the activity might be the most cogent modifications (Meyer and Evans, 1989).

The functional analysis of multiple behaviors provides an alternative, more valid perspective on the treatment of excess behaviors than the simple reductive approach. Excess behaviors seem to have particular functions for the individual. Knowing this, we cannot simply decelerate them and leave the client without equally effective alternative responses. Understanding the systemic organization of behavior within the individual repertoire provides a compelling rationale for viewing interventions not merely as behavior control, but as the development of adaptive repertoires. The recent interest in the function of excess behavior (Durand and Crimmins, and Oliver, this volume) is a most valuable development, but one additional point must be made. We should not be teaching individuals with severe mental handicaps to communicate because they are exhibiting serious excess behaviors, but because communication skills are themselves essential to adaptive behavior and personal satisfaction.

Of course, not all problem behaviors will have easily detectable functions. One of Sturmey et al.'s (1988) subjects and three of Iwata et al.'s (1982) (one third of the clients studied in both cases) showed no variability in excess behaviors across the four environmental conditions. This reveals a limitation to the methodology, and supports the use of more natural situations to assess reponse functions (Durand and Crimmins, 1988). Many behaviors have no obvious function. Some may have a direct organic cause and not be instrumental behaviors. Even so, they will be organized within the total repertoire of the individual, so that a systems analysis of their relationships still suggests the pattern of skill deficits that needs to be modified.

IMPLICATIONS FOR PROGRAM DESIGN AND EVALUATION

The important focus for treatment, clearly, is not simply to change one or two isolated responses, but to have a positive impact upon an individual's total repertoire. To do so, it is important to link the specifics of behavioral intervention with the context of good educational programming and curriculum design. Behavior analysis has a technology for optimizing learning, but in its traditional emphasis upon individual behaviors it has not paid sufficient attention to the establishment of a comprehensive set of functional skills for persons with severe handicaps. It also seems likely that the contingencies of natural learning environments are more powerful than those that can be arranged in a more clinical or therapy-oriented setting, particularly with respect to communication and social skills. This would mean that the focus for behavior analysts might well be in helping to identify and produce the elements of the repertoire that make it possible for persons with severe handicaps to benefit from these natural learning opportunities.

Program design

An analogy might clarify this reorientation. Psychologists seeking to understand the learning process for nonhandicapped children may conduct experiments under relatively artificial learning trial conditions and then extrapolate the implications for learning in the real world. But much of what we do with typical children in school is not specifically supported by this experimental knowledge of learning processes. Because we acknowledge that much remains unknown, schools represent a range of experiences for their children. And schools are greatly influenced by society at large, so that what happens in school reflects general societal values about the socialization process, as well as how children learn academic content. Children will grow up with mixed memories of their school experiences, but at least their schooling took place in contact with friends, family, and the general population. Even if we were to demonstrate that typical children could dramatically increase their academic performance by enrollment in a socially isolating school program, would most people voluntarily choose this option at the expense of social integration? Clearly each individual makes a personal decision in any attempt to reach a balance between academic achievement and social goals. But what has happened to people with severe mental handicap is that others have created clinical or experimental programs— ostensibly to maximize learning and to 'protect' them from social experiences—that would be unacceptable for any other segment of our population.

This process has not only reduced or even eliminated the kinds of social experiences generally regarded as important to personal satisfaction, it has had the paradoxical effect of reducing critical learning experiences as well. The literature on teaching social skills illustrates how this can occur. In social skills instruction, as in other areas, behavior analysts have by and large intervened with single target behaviors taken one at a time, with little regard for the individual's total repertoire or increasing those activities viewed as prerequisites to social competence. In studies purporting to teach social skills, the most common target behaviors are rather simple discrete responses such as eye contact, staying in seat, and following one-step commands (e.g., Lovaas, 1981; Matson *et al.*, 1988). Apparently, assumptions have been made that learning such target behaviors will lead to social competence. There is, however, no direct empirical evidence. It is perhaps an axiom that the ability to follow directions routinely is a critical social skill in many environments, including schools (see Repp and Karsh, this volume). But we know little about how children learn this skill other than the very obvious fact that typical children are not provided with individualized, systematic instruction in following directions.

For children with a severe mental handicap who have not mastered this skill, it seems clear that some settings represent what Staats has called deficit environments (Leduc, Dumais and Evans, 1990; Staats, 1975). It is worth noting that in the Matson *et al.* (1988) study cited earlier, the student was not attending a regular school with nonhandicapped peers, either at baseline or follow-up. It is implausible that the best way to teach social skills is through structured operant conditioning, or that the best way to learn these skills is through a therapist–child instructional dyad. The social environment of the regular school provides the social context and multiple learning opportunities that would be far more supportive of an effort to develop *social competence* than direct instruction alone. The routines of the regular classroom and school would serve as multiple practice trials and nonhandicapped classmates would provide positive models. Further, the possibility that a child who has a severe disability can now develop a friendship with one or more classmates of the same age would also increase motivation to attend to them as models and to please them.

There is now a substantial literature to support the principle that children with even the most severe intellectual and physical disabilities can be served in regular schools, will be accepted by their nonhandicapped peers, and will experience many opportunities to participate in mutually rewarding interactions with those children (e.g., Cole, Vandercook and Rynders, 1988; Meyer and Putnam, 1988). There is evidence that typical children will not only seek out these interactions voluntarily, but that they find them sufficiently rewarding that they continue them for extended periods of time and that friendships develop (Cole, Vandercook and Rynders, 1988; Voeltz and Brennan, 1984). Unless we were to deny the value of such social opportunities for the development of social competence in typical children, what would be the rationale for denying their potential value for children with handicaps?

If intervention occurs in natural environments, several positive collateral effects might result for behavioral clinicians as well as for the client. Firstly, the natural environment allows the therapist to validate socially the importance of a target behavior, rather than assume its validity out of context. Secondly, if a goal truly has social validity, whatever direct instruction might be needed will automatically be augmented by multiple additional trials in that learning environment. Thirdly, the natural environment provides the behavior analyst with an evaluation not only of the validity of the social goal, but also the effectiveness of the instruction through frequent opportunities to probe for generalization. Finally, mastery of a valid social response by a child should lead to positive ripple effects and side effects as peers and other adults come to appreciate these new accomplishments (Evans and Meyer, 1985).

Research design

The traditional format of single-subject research designs has contributed to delaying a focus on such expanded outcomes as the criteria for empirically evaluating behavioral interventions. These designs derive their logic from the ability of the clinician or experimenter to manipulate a given behavior. If behavior analysis is to be treatment—the imparting of new adaptive skills and not the artificial contingency manipulation of a behavior—then such designs have limited usefulness. When teaching new skills, interest must be in whether the client acquired the skill and whether it had the desired effect on quality of life. Some hypotheses about the types of changes likely to be seen, based on prior assumptions about response organization, are necessary. In such strategies, various techniques are available for monitoring the interactions among multiple behaviors.

If it proves difficult to make generalizations about the form of response organization, single-subject methodology will continue to be needed. While group designs have been underused in behavioral interventions with persons who have severe handicaps, we recognize that the diversity within response organization makes it unlikely that there will be only a few new behaviors that can be taught in a variety of contexts. In fact, one of the continuing difficulties in the field is that with the elaborate methods currently available for studying response organization among multiple behaviors in real time, researchers have generally not been able to identify highly consistent patterns within individuals across time and settings. Thus there is a need to pursue some of the more simple and practical methods for including response relationships within our clinical assessments, as we have outlined here.

CONCLUSION

In addition to attending to program quality and extending our treatment designs, the types of outcomes we look for, and their value, need to be continually re-examined. At the most practical level, the assumptions of response organization make it clear that collateral effects will be the rule, not the exception. And because they can as easily be undesirable as desirable, it is essential that we plan to evaluate them systematically, not anecdotally. Assumptions regarding response organization represent clinical hypotheses about treatment. Thus, it should be possible to make explicit predictions regarding the effect of certain interventions on specific response repertoires.

At a more general level, response interrelationships give us another perspective on the meaningfulness of an outcome. In the past, the standard for an effective intervention in behavior modification has really been derived from a comparison with pre-treatment status. An intervention was considered successful if the pre-treatment baseline level was altered in the appropriate direction. Certainly more stringent criteria were often included: for some behaviors, for example, a reduction to zero levels was the goal. Gradually the questions of social validity and clinical significance began to be asked: was the level of change seen the most needed, and, more importantly, was the behavior itself of real significance? We are delighted that these issues are now clearly in the forefront of outcome evaluation methodology, but we feel that they need to be taken further. Response organization provides a central context for considering the meaningfulness of behavior change.

Address for correspondence

Joseph R. Scotti, Department of Psychology, West Virginia University, Morgantown, WV 26506-6040, USA.

REFERENCES

Barlow, D.H. and Hersen, M. (1984) *Single Case Experimental Designs* (2nd edn), Pergamon Press, New York.

Bem, D.J. (1983) Toward a response style theory of persons in situations. In M.M. Page (ed.), *1982 Nebraska Symposium on Motivation: Personality—Current Theory and Research* (pp. 201–232), University of Nebraska Press, Lincoln.

Catania, A.C. (1966) Concurrent operants. In W.K. Honig (ed.), *Operant Behavior: Areas of Research and Application* (pp. 213–270), Appleton–Century–Crofts, New York.

Cole, D.A., Vandercook, T. and Rynders, J. (1988) Comparison of two peer interaction programs: Children with and without severe disabilities. *American Educational Research Journal*, **25**, 415–439.

Cone, J.D. (1979) Confounded comparisons in triple response mode assessment research. *Behavioral Assessment*, **1**, 85–95.

Cook, T.D., Dintzer, L. and Mark, M.M. (1980) The causal analysis of concomitant time series. In L. Bickman (ed.), *Applied Social Psychology Annual* (Vol. 1, pp. 93–135), Sage, Beverly Hills.

Durand, V.M. (1982) Analysis and intervention of self-injurious behavior. *Journal of the Association for the Severely Handicapped*, **7**, 44–53.

Durand, V.M. and Crimmins, D.B. (1988) Identifying the variables maintaining self-injurious behavior. *Journal of Autism and Developmental Disorders*, **18**, 99–117.

Durand, V.M. and Kishi, G. (1987) Reducing severe behavior problems among persons with dual sensory impairments: An evaluation of a technical assistance model. *Journal of the Association for Persons with Severe Handicaps*, **12**, 2–10.

Endler, N.S. (1983) Interactionism: A personality model, but not yet a theory. In M.M. Page (ed.), *1982 Nebraska Symposium on Motivation: Personality—Current Theory and Research* (pp. 155–200), University of Nebraska Press, Lincoln.

Evans, I.M. (1986) Response structure and the triple response mode concept in behavioral assessment. In R.O. Nelson and S.C. Hayes (eds), *Conceptual Foundations of Behavioral Assessment* (pp. 131–155), Guilford Press, New York.

Evans, I.M. (1989) A multidimensional model for conceptualizing the design of child behavior therapy. *Behavioural Psychotherapy*, **17**, 237–251.

Evans, I.M. and Meyer, L.H. (1985) *An Educative Approach to Behavior Problems: A Practical Decision Model for Interventions with Severely Handicapped Learners*, Brookes, Baltimore.

Evans, I.M. and Meyer, L.H. (1987) Moving to educational validity: A reply to Test, Spooner, and Cooke. *Journal of the Association for Persons with Severe Handicaps*, **12**, 103–106.

Evans, I.M. and Scotti, J.R. (1989) Defining meaningful outcomes for persons with profound disabilities. In F. Brown and D. Lehr (eds), *Persons with Profound Disabilities: Issues and Practices* (pp. 315–350), Brookes, Baltimore.

Evans, I.M. and Voeltz, L.M. (1982) *The Selection of Intervention Priorities in Educational Programming of Severely Handicapped Preschool Children with Multiple Behavioral Problems*, Final report, Grant G007901960, US Department of Education, University of Hawaii, Honolulu. Abstracted in *Resources in Education*, July, 1984, ERIC Report No. ED 240-765.

Evans, I.M., Brown, F.A., Weed, K.A., Spry, K.M. and Owen, V. (1987) The assessment of functional competencies: A behavioral approach to the evaluation of programs for children with disabilities. In R.J. Prinz (ed.), *Advances in Behavioral Assessment of Children and Families* (pp. 93–121), JAI Press, Greenwich.

Evans, I.M., Meyer, L.H., Kurkjian, J.A. and Kishi, G.S. (1988) An evaluation of behavioral interrelationships in child behavior therapy. In J.C. Witt, S.N. Elliott and F.N. Gresham (eds), *Handbook of Behavior Therapy in Education* (pp. 189–216), Plenum, New York.

Ferster, C.B. and Skinner, B.F. (1957) *Schedules of Reinforcement*, Prentice Hall, Englewood Cliffs, New Jersey.

Iwata, B.A., Dorsey, M.F., Slifer, K.J., Bauman, K.E. and Richman, G.S. (1982) Toward a functional analysis of self-injury. *Analysis and Intervention in Developmental Disabilities*, **2**, 3–20.

Johnson, W.L., Baumeister, A.A., Penland, M.J. and Inwald, C. (1982) Experimental analysis of self-injurious, stereotypic, and collateral behavior of retarded persons: Effects of overcorrection and reinforcement of alternative responding. *Analysis and Intervention in Developmental Disabilities*, **2**, 41–66.

Johnston, J.J. and Pennypacker, H.S. (1980) *Strategies and Tactics of Human Behavioral Research*, Lawrence Erlbaum, Hillsdale, New Jersey.

Kazdin, A.E. (1978) *History of Behavior Modification: Experimental Foundations of Contemporary Research*, University Park Press, Baltimore.

Kazdin, A.E. (1982) Symptom substitution, generalization, and response covariation: Implications for psychotherapy outcome. *Psychological Bulletin*, **91**, 349–365.

Leduc, A., Dumais, A. and Evans, I.M. (1990) Social behaviorism, rehabilitation, and ethics: Applications for people with severe disabilities. In G.H. Eifert and I.M. Evans (eds), *Unifying Behavior Therapy: Contributions of Paradigmatic Behaviorism*, Springer, New York.

Lichstein, K.L. and Schreibman, L. (1976) Employing electric shock with autistic children. *Journal of Autism and Childhood Schizophrenia*, **6**, 163–173.

Lovaas, I.O. (1981) *Teaching Developmentally Delayed Children: The ME Book*, University Park Press, Baltimore.

Lubinski, D. and Thompson, T. (1986) Functional units of human behavior and their integration: A dispositional analysis. In T. Thompson and M.D. Zeiler (eds), *Analysis and Integration of Behavioral Units* (pp. 275–314), Lawrence Erlbaum, Hillsdale, New Jersey.

Marston, A.R. (1979) Behavior ecology emerges from behavior modification: Side-steps towards a nonspecial profession. *Behavior Modification*, **3**, 147–160.

Matson, J.L., Manikam, R., Coe, D., Raymond, K., Taras, M. and Long, N. (1988) Training social skills to severely mentally retarded multiply handicapped adolescents. *Research in Developmental Disabilities*, **9**, 195–208.

McFall, R.M. (1982) A review and reformulation of the concept of social skills. *Behavioral Assessment*, **4**, 1–33.

McReynolds, P. (1979) The case for interactional assessment. *Behavioral Assessment*, **1**, 237–247.

Meyer, L.H. (1991) Advocacy, research, and typical practices: A call for the reduction of discrepancies between what is and what ought to be and how to get there. In L.H. Meyer, C.A. Peck and L. Brown (eds), *Critical Issues in the Lives of People with Severe Disabilities*, Brookes, Baltimore.

Meyer, L.H. and Evans, I.M. (1989) *Non-Aversive Intervention for Behavior Problems: A Manual for Home and Community*, Brookes, Baltimore.

Meyer, L.H. and Putnam, J. (1988) Social integration. In V.B. Van Hasselt, P.S. Strain and M. Hersen (eds), *Handbook of Developmental and Physical Disabilities* (pp. 107–133), Pergamon, New York.

Meyer, L.H., Evans, I.M., Wuerch, B.B. and Brennan, J.M. (1985) Monitoring the collateral effects of leisure skills instruction: A case study in multiple-baseline methodology. *Behaviour Research and Therapy*, **23**, 127–138.

Mischel, W. (1968) *Personality and Assessment*, Wiley, New York.

Mischel, W. and Peake, P.K. (1983) Analyzing the construction of consistency in personality. In M.M. Page (ed.), *1982 Nebraska Symposium on Motivation: Personality–Current Theory and Research* (pp. 233–262), University of Nebraska Press, Lincoln.

Neel, R.S. and Billingsley, F.F. (1989) *IMPACT: A Functional Curriculum Handbook for Students with Moderate to Severe Disabilities*, Brookes, Baltimore.

Newsom, C., Favell, J.E. and Rincover, A. (1983) The side effects of punishment. In S. Axlerod and S. Apsche (eds), *The Effects of Punishment on Human Behavior* (pp. 285–316), Pergamon Press, New York.

Nisbett, R.E. (1980) The trait construct in lay and professional psychology. In L. Festinger (ed.), *Retrospections on Social Psychology* (pp. 248–271), Oxford University Press, New York.

Pokrzywinski, J., Scotti, J.R. and Hetz, R.N. (1982, May) *Some Effects of Environmental Manipulation on Self-stimulatory Behavior*. Poster presented at the eighth annual convention of the Association for Behavior Analysis, Milwaukee.

Rachlin, H. (1982) Absolute and relative consumption space. In D.M. Bernstein (ed.), *1981 Nebraska Symposium on Motivation: Response Structure and Organization* (pp. 129–168), University of Nebraska Press, Lincoln.

Schefft, B.K. and Lehr, B.K. (1985) A self-regulatory model of adjunctive behavior change. *Behavior Modification*, **9**, 458–476.

Schroeder, S.R. and MacLean, W. (1987) If it isn't one thing, it's another: Experimental analysis of covariation in behavior management data of severe behavior disturbances. In S. Landesman and P.M. Vietze (eds), *Living Environments and Mental Retardation* (pp. 315–338), American Association on Mental Retardation, Washington.

Scotti, J.R., Evans, I.M. and Murphy, R.T. (1988, September) *Differential Effects of Brief Response Interruption: Three Case Studies.* Poster presented at the third World Congress on Behaviour Therapy, Edinburgh, Scotland.

Sidman, M. (1960) *Tactics of Scientific Research*, Basic Books, New York.

Skinner, B.F. (1938) *The Behavior of Organisms*, Prentice-Hall, Englewood Cliffs, New Jersey.

Skinner, B.F. (1953) *Science and Human Behavior*, The Free Press, New York.

Skinner, B.F. (1956) A case history in scientific method. *American Psychologist*, **11**, 221–233.

Staats, A.W. (1975) *Social Behaviorism*, Dorsey Press, Chicago.

Staats, A.W. and Staats, C.K. (1963) *Complex Human Behavior*, Holt, Rinehart & Winston, New York.

Sturmey, P., Carlsen, A., Crisp, A.G. and Newton, J.T. (1988) A functional analysis of multiple aberrant responses: A refinement and extension of Iwata et al.'s (1982) methodology. *Journal of Mental Deficiency Research*, **32**, 31–46.

Terrace, H. (1963) Discrimination learning with and without 'errors'. *Journal of the Experimental Analysis of Behavior*, **6**, 1–27.

Thompson, T. and Lubinski, D. (1986) Units of analysis and kinetic structure of behavioral repertoires. *Journal of the Experimental Analysis of Behavior*, **41**, 219–242.

Voeltz, L.M. and Brennan, J. (1984) Analysis of interactions between nonhandicapped and severely handicapped peers using multiple measures. In J.M. Berg (ed.), *Perspectives and Progress in Mental Retardation, Vol 1: Social, Psychological, and Educational Aspects* (pp. 61–72), University Park Press, Baltimore.

Voeltz, L.M. and Evans, I.M. (1982) The assessment of behavioral interrelationships in child behavior therapy. *Behavioral Assessment*, **4**, 131–165.

Voeltz, L.M. and Evans, I.M. (1983) Educational validity: Procedures to evaluate outcomes in programs for severely handicapped learners. *Journal of the Association for the Severely Handicapped*, **8**, 3–15.

Voeltz, L.M., Evans, I.M., Derer, K.R. and Hanashiro, R. (1983) Targeting excess behavior for change: A clinical decision model for selecting priority goals in educational contexts. *Child and Family Behavior Therapy*, **5**, 17–35.

Wahler, R.G. (1975) Some structural aspects of deviant child behavior. *Journal of Applied Behavior Analysis*, **8**, 27–42.

Wahler, R.G. and Fox, J.J. (1982) Response structure in deviant child–parent relationships: Implications for family therapy. In D.J. Bernstein (ed.) *1981 Nebraska Symposium on Motivation: Response Structure and Organization* (pp. 1–46), University of Nebraska Press, Lincoln.

Wahler, R.G., Sperling, K.A., Thomas, M.R. and Teeter, N.C. (1970) The modification of childhood stuttering: Some response–response relationships. *Journal of Experimental Child Psychology*, **9**, 411–428.

Weld, E.M. and Evans, I.M. (1990) Effects of part versus whole instructional strategies on skill acquisition and excess behavior. *American Journal on Mental Retardation*, **94**, 377–386.

Winterling, V., Dunlap, G. and O'Neill, R.E. (1987) The influence of task variation on the aberrant behaviors of autistic students. *Education and Treatment of Children*, **10**, 105–119.

Section 2

Behavioural Approaches to Functional Communication and Language

Chapter 8

Manual Sign-based Communication for Individuals with Severe or Profound Mental Handicap

PIETER C. DUKER AND BOB REMINGTON

INTRODUCTION

Approximately 80% of people with severe and profound mental handicap fail to acquire effective speech (Garcia and DeHaven, 1974), and for these individuals manual signs of the kind used by deaf people may constitute a viable alternative form of communication. A sign may consist of a single movement of the hand and arm, or a more complex coordinated movement. Although sign language may be used to convey complex messages, and its linguistic status has been widely acknowledged, people with mental handicap are most likely first to use *single* signs, often to convey their needs or desires. The present chapter is concerned with simple signing of these kinds. Some individuals may possess a gestural repertoire that subserves these functions, but that has not been specifically taught. This 'natural sign vocabulary' has instead been inadvertently shaped by an individual's 'verbal community' (Skinner, 1957), his or her family, friends, and caregivers. Following Skinner's terminology, the term 'manding' will be used to describe signing which functions as a request (or de*mand*), and 'tacting' to indicate the signing which functions to label (or con*tact*) objects or events present in the signer's environment (see Goodman and Remington, and Riechle, Sigafoos and Remington, this volume, for a more detailed discussion of these terms).

Selecting individuals for sign teaching

Systems of non-oral communication were first devised for and by individuals with severe hearing deficits, but applications to deaf people

The Challenge of Severe Mental Handicap. Edited by Bob Remington
© 1991 John Wiley & Sons Ltd

who also had mental handicap were reported almost a generation ago (e.g., Hoffmeister and Farmer, 1972). Manual signing is now widely used in schools for all children with mental handicap (Kiernan, Reid and Jones, 1982), but there is a range of physical problems apart from deafness in the presence of which sign teaching may be particularly indicated. For example, people who have suffered neurological damage in Broca's or Wernicke's areas of the cortex (which are thought to mediate speech), or those who carry a diagnosis of microcephaly, Cri-du-Chat syndrome, congenital rubella, and Prader–Willi syndrome, may all benefit from teaching communicative signs (Sanger *et al.*, 1984). Similarly, the communicative functioning of individuals with fragile X syndrome is significantly more retarded than functioning in other cognitive domains (Dykens, Hodapp and Leckman, 1989), and may be enhanced by sign learning. Finally, individuals with Down's syndrome and whose articulation is hindered by a large tongue may be particularly considered for sign training.

Apart from obvious organic problems, there are a range of more psychological indications suggesting that some form of sign teaching programme might be appropriate. For example, if speech training has been repeatedly tried without success, or if—despite therapy—articulation remains incomprehensible or incomplete, signing might be considered. Sign teaching might also be appropriate whenever an intention to communicate is inferred from observing that an individual frequently points to objects or rejects them during interpersonal interactions. Finally, many individuals exhibiting challenging behaviour, like those with natural sign vocabularies, can be said to have acquired a verbal repertoire in the sense that their behaviour has been shaped and maintained by socially mediated consequences (cf. Skinner, 1957). Thus, people showing these very different behavioural topographies may be equally appropriate candidates for signing interventions for exactly the same functional reasons.

Selecting signs for teaching

A primary consideration in selecting a signing vocabulary should concern whether its acquisition will increase individuals' control over their social and physical environment. Such control will be partially dependent on the vocabulary chosen, so for example signs like 'toilet' or 'drink' are more likely to be useful than signs like 'doctor' or 'tree'. In addition, the guessability of the signs, the ease with which they can be produced, and the role of an individual's receptive understanding of the words that to-be-taught signs correspond to, are all important factors affecting sign acquisition. We will briefly consider each of these factors in turn.

Sign guessability

The utility of a signing vocabulary depends on gestures being comprehensible to, or at least guessable by, others in the individual's social environment. Signs differ in the extent to which this is so. For example, Griffith, Robinson and Panagos (1981) and Hoemann (1975) found that 10–30% of the manual signs of American Sign Language were correctly guessed by sign-naive raters. Similarly, Duker and Rikken (1990) assessed the guessability by naive raters of a vocabulary of 58 signs, selected to be taught as mands to a group of individuals with severe and profound mental handicap. University students guessed these signs with an accuracy of 36% on the first occasion, and a sheer second presentation significantly increased the number of correct guesses, suggesting that prolonged exposure to signs may improve comprehension without formal training. Further research is needed to clarify this notion.

Ease of sign production

Several studies have focused on the relationship between performance aspects of communicative signs and how well they are learned and retained. For example, Kohl (1981) found that signs involving touching another part of the body or an object are acquired faster and are retained longer than signs that do not have these features. She also found that signs should preferably have both hands/arms make similar, or complementary movements rather than dissimilar movements. From a teaching standpoint, it is important that signs are 'mouldable', i.e. that a teacher can guide a student's hand to make the sign. For example, it is easier to mould a flat hand sign than one in which the index finger must be pulled out from a clenched fist. Ideally, all signs taught concurrently should differ clearly from each other in all possible respects. For example, it is difficult to teach signs for 'open/close' and 'brick' in the same set, because both use closed fists. Similar difficulties arise in teaching signs for food and drink, as both involve touching the mouth. Generally, if the members of a set of to-be-trained signs show many similarities in their execution (or in their cues which occasion them), sign acquisition will be slower (Griffith and Robinson, 1980). Unfortunately, as an individual's signing repertoire increases, problems of this sort become inevitable.

Speech and signing

As we have seen, a common reason for teaching signing is that it will act as a substitute for speech for some individuals. However, it has also been argued that the acquisition of signing can act as a gateway to vocal communication, in the sense of facilitating speech acquisition in some way. Such a process may well occur under some circumstances, but the fact that many individuals who cannot articulate words can nevertheless understand them should not be forgotten. Although signing may offer a means of expression, it is unlikely to be a first language in the receptive mode. Given this, we can ask whether signs that correspond to items whose names are receptively known are learned faster than signs corresponding to unknown words. There is a possibility that the answer to this question will depend on whether the words are used by the teacher during training (as in the well-known 'total communication' procedure) or left unspoken (as in sign-alone training). The child's receptive word knowledge, and the teacher's use of expressive speech during training, are separate independent variables which may interact. Four possible pairwise comparisons of conditions can therefore be made, and these are shown in Table 8.1. Remington and his associates explored each of them using four separate within-subjects alternating treatments comparisons (Barlow and Hayes, 1979). Known words were selected by a receptive speech pre-test in which the child was required to choose a picture corresponding to a spoken word. All signs in these studies were taught as tacts.

The results of these four studies (see Clarke, 1986; Clarke, Remington and Light, 1986, 1988; Remington and Clarke, 1983) were revealing. Signs

Table 8.1 Alternating treatment comparisons used to assess the effects of training signs for known and unknown words via sign-alone and total communication training procedures

Study	Treatment A	Treatment B
1	Total communication Known words	Total communication Unknown words
2	Sign-alone training Known words	Sign-alone training Unknown words
3	Total communication Known words	Sign-alone training Known words
4	Total communication Unknown words	Sign-alone training Unknown words

for known words were learned faster than signs for unknown words when teachers used total communication. Similarly, when signs for *known* words were taught, total communication was more effective than sign-alone training. However, there were no differences when signs for unknown words were taught by either method, and no differences when signs for either known or unknown words were taught by sign-alone training. To summarize, the four experimental comparisons suggested that knowledge of the word equivalents of the signs *did* facilitate the acquisition of expressive signing, but only when the words were actually spoken during training sessions. Therefore, teachers should begin teaching by using signs corresponding to known words and using total communication. Rather than signing necessarily being a gateway to speech, it seems, paradoxically, that (receptive) speech can sometimes be a gateway to (expressive) signing.

This series of studies also focused on aspects of response generalization, i.e. changes in performance that resulted from teaching but were not themselves directly taught (see Scotti *et al.*, this volume). Depending on the specific circumstances, these included the development, following expressive sign training, of receptive signing, receptive speech, and expressive speech. Instances of transfer of stimulus control of this kind were found in each of the studies, and most of the data could be accounted for using the concept of stimulus equivalence (see Mackay, this volume, for a full account). When signs are taught as tacts, the student experiences three types of stimuli—referents (e.g., pictures or line drawings), signs, and words—and thus nine possible sets of associations between items. These are shown in Table 8.2. Some associations (imitative signing, picture matching, and, in the case of known words, receptive speech) were present prior to training, and the training procedures themselves added to the number of relations between classes. For example, sign-alone training produced picture–sign associations; total communication could produce picture–sign associations, word–sign associations, or both, depending on whether a child attended to one or both stimulus modalities. Of the remaining associations, those which may *emerge* following training are predictable in terms of equivalence relations.

One example should make this clear. Clarke (1986) found that stimulus control of signing by words emerged following sign-alone training *in which words were never used*, but *only* when the word–picture associations were present prior to training, i.e. only if a child had receptive speech. The outcome can be explained thus: known words controlled the selection of their corresponding pictures before sign training, and sign-alone training caused picture stimuli to control signing responses. If these

Table 8.2 The nine possible sets of associations between items assessed in studies of expressive sign training

Name of associative relationship	Performance assessed (given stimulus class/required response category)
Picture matching	Pictures/pictures
Sign imitation	Signs/signs
Verbal imitation	Words/words
Expressive speech	Pictures/words
Receptive speech	Words/pictures
Visual stimulus control	Pictures/signs
Vocal stimulus control	Words/signs
Receptive signing	Signs/pictures
Sign naming	Signs/words

associative relations are transitive, words should also control signs. This cannot happen with *unknown* words since they do not, by definition, control picture selection responses.

PROCEDURES FOR TRANSFERRING STIMULUS CONTROL OF SIGNING

Although transfer of control of signing may emerge in the way outlined above, a number of studies have shown that this does not always occur. When total communication training methods are used, expressive signing may still not come under the control of all of the stimuli present when signing occurs and is reinforced (e.g., Carr *et al.*, 1978; Remington and Clarke, 1983). For example, Carr *et al.* (1978) taught four autistic children to sign in response to being shown referent objects and hearing (and seeing) a teacher speak their names. Subsequent tests, however, revealed that signing was mainly controlled by the presence of the objects, and not by their spoken names or by lip-reading cues provided by the teacher.

When desired forms of stimulus control do not arise 'spontaneously', special training procedures can be developed to ensure their occurrence. For example, Duker and Michielsen (1983) and Duker and Morsink (1984) evaluated a discrete trial procedure using most-to-least prompting to teach individuals with severe mental handicap to respond to verbal cues by signing appropriately. At the start of each trial the trainer pointed to the referent object, named it, and modelled the corresponding sign. Correct responding was reinforced as a mand; errors resulted in physical guidance, which was gradually faded in using a three-step procedure. When the trainee met criterion performance under the conditions described above, the sign-modelling component was omitted, but pointing to and naming an object remained as cues for signing (with modelling faded in again if performance deteriorated). Criterion performance at this stage resulted in withdrawal of the trainer's pointing as a cue for signing, so that by the end of the procedure the trainee would sign reliably on hearing the name of the object. Refinements of this procedure for gaining stimulus control of signs were evaluated in other studies. For example, imposing a 5-second wait time by holding a trainee's hands before allowing a response to the trainer's verbal cue and before presenting of the named object appeared to increase correct responding (Duker, van Doeselaar and Verstraten, 1989). Moreover, repeating the training stimulus at the end of the 5-second interval further improved performance.

The discrete trial training procedures described above are only the first step toward the spontaneous use of communicative signing. Ideally, signing should not be limited to, or controlled by, the trial-by-trial presentation of objects, naming objects, or by repeatedly questioning the individual about his or her possible needs. Rather, broadly defined external stimuli (e.g., presence of an adult) or internal stimuli (e.g., thirst) should occasion signs which function to allow others to know, and thus meet, the signer's needs. Obviously, this implies that spontaneous signing should occur in ways which vary over time and circumstance to reflect an individual's changing motivational flux.

One procedure for moving in the direction of increased spontaneity of signing involves the use of time-delay procedures (Touchette, 1971) to transfer control of signing from training stimuli (i.e., presentation of names or objects) to the question: 'What do you want?' Ideally, a trainee's response to this question will vary over time. To establish this pattern of responding, Duker (1988; see also Coonen and Duker, 1985) combined time-delay with a procedure in which the repeated performance of any sign was physically interrupted. The time-delay procedure involved the trainer gaining a trainee's attention, asking 'What do you want?', and immediately presenting an item which controlled one of the signs in the trainee's repertoire. If he or she responded consistently correctly, a delay of 2 seconds was introduced between asking the next question and presenting an item. Across trials the time-delay was gradually increased until the trainee would reliably respond to the question 'What do you want?' The aim of the study was thus to transfer control of signing from external cues which control tacting to internal cues which control manding. Data were collected within a multiple baseline design across individuals. The results showed a dramatic increase of the number of manual signs to the trainer's question, 'What do you want?' for each of the three trainees. Also, compared to baseline, the number of different signs trainees used increased when the procedure was in effect.

This kind of teaching procedure can perhaps establish more natural signing behaviour within the confines of a discrete-trial training procedure, but ultimately the aim must be to teach individuals with severe and profound mental handicap to sign spontaneously in the settings where they live, work or relax. In the next section we discuss some ways in which this can be facilitated.

SPONTANEOUS COMMUNICATIVE SIGNING

Teaching spontaneous signing

Spontaneous communication may be the ultimate purpose of teaching sign-based communication, but it has been the subject of few studies. In one of the most successful of these, Carr and Kologinsky (1983) demonstrated the effectiveness of a package of imitative prompting, fading, and differential reinforcement for teaching sets of signs as mands to autistic children. Spontaneous signing was defined as a sign occurring without any trainer prompt apart from visual attention. During training sessions, the trainer would present an imitative prompt to the child for one of the manual signs being taught. When the child responded correctly, the trainer would then only present a partial imitative prompt during the next trial. Fading of imitative prompts for that particular sign continued until the child spontaneously signed on two consecutive trials. Spontaneous signed requests were reinforced appropriately, but repetitions of the same sign within a session were extinguished by ignoring repeated instances. Results showed that the procedure rapidly gained control over children's spontaneous and varied communicative signing, and that performance generalized to other attending adults in novel situations.

In residential settings, however, an attending adult may not always be available, so it is important that individuals learn to mand even in the absence of caregivers' initial attention, or learn to mand attention (cf. Reichle, Sigafoos and Remington, this volume). Recently, Duker et al. (1989) showed that staff attention is not equally distributed across all residents, but heavily depends on certain characteristics of these individuals. Staff spend more time on residents who have acquired looking behaviour, who show high frequencies of either adaptive or maladaptive behaviour (not stereotypic behaviours), and who are ambulant (cf. Felce, this volume). Thus, if caretakers' visual attention is established as a discriminative stimulus for signing, we would expect it to be unevenly distributed across individuals.

Duker and Moonen (1985) showed that spontaneous communicative signing could emerge without being directly trained, as a concomitant effect of training caregivers. A training package—consisting of written instruction, modelling, video presentation, visual cueing, feedback, and group discussion—was devised for caregivers of a residential facility. Three individuals with severe and profound mental handicap, one teacher, and 12 caregivers participated in the study. Caregivers were taught to identify appropriate opportunities for communicative signing and, if necessary, administer prompts using a least-to-most procedure. Prompts were initiated when the caregiver was in physical proximity to the trainee and had made eye contact. The three prompting levels for occasioning requests were: first, the question 'What do you want?'; second, this question plus verbally naming an item for which the trainee was learning a manual sign; and third, both of the above, plus pointing to the item, modelling the sign, or moulding it. Data were collected within a multiple baseline design across individuals. The results showed that the package was effective, and that it facilitated spontaneous signing. During the 70 baseline observation sessions (across the three trainees) only three spontaneous communicative signs were recorded. When the programme was instituted, this figure rose to 19 during 121 sessions. Although small in absolute terms, this is a fourfold increase which is remarkable because—by definition—spontaneous signing could not have been directly taught.

A later study by Duker and Moonen (1986), carried out in a classroom setting, using three children with Down's syndrome as participants, assessed the effect of two independent variables, a deprivation procedure and a prompting procedure, on spontaneous communicative manding. The deprivation procedure was designed to establish particular items or activities as reinforcers which could be obtained by the appropriate sign, and is more appropriately described as an *establishing operation* (Michael, 1982). For example, if on signing 'cookie' a trainee is presented a small piece of cookie, he or she will be more inclined to repeat the sign than if the first sign produced the whole cookie. Similarly, when a trainee finds pieces of his or her favourite jigsaw puzzle missing, he or she will be inclined to mand them (see also Reichle, Sigafoos and Remington, this volume). In this study, some desirable consequences were visible to trainees, but out of reach, and others (e.g., activities like listening to music) did not have visible counterparts. The system of least prompts began with the trainer modelling a sign and successively adding other cues; pointing to the target object, verbally naming it, and finally using physical guidance. For each child, three signs were selected for training on the basis of their interest shown in the referents. Only spontaneous signs were recorded, and these were defined as those not preceded by a question (e.g., 'What do you want?'), a teacher's response to a previous sign (e.g., the teacher said: 'No, now something else' when the trainee made the identical gesture twice in a row), or any other visual, verbal, or physical prompt. Both the establishing operation procedure and the prompting procedure were effective in increasing the frequency of trainees' spontaneous signs. The technique of presentation of partial consequences (e.g., a piece of cookie) has the important advantage that it can be easily administered in the classroom setting. It is, however, more effective as a way of strengthening the manding performance of individuals who have already acquired a small repertoire of spontaneous signs, than for establishing such a repertoire *de novo*.

In another, more recent study of spontaneous signing, Seys, Kersten and Duker (1990) assessed how effectively a supervision programme for 15 caregivers facilitated communicative interaction with residents during mealtimes, physical care, and recreation. The supervision programme included instruction, verbal approval, and graphical publicly posted feedback. The nine residents who participated had been involved in a curriculum of teaching procedures to establish communicative signing (see Duker, 1988), and already showed some spontaneous signed manding in their living environments. They had been referred to the programme because they used only a few signs and signed infrequently. Baseline recordings showed that caregivers were already consistent in reinforcing residents for appropriate signing.

Because spontaneity cannot be taught but may emerge as a concomitant effect of training, the programme focused on encouraging caregivers to increase their prompting of signing by asking: 'What do you want?' during interactions. If an individual did not respond, the least-to-most prompting system described above was used to facilitate signing. Additionally, caregivers were taught to identify and use appropriate opportunties for manding by, for example, giving residents unopened boxes or bottles to prompt requests (e.g., 'open'). The results showed that the programme was effective in increasing both caregivers' prompting and their correct identification and use of manding opportunities, and that this in turn significantly increased the number and variety of spontaneous signs used by residents. Follow-up data underlined the long-term effectiveness of the programme.

Problems with apparently spontaneous signing

An important problem in the analysis of manual signing arises from the fact that the form of a sign is not an infallible cue to its function. In a study of speech training with autistic children, Yamamoto and Mochizuki (1988) showed that utterances thought to be functioning as mands were in fact maintained by non-specific consequences. Children were taught to request specific items from an adult, but on some trials were given items that did not correspond with those they had asked for. Because the proferred items were always accepted unquestioningly, it was clear that the children's utterances were not functioning as mands. A remedial procedure was successfully used to teach them both to reject unrequested objects and to accept those they did ask for. Recently, Duker, Dortmans and Lodder (1991) also found that five individuals with severe and profound mental handicap, who had a large signing vocabulary, accepted almost all the noncorresponding items offered following apparent requests, indicating that their signing did not in fact serve a manding function. A training procedure, using prompting, positive practice, and reinforcement, succeeded in increasing manding responses by teaching individuals to repeat their initial sign when a noncorresponding item was given, but accept it when it did correspond with their sign. In retrospect, it is clear that some procedure of this kind is of central importance in mand teaching, particularly in situations where the to-be-manded item is physically present when the request is made.

A second kind of problem arises when individuals who have learned a number of signed mands produce only a fraction of them spontaneously, or show perseverative use of some signs at the expense of others. The need for remediation is urgent if all the items for which mands have been acquired are equally attractive as assessed by independent behavioural measures of preference (see Berg and Wacker, this volume). In a recent study with six individuals with severe and profound mental handicap, Duker and van Lent (in press) found that when teachers failed to respond reliably to high-rate mands, there was a significant increase in the use of previously taught, but underused mands. If manding is considered as a generalized response class (Catania, 1984), it might be expected that extinction through ignoring some class members would render the response topography of the operant more variable, resulting in increased rates of occurrence of previously taught but unused signs. The results showed that, for all six individuals, there was a marked increase in the number of different mands used (mean, 84%; range, 41–209%) when the procedure was introduced.

To summarize, the results of the studies discussed above suggest spontaneous manding can be taught as a two-stage procedure. First, students can be taught on an intensive discrete-trial basis to make signs in the presence of well-defined training stimuli (i.e., as an echoic response to a modelled sign or a tact occasioned by a presented object). This can be followed by procedures capable of transferring stimulus control of signing to the question: 'What do you want?' At a later stage, incidental teaching procedures can be used in the students' natural environment to establish and increase spontaneous and varied signing. Such techniques include presenting incomplete objects or opportunities to behave in preferred ways, and repeatedly asking 'What do you want?', accompanied, if necessary, by temporarily increased levels of prompting. Because signs taught in this way are initially acquired as tacts or echoics, control procedures must be used to establish that they are eventually used as mands. During this second stage of teaching, it may be desirable temporarily to ignore signs emitted at high rates in order to increase or maintain students' variety of communicative signs.

If spontaneous signing can empower individuals by providing effective and relatively effortless ways of controlling their environments, we would expect to see a decline in less appropriate forms of control. In the following section we briefly consider studies relevant to this interpretation.

COMMUNICATIVE SIGNING AND BEHAVIOUR PROBLEMS

Correlational studies by Talkington and associates (Talkington and Hall, 1969; Talkington, Hall and Altman, 1971; Talkington, Hall and Cleland, 1971) have shown that individuals with severe and profound mental handicap who have no communicative behaviours (oral or non-oral) display behaviour problems more often than those who can communicate. In a group comparison study, Gould (1976) found that behaviour problems were significantly associated with absence of communicative behaviours. Although these findings have been interpreted in terms of the well-known frustration–aggression hypothesis, alternative explanations may be more tenable. For example, individuals who can communicate probably receive more attention for appropriate behaviours from caregivers, and this may strengthen behaviours that are functionally or topographically incompatible with problematic behaviours.

Only a few experimental studies have investigated the functional relationship between communicative performance and behaviour problems. One line of research deals with teaching handicapped individuals communicative behaviours that are functionally equivalent to their behaviour problems. This means that some sort of functional analysis of behaviour problems should precede intervention to teach communication (see Durand and Crimmins, and Oliver, this volume). For example, if temper tantrums function to elicit caregivers' help, a functionally equivalent communicative response which elicits help would lead to a decrease of the frequency of the problem behaviour. Similarly, if self-injurious behaviour functions to terminate work on a demanding task, teaching an equivalent verbal response which allows escape would be effective. Carr and Durand (1985) and Durand and Crimmins (1987) have provided evidence that teaching appropriate functional speech can reduce behaviour problems. In another study, Durand and Carr (1987) have shown that apparently 'self-stimulatory' behaviours are not necessarily maintained by reinforcers of a sensory nature, but may instead function to elicit attention or to allow escape and avoidance. Similarly, Horner and Budd (1985) taught a child diagnosed as mentally handicapped with autistic features to use signs to request for objects or activities. Prior to intervention, the child grabbed and yelled when objects were presented, and during mealtimes, instructional sessions, and other activities. The communicative signs that were subsequently taught were a set of specific mands for these objects and events. This produced a sharp decrease in grabbing and yelling, which had thus apparently functioned to inform others to give a particular object or to begin an activity. Teaching functionally equivalent signed manding thus reduced the occurrence of disruptive behaviour with this child.

Unfortunately, it may often be impractical to carry out a complete functional analysis of the behaviour problems of individuals with severe and profound mental handicap, who may be restrained to prevent self-injury, or who are in some other way unable to participate in analogue assessment procedures. Given these circumstances, Durand and Kishi (1987) employed the Motivation Assessment Scale (MAS), a rating scale which makes use of information provided by caregivers to determine the reinforcers controlling problem behaviours (Durand and Crimmins, 1988, and this volume). This information allowed appropriate communicative responses to be selected for teaching. Three individuals were taught symbols to communicate, while two others were taught signs. As in previous studies, the increase of their communicative responding resulted in a concomitant decrease in problem behaviour.

Although all these results are very encouraging, more data are needed to rule out alternative explanations for the experimental effect and thus consolidate the position of interventions based on teaching functionally equivalent communicative behaviour. For example, increased attention concurrent with the beginning of training of communicative behaviours may threaten the internal validity of some results. To explore this possibility, Duker, Jol and Palmen (in press) studied eight individuals with severe and profound mental handicap and with severe forms of challenging behaviour (see Table 8.3).

Their behaviours were observed over an average of 73 daily recording sessions while they were in their home and other environments, such as the classroom or the activity room. An interval recording system was used to record self-injurious behaviour, aggressive behaviour, destructive behaviour, and other behaviour problems (rumination, pica, inappropriate sexual behaviour, stereotypic behaviours). Similarly, each individual's use of communicative signs (i.e., spontaneous signs and signs as response to the question 'What do you want?') was recorded. Two types of signs were distinguished—those that were taught during training sessions (see below) and those that were already in an individual's repertoire. Finally, the number of intervals in which caregivers initiated contact with each individual was recorded. If caregiver contact increased from the baseline to the intervention phase, this would threaten the internal validity of the results and thus undermine the conclusion that teaching functionally equivalent communicative behaviour in itself reduces challenging behaviour. Each individual participating in the study was given one-to-one training to comply with verbal instructions during the baseline phase, and was taught communicative signing during the intervention phase. The rationale for training instruction-following was to control the amount of attention and other reinforcement delivered during the baseline phase in order to ensure that it did not increase when the treatment phase of the study began.

For both types of training, instructional strategies such as most-to-

Table 8.3 Participants in Duker, Jol and Palmen's study of the relationship between signing and behaviour problems

Participant	Age	Degree of mental handicap	Challenging behaviours
H.B.	35	Severe	Self-biting; head-banging/hitting
P.R.	30	Profound	Head-hitting/banging; aggression; stereotypic behaviour
R.S.	26	Profound	Self-biting; head-banging; aggression; destructive and stereotypic behaviour
G.T.	11	Severe	Head-banging; self-biting; screaming; temper tantrums; aggression
M.D.	11	Profound	Head-banging/hitting
M.K.	31	Severe	Head-banging; stereotypic behaviour
P.V.	32	Severe	Self-biting; head-hitting; aggression; spitting
A.M.	23	Profound	Self-biting; screaming; stereotypic behaviour

least prompting, time-delay, and reinforcement were used during four 30-minute sessions each week. Sessions were conducted in a training room. Caregivers working in the individuals' natural environment were instructed to prompt them to respond to the verbal instructions during baseline, and to the question 'What do you want?' during intervention. Moreover, caregivers were told to respond appropriately to individuals' spontaneous signs by providing them with the consequences that corresponded to their signed requests. The selection of verbal instructions and communicative signs was based on interviews with caregivers. They identified a potential set of 68 signs and selected at least ten signs for each individual. These signs could be used to request preferred items and activities to which individuals had no free access while in their natural environment, and which could be used at least once during the day. For example, there were signs to request listening to music, going outside, and working with clay.

Data were collected within a multiple baseline design across individuals to further reduce threats to the internal validity of the results. Further data were obtained during a follow-up phase during which no training occurred. Reliability assessments for recording were conducted in 29% of the recording sessions, approximately equally distributed across the phases of baseline, intervention, and follow-up. The mean reliability for recording behaviour problems was 90.2% (range: 25–100%); communicative gestures, 88.8% (range: 47–100%); and caregivers' initiations, 97% (range: 73–100%).

During baseline none of the individuals used the to-be-trained signs. In the intervention period, however, seven of the eight individuals both learned new communicative signs and increased their use of signs that they already had in their vocabulary (only A.M. failed to learn the signs selected, and her data will not be considered further here). There was a mean increase to 0.81% (range: 0.2–1.7%) of the intervals in which trained signs occurred during the intervention phase, and this increased further during the follow-up phase to 3.16% of intervals. Although relatively modest, the increases between the means of baseline and intervention and intervention and follow-up were statistically significant in both cases (Wilcoxon signed ranks tests: $T = 0$, $p = 0.009$, one-tailed). Signs that individuals had previously acquired also increased between phases of baseline and intervention, and intervention and follow-up. However, in this case, only the latter increase was significant ($T = 0$, $p = 0.014$).

For clarity, data showing the effect of sign teaching on the four forms of challenging behaviour monitored are presented in Table 8.4, which shows the mean percentage of intervals containing these actions during baseline, intervention, and follow-up. Across the seven individuals (excluding A.M.), a statistically significant mean decrease of 39.4% of intervals of self-injurious behaviour occurred between baseline and intervention ($T = 0$, $p = 0.009$). The difference between the intervention phase and follow-up was not statistically significant ($T = 10$, $p = 0.249$).

Table 8.4 also shows the mean percentages for aggression, destruction, and other behaviour problems during baseline, intervention, and follow-up for each of the seven individuals. The mean percentage of intervals containing aggression also declined during the intervention phase although, due to the small number of individuals who behaved in this way ($n = 5$), no statistical analysis was possible. The same holds true for destructive behaviour, although a decrease of the mean percentage of intervals in which destructive behaviours occurred also declined and, except for one person (H.B.), remained at zero levels during the follow-up phase. With respect to the six individuals exhibiting other behaviour problems, a significant mean decrease of 39% of intervals of this category occurred during the intervention ($T = 2$; <0.04), but no difference was found between intervention and follow-up.

Surprisingly, caregivers initiated *fewer* interactions with individuals during intervention than during the baseline phase (mean percentages of intervals 10.69 and 8.41, respectively). This decrease was statistically significant ($T = 3$; $p = 0.03$). The mean percentage of intervals containing caregiver initiatives increased slightly to 10.19% in the follow-up phase relative to the intervention phase, although this change was not statistically significant. The fact that the number of interactions did not rise significantly during intervention or follow-up means that increased attention by caregivers cannot provide an alternative explanation for the

Table 8.4 Mean percentage of intervals of self-injurious behaviour, aggression, destruction and other problem behaviours during the baseline (BL), intervention (INT) and follow-up (FU) periods of Duker, Jol and Palmen's study

Subjects	Self-injurious behaviour			Aggression			Destruction			Other behaviour problems		
	BL	INT	FU	BL	INT	FU	BL	INT	FU	BL	INT	FU
H.B.	3.0	2.3	5.0	3.4	1.0	1.7	1.8	0.6	1.5	9.5	4.2	3.0
P.R.	5.5	1.9	5.5	0.1	0.0	0.0	0.7	0.0	0.0	8.2	3.9	4.2
R.S.	4.9	4.2	3.3	0.4	0.3	0.2	1.8	0.0	0.0	5.5	1.4	2.0
G.T.	2.7	1.4	0.0	0.1	0.0	0.0	2.4	0.2	0.0	20.0	12.3	13.2
M.D.	24.0	12.8	22.9	0.0	0.0	0.0	0.0	0.0	0.0	0.0	0.0	0.0
M.K.	13.7	13.0	11.6	0.0	0.0	0.0	0.0	0.0	0.0	1.5	1.0	0.0
P.V.	1.8	0.5	0.2	0.1	0.0	0.0	0.1	0.0	0.0	4.3	7.3	0.6

improvements in challenging behaviour which occurred when participants were taught communicative signing.

Overall, then, Duker, Jol and Palmen's results confirm that teaching signs to individuals with severe and profound mental handicap who have no functional speech can be a fruitful procedure for decreasing the frequency of their self-injurious behaviour. At the very least, this approach might be considered as a useful supplement to existing procedures for reducing behaviour problems (see, for example, Jones, this volume). The results support and extend Durand and Kishi's (1987) and Horner and Budd's (1985) work, and underline the need for a functional analysis of behaviour problems. Such an analysis should focus on the motivational determinants of individuals' behaviour problems, a position taken by Carr as early as 1977. From a theoretical point of view, the present results might be explained in terms of response covariation (Kazdin, 1982; Scotti *et al.*, this volume), whereby a change in one behaviour can affect other behaviours in the same individual which are not manipulated directly, and irrespective of the topographical relationship between them.

CONCLUSIONS

In the present chapter, we have focused on the use of manual signs as alternatives to speech for individuals with severe or profound mental handicap. We have seen that a number of factors can affect the speed with which manual signs are acquired, and the impact that they have on the social environment of the individuals that acquire them. These factors include the guessability of the signs by non-signing caregivers, the motor difficulty involved in producing the signs and the ease with which they can be prompted, and the facilitatory effect of a receptive speech vocabulary on the acquisition of corresponding signs. Because signs are often taught in discrete trial training sessions conducted away from learners' living environments, some of the most important issues concern transfer of stimulus control of signing. We have reviewed some of the procedures which can facilitate this kind of transfer to make signing more spontaneous and unprompted, and discussed some of the difficulties inherent in the concept of spontaneity. Finally, we have examined the relationship between manual sign learning and challenging behaviour.

Once spontaneous communicative signing begins to occur in natural environments, it creates several potential difficulties to caregivers. First, signs are often low in salience and are difficult to identify by caregivers against a background of other motoric responses of the individuals present. This might be circumvented by teaching signers to behave in ways that serve as discriminative stimuli for caregivers' attention (cf. Reichle, Sigafoos and Remington, this volume). If attempts to sign are not recognized and reinforced individuals' signing behaviour will extinguish, or a reversion to earlier forms of communicative behaviour (e.g., natural signing, pointing) will occur. Another major source of difficulty for individuals who have learned to sign is that the social part of their living environment may have adapted itself to their previous noncommunicative status. For example, people may be taken to the bathroom at fixed times despite the fact that they have learned to use a manual sign to mand the toilet. There are undoubtedly many more difficulties related to the implementation of intervention to establish sign-based communication for individuals with severe or profound mental handicap. Nevertheless, we now know enough about how to teach these skills, and the benefits that such teaching is likely to produce, that the application of this knowledge is essential. A repertoire of signs may lead not only to a decrease in behaviour problems but, more importantly, it provides individuals with the means to control their social and physical environment to a degree that a purposeful interaction with others is possible.

Address for correspondence

Pieter C. Duker, Process Research Group, Instituut voor Orthopedagogiek, University of Nijmegen, Erasmusplein 1, Postbus 9103, Nijmegen 6500 HD, The Netherlands.

REFERENCES

Barlow, D.H. and Hayes, S.C. (1979) Alternating treatments designs: One strategy for comparing the effects of two treatments in a single subject. *Journal of Applied Behavior Analysis*, **12**, 199–210.

Carr, E.G. (1977) The motivation of self-injurious behavior: A review of some hypotheses. *Psychological Bulletin*, **84**, 800–816.

Carr, E.G. and Durand, V.M. (1985) Reducing behavior problems through functional communication training. *Journal of Applied Behavior Analysis*, **18**, 111–126.

Carr, E.G. and Kologinsky, E. (1983) Acquisition of sign language by autistic children. II: Spontaneity and generalization effects. *Journal of Applied Behavior Analysis*, **16**, 297–314.

Carr, E.G., Binkoff, J.A., Kologinsky, E. and Eddy, M. (1978) Acquisition of sign language by autistic children. I. Expressive labeling. *Journal of Applied Behavior Analysis*, **11**, 489–501.

Catania, A.C. (1984) *Learning*, Prentice-Hall, Englewood Cliffs, New Jersey.

Clarke, S. (1986) An evaluation of the relationship between receptive speech and manual sign language with mentally handicapped children. Unpublished PhD thesis, University of Southampton.

Clarke, S., Remington, B. and Light, P. (1986) An evaluation of the relationship between receptive speech skills and expressive signing. *Journal of Applied Behavior Analysis*, **19**, 231–239.

Clarke, S., Remington, B. and Light, P. (1988) The role of referential speech in sign learning by mentally retarded children: A comparison of total communication and sign-alone training. *Journal of Applied Behavior Analysis*, **21**, 419–426.

Coonen, E. and Duker, P. (1985) Het trainen van gegeneraliseerd gebruik van gebaren bij ontwikkelingsgestoorden. *Tijdschrift voor Orthopedagogiek*, **24**, 298–305.

Duker, P. (1988). *Teaching the Developmentally Handicapped Communicative Gesturing: A How-to-do Book*, Swets, Berwyn.

Duker, P. and Michielsen, H. (1983) Cross-setting generalization of manual signs to verbal instructions with severely retarded children. *Applied Research in Mental Retardation*, **6**, 147–158.

Duker, P. and Moonen, X. (1985) A program to increase manual signs with severely/profoundly mentally retarded students in natural environments. *Applied Research in Mental Retardation*, **6**, 147–158.

Duker, P. and Moonen, X. (1986) The effect of two procedures on spontaneous signing with Down's syndrome children. *Journal of Mental Deficiency Research*, **30**, 342–352.

Duker, P. and Morsink, H. (1984) Acquisition and cross-setting generalization of manual signs with severely retarded children. *Journal of Applied Behavior Analysis*, **17**, 93–103.

Duker, P. and Rikken, A. (1990) Assessing transparency of communicative gestures for mentally handicapped individuals. *International Journal of Rehabilitation Research*, **12**, 318–320.

Duker, P. and van Lent, C. (in press) Inducing variability in communicative gestures used by severely retarded individuals. *Journal of Applied Behavior Analysis*.

Duker, P., van Doeselaar, C. and Verstraten, A. (1989) The effect of response-delay on communicative gesturing with mentally handicapped individuals. Unpublished manuscript.

Duker, P., Dortmans, A. and Lodder, E. (1991) Establishing the manding function of communicative gestures. Unpublished manuscript.

Duker, P., Jol, K. and Palmen, A. (in press) The collateral decrease of self-injurious behavior with teaching communicative gestures to severely/profoundly mentally handicapped individuals. *Behavioral Residential Treatment*.

Duker, P., Boonekamp, J., ten Brummelhuis, Y., Hendrix, Y., Hermans, M., van Leeuwe, J. and Seys, D. (1989) Analysis of ward staff initiatives towards mentally retarded residents: Clues for intervention. *Journal of Mental Deficiency Research*, **33**, 55–67.

Durand, V.M. and Carr, E.G. (1987) Social influences on 'self-stimulatory' behavior: Analysis and treatment application. *Journal of Applied Behavior Analysis*, **20**, 119–132.

Durand, V.M. and Crimmins, D.B. (1987) Assessment and treatment of psychotic speech in an autistic child. *Journal of Autism and Developmental Disorders,* **17,** 17–28.

Durand, V.M. and Crimmins, D.B. (1988) Identifying the variables maintaining self-injurious behavior. *Journal of Autism and Developmental Disorders,* **18,** 99–117.

Durand, V.M. and Kishi, G. (1987) Reducing severe behavior problems among persons with dual sensory impairments: An evaluation of a technical assistance model. *Journal of the Association for Persons with Severe Handicaps,* **12,** 2–10.

Dykens, E., Hodapp, R. and Leckman, J. (1989) Adaptive and maladaptive functioning of institutionalized and noninstitutionalized Fragile X males. *Journal of the American Academy of Child and Adolescent Psychiatry,* **28,** 427–430.

Garcia, E. and DeHaven, E.D. (1974) Use of operant techniques in the establishment and generalization of language. *American Journal of Mental Deficiency,* **79,** 169–178.

Gould, G. (1976) Language development and non-verbal skills in severely mentally retarded children: An epidemiological study. *Journal of Mental Deficiency Research,* **20,** 126–146.

Griffith, P.L. and Robinson, J. (1980) Influence of iconicity and phonological similarity on sign learning by mentally retarded children. *American Journal of Mental Deficiency,* **85,** 291–298.

Griffith, R., Robinson, J. and Panagos, J. (1981) Influence of iconicity and phonological similarity on sign learning by mentally retarded children. *Journal of Speech and Hearing Disorders,* **46,** 388–397.

Hoemann, H. (1975) The transparency of meaning of sign language gestures. *Sign Language Studies,* **7,** 151–161.

Hoffmeister, R.J. and Farmer, A. (1972) The development of manual sign language in mentally retarded deaf individuals. *Journal of Rehabilitation of the Deaf,* **6,** 19–26.

Horner, R.H. and Budd, C.M. (1985) Acquisition of manual sign use: Collateral reduction of maladaptive behavior, and factors limiting generalization. *Education and Training in Mental Retardation,* **20,** 39–47.

Kazdin, A.E. (1982) Symptom substitution, generalization, and response covariation: Implications for psychotherapy outcome. *Psychological Bulletin,* **91,** 349–365.

Kiernan, C., Reid, B. and Jones, L. (1982) Signs and symbols: A review of literature and survey of the use of non-vocal communication systems. *Studies in Education, No. 11,* University of London Institute of Education.

Kohl, F. (1981) Effects of motoric requirements on the acquisition of manual sign responses by severely handicapped students. *American Journal of Mental Deficiency,* **85,** 396–403.

Michael, J. (1982) Distinguishing between discriminative and motivational functions of stimuli. *Journal of the Experimental Analysis of Behavior,* **37,** 149–155.

Remington, B. and Clarke, S. (1983) Acquisition of expressive signing by autistic children: An evaluation of the relative effects of simultaneous communication and sign-alone training. *Journal of Applied Behavior Analysis,* **16,** 315–328.

Sanger, D., Stick, S., Sanger., W. and Dawson, K. (1984) Specific syndromes and associated communication disorders: A review. *Journal of Communication Disorders,* **49,** 385–405.

Seys, D., Kersten, H. and Duker, P. (1990) Evaluating a ward staff program for increasing spontaneous and varied communicative gesturing with individuals who are mentally retarded. *Behavioral Residential Treatment,* **5,** 318–328.

Skinner, B.F. (1957) *Verbal Behavior*, Appleton–Century–Crofts, New York.

Talkington, L. and Hall, S. (1969) Hearing impairment and aggressiveness in mentally retarded. *Perceptual and Motor Skills*, **28**, 303–306.

Talkington, L., Hall, S. and Altman, R. (1971) Communication deficits and aggression in the mentally retarded. *American Journal of Mental Deficiency*, **76**, 235–237.

Talkington, L., Hall, S. and Cleland, C. (1971) Behavioral correlates of noncommunicators. *Psychological Records*, **21**, 213–217.

Touchette, P. (1971) Transfer of stimulus control: Measuring the moment of transfer. *Journal of the Experimental Analysis of Behavior*, **15**, 347–354.

Yamamoto, J. and Mochizuki, A. (1988) Acquisition and functional analysis of manding with autistic students. *Journal of Applied Behavior Analysis*, **21**, 57–64.

Chapter 9

Beginning an Augmentative Communication System with Individuals who Have Severe Disabilities[1]

JOE REICHLE, JEFF SIGAFOOS AND
BOB REMINGTON

INTRODUCTION

The past fifteen years have produced remarkable improvements in our ability to establish functional communication skills among people with the most extreme mental and physical handicaps. Often, such individuals have not benefited much from intervention programs designed to teach speech: for them, the development of communication systems using gestural or graphic modes which can act as an augmentative or alternative to speech represents a major advance. Research has provided procedures of proven effectiveness for establishing functional communication skills, giving teachers an array of options for designing intervention programs.

Once a decision has been made to use augmentative or alternative communication, the next choice that must be made is which system should be used to supplement or replace the vocal mode. Sign language and other gestural mode systems are appropriate for many people (see Duker and Remington, this volume). Graphic, or symbol-based, systems represent the other option. Because many individuals can sometimes utilize a combination of vocal, gestural and graphic modes, matching

[1] Preparation of this work was supported in part by Contract No. 300–82–0363 awarded to the University of Minnesota from the Division of Innovation and Development, Special Education Programmes, US Department of Education. The opinions expressed herein do not necessarily reflect the position or policy of the US Department of Education and no official endorsement should be inferred.

modes to communicative contexts is a critical issue in intervention. In this chapter, we will consider in detail the use of graphic modes, although many of the issues which arise are relevant to any form of communication.

The choice of a graphic-based system raises a host of additional questions. First, how should the symbol type be selected so that its use might be most easily acquired, maintained and generalized? Graphic symbols include photos, line drawings, and product logos. We also need to know the optimal level of specificity for the symbols (from general, e.g. 'food', to specific, e.g. 'Oreo'). Secondly, there is an issue concerning how symbols should be accessed. In direct selection, learners choose a symbol by touching it. Alternatively, a scanning technique provides choices sequentially, and when the desired symbol is reached the learner indicates this with a discrete response (e.g., a head nod). We will discuss both of these techniques.

Once the system has been selected, other obstacles to its implementation remain. One major difficulty concerns the controversy regarding the point in a learner's cognitive development at which such interventions should first be attempted. It has been argued that learners who do not show certain levels of cognitive development will not benefit from intervention. We will argue that the difficulties proposed are exaggerated, and that intervention need not necessarily await the achievement of particular developmental targets.

Another important issue faced by teachers concerns their choice of which specific functional classes of communicative behavior should be taught. We will describe two functional classes, which correspond loosely to requests and provisions of information ('mands' and 'tacts'), and outline interventions for establishing them. We will also consider which of these classes is best taught initially, and discuss the nature of generalization between them. We will look in some detail at how situational factors affect symbol use within functional classes. At a more applied level, we will show the importance of matching learners' communicative repertoires to the classes that will best serve them in their natural environments. We will discuss ways in which control over symbol use can be established so as to promote spontaneous, rather than prompted, communication (e.g., requesting food when hungry).

In the past, communication intervention programs often focused on speech and emphasized the acquisition of grammatical structures, sometimes to the detriment of teaching skills that enable learners to convey their needs efficiently. The resulting period of failure provided ample opportunity for socially inappropriate behaviors to enter their repertoire to fill the communicative void (see Durand and Crimmins, this volume). The early introduction of an augmentative system, together with intervention programs designed to teach functional communication skills, represents a powerful alternative to these earlier approaches.

SELECTING AND USING SYMBOLS FOR ALTERNATIVE COMMUNICATION

Selecting a symbol set

Typically, graphic communication systems consist of line drawings, photographs, or more abstract symbols that learners are taught to select in ways that are functionally equivalent to speaking a word or phrase. Typically, symbols are housed in a small fabric wallet, in a notebook, on a communication board, or lap-tray. Graphic mode communication systems offer several distinct advantages for a person with severe disabilities. First, graphic mode systems are community friendly: a graphic with a printed message below it is understandable even to those with no prior experience with the system or its user. Secondly, graphic representations permit very explicit representations of referents. For example, the logos on packages may be used to represent their contents. Finally, symbols offer a permanent display, lessening the memory burden on the learner.

Given that graphics are suitable for an individual, several specifics of the chosen system and how to teach it must be determined. For example, there are a plethora of two-dimensional symbol systems from which the teacher can select (e.g., Rebus, Bliss, Pic, Pic Syms).

Rebus symbols, for example, are relatively more guessable (iconic) to a naive communication partner than Bliss symbols. It is possible to decide which system to adopt for a particular learner by comparing the ease of the acquisition of symbols selected from different systems. There are several empirically based reports which make this kind of comparison. Hurlbut, Iwata and Green (1982), for example, compared Bliss and more iconic Rebus-like symbol responses. In the acquisition phase, participants were shown an object and asked 'What is this?' Correct responses (indicating the corresponding symbols from *either* the Bliss *or* iconic symbol sets) were reinforced. A participant might, for example, name a 'watch' by pointing to a Bliss symbol for this item, but name a 'shirt' by pointing to an iconic symbol for 'shirt'. Following acquisition, probes were implemented to assess performance with both symbol systems. For all three multiply handicapped participants, the more iconic symbols excelled in measures of acquisition, generalization, maintenance, and spontaneous use. In addition, that superiority typically became apparent in less than five training sessions. In a similar study, Clark (1981) employed intervention procedures with normal pre-schoolers to compare recall rates for Bliss, Rebus, and printed words. Iconic symbols were again found to be superior. Thus, large differences in performance on graphics systems may often be attributed to the type of symbols used.

This raises the additional question, however, of which type of graphic symbol is the more iconic. In fact, some group comparison studies (e.g., Mirenda and Locke, 1989) have found color photographs to be superior to both monochrome photographs and line drawings. It is, however, entirely possible that because of idiosyncratic learning histories, some learners may more readily acquire symbols assumed to be less iconic. For example, learners familiar with the Bliss system might perform as well with novel Bliss symbols as with an iconic symbol system. Determining the impact of the symbol iconicity variable is thus an empirical question.

Finally, although it would be more orderly if all symbols within a particular symbol collection or symbol system were of equal guessability, it appears that they are not: within symbol collections there may be significant variability (Bloomberg, 1984). This lack of homogeneity makes it virtually impossible to choose a single symbol system if the criterion is finding the most guessable symbols.

Because systematic evaluation of individual learners' performance of the kind adopted by Hurlbut, Iwata and Green (1982) is often difficult to implement in applied settings, there is a need to develop and validate assessment procedures that are manageable under more typical educational conditions. Given these kinds of difficulties, it may be most practical to take advantage of any symbol systems which already operate in a learner's environment. For example, some learners may have already been exposed to many incidental pairings of a product logo with the receipt and consumption of the product itself. These pairings suggest that, through classical conditioning, learners will associate the logo with the product, and thus rapidly learn to use the former symbolically.

Clearly, selecting a communication system represents a particularly challenging task. The aim is to choose symbols that are the most readily identifiable to the learner, and thus most rapidly learned and best maintained, but it is also important to select those symbols that are the easiest to present in a small display. In some respects, this issue is more involved than simply selecting a symbol type that, in the short run, is most easily acquired and best maintained. For example, Bliss symbols may initially be chosen because research suggests that they are acquired more easily than printed words (Clark, 1981). The real issue, however, may be how many teaching opportunities would be needed to teach the printed word directly in comparison with those needed first to teach Bliss symbols plus those required to shift stimulus control from the Bliss symbols to the printed words.

Another selection issue concerns deciding how specifically to represent initial vocabulary. Often, communication program content is based on normal developmental sequences. For example, Bloom and Lahey (1974) suggested teaching vocabulary that represented an intermediate level of specificity, based on available data describing vocabulary acquisition among intellectually normal children. For example, in the hierarchy collie/dog/animal, 'dog' would be taught first. It was argued that, over time, the learner would acquire both more specific and more general descriptors. This is certainly true of normal language development (Anglin, 1977). However, typically these results are obtained in tasks which involve learning the names of objects. It is unclear, therefore, if similar advantages would pertain when teaching communicative behavior which functions to request or reject objects or activities. Nevertheless, an intermediate level of specificity *might* serve as a compromise that maximizes the number of opportunities for using a request successfully while minimizing the probability that a listener will not understand what is needed. For example, listeners may be less likely to misunderstand the request 'juice' than a more general type of request, such as 'want'. In addition, a request for 'juice' symbol can be reinforced even when one particular flavor of juice is not available. We will return to the issue of the specificity of vocabulary later when we discuss functional classes of communicative behavior.

Choosing a technique to access the communication board

Decisions related to the design of graphic communication systems are not limited to questions of symbol type, but also concern how a learner can best select a displayed symbol. Many can use direct selection by pointing with a finger, hand, or perhaps a mouth stick. Others who, because of motor impairments, cannot point directly may require a method that circumvents direct selection. 'Scanning' is an alternative selection technique in which the listener (or a microcomputer) offers a series of discrete symbol choices to the learner. When a symbol corresponding to the desired message is offered, the learner must emit a discrete 'selection' response. With augmentative communication systems, direct selection usually allows symbols to be accessed relatively quickly. However, for persons with severe motor deficits, symbols may have to be inordinately large, or spaced very far apart, for effective direct selection. Here, the use of a scanning selection technique allows symbols to be smaller and placed close together on the learner's communication board to save space.

Without some quantifiable comparison of performance using measures such a speed of symbol access and endurance in repetitively selecting symbols, there is a danger that the choice of selection technique can become arbitrary. In addition, a learner might occasionally benefit from both direct selection and scanning techniques depending upon the situation. This is analogous to what happens among normal children interacting with their caregivers. For example, when a 2-year-old child who wants some ketchup cannot *say* 'ketchup', she points to the condiments at the center of the table and says 'want it'. Her father may then touch each condiment saying 'this one?' as he does so. When he touches the ketchup, the child nods approvingly. Conversely, had she wanted milk she would simply have said 'milk' since she was able to produce that word. Thus, in some situations, normal children rely on a combination of scanning and direct selection to communicate.

COGNITIVE PREREQUISITES

Once a symbol set and a means of selecting symbols has been chosen, it may be possible to begin teaching it. However, as late as 1980, prominent scholars were suggesting that the successful implementation of an augmentative communication system was predicated on a number of cognitive prerequisites which are often absent in the most likely candidates for communication intervention (Chapman and Miller, 1980; Shane, 1980). The basis for this view was deeply rooted in classes of behavior exhaustively described by Piaget (1929). Frequently cited behavioral prerequisites have included evidence of more sophisticated aspects of imitation, object permanency and means/end behavior. It was assumed that unless or until learners developed behaviors characteristic of these underlying cognitive abilities, implementation of procedures to teach communicative skills would not be successful. This meant that many persons with severe disabilities were, in effect, without intervention options.

Rather than postponing attempts to teach functional communication skills until the learner attains a certain level of cognitive development, it may be possible to intervene directly, either by teaching sufficient exemplars of the cognitive class or by circumventing the need for behaviors in that class altogether. We will consider several cognitive classes that have received significant attention as 'prerequisites'.

Imitation

Imitation involves performance of a vocal or motor behavior modeled by another. There is ample evidence to show that people with severe disabilities can be taught to imitate speech and gestures (Baer, Peterson and Sherman, 1967; Lovaas *et al.*, 1966). In the gestural mode, imitation is taught by the teacher modeling the sign to be taught, then physically guiding or 'molding' the learner's hand(s). Correct responding is reinforced, and 'molding' is faded across teaching opportunities until the learner imitates the teacher's model without prompting. Because learners with severe disabilities can be taught to imitate directly, the initial absence of an imitative repertoire need not prevent intervention aimed at establishing communicative behavior.

It could be argued that the fact that most children learn to imitate at about the same time that their communicative production repertoire begins to expand does not necessarily establish imitation as a cognitive prerequisite. At least some (i.e., Lovaas *et al.*, 1966) felt that imitation training was important, not because imitation was a cognitive prerequisite, but rather because providing an imitative model represented an efficient response prompt. There are few prompting techniques that can be implemented to ensure that non-vocal learners will attempt to speak a word associated with a referent. That is, vocal forms of behavior are not as easily prompted as attempts at graphic or gestural mode communication. Consequently, the initial importance of establishing an imitative repertoire may be somewhat specific to the establishment of communication in the vocal mode.

Object permanency

Object permanency is another Piagetian cognitive class which has been proposed as a prerequisite for communication intervention. The basis for this is the assumption that before learners can be taught to communicate with reference to objects, they must first have developed the concept that objects continue to exist even when they may not be currently present or visible. Children are said to exhibit this cognitive skill when they produce behaviors such as searching for a previously visible, but now hidden, object. It is possible, however, that a well-designed program could be implemented for teaching this skill to learners with severe disabilities. Consider, for example, a learner who will reach for and take a preferred food item. Initially, the item may be placed in full view, perhaps, for example, in a cupboard with the door open. Once a history of reaching for the item is established in this fully visible state, the cupboard door could be gradually closed. At each step of this process, less of the preferred item would remain visible until, at some point, the learner would be required to open the cupboard door to obtain it. At this stage the learner is engaging in behavior which, if generalized, would be said to reveal the underlying Piagetian concept of object permanency. Object permanency is also relevant to the mode of communication. While both signs and spoken words are somewhat transient in nature, the vocabulary items used in symbol systems are relatively permanent and may thus reduce the constraints on performance implied by 'out-of-sight, out-of-mind' characterization of lack of object permanency.

Means–end

Means–end represents a cognitive class of behavior evidenced in the strategies that children use to obtain desired items and events. Normally developing children between 12 and 18 months begin using adults as agents of procurement, for example, by attracting an adult's attention before pointing to a toy placed out of reach. Means–end behavior can thus be seen in the behavior emitted by a speaker to recruit the attention of a potential listener. Logically, this type of behavior can be viewed as a sequence of two quite separable component skills: recruiting the attention of a listener and producing the desired message. Of course, in vocal communication, the two functions are interlinked. The localized auditory stimulation produced as a person speaks implicitly requests the attention of his listener.

In traditional interventions, opportunities to communicate were often provided only when the learner already had the attention of the teacher. Under these conditions, there is no need for the learner to engage in a separate attention-recruiting behavior. Keogh and Reichle (1985) have suggested that a teacher could choose either component skill as an initial intervention target or address both concurrently. Reichle (1989) therefore taught a participant both component behaviors. Initially, intervention established discriminative use of graphic symbols to request preferred items. During this part of the study, the participant always had the attention of the teacher. After the discriminated requesting using symbols was established, probe opportunities were introduced in which the participant did not have the teacher's attention, and data were obtained to determine if he would seek to attract it before making a request. Because he did not, steps were taken to teach him to use an attention-recruiting signal. During approximately 75% of the requesting opportunities, the teacher initially avoided attending. For example, when the participant arrived in a new environment (e.g., the kitchen of his home), a preferred object was present, perhaps placed on the table, but as he attempted to reach it a second adult directed him to the teacher and prompted an attention-getting response (moving 3–6 feet to the teacher, tapping her on the shoulder).

Figure 9.1 shows how such a procedure worked with Al, a 27-year-old individual described as autistic. At the start of intervention, Al had no formal communicative repertoire: he did not speak, use signs, or symbols, and a measure of infant development (Uzgiris and Hunt, 1975) showed that he did not attempt to use others as agents. During the baseline phase of this study, Al signaled his desire for objects by attempting to get them directly, rather than using symbols as requests, or attempting to recruit the attention of a listener.

During intervention, Al was taught to request access to each of two items (a radio and a Diet Coke) by pointing to line drawings of those objects. In keeping with the more general intervention procedures described by Keogh and Reichle (1985), requests for the two items were taught, initially when the teacher was attending to the participant. On half of these occasions, Coke was presented in an array of items available as snacks during break time, but access to the radio was not available. On the remaining opportunities, Coke was replaced by the radio. This ensured that the teacher could determine whether Al's requests were

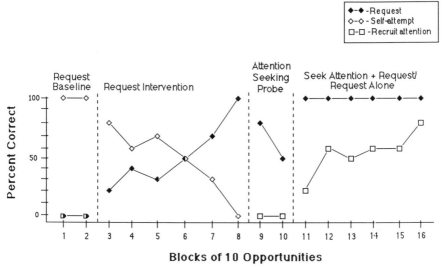

Figure 9.1 The effect of teaching an attention recruiting response to a man with autism (see text for explanation).

correct. (Only requests for the currently available item were considered correct.) The availability of an item thus constituted part of the antecedent condition under which pointing to a line drawing would be reinforced by access to the corresponding object.

Once requests for these two items were established, probes were used to determine what Al would do during requesting opportunities when the teacher was not attending to him. Objects were placed near him, but in a locked cabinet with windows (allowing the desired items to be easily seen), and no listener was present. Al's typical response during the probes was to emit the previously learned requests without attempting to obtain an adult's attention. Figure 9.1 shows, however, that the subsequent intervention ('seek attention + request/request alone') was highly successful. Al was taught to move to a listener and tap his or her shoulder to recruit attention on those occasions when he did not have it, thus establishing the conditional use of a communicative behavior. In the presence of an attending listener, Al's use of symbols as requests resulted in reinforcement; but in the absence of a listener, Al learned to refrain from requesting until he had obtained a listener's attention.

In the context of establishing an initial communicative repertoire, it is unclear what represents the most beneficial strategy for sequencing the teaching of the two skills that have just been described. There are at least three possibilities: teach attention-getting followed by discriminative use of symbols; teach symbol discrimination followed by attention-seeking; or teach both concurrently. At present, there are no empirical data that address this issue. It is possible that the most efficient sequencing strategy is learner specific. For example, with learners who typically isolate themselves from others, teaching the use of symbols as a means of requesting before establishing communicative partners as mediators may be most efficient. Conversely, for many other learners, attention may serve as a very powerful reinforcer.

To summarize, there are empirical data suggesting that certain cognitive classes of behavior may not need to emerge 'naturally' before successful attempts can be made to establish an initial communicative repertoire. Reichle and Karlan (1985) reviewed the data regarding the relationships among the acquisition of an initial augmentative communication repertoire and imitation, object permanency, and means–end. They concluded that the presence of each of the classes of behavior commensurate with a level of performance of a normal child between 12 and 18 months (sensorimotor stage 5) might potentially facilitate the acquisition of an initial repertoire of communicative behavior. That is, it may require less intervention to establish communicative repertoires in such individuals than in others not yet at this stage. However, there was no evidence to suggest that the presence of these classes of behavior constituted a prerequisite, i.e. that communicative behaviors could not be established among learners thought to be functioning below sensorimotor stage 5 (as evidenced by the lack of imitative or object permanency behavior). Interestingly, both groups of authors who carried out the original work in this area (Chapman and Miller, 1980; Shane, 1980) have most recently suggested that the cognitive skills previously cited should no longer be considered prerequisites for the implementation of communication intervention (e.g., Shane and McCormick, in press).

TEACHING FUNCTIONAL CLASSES OF COMMUNICATIVE BEHAVIOR

Functional classes of communicative behavior

Communicative behavior may be emitted for a variety of reasons. For example, when thirsty, one might request a beverage. When offered a trip to the dentist, one may decline the offer. On a sunny day, one may comment to a neighbor about how warm it is. Each of these situations involves different reasons for interacting, or different communicative intents. Interestingly, communicative intents are not necessarily vocabulary specific. For example, a person can say 'cookie' to direct a listener's attention to a cookie that has fallen on the floor (comment/provide information), or to object when everyone else in the room was given one (protest), or upon seeing cookies in a shop window, to obtain one (request). A learner's skill in using a particular vocabulary item across different functional classes constitutes an important area of generalized use of communication that has received only limited attention in the literature (see also Goodman and Remington, this volume).

In a functional analysis of communicative behavior, an important distinction has been made between two classes of behavior which are frequently taught to learners with severe disabilities. These two classes have been termed mands and tacts. Skinner (1957) defined a mand as 'a verbal operant in which the response is reinforced by a characteristic consequence and is therefore under the functional control of relevant conditions of deprivation or aversive stimulation' (pp. 35–36). In more familiar terms, mands include 'requesting' and 'rejecting' utterances. For example, when thirsty, a learner may point to a 'water' symbol. This behavior is reinforced as a mand when the teacher then supplies the learner with a glass of water. A tact, in contrast, is defined as 'a verbal operant in which a response of a given form is evoked . . . by a particular object or event or property of an object or event' (pp. 81–82). One type of tact, then, consists of naming objects to comment or provide information. A passenger in an airplane on a transatlantic flight may look out the window and say 'water'. Under these conditions the passenger sitting next to her is likely to provide some type of social reinforcement (e.g., 'Yes. I see. And quite a lot of it') rather than attempting to supply a glass of water. Traditionally, communication intervention programs for persons with severe disabilities have not distinguished clearly between mands and tacts. A learner might, for example, be shown an object and asked 'What is this?' When the object was correctly named, the learner would often be given that object as a consequence. In this type of intervention sequence, the antecedent is more akin to a tact, whereas the consequence is more akin to a mand.

Recently, intervention programs have recognized the importance of distinguishing between procedures for establishing mands and tacts (e.g., Cipani, 1988; Keogh and Reichle, 1985; Sundberg, 1980). Although the same symbol can be used in both functional contexts, there is a growing database which suggests that responses taught as names (tacts) will not necessarily generalize to a requesting (mand) task, and vice versa. This functional independence of mands and tacts has been demonstrated with pre-school children (Lamarre and Holland, 1985) and among individuals with severe disabilities (Hall and Sundberg, 1987; Romski, Sevcik and Pate, 1988; Sigafoos, Doss and Reichle, 1989). Evidence such as this suggests that learners will often need separate intervention procedures that systematically establish both mands and tacts, and this raises a number of questions concerning how best to teach these functions.

Teaching initial mand and tact repertoires

Although we suspect that it is beneficial to establish discrimination between manding and tacting in the early phases of learning a communicative repertoire, it is unclear whether this should be done initially by making some symbols specific to one or other functional relationship, or whether it is possible to teach the functional discrimination using the same symbols. For example, is it possible first to teach a learner to name an object (e.g., 'What is this?' Answer: 'Coke'), and second, that on some occasions, those prefaced by 'What do you want?', 'Coke' can actually be used to obtain the item (i.e., a request)? There are data indicating that when specific symbols are mastered first as requests, learners have difficulty using them to express a tacting function. Savage-Rumbaugh (1984), for example, experienced difficulty in teaching chimps to use lexigrams acquired as mands in a tacting context. Chimps made many errors, showed emotional disturbance, and eventually responded less frequently. Thus, it appears that reinforcing the learner with an item that matches the symbol, as in manding function, establishes a certain expectancy which, when violated, produces deterioration in the discriminative use of the symbol. It is unclear whether reversing the order in which vocabulary is assigned functions by teaching tacting first would ameliorate the problem just described.

Thus far, our discussion has focused on mands that result in the learner procuring objects. Rejecting also can be thought of as a variety of mand which operates in a negative rather than a positive reinforcement paradigm. Occasionally we have encountered learners with little interest in sharing information with others, but who are motivated to avoid certain everyday events. The issue of sequencing initial communicative functions becomes slightly more complex when one considers adding an initial repertoire of rejecting as an intervention option.

One program we developed illustrates the potential pitfalls of establishing rejecting as the initial communicative function taught. It was difficult to identify objects or events that were attractive to Michael, a man with developmental disabilities, but very easy to identify foods and activities that he found undesirable. Consequently, we implemented a program to teach generalized rejecting as his first communicative behavior. Michael readily acquired a generalized reject gesture, but as he became more proficient in producing it, we noticed that it got harder to create instructional opportunities. Michael had come to anticipate that when individuals approached him, there was a fair chance that he would be offered something aversive. Because staff never offered strong reinforcers, Michael had learned that the wisest strategy was to keep his distance from them. In effect, the program taught him to be more self-isolative. This extreme example reveals the potential difficulty of teaching rejecting in the absence of other concurrently implemented communicative responses. Teachers run the risk of establishing themselves as conditioned negative reinforcers.

There are a number of further options available when attempting to determine which functional classes of behavior to establish as a learner's initial communicative repertoire. These relate to the specificity of the symbols taught. For example, the symbol 'want' could be taught as a generalized mand which can be used in a range of situations, or more specific mand symbols (e.g., coke, radio) could be taught. One alternative is to teach generalized and explicit requesting concurrently; a second is to teach generalized mand symbol concurrently with more specific symbols taught as tacts. Eventually, it might be possible for a learner to combine these skills to produce specific requesting chains that consist of 'want + (object name)'. Keogh and Reichle (1985) reasoned that being able to request objects by combining symbols (e.g., 'want milk'), and to name objects with single symbols (e.g. 'milk'), would be highly advantageous.

Keogh and Reichle (1985) developed the argument for beginning requesting intervention by teaching a single symbol ('want') that could act as a generalized request for a large class of objects. There are two advantages to this approach. First, the teacher can maximize teaching opportunities by avoiding the possibility that a learner might satiate on a single type of item that is likely to be requested. For example, the use of the symbol for 'cola' as a request would be limited significantly by the learner's eventual satiation with fizzy drinks. However, teaching a highly generalized symbol 'want' allows a wide variety of other items to be used should the learner become satiated on any one item. Similarly, using a generalized symbol as an initial intervention target could result in a significantly greater number of different teaching opportunities across a range of settings and situations than would have been available if an explicit symbol were utilized. This may be particularly important for people with the most severe handicaps. The primary disadvantages in establishing specific requests occur if learners quickly satiate on item(s) requested, or if their preferences shift over time such that some specific mands may no longer be relevant. Conversely, the primary advantage of teaching specific mands is that they will be more informative to listeners, lessening their need to rely on situational content to aid understanding. An additional advantage of teaching more specific mands during the initial stages of intervention relates to the possibility of capitalizing on past learning experiences by using specific product logos as graphic symbols. Table 9.1 summarizes advantages and disadvantages associated with highly generalized and more explicit mands.

Generalization of communicative intents to more complex situations

Although evidence suggests that individuals with severe disabilities do not readily generalize the use of a symbol across different functional classes of communicative behavior (e.g., mands and tacts), it is also important to know how well learners generalize their use within a single class of functional communication.

The bulk of existing language generalization research has focused stimulus generalization across persons, settings, and characteristics of actual referents. Investigations of response generalization, for the most part, have focused on the combinations of previously established vocabulary into unique previously untrained structures (Remington, Watson and Light, 1990). Within a single functional class (e.g., mands), however, subtle generalization issues still remain unexplored. For

Table 9.1 Advantages and disadvantages of generalized and explicit mands

Generalized	Explicit

Advantages

Generalized	Explicit
1. Reduces the influence that satiation might play 2. Reduces the influence that a shift in the learner's preferences over time might play 3. Provides the learner with communicative behavior that can be used in a greater variety of situations 4. Allows the interventionist to conduct a potentially greater number of intervention opportunities dispersed throughout the learner's day	1. Allows the listener to rely less on redundant contextual information to decipher message 2. Maximizes the possibility that the learner may already discriminate among some product logos that have been associated with highly reinforcing items

Disadvantages

Generalized	Explicit
1. Increases the communicative demands on the listener to decipher the learner's message Consequently, more generalized symbols tend to be less useful in community environments	1. Reduces the variety of situations in which a symbol can be used 2. Potentially limits the range of intervention opportunities 3. Increases the potential influence that satiation may have on program implementation 4. Increases the possibility that shifting preferences could sabotage program

example, we usually think of a generalized rejecting response 'no thanks' as a mand used to avoid undesired items. To maximize the probability that this relationship is established, teachers select highly non-preferred items as the focus of intervention. Interestingly, however, a relatively large proportion of rejecting responses follow the offer of an item that is usually reinforcing but, because of experience in the immediate past (e.g, habituation or satiation), has temporarily lost its reinforcing properties. For example, after drinking five cups of coffee, we may say 'no thanks' when offered a sixth. To investigate this issue, we examined whether participants with severe intellectual delays would use a generalized reject gesture after satiation. All were first taught to emit the gesture in the presence of highly nonpreferred objects/events. Two probe conditions were then implemented. During one, we offered objects/events that were highly undesirable, but had never been used before in the study. During the other probe condition, participants were *repeatedly* offered preferred items or activities to create a state of satiation. Both types of opportunity continued until participants either emitted the generalized reject gesture or engaged in any discrete behavior that could be reliably coded as escape. Participants readily generalized the use of the gesture only to those items that had a history of being highly nonpreferred. In a separate case study (Reichle, 1987), a participant was taught to use a generalized reject symbol to avoid items that were nonpreferred, and a generalized request symbol to obtain items that functioned as reinforcers. Objects associated with these two response classes did not overlap. After initial training, satiation was used to create probe opportunities in which the participant would be motivated to reject an item that had previously occasioned only a requesting response. The participant, who regularly requested coffee at breakfast, was offered up to six refills, and any escape/avoidance behavior following each offer was recorded. Although he readily became satiated, and either stopped drinking coffee or left the environment, the participant failed to use the rejecting gesture that he had been taught. However, in the same setting when offered a normally nonpreferred beverage, he readily used the rejecting gesture. It thus appears from both these studies that, for handicapped learners, a rejecting response does not generalize from external stimuli to internal cues associated with satiation. Effective intervention must therefore address the subtleties of prior exposure and reinforcement history relating to potential positive and negative reinforcers.

There are many instances in which very subtle aspects of the environment appear to serve as discriminative stimuli occasioning particular forms of communicative behavior. Utterances manding one's removal from a situation or termination of an activity provide some examples. Leave-taking may be cued by undesirable settings (e.g., the dentist's office); a setting which, although normally enjoyed, proves disappointing (e.g. a cinema visit to a boring movie); or the need to quit doing something interesting to meet an obligation (e.g., stop shooting baskets to practice piano). Finally, a leave-taking utterance may be emitted to quit a situation without terminating a social interaction, as when 'let's go' means 'let's leave together'.

Often, initial communicative exchanges with learners are characterized by an adult initiation followed by a single response (Reichle, York and Eynon, 1989). As communicative behavior becomes more sophisticated, initiation is likely to be followed by a sequence of utterances that first maintain the exchange, and finally terminate it. We know very little about how well learners with severe handicaps can be taught to initiate, maintain, and terminate interactions. The majority of investigators who have attempted to teach conversational skills have focused on establishing information sharing. For example, Gaylord-Ross *et al.* (1984) taught students with severe handicaps to use communication boards to share information with their normal peers. Although this function is important, for some learners it may not be the most salient. Rather, they may be more inclined to engage in extended chains of interaction that focus on obtaining or maintaining access to an activity, or obtaining sustained assistance during work activity (e.g., cleaning a room as long as another individual is working alongside them).

Regardless of the reason for more sustained interactions, learners should eventually be able to use their communicative repertoire to initiate, maintain and terminate interactions. Although some symbols may be unique to one or other of these components, we suspect that most can be used across all three. If learners have difficulty generalizing the use of vocabulary across communicative intents such as requesting, rejecting, and describing, it is questionable whether communicative intents will generalize across the temporal components of an interaction. As yet, we know very little about how graphic symbol-based communication can be used to initiate, maintain and terminate interactional exchanges, or how these functions can be taught. This area would appear to be a critical topic for future empirical scrutiny.

MORE SUBTLE ISSUES IN ESTABLISHING SPONTANEOUS COMMUNICATION

Clearly, our ability to establish an initial communicative repertoire has improved significantly in recent years. Nevertheless, several areas remain problematic. Repertoires taught to learners with developmental disabilities are often characterized by a lack of spontaneity (Carr and Kologinsky, 1983; Charlop, Schreibman and Thibodeau, 1985; Gobbi *et al.*, 1986; Halle, 1987). Although various definitions for spontaneity have been offered, most define it by default. Spontaneous communication has been defined as that which occurs in the absence of an imitative model (Bricker and Bricker, 1974; Charlop, Schreibman and Thibodeau, 1985), or in the absence of explicit instructions such as 'Tell me what you want', or 'What's this?' (Beisler and Tsai, 1983; Hart and Risley, 1968). Communicative behavior that is occasioned by the speech of others, although important, is often less functional than that for which interoceptive states serve as discriminative stimuli (e.g., requests for food and drinks that are prompted by hunger and thirst, respectively).

Several investigators (e.g, Charlop, Schreibman and Thibodeau, 1985; Halle, 1987) have suggested that the stimuli controlling a repertoire of verbal behavior can be arranged along a continuum of spontaneity. Generally, when a given class of verbal behavior is controlled by physical prompts, imitative models, or questions, it is considered less spontaneous than if controlled by contextual cues (e.g., requesting help to open a stuck door) or interoceptive stimuli (e.g., requesting water when thirsty). Bringing communicative behavior under the control of more natural discriminative stimuli presents some unique challenges worth considering in greater detail.

Contextual cues and interoceptive states with motivating functions can themselves be viewed as distinct. Michael (1982, 1987, 1988) distinguished these two types of motivational variables, referring to the former as 'conditioned' and the latter as 'unconditioned' establishing operations. An establishing operation is 'any change in the environment which alters the effectiveness of some object or event as reinforcement and simultaneously alters the momentary frequency of the behavior that has been followed by that reinforcement' (Michael, 1982, pp. 150–151). For example, deprivation with respect to food is an environmental change that alters the significance of food by making it an effective type of reinforcement. Because of this change, behaviors which in the past resulted in access to food, such as picking, or requesting, an apple, are more likely to occur.

Establishing operations that do not depend on a past learning history are said to be 'unconditioned'. No one has to learn to be hungry or thirsty, and a hungry person does not need to learn the reinforcing effect of food nor a thirsty person that of water. (Of course, the actual behaviors which result in food or water are subject to selection by contingencies.) The other type of establishing operations ('conditioned' establishing operations) depend upon a learning history. For example, a person must learn that if confronted with apple sauce, steak, or salad, then spoons, knives, or forks (respectively) have reinforcing effects. The receipt of, say apple sauce, is thus an establishing stimulus; that is, a change in the environment that renders spoons reinforcing, thereby increasing the momentary frequency of any behavior which has in the past resulted in obtaining a spoon (e.g., searching the kitchen, asking for a spoon).

Bringing communicative behavior such as requesting under the control of such conditioned establishing operations is, in principle, no different from that used to develop control by questions, objects, or persons, and transfer of stimulus control procedures have been successfully used (see also Duker and Remington, this volume). The unique challenge, however, is in creating the motivational conditions under which requesting will occur. Hall and Sundberg (1987) manipulated conditioned establishing operations by withholding from two adolescents with severe intellectual impairments the utensils (e.g., can opener, cup) required to complete activities (e.g., opening a can of fruit, making soup). Time-delay and prompt/fading procedures were used to transfer control of sign production from imitative models or displayed objects to the conditioned establishing operations. Eventually, spontaneous requests for utensils occurred appropriately. Once the utensils had been obtained, the chain of behaviors leading to the terminal reinforcer (e.g., eating the soup) could proceed. Sigafoos, Doss and Reichle (1989) created similar conditioned establishing operations by withholding the utensils required to access previously requested foods and beverages. Spontaneous requests for these utensils were established by fading control from the presence of the objects.

Reichle, Anderson and Schermer (1986) manipulated the difficulty of unwrapping the twist tie of a bread package to establish spontaneous requests for assistance in an adult with autism. After the participant had requested bread in a sandwich-making task, he was confronted with either a loosely or tightly wrapped package. In the former case, he could continue with the task independently, but he could not access the bread from the tightly wrapped bag. Under the latter condition, he was taught to point to a 'help' symbol. His mand was reinforced by unwrapping the package. These studies have each extended transfer of stimulus control procedures to bring requests under the control of conditioned establishing operations created by arranging the environment to provide opportunities for requests. Teaching the appropriate *conditional* use of symbols in this way is essential for flexible communication.

Goetz, Gee and Sailor (1985) investigated a different method of creating motivational conditions. Two adolescents with severe mental handicaps learned to point to an appropriate symbol either to initiate a task such as toast-making, or to continue with it when it was interrupted. Participants made unprompted symbol selections more frequently during opportunities provided by interruptions of the activity (where symbol use resulted in continuation of the task) than they did to initiate the activity. Hunt *et al.* (1986) later replicated the superiority of this 'interrupted behavior chain strategy'. One explanation for its efficacy is that continuation of an in-progress task not only gets participants back 'on track' towards the terminal reinforcer (e.g., eating the toast), but also provides negative reinforcement through escape from the aversive stimulation of task interruption. Both Goetz, Gee and Sailor (1985) and Hunt *et al.* (1986) showed that such interruptions were somewhat upsetting. In addition, stimuli associated with completing later steps in a chain of behaviors often function as more powerful positive (conditioned) reinforcers than do changes resulting from earlier steps. Interrupted-chain strategies may therefore work in part because reinforcers more closely follow the communicative responses made in the midst of an interrupted task than those made at its inception.

One rationale frequently offered for teaching verbal behavior to persons with developmental disabilities is to help them to 'express wants and needs'. For example, requests for a warm sweater or for the cooling effects of a fan are most spontaneous (and beneficial) when the speaker is too cold or too warm (respectively). But the terms 'hunger', 'thirst', 'cold', and 'warm', as used above, refer to private events (Skinner, 1945, 1953), which—by definition—cannot be independently verified by direct means (Schnaitter, 1978). This presents a significant challenge. Bringing verbal behavior under stimulus control depends upon differential reinforcement with respect to the presence of the relevant stimuli, but if the presence of the relevant controlling variables (e.g., hunger, thirst) cannot be verified independently, mands cannot be differentially reinforced with respect to them—at least not in a very precise manner.

The problem created by privacy has not been adequately addressed when teaching verbal behavior to persons with severe handicaps. In teaching requests for edibles, for example, it has usually been assumed, often safely, that the learners were hungry. Request teaching has also been incorporated into mealtime or snack routines (Gobbi *et al.*, 1986; McCook *et al.*, 1988) which may increase the probability of contacting a relevant state of deprivation, and the subsequent consumption of requested edibles has been taken as evidence that the relevant motivational condition (i.e., hunger) was present.

Skinner (1945) described several ways a verbal repertoire controlled by private establishing operations could be set up. First, interoceptive states can be inferred by certain 'public accompaniments'. Thus we may infer that a person sitting in the Florida sun is hot, and 'goose flesh' frequently appears when one is cold. These public accompaniments could then set the occasion for teaching individuals to request a cold beverage or a warm coat, which may perhaps facilitate eventual control by the establishing operations themselves. Second, the appearance of collateral behavior may indicate an interoceptive state. For example, people fanning themselves are usually hot, and those who shiver cold. The appearance of these behaviors provides natural opportunities to facilitate communication controlled by the relevant establishing operation. For example, a teacher may approach a shivering learner, ask 'What do you need?', and prompt a request for a warm sweater. Over successive opportunities the prompts are faded, until the person 'spontaneously' requests warm clothes when cold. Third, information concerning a person's past history can be used to infer certain bodily states. For example, someone who has not eaten recently may be assumed, often correctly, to feel hungry. While it is ethically questionable to withhold food deliberately to create a relevant motivational state, teachers can make use of naturally occurring periods of deprivation as opportunities to teach mands for food. Another possibility is to establish control by some verifiable public stimulus, (e.g., the presence of food items), maintain that control through intermittent reinforcement, and hope for generalization to private accompaniments. This is no doubt how much verbal behavior comes under the control of private events for many speakers. For people with severe handicaps, however, it may be too much to simply assume this will occur (see Goodman and Remington, this volume).

At present, few studies have demonstrated procedures for bringing verbal behavior under the control of private interoceptive states (cf. Carr and Kologinsky, 1983) although, in principle, such control should be possible. Skinner's (1945) analysis of how the verbal community ordinarily creates such control may provide a framework for developing effective intervention procedures. However, Skinner was not at that time concerned with manding, but with how speakers learn to name (tact) private stimuli. For example, how does the verbal community teach a speaker to call a particular sensation a 'sharp pain' when it has no direct access to what is felt? The same problem arises when teaching a person with severe handicaps to tact internal states (e.g., toothache, fever). The problem of privacy is thus relevant to both manding and tacting, although there are important distinctions between these forms of verbal behavior. Much of the needed empirical work in facilitating the display of spontaneous verbal behavior may depend upon the classification of response classes and the definition of spontaneity within those response classes. Classification of verbal behavior is based upon the reinforcing practices of the verbal community. Skinner's (1957) analysis of these practices may, therefore, have much to offer those who teach verbal behavior to persons with developmental disabilities.

CONCLUSIONS

In spite of considerable progress in our ability to establish a beginning repertoire of communication for those with severe and multiple handicaps, a number of issues remain to be resolved. For instance, even though the bulk of recent empirical data suggests that cognitive 'prerequisites' are not in fact essential to the establishment of early communicative behavior, speech/language pathologists continue to behave as if they were. Similarly, the choice of augmentative communication system and symbol selection technique is frequently based on personal preference or assumed knowledge, rather than data provided by the learner. This less than data-based strategy is also prevalent in the selection of both initial communicative behaviors and level of symbol specificity used in symbol systems.

We have focused on the teaching of generalized and explicit requesting and rejecting. There are few data to help determine which type of communicative behavior would most easily be established initially, or if various classes should be taught concurrently. Although intervention to teach rejecting as an initial component of communicative behavior is rare (and may be difficult), it could provide a useful initial repertoire for individuals with excessive behavior that serves escape/avoidance functions.

There are aspects of generalization that have not been studied extensively in the communication literature. We have learned that functional classes of behavior do not necessarily correspond to pragmatic classes of behavior. Important issues that require further empirical scrutiny involve the conditions necessary to promote generalization of communicative behavior across functional response classes. Equally important is identifying subclasses of conditions within communicative functions that may influence use. Typically, spontaneity has been seen as a critical characterization of efficient communicators. However, equally important may be learners' ability to use a specific communicative function such as requesting at junctures of a conversation that involve initiation, maintenance, and termination of interaction. To date, we have very little data on this topic. These subtle aspects of generalization are critical if the goal of intervention is to establish a full range of use of the communicative behavior established.

The 1970s demonstrated that we could teach a repertoire of communicative behavior to persons with severe disabilities. It is apparent that such repertoires can be established at simple yet highly functional levels among learners who only 15 years ago were not candidates for communicative intervention. The 1980s have focused more on the conditions under which communicative behavior occurs: the 1990s will see further growth in scrutiny of the correspondence between functional analyses of behavior and what linguists have described as pragmatic classes of behavior.

Address for correspondence

Joe Reichle, Department of Communication Disorders, University of Minnesota, 115 Shevlin Hall, 164 Pillsbury Drive S.E., Minneapolis, Minnesota 55455, USA.

REFERENCES

Anglin, J.M. (1977) *Word, Object, and Conceptual Development*, Norton, New York.

Baer, D.M., Peterson, R. and Sherman, J. (1967) The development of imitation by reinforcing behavioral similarity to a model. *Journal of the Experimental Analysis of Behavior*, **10**, 405–416.

Beisler, J.M. and Tsai, L.Y. (1983) A pragmatic approach to increase expressive language in young autistic children. *Journal of Autism and Developmental Disorders*, **13**, 287–303.

Bloom, L. and Lahey, M. (1974) *Language Development*, Merrill, Columbus.

Bloomberg, E. (1984) The comparative translucency of initial lexical items represented by five graphic symbol systems. Unpublished master's thesis, Purdue University, West Lafayette, Indiana.

Bricker, W.A. and Bricker, D.D. (1974) An early language training strategy. In. R.L. Schiefelbusch and L.L. Lloyd (eds), *Language Perspectives: Acquisition, Retardation, and Intervention* (pp. 431–468), University Park Press, Baltimore.

Carr, E.G. and Kologinsky, D. (1983) Acquisition of sign language by autistic children. II: Spontaneity and generalization effects. *Journal of Applied Behavior Analysis*, **16**, 297–314.

Chapman, R. and Miller, J. (1980) Analyzing language and communication in the child. In R. Schiefelbusch (ed.), *Nonspeech Language and and Communication: Analysis and Intervention* (pp. 159–196), University Park Press, Baltimore.

Charlop, M.H., Schreibman, L. and Thibodeau, M.G. (1985) Increasing spontaneous verbal responding in autistic children using a time delay procedure. *Journal of Applied Behavior Analysis*, **18**, 155–166.

Cipani, E. (1988) *Behavior Analysis Language Program (BALP): Therapy, Assessment, and Training Practices for Personnel Working with People with Severe Handicaps*, Bellevue, Washington.

Clark, C.R. (1981) Learning words using traditional orthography and the symbols of Rebus, Bliss and Carrier. *Journal of Speech and Hearing Disorders*, **46**, 191–196.

Gaylord-Ross, R.J., Haring, T.G., Breen, C. and Pitts-Conway, V. (1984) The training and generalization of social interaction skills with autistic youth. *Journal of Applied Behavior Analysis*, **17**, 229–247.

Gobbi, L., Cipani, E., Hudson, C. and Lapenta-Neudeck, R. (1986) Developing spontaneous requesting among children with severe mental retardation. *Mental Retardation*, **24**, 357–363.

Goetz, L., Gee., K. and Sailor, W. (1985) Using a behavior chain interruption strategy to teach communication skills to students with severe disabilities. *Journal of the Association for Persons with Severe Handicaps*, **10**, 21–30.

Hall, G. and Sundberg, M.L. (1987) Teaching mands by manipulating conditioned establishing operations. *Analysis of Verbal Behavior*, **5**, 41–53.

Halle, J.W. (1987) Teaching language in the natural environment: An analysis of spontaneity. *Journal of the Association for Persons with Severe Handicaps*, **12**, 28–37.

Hart, B. and Risley, T.R. (1968) Establishing use of descriptive adjectives in the spontaneous speech of disadvantaged preschool children. *Journal of Applied Behavior Analysis*, **1**, 109–120.

Hunt, P., Goetz, L., Alwell, M. and Sailor. W. (1986) Using an interrupted behavior chain strategy to teach generalized communication responses. *Journal of the Association for Persons with Severe Handicaps*, **11**, 196–204.

Hurlbut, B.I., Iwata, B.A. and Green, J.D. (1982) Nonvocal language acquisition in adolescents with severe physical disabilities: Bliss symbol versus iconic stimulus formats. *Journal of Applied Behavior Analysis*, **15**, 241–258.

Keogh, B. and Reichle, J. (1985) Communication intervention for the 'difficult-to-teach' severely handicapped. In S. Warren and A. Rogers-Warren (eds), *Teaching Functional Language* (pp. 157–196), Pro-Ed, Austin.

Lamarre, J. and Holland, J.G. (1985) The functional independence of mands and tacts. *Journal of Experimental Analysis of Behavior*, **43**, 5–19.

Lovaas, O.I., Berberich, J.P., Perloff, B.F. and Schaeffer, B. (1966) Acquisition of imitative speech by schizophrenic children. *Science*, **151**, 705–707.

McCook, B., Cipani, E., Madigan, K. and LaCampagne, J. (1988) Developing requesting behavior: Acquisition, fluency, and generality. *Mental Retardation*, **26**, 137–143.

Michael, J. (1982) Distinguishing between discriminative and motivational functions of stimuli. *Journal of Experimental Analysis of Behavior*, **37**, 149–155.

Michael, J. (1987) Advanced topics in behavior analysis. Unpublished manuscript, Western Michigan University, Kalamazoo.

Michael, J. (1988) Establishing operations and the mand. *Analysis of Verbal Behavior*, **6**, 3–9.

Mirenda, P. and Locke, P.A. (1989) A comparison of symbol transparency in nonspeaking persons with intellectual disabilities. *Journal of Speech and Hearing Disorders*, **54**, 131–140.

Piaget, J. (1929) *The Child's Conception of the World*, Harcourt, Brace & World, New York.

Reichle, J. (1989) Teaching an individual with severe handicaps to request items and request attention. Unpublished manuscript, University of Minnesota, Minneapolis.

Reichle, J., Anderson, H. and Schermer, J. (1986) Establishing the discrimination between requesting objects, requesting assistance and 'helping yourself'. Unpublished manuscript, University of Minnesota, Minneapolis.

Reichle, J. and Karlan, G. (1985) The selection of an augmentative system in communication intervention: A critique of decision rules. *Journal of the Association for Persons with Severe Handicaps*, **10**, 146–156.

Reichle, J., York, J. and Eynon, D. (1989) Influence of indicating preferences for initiating, maintaining, and terminating interactions. In F. Brown and D. Lehr (eds), *Persons with Profound Disabilities: Issues and practices* (pp. 191–212), Brookes, Baltimore.

Remington, B., Watson, J. and Light, P. (1990) Beyond the single sign: A matrix-based approach to teaching productive sign combinations. *Mental Handicap Research*, **3**, 33–50.

Romski, M.A., Sevcik, R.A. and Pate, J.L. (1988) Establishment of symbolic communication in persons with severe mental retardation. *Journal of Speech and Hearing Disorders*, **53**, 94–107.

Savage-Rumbaugh, E.S. (1984) Verbal behavior at a procedural level in the chimpanzee. *Journal of Experimental Analysis of Behavior*, **41**, 223–250.

Schnaitter, R. (1978) Private causes. *Behaviorism*, **6**, 1–12.

Shane, H. (1980) Approaches to assessing the communication of nonoral persons. In R.L. Schiefelbusch (ed.), *Nonspeech language and Communication: Analysis and Intervention*, University Park Press, Baltimore.

Shane, H. and McCormick, L. Unpublished manuscript, University of Kansas, Lawrence.

Sigafoos, J., Doss, S. and Reichle, J. (1989) Developing mand and tact repertoires in persons with severe developmental disabilities using graphic symbols. *Research in Developmental Disabilities*, **10**, 183–200.

Skinner, B.F. (1945) The operational analysis of psychological terms. *Psychological Review*, **52**, 270–277.

Skinner, B.F. (1953) *Science and Human Behavior*, Macmillan, New York.

Skinner, B.F. (1957) *Verbal Behavior*, Prentice-Hall, Englewood Cliffs, New Jersey.

Sundberg, M.L. (1980) Developing a verbal repertoire using sign language and Skinner's analysis of verbal behavior. Unpublished doctoral dissertation, Western Michigan University, Kalamazoo.

Uzgiris, I. and Hunt, J.M. (1975) *Assessment in Infancy: Ordinal Scales of Psychological Development*, University of Illinois Press, Urbana.

Chapter 10

Teaching Communicative Signing: Labelling, Requesting and Transfer of Function[1]

JULIE GOODMAN AND BOB REMINGTON

INTRODUCTION

Many people with severe mental handicap or autism never acquire language. Ager (1985) notes that the incidence of speech disorders, including total absence of speech, tends to vary directly with the degree of intellectual impairment, and that speech difficulties are generally more extreme than would be expected in relation to the rest of an individual's abilities. These findings motivate the continued search for language programmes that are effective in teaching people with severe learning difficulties to communicate. Increased use of manual signs has helped considerably in providing a means of communication for such people and, in that sense, signing can act as a substitute for speech.

In this regard, a major concern should be to ensure that signing is of real communicative value to the user in that it increases functional control over his or her environment. There are, however, various problems with the signing literature, not least of which is the fact that relatively few researchers have directed their attention towards how best to teach people initial signing skills capable of producing such control. Although the relevance of variables such as iconicity and performance difficulty have been well documented, certain training techniques have been adopted, and are in widespread use, often without much research evidence to support their effectiveness (see Kiernan, 1983, for review). For example, the well-known UK sign-teaching programme, Makaton

[1] This research was supported by an Economic and Social Research Council Linked Studentship (Award C00428525031).

The Challenge of Severe Mental Handicap. Edited by Bob Remington (see, for example, Walker, 1978), recommends adherence to a structured training sequence based on a developmental model, and teaching within a formal training situation. Total communication (Creedon, 1973), in which speech and sign are used in parallel, is also recommended. Here, the teacher presents a referent, names it, prompts the child to perform the sign, and reinforces correct performance either socially or tangibly (e.g., with a small edible item). The prompt is gradually faded using behavioural techniques. This procedure teaches the child to *label* or *name* referents, in that signs are eventually occasioned by some property of the referent, and reinforced non-specifically with respect to that property (e.g., naming a drink would not result in being given that drink). Skinner (1957) defined this class of verbal behaviour as the *tact*.

The kind of tact training procedure described above has been studied in depth by a number of researchers, partly because it provides a convenient procedure for examining important variables in sign language acquisition. For example, Clarke, Remington and Light (1986, 1988), Remington and Clarke (1983), and Barrera, Lobato-Barrera and Sulzer-Azaroff (1980) all used a tact training procedure incorporating non-specific reinforcement to examine the role of speech in sign language acquisition. Similarly, Konstantareas, Oxman and Webster (1978) investigated the role of iconicity in the acquisition of signed tacts. Motoric aspects of sign such as production mode (e.g. contact versus no contact with hands and body during signing) (Doherty and Lloyd, in press; Kohl, 1981), and performance difficulty (see Kiernan, 1983, for review) have also been investigated using a tacting procedure.

Study 1: Comparing methods of teaching initial sign acquisition

Although teaching methods based on tacting are demonstrably successful in terms of the initial acquisition of signs, it is questionable whether once acquired they will be used in a truly communicative way outside of teaching sessions. One way in which greater generalization might be facilitated involves changing the reinforcement contingency for signing, and this can be achieved by making the reinforcer specific to the referent. For example, when a child signs 'drink' in the presence of a drink, the response would be reinforced by presentation of the drink. This 'requesting' procedure, which in some ways resembles *manding* (Skinner, 1957; but see p. 219) has been successfully used by Carr *et al.* (1978) to teach five signs to children with autism. Carr and Kologinsky (1983: Experiment 1: 'Sign label pre-training') used a similar technique to establish an initial sign repertoire prior to attempting to facilitate 'spontaneous' sign use. This kind of procedure seems more natural than the tact training, but, because both methods have reportedly produced acquisition of signing, it seemed sensible to compare them directly.

The aim of our first study (Goodman, 1990) was twofold. First, we wished to see whether signs were acquired faster using one or other teaching method; and secondly, we wanted to examine whether either approach was superior in terms of generalization to naturalistic contexts. Although we could find no research directly relating to the generalization issue, three studies that had evaluated reinforcer specificity in relation to the acquisition of speech comprehension were available. Working with children with developmental disabilities, Janssen and Guess (1978), Saunders and Sailor (1979), and Litt and Schreibman (1981) compared acquisition of receptive speech functions in relation to preferred toy or food item (a) when reinforcement corresponded to the item pointed to by the child in response to a word spoken by the teacher (i.e., specific reinforcement) and (b) when other, equally preferred reinforcers were presented for correct naming. The latter, non-specific, reinforcement procedure was instantiated in slightly different ways in each study, but the essential feature of all such conditions is the removal of a correlation between the antecedent stimulus and the reinforcer.

Our study differed from those above in that it involved a comparison of *sign* acquisition in the *expressive* mode. We compared specific and non-specific reinforcers using an alternating treatments design (Barlow and Hayes, 1979), and replicated the comparison across four children with severe mental handicap. Two sets of five equally preferred snack foods were identified for each child using paired comparison methods, and expressive signs corresponding to each of these items were taught using total communication. Request training took the form of teaching the child to perform a sign in the presence of specific preferred food items which were then presented as reinforcers for correct signing. Tact training followed the procedure often adopted to teach signs, with the reinforcer varying randomly from trial to trial, but always being different from the stimulus item. Children took part in one of each kind of session each day, with the order of sessions counterbalanced across days.

The two less able participants (in terms of mental age, language ability, receptive knowledge of signs, and of words corresponding to signs) fared far better under request training than tact training. They acquired requests in approximately two thirds of the time it took them to acquire tacts (29 versus 44, and 25 versus 35 sessions for requests and tacts respectively), and the differences were most marked early in training. For the two more able children, however, there was much less difference in acquisition rate between teaching methods (14 versus 17, and 17 versus 17 sessions). None of the children showed differences between conditions in terms of either maintenance over four weeks, or generalization to a new teacher; both conditions produced high levels of performance.

The superiority of request training over tact training is in line with earlier research (e.g., Litt and Schreibman, 1981). It may have arisen because, in the former condition, the functional relationship between the stimulus object, the sign and the reinforcer allowed greater control over reinforcement. The consequences of correct signing were only fully controllable in the request situation, thus providing a child with a tool to obtain a desired reinforcer directly. An alternative explanation may be that children may have had a history of successful requesting with natural signs (see Duker and Remington, this volume). If the tacting function is unfamiliar, some prerequisite skills would be lacking, thus slowing acquisition. Moreover, as Savage-Rumbaugh (1984) found in studies with 'linguistic' chimpanzees, a prior history of requesting particular items could actively interfere with learning to tact those same items with the same lexigram (see Reichle, Sigafoos and Remington, this volume). The fact that the difference between requests and tacts was apparent only for the less able children perhaps favours this kind of interpretation but, whatever the explanation, the finding clearly has important implications for teaching, suggesting that reinforcer specificity may greatly facilitate initial sign acquisition.

We devised two post-tests to assess the functional utility of the signs trained in naturalistic settings. First, we concentrated on examining requesting functions because the immediate reinforcement of successful requests seemed to be the key to sustainability. We thus compared signs in terms of their effective use in a simulated 'cafeteria' situation where items corresponding to signs taught by both methods were available and could be requested. This test suggested that differences in teaching method were not important; children were apparently able to use signs acquired as both requests and tacts to ask for food items. A second post-test, conducted to assess use of signs as labels, also showed that, regardless of initial teaching method, signs could apparently serve a tacting function.

ATTEMPTS TO PRODUCE SPONTANEOUS COMMUNICATION

Establishing events and the functional control of requesting behaviour

Given that what appeared to be successful transfer across language function occurred readily regardless of the mode in which signs were initially taught, the superiority of using a request-based format for the initial teaching of signs seemed to be secure. Despite this, we had both theoretical and empirical reasons for doubting the findings of the post-tests. At the theoretical level, Skinner (1957) had proposed that different language functions, specifically tacting and requesting (or manding), are separately acquired. He argued that the same vocabulary item (i.e., a single word, sign, or symbol) can serve both functions, that these functions can be established separately, and that transfer is not inevitable but only occurs under special circumstances. Moreover, Lamarre and Holland (1985) provided empirical evidence to support this idea. They conducted a study in which mainstream pre-school children were taught to use the phrases 'on the left' and 'on the right' as either tacts (to *describe* the placement of toys) or mands (to *request* particular placements), and found that transfer between functions did not readily occur in either direction.

Because our results were anomalous with both theory and research, we reconsidered our transfer test procedures. In both requesting and tacting tasks, the possibility existed that the functions of the children's signing could have been misinterpreted. For example, it may have been that, in the cafeteria situation, we regarded children's signs as requests when in fact they were simply tacts for visible items as far as the children were concerned. Conversely, in our test of tacting, the children may in fact have been unsuccessfully attempting to request the items they were shown.

In retrospect, this problem arose because our procedure for teaching requesting was not based sufficiently closely on the definition of manding provided by Skinner. He defined the mand as 'a verbal operant in which the response is reinforced by a characteristic consequence *and is therefore under the functional control of relevant conditions of deprivation or aversive stimulation*' (italics added). In our request training situation, each sign was 'reinforced by a characteristic consequence', but signing was always under the functional antecedent control of the food items that were used to cue correct signing (as well as to reinforce it). Skinner's definition emphasizes that manding is not controlled in this way; for example a mand for aspirin is controlled by a headache, not by a preferred tablet. This problem arises even in the well-designed experiments of Carr and associates (1978, 1983), both of which include the characteristic consequences unique to mands, but do not ensure the functional control by deprivation or aversive stimulation that is also required.

A theoretical paper by Michael (1982) has substantially clarified the nature of the kind of events that can exert functional control of manding. Michael uses the term *establishing operation* to refer to any change in the environment which alters the effectiveness of some object or event as a reinforcer, and at the same time alters the momentary probability of behaviours that have been followed by that reinforcer. For example, ingestion of a salty snack would establish water as a reinforcer, and increase the likelihood of responses that had previously been successful in securing water. Simple water deprivation would have a similar establishing effect, but proferring of a glass of water would not. At most, this would serve a discriminative function. For example, it might be the case that a thirsty child would be reinforced for signing 'water' only when water was being offered. Michael is at pains to point out the difference between the discriminative and the establishing functions of environmental events. In a further refinement of the basic principle, Michael points out that some environmental events serve as *establishing stimuli*. For example, a bowl of cereal may be a *discriminative* stimulus for eating, but eating is not possible without an appropriate tool (i.e., a spoon). Thus, the cereal bowl *also* functions as an *establishing* stimulus, i.e., a stimulus in whose presence the spoon will function as a reinforcer. If the child signs 'spoon', and a spoon is provided by an adult, the child can successfully gain access to the more basic reinforcer (eating the food). Signing 'spoon' is thus a mand that forms part of a larger unit of behaviour evoked by the sight of the cereal bowl and reinforced by eating.

The key feature of Michael's account is that manding is dependent on establishing operations or stimuli (generically, 'establishing events'). The stimuli which serve discriminative functions for tacting may be absent when manding occurs (e.g., in the previous examples, manding water, or a spoon, would occur when these stimuli were *not* present, under the control of establishing operations (prior consumption of salty food) or establishing stimuli (cereal bowl)). Manding thus appears 'spontaneous' both because it is occasioned by establishing events which are not typically manipulated by a teacher or experimenter and because these events are not 'named' by the mand.

Mand teaching: Programmed transfer

Michael's framework has several implications for the issues of teaching manding and assessing transfer of function. The kinds of problems alluded to in the post-tests following our comparison study have also bedevilled other research that has attempted to teach signs or symbols as mands. Most such studies have attempted to transfer control from discriminative stimuli to establishing events.

Carr and Kologinsky (1983), for example, devised a transfer procedure involving prompting, fading and differential reinforcement to teach six autistic children to use their existing sign repertoire to make spontaneous requests of adults. First, a sign label pre-training procedure, almost identical to our specific reinforcement procedure, was conducted to bring signing under the *discriminative* control of the items that were used as reinforcers. A subsequent period of baseline observation showed, however, that children virtually never used these signs to request concealed food items from an attending adult. Next, Carr and Kologinsky arranged sessions consisting of two parts: a maintenance period followed by a training period. During maintenance, the adult simply attended to the child, and reinforced signed requests with the corresponding items which, again, were concealed. In the immediately following training period, the adult approached the child, gained eye contact, presented an imitative prompt to sign one of the ten concealed food items, and reinforced correct imitation with that item. The prompts were gradually faded and training on a sign was considered complete when the child spontaneously made the sign in a subsequent session during the maintenance period (i.e., in the absence of any prompt other than adult attention). The procedure was successful across all three subjects. In a second experiment, Carr and Kologinsky also showed that the use of signs functioning as requests would, with appropriate training, generalize to other adult 'requestees' and new physical settings.

Carr and Kologinsky suggested that 'spontaneity may be facilitated when language is brought under the control of broadly defined stimuli, such as adult attention, rather than narrowly defined stimuli such as the presence of specific objects or verbal prompting in the form of questions' (1983, p. 297). However, this conclusion in itself raises the possibility that the signs taught were not in fact functioning as mands. Control by discriminative stimuli, however broadly defined, is not the same as control by establishing operations or stimuli. Carr and Kologinsky were able to provide only anecdotal evidence that signs were sensitive to establishing events. Although children were said to be more likely to make requests for fluid if they had just had salty food, or requests for toys or activities if they had come to the session directly after classroom snacks, no systematic manipulation of establishing operations or stimuli was attempted.

Evidence of antecedent control can provide the most powerful method of demonstrating that 'spontaneous' signing is in fact subserving a manding function. The central requirement is that control of manding must be conditional on the presence of particular antecedent establishing events. For example, a learner must be able to make at least two conditional discriminated mands, for example appropriately requesting either a can opener or nutcrackers, when presented with the establishing stimuli of an unopened can or uncracked nut. Magpusao and Cipani (1989) describe a study in which manding was occasioned by the absence of an item necessary to complete a task. However, it is not clear from their report that *different* mands, conditional on particular establishing events, were acquired.

A supplementary method of evaluating whether verbal behaviour is functioning as a mand has been proposed by Yamamoto and Mochizuki (1988). They used a 'social behaviour chain' technique in which a teacher established the reinforcing value of specific objects by instructing autistic students to request those objects from a second adult. This allowed probes in which objects other than those manded were offered by the second adult (using the verbal response 'Give me—'). Before a remedial procedure was introduced, children would accept items that they had not requested, thus indicating that their verbal behaviour was not serving a manding function. Presumably, their 'requests' were in fact simply 'echoics' (Skinner, 1957), i.e. repetitions of the instructions.

STUDIES OF EMERGENT TRANSFER OF LANGUAGE FUNCTIONS

These considerations led us to devise a procedure which would enable more precise examination of the issue of transfer of function, from mand to tact and vice versa. In order to do this, it was essential to remove the ambiguity surrounding the previously used requesting tasks by ensuring that stimulus items manded were not present when mands were emitted, so that their control could be unequivocally attributed to establishing events. Control should also be conditional in the sense that different establishing events reliably resulted in different mands.

To achieve this, without manipulating our participants' access to important reinforcers, we devised a novel, game-like situation which required children to 'ask for' things they needed to complete an operation which in turn had reinforcing consequences. We used a simple formboard with five circular 'puzzle pieces', each with a picture of a different animal on it. Each piece 'belonged in' one of the five distinctively coloured circular recesses (see Figure 10.1). Thus, during mand training, the appearance of a single uncovered recess provided an establishing stimulus for manding the final, missing puzzle piece. Placing that piece successfully completed the task, and was reinforced with a small edible item. Because each of the five pieces could be missing on different trials, the formboard allowed participants to produce five appropriate mands for puzzle pieces conditional on the five establishing stimuli.

The signs used in mand teaching were based on British Sign Language signs for the animals depicted on the puzzle pieces. Therefore, when we wished to teach tacting, these same signs were used, the puzzle pieces themselves acted as discriminative stimuli, and correct tacting was

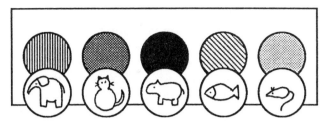

Figure 10.1 The formboard used to study transfer of function. Each 'puzzle piece' 'belonged in' one of the five distinctively coloured recesses.

reinforced non-specifically. The procedure thus allowed the same sign forms to be taught in the service of either a manding or a tacting function. Our general strategy was to teach one function and use probe procedures to look for the collateral emergence of signing subserving the other function.

Two studies were conducted (Goodman, 1990), again using single-subject experimental procedures with replications across children. In the first, children were taught to tact, and mand emergence was concurrently tested for, using a probe procedure. In the second, the procedure was reversed, that is, mands were taught (using a new sign set) and transfer to tact usage was probed. The use of probe trials interspersed between training trials had the advantage of revealing exactly when emergence of transfer occurred.

Study 2: Tact to mand transfer

Two children with severe mental handicaps (and with poor receptive and absent expressive speech skills) served as participants. First, they were taught the correspondences between the coloured recesses and puzzle pieces. On each trial, four of the recesses were blanked off, leaving one colour exposed. The teacher then gave the child the five puzzle pieces, cued the child's attention to the empty recess, and asked 'What goes/lives here?' The child was trained to place the correct piece in the recess using physical prompting and fading techniques. Correct placements were reinforced with a small edible item. This colour–picture matching-to-sample procedure (see Mackay, this volume) thus ensured that each recess could function as an establishing stimulus for 'wanting' one of the puzzle pieces. In subsequent mand probes, participants would again experience an empty recess and should—if tact to mand transfer occurred—be able to sign for the missing piece. Following pre-tests which established that they could not use the animal signs as either mands or tacts, five signs were trained as tacts for the puzzle pieces using a non-specific reinforcement procedure. During this phase, probes were concurrently conducted to assess transfer to mand usage by presenting participants with the formboard with a single piece missing, and waiting to see if manding occurred. Because puzzle pieces were not present during probes, they obviously could not function as discriminative stimuli. Therefore, correct signs could not be tacts, and their presence must indicate that transfer of function to manding had occurred. Correct performance on probe trials was *not* reinforced.

Both children rapidly learned to select the picture from a choice of five which corresponded to the exposed coloured recess in the formboard during phase one. During tact training, each participant gradually learned signs to tact all five pictures. Moreover, mand probe trials revealed that transfer of function to the mand situation occurred almost immediately a sign had been reliably acquired as a tact. Figure 10.2 shows that for one (representative) participant, correct manding performance improved in parallel with the improvement in tacting performance, but lagged slightly behind.

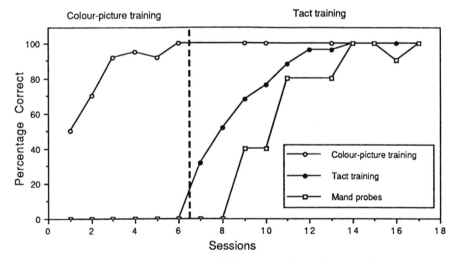

Figure 10.2 Tact to mand transfer. Data for one subject showing the acquisition of tacting, and the emergence of appropriate manding as a function of training sessions.

Study 3: Mand to tact transfer

A subsequent study was conducted with six different participants to establish whether transfer in the opposite direction (from mand to tact function) could also occur. The procedure was similar to that used in the previous study. Manding was taught by prompting participants to make the appropriate sign conditional on the presence of each coloured recess. Correct signing was then reinforced by presentation of the corresponding piece, the insertion of which into the recess was itself reinforced with an edible item. Concurrent with mand training, the acquisition of the tacting function was probed. The procedure involved presentation of a number of pictures for which participants had previously acquired signed tacts (a 'warm-up' procedure), followed by probes with the puzzle pieces which had not previously occasioned signing. Only three children learned to mand in the time available for training, but in each of these cases tacting developed as a collateral repertoire. The data from one of these participants, shown in Figure 10.3, indicate that tacting emerged in parallel with, but a little behind, manding. This also shows probe trials used to assess the emergent acquisition of picture–colour matching skills. All three participants showed the same pattern: picture–colour matching skills emerged in close synchrony with tacting.

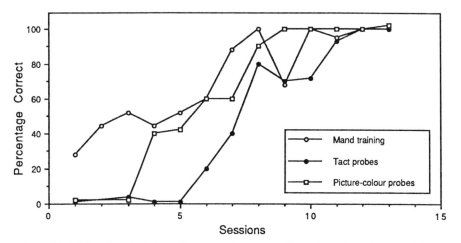

Figure 10.3 Mand to tact transfer. Data for one subject showing the acquisition of manding, and the emergence of appropriate tacting as a function of training sessions.

STIMULUS EQUIVALENCE AND TRANSFER ACROSS LANGUAGE FUNCTIONS

Earlier explanations of transfer

In one sense the above results are unsurprising. Most parents know to their cost that a child who learns the name of a new product in a sweetshop, or from a TV commercial, can subsequently mand that product. Thus, transfer of verbal behaviour across functions seems quite natural. Indeed, while Skinner's account of mand and tact acquisition suggests that the different functions *can* be acquired independently of one another, he provided a number of possible supplementary explanations for the fact that transfer is so often observed. For example, there may be what Lamarre and Holland (1985) have described as 'mixing of the two functional types at the time of acquisition' (p. 17). This may occur in several ways but, essentially, these explanations reduce to having stimuli relevant to tacting present when manding is reinforced (or vice versa), and 'erroneously' reinforcing mands non-specifically (or tacts specifically). These accounts are difficult to reconcile with the data reported above for two reasons. First, we took great care to avoid the mixing of types by ensuring that the contingencies for manding were quite different from those of tacting. Second, the effect that we observed was not simply the facilitated acquisition of non-trained forms, but their immediate transfer and appropriate use in the absence of reinforcement.

Catania (1984) concedes that such direct transfer can occur, and reconceptualizes manding as 'a single class of responses, characterized by including the verbal response that in other circumstances tacts the reinforcing consequences' (p. 237). Difficulties with this account are also apparent. First, it avoids the problems that Skinner discussed but only by failing to specify the circumstances necessary for the establishment of the class. Secondly, it does not seem to explain how a specific subclass of manding is uniquely controlled by a relevant establishing event when the discriminative stimulus for the corresponding tact is absent. Finally, it does not account for transfer from mand to tact functions.

A new explanation of transfer

We believe it might be possible to build an explanation for transfer of function, which is more helpful with respect to understanding the process involved, using the concept of stimulus equivalence (Sidman and Tailby, 1982). The basic prerequisites for equivalence and its defining characteristics are described in detail in the following chapter (Mackay, this volume) but, essentially, equivalence is a phenomenon which arises from matching-to-sample procedures not dissimilar from those used to teach manding and tacting. Any matching-to-sample task consists of choosing the appropriate comparison stimulus when a particular sample stimulus is presented. For example, in Figure 10.4, matching between set A and set B (A–B) would be achieved by teaching a participant to choose the **square** comparison stimulus when the **X** sample was presented, and the **triangle** comparison when the **O** sample was presented. Responses deemed correct would be reinforced, erroneous choices ignored. Similarly, A–C matching would be achieved when a participant reliably selected **K** on presentation of **X**, and **J** on **O**. Teaching these conditional matching skills often leads to the emergence of untrained matching skills characterized by reflexivity, symmetry, and transitivity, which together are the defining characteristics of stimulus equivalence (Sidman and Tailby, 1982). Reflexivity involves the emergence of correct matching of comparisons stimuli to identical samples (A–A, B–B, C–C). Symmetry is the emergence of matching performances in which sample and comparison functions are reversed from those trained (B–A, C–A). Finally, transitivity is the combination of taught relationships, or emergent symmetrical relationships, to produce yet more untaught matching performances (B–C, C–B). At this point, the **X**, **square**, and **K** stimuli are said to be equivalent (as are **O**, **triangle**, and **J** stimuli). Equivalence, as defined by reflexivity, symmetry and transitivity, can also emerge when the two taught performances are A–B and B–C matching (see Mackay, this volume, for a much fuller account).

It is clear that matching relationships, such as those described above, are important in the sign-teaching paradigms used to teach manding and tacting. Broadly speaking, we believe that for children to show transfer of function from tact to mand and vice versa, they must have

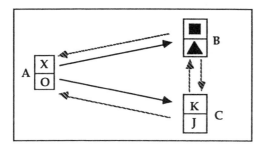

Figure 10.4 The conditional matching performances involved in stimulus equivalence. When two relations (e.g., A–B and A–C) are taught, the remainder (B–A, C–A, C–B, B–C) may emerge without explicit training.

learned the necessary matching relations between the stimulus sets
involved in the formboard game. In this context, the stimulus sets are
the coloured recesses, the puzzle pieces, and the manual signs. These
are shown on Figure 10.5 which, for simplicity, includes only two of the
five stimuli each set. The relationships taught in the course of either
mand or tact training appear sufficient for the emergence of the untaught
function through equivalence.

First consider tact to mand transfer. Insertion training established A–B
matching relationships between the coloured recesses (set A), and their
corresponding puzzle pieces (set B). Tact training involved producing a
set of conditional B–C matches between the animal pictures on the puzzle
pieces (set B) and the signs (set C). Both the A–B and B–C conditional
matching performances are reinforced non-specifically. These are normally
sufficient conditions for equivalence to develop between the corresponding items in each of the stimulus sets $(A_1-B_1-C_1, \ldots, A_5-B_5-C_5)$.
Under these circumstances, a transitive A–C relationship would emerge,
consisting of a set of conditional matching performances in which each
sample was a coloured recess, and the correct comparison was its
corresponding sign. These performances occur in such a way that they
can be reinforced as mands, with each sign occasioned by its relevant
establishing stimulus.

If this interpretation is correct, the frequently observed failure of tact
teaching to produce 'spontaneous' manding in natural settings (see, for
example, Poulton and Alggozine, 1980) may be because the A–B
relationship between establishing events and their reinforcers has not

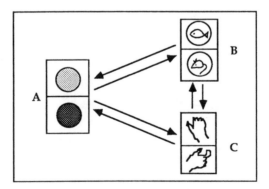

Figure 10.5 The relations between establishing stimuli (set A), 'puzzle pieces'
(set B) and signs (set C) in the transfer of function task. For ease of presentation,
only two of the five items in each set are shown.

been learned. Essentially, failure to transfer may mean that, in a sense, individuals do not know what they need.

The observed transfer from mand to tact functions can be handled somewhat similarly. The mand training procedure established conditional control of signs (set C) by coloured recesses (set A) acting as establishing stimuli (the A–C relation). There are two possible accounts of how the remaining relationship necessary for equivalence was acquired. First, B–A matching may have been incidentally acquired as part of the mand training procedure. Recall that a correct signed mand was reinforced with the corresponding puzzle piece (set B), and the child was then reinforced with an edible item for placing this piece in the available coloured recess (set A). Under these conditions, B–A matching could have been acquired incidentally, although the relevant conditional discriminations were not taught using *differential* reinforcement because, with only one available recess, alternatives were impossible. All of the children who showed mand-to-tact transfer also showed the emergent acquisition of B–A (picture–colour) matching (see Figure 10.3). If this explanation is correct, emergent tacting (B–C) would require transitivity between B–A and A–C relations.

However, another explanation for the two conditional relations necessary for equivalence is suggested by very recent work by Dube and his associates (Dube *et al.*, 1987, 1989). Within a standard equivalence paradigm, Dube *et al.* used procedures for teaching two conditional relationships (e.g., A–B and B–C) which involved 'performance-specific contingencies' in which reinforcers that were specific to each putative stimulus class were employed. For example, A_1–B_1 and B_1–C_1 were reinforced with a particular food item, F_1, and A_2–B_2 and B_2–C_2 were reinforced with a different food item, F_2. Subsequent tests revealed that the food items themselves had also entered the equivalence classes (i.e., A_1–B_1–C_1–F_1 and A_2–B_2–C_2–F_2). The specific reinforcement contingency is, of course, highly similar to our mand training procedure, in which correct signing was reinforced by specific puzzle pieces. Thus, mand training alone might be sufficient to produce both the A–C relationships (between coloured recess establishing stimuli (set A) and signs (set C)), and the C–B relationships (between signs (set C) and pictures functioning as specific reinforcers (set B)). If so, tacting (the B–C relation) would emerge by symmetry of the C–B relation.

This application of the stimulus equivalence framework is an attempt to provide a more comprehensive and testable explanation of the occurrence, and non-occurrence, of transfer across mand and tact functions. However, it is not without problems. First, it is post hoc. Our primary interest was in developing a test of whether transfer occurred and we did not carry out all of the procedures necessary to check for the emergence of reflexivity, symmetry and transitivity. Nevertheless, the explanation is in line with our data, and provides a framework for more thorough investigation of the processes involved.

The second problem is that we have treated the signs that were taught as 'stimuli', whereas they are perhaps more readily seen as 'responses'. We are not sure of the importance of this distinction. The modelling and prompting of signing during both mand and tact training procedures provided many opportunities for participants to observe signs as stimuli arising from the teacher's, or their own, behaviour. In the same vein, signs might be regarded as 'constructed stimuli' (Mackay, 1985; see also Mackay, Chapter 11 this volume). Mackay taught participants to construct colour words from letter tiles (a set of responses), conditional on the presence of colour patches as stimuli. Subsequent tests showed that this procedure allowed the same written words, this time presented directly as stimuli, to take part in emergent two-way symmetrical relationships with the colour patches (colour–word and word–colour), although neither of these relations was taught.

A third problem, which relates both to our data and its interpretation, concerns why one other major study (Lamarre and Holland, 1985) failed to find transfer between mand and tact repertoires. Assuming neither study could be faulted in terms of internal validity, how might the difference be explained? Lamarre and Holland claim that transfer cannot always be expected, and although this conclusion is reasonable the experimental situation they used to look for it was somewhat unusual. Specifically, their criterion for deciding whether a response was a mand paid no attention to the establishing event concept discussed earlier. The mands that they trained consisted of verbal responses prompted by the experimenter's question 'Where do you want me to put [object P]?' when participants were presented with a pair of objects (P and Q). Participants were trained to say 'on the left (right)'. Lamarre and Holland claim that 'proper placement of the objects by the experimenter was a *sufficient reinforcing stimulus*, as evidenced by the (appropriate) prepositional phrase being repeated in subsequent mands' (1985, p. 7 italics added). However, this appears to be a rather weak conception of a mand since it does not specify why placement of an object P on one side or the other of an object Q on any trial should be reinforcing. No establishing event is involved, and placement results in no further consequence for the child. Lamarre and Holland checked 'that the specific position (of placement) was discriminated' (p. 8) by occasionally placing an object in the alternative position to that 'manded'. However, the fact that participants could detect the correspondence between their own verbal behaviour and the experimenter's placements does not mean that their responses had functioned as mands. They might simply have been an intraverbal response to the experimenter's 'Where . . .?' question (cf. 'How are you?' 'Fine, thanks', Skinner, 1957, p. 72). The key point is that there is still no evidence that apparent 'mands' were 'under the functional control of relevant conditions of deprivation or aversive stimulation' (Skinner, 1957). If this interpretation is correct, then there is no reason to expect transfer based on equivalence within the Lamarre and Holland procedure, because one of the three sets of stimuli necessary for the formation of equivalence—the establishing events—are altogether absent.

A final question this account must face concerns its ecological validity. Do the stimulus relations which give rise to equivalence in the somewhat artificial task we devised to study transfer resemble those which exist in the natural environment? There seems little reason to doubt that such resemblances exist. For example, the A–B associations between coloured recesses and puzzle pieces reflects a simple recognition that particular environmental changes are reinforcing given the occurrence of discriminable establishing events—that food will satisfy hunger, or that a pen will allow a cheque to be written. Similarly, the A–C relations between coloured recesses and signs model the relations between discriminable establishing events and mands. People ask for heat when they feel cold, and matches when a fire is to be lit. Finally, B–C links between puzzle pieces and signs correspond to the relationship that exists in a naming context between words and their referents.

In sum, the stimulus equivalence model provides an analytical framework within which the prerequisite stimulus relationships involved in functional communication can be assessed and, where necessary, developed through specific teaching interventions.

CONCLUSION

Poulton and Alggozine (1980), in their review of literature on sign language use by individuals with mental handicaps, stated that: 'The literature specifically supports the notion that manual signing can facilitate word–object associations. It does not, however, support the contention that retarded persons attain a functional communication system based on manual signing, or that manual signing has become a primary mode of communication for nonverbal retarded individuals' (1980, p. 51).

We think that there is now cause for a little more optimism, particularly with the recent focus on establishing functional communication which indicates the direction for the development of research and teaching practice. Poulton and Alggozine's review was largely an evaluation of training programmes which, in the main, taught tact relationships. Once students could produce signs that corresponded with presented objects, they were given credit for 'knowing the meaning' of the signs.

Poulton and Alggozine concluded that students did not use their signs outside the training situation and that their repertoire was not like that of typical children. From the present perspective, this is not surprising because researchers only taught one part of a verbal repertoire and expected the other functions somehow to emerge spontaneously. There is no reason to believe that this will occur. Nevertheless, the studies reported above provide a behavioural explanation of how generalization across language function may, under some circumstances, arise without necessarily having to train all possible language functions separately. From the practitioner's viewpoint, this is an important consideration. Before this kind of transfer can be achieved routinely, however, we will need to know a great deal more about the processes of stimulus equivalence.

Address for correspondence

Julie Goodman, Department of Psychology, University of Southampton, Highfield, Southampton SO9 5NH, UK.

REFERENCES

Ager, A.K. (1985) Alternatives to speech for the mentally handicapped. In F. Watts (ed.), *New Developments in Clinical Psychology*, Wiley, Chichester.

Barlow, D.H. and Hayes, S.C. (1979) Alternating treatments design: One strategy for comparing the effects of two treatments in a single subject. *Journal of Applied Behavior Analysis*, **12**, 199–210.

Barrera, R.D., Lobato-Barrera, D. and Sulzer-Azaroff, B. (1980) A simultaneous treatment comparison of three expressive language training programs with a mute autistic child. *Journal of Autism and Developmental Disorders*, **10**, 21–37.

Carr, E.G. and Kologinsky, E. (1983) Acquisition of sign language by autistic children. II: Spontaneity and generalization effects. *Journal of Applied Behavior Analysis*, **16**, 297–314.

Carr, E.G., Binkoff, J.A., Kologinsky, E. and Eddy, M. (1978) Acquisition of sign language by autistic children. I: Expressive labeling. *Journal of Applied Behavior Analysis*, **11**, 489–501.

Catania, A.C. (1984) *Learning*, Prentice-Hall, Englewood Cliffs, New Jersey.

Clarke, S., Remington, B. and Light, P. (1986) An evaluation of the relationship between receptive speech skills and expressive signing. *Journal of Applied Behavior Analysis*, **19**, 231–239.

Clarke, S., Remington, B. and Light, P. (1988) The role of referential speech in sign learning by mentally retarded children: A comparison of total communication and sign-alone training. *Journal of Applied Behavior Analysis*, **21**, 419–426.

Creedon, M.P. (1973, March) Language development in nonverbal autistic children using a simultaneous communication system. Paper presented at the biennial meeting of the Society for Research in Child Development, Philadelphia.

Doherty, J.E. and Lloyd, L.L. (in press) Effects of production mode, translucency and manuality on sign acquisition by adults with mental retardation. *Augmentative and Alternative Communication.*

Dube, W.V., McIlvane, W.J., Mackay, H.A. and Stoddard, L.T. (1987) Stimulus class membership established via stimulus–reinforcer relations. *Journal of the Experimental Analysis of Behavior*, **47**, 159–175.

Dube, W.V., McIlvane, W.J., Maguire, R.W., Mackay, H.A. and Stoddard, L.T. (1989) Stimulus class formation and response–reinforcer relations. *Journal of the Experimental Analysis of Behavior*, **51**, 65–76.

Goodman, J.M. (1990) *Acquisition and Transfer of Language Function.* Unpublished doctoral dissertation, Unversity of Southampton.

Janssen, C. and Guess, D. (1978) Use of function as a consequence in training receptive labeling to severely and profoundly retarded individuals. *AAESPH Review*, December, 246–258.

Kiernan, C. (1983) The exploration of sign and symbol effects. In J. Hogg and P. Mittler (eds), *Advances in Mental Handicap Research* (Vol. 2), Wiley, Chichester.

Kohl, F.L. (1981) Effects of motoric requirements on the acquisition of manual sign responses by severely handicapped students. *American Journal of Mental Deficiency*, **85**, 396–403.

Konstantareas, M.M., Oxman, J. and Webster, C.D. (1978) Iconicity: Effects on acquisition of sign language by autistic and other severely dysfunctional children. In P. Siple (ed.), *Understanding Language Through Sign Language Research*, Academic Press, London.

Lamarre, J. and Holland, J.G. (1985) The functional independence of mands and tacts. *Journal of the Experimental Analysis of Behavior*, **43**, 5–19.

Litt, M.D. and Schreibman, L. (1981) Stimulus-specific reinforcement in the acquisition of receptive labels by autistic children. *Analysis and Intervention in Development Disabilities*, **1**, 171–186.

Mackay, H. (1985) Stimulus equivalence in rudimentary reading. *Analysis and Intervention in Developmental Disabilities*, **5**, 373–387.

Magpusao, B. and Cipani, E. (1989) Spontaneous requesting—acquisition, generalisation and discriminative components: A single case study. *Mental Handicap Research*, **2**, 61–72.

Michael, J. (1982) Distinguishing between discriminative and motivational functions of stimuli. *Journal of the Experimental Analysis of Behavior*, **37**, 149–155.

Poulton, K.T. and Alggozine, B. (1980) Manual communication and mental retardation: A review of research and implications. *American Journal on Mental Deficiency*, **85**, 145–152.

Remington, B. and Clarke, S. (1983) Acquisition of expressive signing by autistic children: An evaluation of the relative effects of simultaneous communication and sign-alone training. *Journal of Applied Behavior Analysis*, **16**, 315–327.

Saunders, R.R. and Sailor, W. (1979) A comparison of three strategies of reinforcement on two-choice learning problems with severely retarded children. *AAESPH Review*, **4**, 323–333.

Savage-Rumbaugh, E.S. (1984) Verbal behaviour at a procedural level in the chimpanzee. *Journal of the Experimental Analysis of Behavior*, **41**, 223–250.

Sidman, M. and Tailby, W. (1982) Conditional discrimination vs. matching to sample: An expansion of the testing paradigm. *Journal of the Experimental Analysis of Behavior*, **37**, 5–22.

Skinner, B.F. (1957) *Verbal Behavior*, Appleton–Century–Crofts, New York.

Walker, M. (1978) The Makaton Vocabulary. In T. Tebbs (ed.), *Ways and Means*, Global Educational, Basingstoke.

Yamamoto, J. and Mochizuki, A. (1988) Acquisition and functional analysis of manding with autistic students. *Journal of Applied Behavior Analysis*, **21**, 57–64.

Chapter 11

Stimulus Equivalence: Implications for the Development of Adaptive Behavior[1]

HARRY A. MACKAY

INTRODUCTION

People with mental handicap or autism often lack elementary skills essential for adjustment to the everyday demands of life in the community. Many have little functional language skill, and cannot read, spell, or write. Many also display few or no numerical skills and have not learned to use money. Recent research on stimulus equivalence has been concerned with the analysis of the kinds of complex behavioral repertoires that such individuals lack. For example, some studies outline procedures that effectively establish the rudiments of functional reading and spelling skills (e.g., Mackay and Sidman, 1984), pre-arithmetic performances (Gast, VanBiervliet and Spradlin, 1979), and the equivalences between different coin sets and prices that are necessary for money use (e.g., Stoddard *et al.*, 1989). Matching-to-sample (MTS) and related techniques are central to these studies. Thus, the specification of these procedures, the assessment of their behavioral outcomes, and the delineation of important precursors and prerequisites, provide an important focus of this chapter.

As we will see, stimulus equivalence research has obvious practical and educational value. Its significance is further increased because it provides the basis for development of a technology for establishing generative behavioral repertoires; instructional sequences that engender

[1] The preparation of this chapter was supported in part by Grants HD17445 and HD25995 from the National Institute of Child Health and Human Development and Grant RR07143 from the Department of Health and Human Services. Support of the Massachusetts Department of Mental Retardation (Contract No. 3404-8403-306) also is acknowledged. I thank Dr L.T. Stoddard for his comments in a previous version of this manuscript.

performances not explicitly trained. Progress in understanding the procedures that yield such emergent behavior thus is likely to suggest highly efficient teaching methods—ones that do not require explicit instruction of each of the myriad of individual subperformances encompassed in pre-reading, pre-arithmetic, and money skill repertoires. In addition, research on stimulus equivalence can elucidate the role of variables that affect the acquisition of these complex repertoires that often are viewed in terms of cognitive and linguistic processes.

Much of the research described here was conducted in laboratory settings and some involved participants who did not have learning disabilities. To date, only little systematic application appears to have been attempted in classrooms and other treatment settings. The challenge for teachers, psychologists, and other professionals, then, will be the creative application of the empirical findings that have emerged from the research conducted so far.

MATCHING-TO-SAMPLE PROCEDURES AND STIMULUS EQUIVALENCE

The basic tasks

MTS is a conditional discrimination procedure in which two (or more) comparison stimuli are presented simultaneously to the student on each trial (e.g., pictures of a CAT and a DOG). The positive comparison (S+), the one to be selected on a given trial, is determined by a third, conditional stimulus, the sample. In one form of this task, called *identity matching*, the sample and the positive comparison are physically the same. Thus, some trials begin with presentation of the CAT as the sample. After the student responds to the sample, the CAT and DOG comparisons appear simultaneously. In this instance, selection of CAT (S+) is reinforced by delivery of a penny, a candy, a token, praise, or some other stimulus that maintains the student's behavior. The picture of the DOG is the incorrect comparison (S−). When it is selected, in error, no reinforcer is delivered. The stimuli are merely removed and replaced, after a brief intertrial interval, by the sample for the next trial. The sample stimuli and the positions (left and right) of the comparison stimuli change unsystematically from trial to trial. Thus, on other trials, DOG is the sample. On these trials, the comparison DOG is now the S+ to be selected, and CAT is S−.

These four-term, sample–comparison–response–reinforcement contingencies (Sidman, 1986) typically generate a performance in which the student reliably selects the comparison stimulus specified as correct in the presence of each sample. That performance alone, however, does not constitute evidence that the student's behavior is controlled by relations of identity between the sample and comparison stimuli. Such an inference requires explicit tests of *generalized* identity matching using additional stimuli (e.g., pictures of a car, a bed, etc.). Successful performance in such tests can be taken for granted in normally capable children (cf. Stromer and Stromer, 1989). Many students with mental handicap, however, fail such tests, and therefore cannot be said to have been 'identity matching'. Their performance, instead, must be characterized only in terms of learning the specific conditional, or 'if . . . then . . .', relations specified by the training contingencies; if CAT then CAT, if DOG then DOG.

Another form of MTS task, called *arbitrary matching*, involves four-term contingencies just like those described previously, but the sample and comparison stimuli are physically different (e.g., pictures and printed words, numerals and dot quantities). Arbitrary matching procedures establish relations that resemble semantic (meaning) relations. For example, picture-printed word matching resembles a form of elementary reading. Thus, it often seems reasonable to suggest that the printed words 'stand for' or 'represent' the pictures (or that the numerals are 'symbols' for the dot quantities). This conception, however, involves the assumption that each sample and its positive comparison (e.g., the respective pictures and words, numerals and dot quantities) constitute a class of equivalent stimuli. As we will see, explicit tests are needed to verify this assumption. These tests, derived from elementary logic, evaluate whether the empirical relations between stimuli satisfy the three necessary properties of any equivalence relation: *reflexivity, symmetry,* and *transitivity*. The procedures for assessing these relational properties are described in the next section. It is important to note, however, that a student 'whose performance fails to display any one of these properties cannot be said to have been doing arbitrary matching; the stimuli involved in the procedure would bear only a conditional, or "if . . . then . . ." relation to each other, with no relation of equivalence' (Mackay and Sidman, 1984, p. 494).

Prerequisites of equivalence

Reflexivity, symmetry, and transitivity are the three prerequisites that must be satisfied before inferring that stimuli have become members of an equivalence class. Each can be specified operationally by MTS tests (Sidman and Tailby, 1982). The paradigm is illustrated in Figure 11.1

using three sets of visual stimuli that are important for numerical performances: printed numerals (A), and their printed names (B) and dot quantities (C). Reflexivity requires the demonstration of generalized identity MTS performance. The participant must match each printed numeral to itself, each printed word to itself, and each dot quantity to itself without explicit reinforcement. Symmetry refers to relations between two members of a class and is evaluated by tests for reversibility of the functions of the sample and comparison stimuli. Thus, a child who has learned the AB relations by doing numeral : word (sample : comparison) matching must also do word : numeral matching, BA, without explicit reinforcement. The third requirement, transitivity, refers to the relations between three members of a class. The child who has been taught the AB, numeral : word relations, and the BC, word : dot-quantity relations, must prove capable of AC, numeral : dot-quantity matching, again without explicit reinforcement.

Because AC transitive relations can emerge in the absence of symmetry in the directly trained performances, the existence of symmetry must be evaluated by separate tests. However, other procedural variants permit the simultaneous evaluation of symmetry and transitivity and, hence, a direct test of equivalence (Sidman and Tailby, 1982). For example, assume that the AB and AC tasks that share the same sample are trained. If the directly trained AB relations are symmetric (thus yielding BA), the combination of BA with AC will yield BC via transitivity. Emergence of the conditional relations BC (and CB) requires the directly trained relations, AB and AC, to be both symmetric and transitive. Similar logic can be applied to the case in which the training relations share comparisons rather than samples, e.g. AB and CB.

The procedures that yield equivalence class formation have significant educational implications because they make possible the occurrence of adaptive behavior in environments to which the student has never been exposed. Relevant quantitative considerations about the training that is

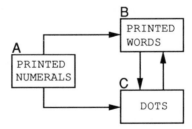

Figure 11.1 Illustration of the stimulus equivalence paradigm. See text for explanation.

necessary and about potential transitive outcomes have been discussed by Fields, Verhave and Fath (1984). The smallest number of training relations required to establish a class is $(N-1)$, where N is the number of stimuli in a class. The total number of derived transitive relations is $(N-2)(N-1)/2$. Thus, with a set of four stimuli, (A, B, C, and D), a minimum of three relations (e.g., A–B, A–C, A–D) must be trained in order to establish relations between all stimuli, and three transitive relations may be derived (B–C, B–D, C–D). In general, the ratio of trained to untrained performances increases with the class size. For example, to establish a five-member class, four training relations are required, but six transitive relations can be derived. In addition, the yield of untrained performances is increased by the emergence of symmetric relations.

The tests for reflexivity, symmetry, and transitivity are critical for evaluation of students' performance because they provide a way of determining whether more has been learned than is observed in the current performance. According to the logic of equivalence, only when all three tests are positive, thus confirming the formation of equivalence classes, can it be said that a numeral, a name, and a quantity of dots mean the same thing. Furthermore, the 'emergence of equivalence from conditionality permits behavior analysis to account for the establishment at least of simple semantic correspondences without having to postulate a direct reinforcement history for every instance. Instead of appealing to cognitions, representations, and stored correspondences to explain the initial occurrrence of appropriate new behavior, one can find a complete explanation in the four-term units that are the prerequisites for the emergent behavior' (Sidman, 1986, p. 236).

SIDMAN'S BASIC STUDY: EQUIVALENCE AND READING

Sidman (1971) reported the initial study using the stimulus equivalence paradigm to teach a rudimentary reading repertoire to a youth with a moderate mental handicap. Figure 11.2 outlines the paradigm which, in contrast with the preceding example with only visual stimuli, included stimulus names spoken to, and by, the student. The lettered boxes designate the categories of stimuli used—these were 20 dictated picture names (A), and their corresponding pictures (B) and printed names (C). The box marked 'D' represents names produced by the student. The arrows point from the sample to the comparison stimuli of the four MTS tasks used in the critical teaching and testing, and from the stimuli to the oral naming performances of oral naming tests.

Preliminary tests indicated that the youth could match picture comparisons (B) to their dictated names (A) when he entered the study. He thus demonstrated the auditory comprehension performance designated by the AB relations between corresponding dictated and visual stimuli. He also named the pictures orally, thus demonstrating the BD performance. MTS training then taught the youth to select printed picture names conditionally upon their corresponding dictated names (AC relations), a form of auditory-receptive reading performance. After he mastered this task, the two performances of matching printed words to pictures (BC) and pictures to printed words (CB) emerged without training. These emergent performances, which define two forms of visual reading comprehension, confirmed the formation of 20 three-member classes of equivalent stimuli. For example, one class consisted of the dictated word 'bee', a picture of a bee, and the printed word 'bee'; another class consisted of the dictated word 'car', a picture of a car, and the printed word 'car'. The CD performance of orally naming the printed words, a rudimentary form of oral reading, also emerged without explicit training.

As suggested previously, the equivalence paradigm allows great economy of teaching. Sidman's student had already learned 20 AB and 20 BD relations and was directly taught 20 AC relations. Without additional training, he then demonstrated 60 more—20 BC and 20 CB relations, and the 20 word-naming relations.

The teaching paradigm illustrated in Figure 11.2 has also been shown to be effective with more severely mentally handicapped students who were unable to match the pictures to their dictated names or to name the pictures or the printed words orally prior to training (Sidman and Cresson, 1973). Nevertheless, naming performances frequently emerge after exposure to the auditory–visual MTS training. It is of practical and theoretical interest, however, that naming frequently may not occur during the actual training itself (see below).

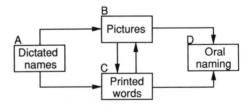

Figure 11.2 Illustration of stimulus equivalence paradigm used by Sidman (1971). See text for explanation.

The gradual emergence of outcome performances

Many students, like Sidman's, display the critical emergent conditional discriminations (and the naming performances as well) in the first outcome tests given after training. But what can the teacher do if a student fails to demonstrate these performances immediately?

One possibility is simply to repeat the tests. Some investigators have reported that equivalence classes may develop gradually across unreinforced test repetitions (e.g., Sidman, Willson-Morris and Kirk, 1986; Spradlin, Cotter and Baxley, 1973; Green, 1991; Stromer and Osborne, 1982). While these observations suggest a useful practical step that may be taken they also have raised important issues concerning equivalence class formation and the variables that influence it (e.g., Lazar, Davis-Lang and Sanchez, 1984; Saunders, Wachter and Spradlin, 1988; Sidman, Willson-Morris and Kirk, 1986; Stoddard and McIlvane, 1986). For example: is the baseline training sufficient for formation of equivalence classes or is class formation dependent on experiencing the outcome tests? Do uncontrolled features of the teaching environment sometimes involve a 'sorting out process' [because] 'the stimuli chosen on some trials were determined by class memberships that proved to be invalid on other trials' (Sidman, Kirk and Willson-Morris, 1985, p. 60). What aspects of the test conditions (e.g., the presence or absence of baseline performances) facilitate or hinder the display of equivalence relations? Further research is needed to answer such questions and to identify manipulable variables that might foster the desired outcomes.

Also relevant here are considerations about the relations between reflexivity, symmetry, and transitivity. It is conceivable that the three requirements for equivalence are hierarchical; reflexivity may be a precondition for symmetry, and symmetry may be a precondition for transitivity (Stoddard and McIlvane, 1986; Spradlin and Saunders, 1984; Sidman, Willson-Morris and Kirk, 1986). If so, equivalence class formation may be facilitated, or even 'programmed', by careful arrangement of the order in which the tests for its prerequisites are presented. Perhaps tests for reflexivity should be given first, and followed by tests for symmetry, and then transitivity.

Although relevant data are sparse, some support the notion that symmetric performance may be a critical precursor of transitive perform- ance (e.g., Green, 1991; Sidman, Willson-Morris and Kirk, 1986). For example, Sidman, Willson-Morris and Kirk (1986) used combined tests for symmetry and transitivity to evaluate the formation of equivalence relations among visual stimuli. Three students initially failed these tests. Direct tests for symmetry of the trained relations were given next, and two of these students immediately displayed good performance on them.

Both then passed the combined tests. The third student failed on only one of the combined tests and, then, also on the direct symmetry test related to it. His performances on the other combined test, and its related direct test of symmetry, were positive. After this student received direct training on the missing symmetry performance, he succeeded on the combined test that he had failed previously.

Systematic replications and extensions

Sidman's original findings have been systematically replicated and extended in repeated studies showing that appropriate conditional discrimination training can yield performances that were not explicitly trained (e.g., Gast, VanBiervliet and Spradlin, 1979; Hollis, Fulton and Larson, 1986; Lazar, 1977; Mackay and Sidman, 1984; Stoddard et al., 1989; Spradlin and Dixon, 1976; Sidman and Cresson, 1973; Sidman, Cresson and Willson-Morris, 1974; Sidman, Kirk and Willson-Morris, 1985; Sidman, Willson-Morris and Kirk, 1986; Stromer and Osborne, 1982; Wetherby, Karlan and Spradlin, 1983). A broad range of students have participated, including: normally capable pre-school and school-age children and adults; people with mental handicap and autism representing all but the most profound levels of developmental retardation, many diagnostic categories, and a wide age range (up to the eighth decade). Patients with brain injuries, and deaf children also have participated in some studies.

Only one study with human students reported failure to observe the emergence of equivalence after conditional discrimination training. Devany, Hayes and Nelson (1986) found that 'language-able' normal children and those with mental handicap formed classes of equivalent visual stimuli whereas 'language-impaired' children (matched to the mental ages of the language-able children) did not. Replication of Devany et al.'s observations (including formal specification of students' language capabilities) is important because they are relevant to the broad issue of the relationship between stimulus equivalence and language. Some have suggested that processes involved in emergent performances may be fundamental to language acquisition (e.g., Catania, 1984; Mackay and Sidman, 1984; Sidman, 1986)—a view consistent with the failure of investigations to demonstrate equivalence and its prerequisites in nonhuman animals (cf., D'Amato et al., 1985; Sidman et al., 1982; but see McIntire, Cleary and Thompson, 1987). On the other hand, others have suggested (e.g., Devany, Hayes and Nelson, 1986; Lowe, 1986) that emergent performances may be mediated by subjects' language capabilities.

Visual and auditory stimuli have been used most commonly as the samples and comparisons in table-top and automated (e.g., computer-controlled) tasks. However, recent research has shown that spatial and gustatory stimuli may also participate in equivalence classes (Mackay and Ratti, 1990; Hayes, Tilley and Hayes, 1988), and two studies suggest that specific reinforcing stimuli, e.g. types of food, may be members of equivalence classes together with sample and comparison stimuli (Dube et al., 1987, 1989).

Typically, subjects have responded to stimuli merely by touching them. The use of oral naming by some investigators and manual signing by others (e.g., Clarke, Remington and Light, 1986, 1988; Osborne and Gatch, 1989; Remington and Clarke, 1983; VanBiervliet, 1977), however, has extended the range of behavior relevant to equivalence. Such responses also have substantial applied significance; they provide forms of verbal communication. In other work, procedural modifications have required students to construct the stimuli that are to participate in equivalence classes. For example, a form of spelling has been included in the network of relations shown in Figure 11.2 by teaching students to select individual anagram letters to construct the words (Mackay and Sidman, 1984; see below). Stoddard et al., (1989) illustrate the application of the constructed response procedure to money skills.

The existing literature illustrates a variety of the quantitative features of possible procedures, their outcomes, and the teaching variables that may influence class formation. Equivalence class formation has been demonstrated using from two to 20 classes. The number of stimuli in each class has varied from three (the minimum) to nine (eight visual and one auditory; Saunders, Wachter and Spradlin, 1988). It has also been shown that existing equivalence classes may be expanded readily by establishing a relation (e.g., via MTS) between a new stimulus and one member of an existing class (Sidman, Kirk and Willson-Morris, 1985). Further, Spradlin and Saunders (1986) found that for participants with a mental handicap MTS training with four sample stimuli each related to a single comparison (many-to-one training) yielded equivalence relations among the samples. In contrast, training that related a single sample to each of four comparisons (one-to-many training) failed to yield equivalence relations among the comparison stimuli. These results suggest that the direction of the stimulus–stimulus relations established during training may be important for later demonstration of equivalence class formation (see Stoddard and McIlvane, 1986, for discussion of this research). Stromer and Stromer (1990a, b) have demonstrated that each component of a complex sample may enter into the same equivalence class. Their procedure thus suggests that the paired presentation of stimuli during training may yield instructional gains. Finally, the conditions that result in the merging of two existing classes have been explored. For example, the stimuli in each class may be made equivalent to one another by establishing matching relations between one member of one class and one member of the other class (Sidman, Kirk and Willson-Morris, 1985; see also Saunders et al., 1988). The formal analyses provided by Fields, Verhave and Fath (1984) and Fields and Verhave (1987) may serve as a guide to further empirical investigation of such quantitative variables.

Innovative extensions of the general conditional discrimination methods have been developed by some investigators. MacDonald, Dixon and LeBlanc (1986) investigated the use of observational learning methods in establishing equivalence classes. In a particularly creative study, Silverman et al. (1986) illustrated the relevance of concepts derived from stimulus equivalence research to social behavior and to complex verbal behavior. (For useful discussion of these two studies and suggestions for additional work, see Stoddard and McIlvane, 1986). In addition, contextual control of equivalence relations has been demonstrated (Bush, Sidman and DeRose, 1989).

Finally, a few studies have investigated whether all members of an equivalence class will perform the same functions in contexts differing from the MTS context in which the classes were established (e.g., Lazar and Kotlarchyk, 1986; DeRose et al., 1988). In addition, others have examined whether existing stimulus functions will transfer to other class members when that stimulus is added to the class (e.g., Sidman et al., 1989). In general, such studies concern the relationship between equivalence classes and stimulus classes that are comprised of stimuli that perform the same functions (as discriminative stimuli, as members of sequences and so on). Some of these studies involve relationships between equivalence classes and sequence classes and thus may be relevant to the analysis of syntactic behavior (see below).

Equivalence classes and stimulus names

The student in Sidman's (1971) study—and others since then—demonstrated emergent visual matching performances after auditory–visual, receptive training. The performance of producing the same oral name for each of the stimuli in a class also emerged. The function of the names spoken to and by the student remains a question; however, that has prompted considerable discussion about the nature and basis of equivalence classes. For example, is the naming critical for equivalence? Do common names applied to all stimuli in a class serve as differential responses that mediate class formation? The issue has much in common with earlier response mediation accounts of stimulus equivalence and 'mediated generalization' (cf. Jenkins, 1963; Jenkins and Palermo, 1964). However, although there is little doubt that differential responses can mediate the formation of stimulus classes, several difficulties face a response-mediation interpretation of the development of equivalence relations.

In the paired-associate procedures often used in the earlier studies, training included the production of names. In contrast, Sidman's and other similar studies of stimulus equivalence used MTS procedures to establish receptive auditory–visual performances; naming was not explicitly taught. With respect to the matching performances, then, it appears just as plausible to suggest that naming was an outcome of stimulus equivalences yielded by the training as it is to infer that naming mediated the formation of equivalences. Also inconsistent with a response mediation account are the findings of studies demonstrating the formation of entirely visual classes (e.g., Green, 1990; Sidman, Kirk, and Willson-Morris, 1985; Stromer and Osborne, 1982). In this instance, if the application of common names underlies the emergence of equivalence relations, then the students themselves would have to supply these names—and several investigators have reported that this may not occur (Sidman et al., 1982; Lazar, Davis-Lang and Sanchez, 1984; Sidman, Willson-Morris and Kirk, 1986). These observations are consistent with the general finding that young normally capable children and individuals with mental handicaps often fail to produce mediating behavior without direct instructions to do so (e.g., Constantine and Sidman, 1975; Ellis, 1979).

Other evidence also indicates that stimulus equivalence may be independent of naming. Sidman and Tailby (1982) reported that new conditional discriminations may emerge before students apply names to the stimuli involved. The students in Lazar, Davis-Lang and Sanchez's (1984) study demonstrated equivalence class formation although they almost always gave different names for the stimuli in each class. Apparently, then, common names are not necessary for equivalence class formation. In addition, naming does not appear to provide a sufficient basis for the emergence of equivalence relations. Sidman and Tailby (1982), for example, reported that students may name stimuli before they are able to match these stimuli to their dictated names—an auditory–visual performance that is required to support the inference of class formation.

As Sidman and Tailby (1982) stated, 'the dichotomy . . . between classes defined by naming and classes defined by equivalence is not surprising: the relation "is name of", does not possess the defining properties of an equivalence relation' (p. 21). Classes that are defined in terms of common naming responses, however, may be characterized as functional classes because each stimulus in a class controls the same response (Goldiamond,

1966). It may be, then, that functional (naming) and equivalence (matching) classes are independent outcomes of the training procedures (cf. Sidman, Willson-Morris and Kirk, 1986), 'and not that one (equivalence) depends upon the other (naming)' (Saunders, 1989, p. 383). This notion is consistent with the view that direct stimulus–stimulus (sample-comparison) relations underlie the formation of stimulus equivalence (Lazar, Davis-Lang and Sanchez, 1984; Mackay, 1985; Sidman, 1986; Stoddard and McIlvane, 1986). However, just as suggested previously, it is possible that names may serve important functions that facilitate the formation of equivalence relations. Indeed, some evidence suggests that classes that involve dictated names may form more readily than classes that do not (Sidman, Willson-Morris and Kirk, 1986; Green, 1990). In Green's study, five women with mental handicaps were taught two classes that contained three visual stimuli (arbitrary forms) and two that each contained one auditory stimulus (or spoken syllable) and two visual stimuli. Four of these students required repeated testing, before they demonstrated equivalence with the stimuli from the all-visual classes. In contrast, all were immediately successful on the equivalence tests with stimuli from the auditory–visual classes. The difference between classes also appeared with a sorting task. All students immediately grouped the visual stimuli from the auditory–visual classes whereas only two did so with the stimuli that made up the all-visual classes.

The results of these studies are important and require follow-up. They help to elucidate the nature and the basis of equivalence classes and add to our meager knowledge about the variables that may facilitate or hinder equivalence formation. There are also worthwhile applications.

Practical and educational implications

Oral naming is often a critical ingredient in initial reading instruction, as with the common 'look–say' method in which the meaning of a word is established by teaching children to give the same name to a printed word and to its referents, e.g. a picture and an object. The training thus establishes the picture, the object, and the text as members of the same functional class because they each control the same response. However, these children may then be capable of selecting the appropriate printed word and its 'referent' when another individual says the word aloud, thereby demonstrating emergent performances that suggest the formation of equivalence relations. The 'look–say' method thus may be considered a reversal of the sequence of events described in refernce to Sidman's (1971) study. Students are explicitly taught the BD and CD oral naming performances shown in Figure 11.2; the BC, CB, AB, and AC performances then emerge.

With the 'look–say' method, a teacher must be present to monitor the children's naming responses. For this reason, MTS procedures that establish rudimentary spoken and textual language forms, even in individuals with severe learning disabilities, may have relative practical advantages. Many individuals who have not yet learned to read often are already capable of matching stimuli like pictures, colors, and numbers to their dictated names, and can name these stimuli orally. In other words, they already possess important prerequisites that would allow training to be conducted via auditory–visual matching tasks or entirely in the visual modality, e.g. with pictures and printed words. The presentation of these auditory and visual stimuli can be automated readily via computer (see Dube and McIlvane, 1989). Thus, practical methods are available for introducing rudimentary reading tasks to many severely handicapped individuals without the continuous involvement of a teacher. Auditory–visual instruction, however, may be more fruitful than visual–visual because it may be used with many words that cannot be related to pictures, e.g. verbs (walk, run, lift, etc.) that are already in the student's receptive vocabulary. The technology is not currently widely available that would permit the teaching of visual relations between printed words and moving pictures of these actions.

Aspects of the preceding discussion may be relevant to non-oral modes of communication such as manual signing. For example, Clarke, Remington and Light's (1986, 1988) studies of 'sign-alone' and 'total communication' training illustrate relations between expressive and receptive signing that are analogous to the relations between expressive and receptive performances involved in 'look–say' reading instruction. In a procedure that bears a formal resemblance to the one used by Stromer and Stromer (1990a, b), children with mental handicaps and autism learned to produce manual signs conditionally upon paired presentations of dictated picture names and pictures. This expressive training resulted in receptive stimulus control of picture selection by manual signs, an outcome like that produced by the look–say method of reading instruction. In addition, Clarke, Remington and Light (1988) observed that acquisition of signed picture naming was faster and retained better when the dictated picture names (with which the signs were paired) already controlled picture selection. Although selective control by picture or spoken stimuli may limit the transfer of stimulus control produced by training, the 'results suggest that the selection of referents on the basis of a child's receptive vocal repertoire may facilitate signing acquisition and retention. A simply administered pretest thus

can provide an efficient means of selecting appropriate training items'
(Clarke, Remington and Light, 1986, p. 237).

More generally, the formation of equivalence classes that include
receptive and expressive performances may facilitate the development of
functional social behavior and communication. Such performances extend
the range and the forms of behavior controlled by each stimulus in a
class because they establish components of the student's repertoire as
'listener' and as 'speaker'. In turn, these repertoires introduce the
possibility of social interactions in a way that exposes the behavior
involved to the reinforcement contingencies that occur naturally in the
community. In this respect, it is worth noting that equivalence classes
and functional classes may share the characteristic that reinforcement of
only some of the relations involved will serve to maintain all of the
relations in the class (cf. Sidman and Tailby, 1982).

EQUIVALENCE AND SPELLING

Constructed stimuli

Figure 11.3 outlines an expansion of the equivalence paradigm that
illustrates how forms of spelling may be included. In one study (Mackay,
1985), each of three boys with severe mental handicap could perform
only the AB and BD tasks when the study began. They were then taught
the task BE which required them to construct printed words letter by
letter in response to colored patch samples. Figure 11.4 illustrates the
stimulus cards used in the program for teaching the word *black*. In each
trial, one of the cards was placed on the table with five small tiles (the
choice pool) on each of which was printed one letter: b, l, a, c, or k. For
the final performance, the card had a black patch at the left and five lines
to the right (bottom panel). The task was to place the letter tiles above
the lines in the order required to construct the word *black*. If the student
did so, he received praise and a token.

The initial card in the teaching sequence is shown at the top in Figure
11.4. The word *black* printed above the lines on this card served to
prompt selection of successive letters from the choice pool. Thus, the
student merely placed individual letter tiles on the matching letters in
the prompt word in order, left to right. As training progressed across
successive program cards, the prompt letters were removed one at a time.
On the final trials, without prompt letters, the black patch alone occasioned
construction of the printed word. Additional programs were developed
to teach construction of the words *red*, *green*, *blue*, *orange*, and *yellow*.

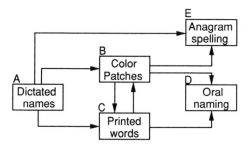

Figure 11.3 Illustration of stimulus equivalence paradigm including anagram word construction. See text for explanation.

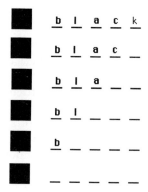

Figure 11.4 Illustration of teaching program stimulus cards used by Mackay (1985).

Training was given with one word at a time with final performance tests of cumulative words learned after each training series. Post-training tests given after all six words had been trained then assessed whether the MTS performances AC, BC, and CB had emerged as well as the word-naming performance CD. If the word construction training established each printed color word as a compound stimulus related to the corresponding color patch, then all of those relations could emerge, thus confirming the formation of equivalence classes. All three boys demonstrated these emergent post-test performances, a result that has been replicated systematically. For example, the critical emergent performances have been obtained when dictated color names rather than patches of color were the samples during training (Lazar and Mackay, 1982; see also Mackay and Sidman, 1984) Other response forms have also been examined—oral spelling of picture names (Stromer, in press) and writing the names of numerals (Mackay and Sidman, 1984); subsequent matching tests involving the dictated names, the pictures or numerals, and the printed names yielded similar emergent outcomes.

Educational significance

The preceding studies are consistent with others that illustrate circum-stances under which training in spelling may yield reading performances (cf. Chomsky, 1971; Ehri and Wilce, 1987; Lee and Sanderson, 1987). Their educational significance is enhanced, however, when viewed in the context of the equivalence paradigm. In the original paradigm (Figure 11.2), which does not include spelling, two tasks were trained directly (e.g., AB and AC) and four other performances then emerged. In the modified paradigm (Figure 11.3), two tasks again were taught directly (e.g., AB and BE), but six other performances then emerged. The training, which required explicit behavior with respect to each letter in a word, may also have other advantages. Such training would tend to discourage (if not eliminate) control of reading by restricted aspects of the words (e.g., initial letter, last letter, general outline, etc.) and thus minimize the occurrence of errors related to such sources of stimulus control.

The variables that may be critical to the emergent outcomes after spelling (or writing) training are not well understood. Data from other research illustrate the complexities of the problem. Some findings suggest, for example, that reading and spelling may be functionally independent. For example, instruction in reading printed words does not necessarily improve spelling. As Lee and Sanderson (1987, p. 7) found, 'a reader can read (or, better, text) the same word he or she cannot spell (i.e., write in standard form) on another occasion' (see also Stromer, in press, for an example with oral spelling). In addition, spelling may occur in the absence of reading (cf. Lee and Pegler, 1982).

From the perspective of the present analysis, such results are not surprising. Reading and spelling may function independently because the potential forms of stimulus control involved in each repertoire may differ. Continued research is needed to elucidate the conditions that may engender or prevent such functional independence. In this respect, Lee and Pegler's (1982) data may be instructive in suggesting relevant variables that may promote the interdependence of reading and spelling. These investigators found (with normally capable children who had deficient reading skills) that written spelling from dictation improved with overtraining on oral reading. Additional analysis also showed that the variable responsible for the improved spelling was repeated exposure to the printed words rather than repeated opportunities to say the words aloud. However, the study left unanswered questions about the prerequisites for learning to produce the individual elements (i.e., the letter names) in sequence. Whether the procedure of merely exposing the children to the printed words without requiring oral reading involved primarily receptive or expressive components remains unclear. Apparently the children often rehearsed spellings audibly or subvocally, thus rendering their performance, if not the task requirements, expressive rather than receptive. Perhaps that behavior was necessary to 'decompose' the compound printed word stimuli into the constituent elements critical for the spelling. If so, would the results of the procedure differ for individuals with mental handicaps who often fail to make use of such behavior even when they are capable of it (Constantine and Sidman, 1975; Mackay and Ratti, 1990; see also Ellis, 1979)?

EQUIVALENCE AND SYNTACTIC BEHAVIOR

The use of meaningful two-word utterances by young children is an early indicator of novel verbal behavior that provides a basis for the development of syntax (cf. Brown, 1958). The emergence of untrained equivalence relations may exemplify the development of the simple semantic (meaning) relations involved in such behavior, as suggested previously. But what of the systematic sequential properties (e.g., 'first' and 'second' in two-word utterances) that also characterize the relations between words?

In the context of the present analysis, it is conceivable that the words (stimuli) that comprise equivalence classes may come to participate also in functional sequence classes. For example, acquisition of a few two-word utterances may result in the emergence of two classes of words, each consisting of those words that had served an equivalent serial function (first and second) in different utterances. Potentially, the words in each sequence class may be considered members of the same grammatical class—adjectives and nouns, nouns and verbs, etc.

Consider a child who has learned to name the colors red, green, and blue and the objects bus, ball, and car, and then is taught to say 'red bus' and 'green ball' in the presence of these objects. The repetition of these utterances clearly would be a direct function of the training. However, the child may also produce the novel utterances 'red ball', 'green bus', and 'blue car' appropriately when shown these objects. These novel generative performances suggest that 'red', 'green', and 'blue' belong to the class 'first', and 'bus', 'ball', and 'car' to the class 'second' as well as to meaning classes.

Although speculative, this account is consistent with studies that have examined the relationship between equivalence classes and sequence classes. For example, in a study with 6-year-old children, Lazar and Kotlarchyk (1986) established two three-member equivalence classes with visual stimuli. Next, the children were trained to touch two of these stimuli in order: first, one stimulus from one class, and second, one stimulus from the other class. Finally, sequence tests with the remaining stimuli were presented—two stimuli, one from each equivalence class appeared on each test trial. The children touched these test stimuli in the order, first and second, that was consistent with the class memberships established earlier; no explicit sequence training was required. The results suggested that one equivalence class now could be considered the class 'first' and the other the class 'second'. Lazar and Kotlarchyk also demonstrated that the sequential functions of stimuli in each class could be brought under second-order conditional control. The children were presented with one stimulus from each equivalence class (patches of green and red respectively) and trained to touch these stimuli in two different orders conditionally upon the presence of another stimulus (tone A or tone B). When tone A was presented, they had to touch green first and then red. When tone B was presented they had to touch red first and then green. Next, in critical tests using other stimuli from the two equivalence classes, the children touched stimuli from class 1 first and stimuli from class 2 second in the presence of tone A. The order was reversed in the presence of tone B.

The relevance of second-order control to syntax may be seen in the following illustration. After training like that described above, a child orders the printed words THE, RED, and TRUCK, in different ways conditionally upon the presence of the word IS. If classes of color words and object words had previously been established, the child should then produce the novel sequences THE GREEN BALL and THE BALL IS GREEN. The possibility for the development of longer sequences like these has been investigated by Sigurdardottir, Green and Saunders (1990). In related work, Wulfert and Hayes (1988) provide extensive discussion of the potential relevance of such findings for rudimentary grammatical development. A particularly important feature of such research is the demonstration that 'the environment can establish rather sophisticated control over sequential responses to symbols and that from few training exemplars a very large and flexible number of untrained sequences can arise' (Wulfert and Hayes, 1988, p. 140).

At present, the literature contains no research with mentally handicapped individuals that directly concerns the issues just discussed. It may be noted, however, that the foregoing work has features in common with matrix training procedures used recently to examine language development in individuals with mental handicap (e.g., Goldstein, Angelo and Mousetis, 1987; McCuller and Salzberg, 1984; Remington, Watson and Light, 1990; Wetherby and Striefel, 1978).

EQUIVALENCE AND MEMORY

Personal experience and anecdotal accounts of the long-term stability of performances based on equivalence class formation have suggested to this author that the relational learning described here is relevant to the study of memory. People with mental handicap often have shown excellent retention of equivalence classes across absences lasting up to a month due to vacations or periods of illness. Systematic examination of the retention of equivalence classes is only beginning, however. In one of few systematic studies of retention, Saunders, Wachter and Spradlin (1988) found that eight-member equivalence classes 'remained intact' for some students with test–retest periods that lasted up to five months. These investigators also observed that erratic performance could be perfected without direct reinforcement. In accounting for this outcome, Saunders and colleages suggested that the network of relations that was established directly and indirectly may have provided multiple determination of each relation within a class. Thus, the 'stimulus control of the intact relations may have served as the basis for ultimately recovering all the relations involved in the stimulus class' (p. 113). For example, consider a three-member equivalence class containing the visual stimuli A, B, and C. Such a class involves six stimulus–stimulus relations: AB, AC, and BC, and their symmetric counterparts, BA, CA, and CB. Even if only two of these relations remain intact in any combination (e.g., AB and BC, or AC and CB, etc.), that would provide sufficient basis for recovery of the remainder.

Further pursuit of this notion suggests that class size and the availability of stimulus names may be variables of considerable interest. With respect to class size, one might expect that larger classes would show greater stability over time than smaller classes. For instance, in comparison with the preceding example, a four-member class has 12 constituent relations, and only three of them must be intact (again in any combination) in order to derive the remainder. Similarly, the availability of a spoken name for the stimuli in a class potentially increases the number and the nature of the relations in the class. For example, suppose that stimulus A in the earlier three-member example was a dictated name rather than a visual stimulus. In this case, three stimulus–response relations, AD, BD, and CD, might be added to the class. Thus, if naming performances emerge, classes that include the names may be remembered better than classes of visual stimuli.

It is of interest with respect to these notions that Fields *et al.* (1990) recently noted the formal similarities between studies of equivalence relations and research on semantic memory networks or knowledge structures (cf. Anderson, 1981). Furthermore, Green *et al.* (1990) suggested that class size might be a quantitive index of the richness of the student's 'knowledge base (semantic network) (Chi, 1976)'.

The relevance of equivalence class formation to short-term memory processes, rather than long-term retention, was examined by Mackay and Ratti (1990). Specifically, they investigated the role of equivalence class formation in a delayed recognition span test with three individuals with mental handicap. The stimuli for the span test were the positions of discs on the nine-position (3×3) test-board. The three participants with learning disabilities, however, had no names for these spatial stimuli and, thus, had no basis for the kind of verbal mnemonic code that might facilitate span performance. Pre-tests showed, however, that each student was able to match printed numerals (1–9) to their corresponding names and to name these stimuli orally—performances that were critical to the design of training that might enable the use of a verbal mnemonic strategy. In this training, an arbitrary MTS procedure was used to relate each numeral to a position on the recognition span test board. Tests then confirmed the formation of nine equivalence classes each comprised of a position, a numeral, and the numeral name. In addition, students displayed the emergent performance of labelling the recognition-span, test-board positions with the numeral names. Repetition of the span test then showed that student-produced numeral names served to yield dramatically improved span performance. Thus, training established equivalence classes and functional (naming) classes that were the basis for behavior that may define a form of 'encoding' that facilitates short-term remembering. This study, thus, may suggest novel ways to analyze and to teach the prerequisites for behavior that constitutes the basis of rudimentary forms of strategy use in individuals with mental handicap who are said to display mediational deficiencies (cf. Ellis, 1979).

CONCLUSION

Individuals with mental handicap often do not respond to standard instructional methods because these methods typically depend heavily on verbal instruction. Furthermore, these individuals frequently display multiple behavioral deficits. Remediation of each of these deficits individually can be time consuming, impractical, and beyond the reach of available resources. The instructional methods described in this chapter, however, can make effective remediation an attainable goal. These methods may enhance teaching effectiveness because they do not rely on verbal instruction. They can also increase the efficiency of instruction because they can engender new behaviors that emerge without direct training, define conditions that may determine whether functional behaviors will appear in novel situations, and lead to coordination of complex repertoires of behavior (e.g., receptive and expressive repertoires, reading and spelling performances). Technological advances that enable the use of microcomputers may further increase the number of individuals with mental handicaps who can be exposed to the kind of instruction they require. Several examples of rudimentary pre-academic skills that are well suited to computer presentation were described in this chapter. Finally, the straightforward logic that provides an analytic framework for the approach described here may be particularly useful in the analysis and design of teaching and remediation methods. More generally, this approach is valuable because it emphasizes variables that directly influence behavior acquisition. Such an emphasis helps to ensure that the results of experimental analyses of behavior often have direct implications for applied behavior analysis.

Address for correspondence

Harry A. Mackay, Behavior Analysis Department, Eunice Kennedy Shriver Center, 200 Trapelo Road, Waltham, Massachusetts 02115, USA.

REFERENCES

Anderson, J.R. (1981) Concepts, propositions, and schemata: What are the cognitive units? In J.H. Flowers (ed.), *Nebraska Symposium on Motivation*, (Vol. 28, pp. 121–162), University of Nebraska Press, Lincoln.
Brown, R.W. (1958) *Words and Things*, Free Press, New York.
Bush, K.M., Sidman, M. and deRose, T. (1989) Contextual control of emergent equivalence relations *Journal of the Experimental Analysis of Behavior*, **51**, 29–45.
Catania, A.C. (1984) *Learning* (2nd edn), Prentice-Hall, Englewood Cliffs, New Jersey.
Chi, M.T.H. (1976) Short-term memory limitations in children: Capacity or processing deficits. *Memory and Cognition*, **4**, 559–572.
Chomsky, C. (1971) Write first; read later. *Child Education*, **47**, 296–299.
Clarke, S., Remington, B. and Light, P. (1986) An evaluation of the relationship between receptive speech skills and expressive signing. *Journal of Applied Behavior Analysis*, **19**, 231–239.

Clarke, S., Remington, B. and Light, P. (1988) The role of referential speech in sign learning by mentally retarded children: A comparison of total communication and sign-alone training. *Journal of Applied Behavior Analysis*, **21**, 419–426.

Constantine, B. and Sidman, M. (1975) Role of naming in delayed matching-to-sample *American Journal of Mental Deficiency*, **79**, 680–689.

D'Amato, M.R., Salmon, D.P., Loukas, E. and Tomie, A. (1985) Symmetry and transitivity of conditional relations in monkeys (*Cebus apella*) and pigeons (*Columba livia*). *Journal of the Experimental Analysis of Behavior*, **44**, 35–47.

deRose, J.C., McIlvane, W.J., Dube, W.V. and Stoddard, L.T. (1988) Stimulus class formation and functional equivalence in moderately retarded individuals' conditional discrimination. *Behavioral Processes*, **17**, 167–175.

Devany, J.M., Hayes, S.C. and Nelson, R.O. (1986) Equivalence class formation in language-able and language-disabled children *Journal of the Experimental Analysis of Behavior*, **46**, 243–257.

Dube, W.V. and McIlvane, W.J. (1989) Adapting a microcomputer for behavioral evaluation of mentally retarded individuals. In J.A. Mulick and R.F. Antonak (eds), *Transitions in Mental Retardation* (Vol. 4, pp. 104–127), Ablex, Norwood, New Jersey.

Dube, W.V., McIlvane, W.J., Mackay, H.A. and Stoddard, L.T. (1987) Stimulus class membership established via stimulus–reinforcer relations. *Journal of the Experimental Analysis of Behavior*, **47**, 159–175.

Dube, W.V., McIlvane, W.J., Maguire, R.W., Mackay, H.A. and Stoddard, L.T. (1989) Stimulus class formation and stimulus–reinforcer relations. *Journal of the Experimental Analysis of Behavior*, **51**, 65–76.

Ehri, L.C. and Wilce, L.S. (1987) Does learning to spell help beginners learn to read words? *Reading Research Quarterly*, **22**, 47–65.

Ellis, N.E. (1979) *Handbook of Mental Deficiency, Psychological Theory and Research*, Erlbaum, Hillsdale, New Jersey.

Fields, L. and Verhave, T. (1987) The structure of equivalence classes. *Journal of the Experimental Analysis of Behavior*, **48**, 317–332.

Fields, L. Verhave, T. and Fath, S. (1984) Stimulus equivalence and transitive associations: A methodological analysis. *Journal of the Experimental Analysis of Behavior*, **42**, 143–157.

Fields, L., Adams, B.J., Verhave, T. and Newman, S. (1990) The effect of nodality on the formation of equivalence classes. *Journal of the Experimental Analysis of Behavior*, **53**, 345–358.

Gast, D.L., VanBiervliet, A. and Spradlin, J.E. (1979) Teaching number–word equivalences: A study of transfer. *American Journal of Mental Deficiency*, **83**, 524–527.

Goldiamond, I. (1966) Perception, language, and conceptualization rules. In B. Kleimuntz (ed.), *Problem Solving* (pp. 183–224), Wiley, New York.

Goldstein, H., Angelo, D. and Mousetis, L. (1987) Acquisition and extension of syntactic repertoires by severely retarded youth. *Research in Developmental Disabilities*, **8**, 549–574.

Green, G. (1990) Differences in development of visual and auditory–visual equivalence relations. *American Journal on Mental Retardation*, **95**, 260–270..

Green, G., Mackay, H.A., McIlvane, W.J., Saunders, R.R. and Soraci, S.A. (1990) Perspectives on relational learning in mental retardation *American Journal on Mental Retardation*, **95**, 249–259.

Hayes, L.J., Tilley, K.J. and Hayes, S.C. (1988) Extending equivalence class membership to gustatory stimuli. *The Psychological Record*, **38**, 473–482.

Hollis, J.H., Fulton, R.T. and Larson, A.D. (1986) An equivalence model for vocabulary acquisition in hearing-impaired children. *Analysis and Intervention in Developmental Disabilities*, **6**, 331–348.

Jenkins, J.J. (1963) Mediated associations: Paradigms and situations. In C.N. Cofer and B.S. Musgrave (eds), *Verbal Behavior and Learning: Problems and Processes* (pp. 210–245), McGraw-Hill, New York.

Jenkins, J.J. and Palermo, D.S. (1964) Mediation processes and the acquisition of linguistic structure. In *The Acquisition of Language*, Monographs of the Society for Research in Child Development, **29**, No.1, 141–169.

Lazar, R. (1977) Extending sequence-class membership with matching to sample. *Journal of the Experimental Analysis of Behavior*, **27**, 381–392.

Lazar, R., Davis-Lang, D. and Sanchez, L. (1984) The formation of stimulus equivalence in children. *Journal of the Experimental Analysis of Behavior*, **41**, 251–266.

Lazar, R. and Kotlarchyk, B.J. (1986) Second-order control of sequence-class equivalences in children. *Behavioural Processes*, **13**, 205–215.

Lazar, R. and Mackay, H.A. (1982) Teaching spelling via stimulus equivalences. Exceptional Children Educational Resources, 14:EC142410, National Institute of Education, Washington, DC.

Lee, V.L. and Pegler, A.M. (1982) Effects on spelling of training children to read *Journal of the Experimental Analysis of Behavior*, **37**, 311–322.

Lee, V.L. and Sanderson, C.M. (1987) Some contingencies of spelling. *Analysis of Verbal Behavior*, **5**, 1–13.

Lowe, C.F. (1986) The role of verbal behavior in the emergence of equivalence. Paper presented at the meeting of the Association for Behavior Analysis, Milwaukee, Wisconsin.

MacDonald, R.P.F., Dixon, L.S. and LeBlanc, J.M. (1986) Stimulus class formation following observational learning. *Analysis and Intervention in Developmental Disabilities*, **6**, 73–87.

Mackay, H.A. (1985) Stimulus equivalence in rudimentary reading and spelling. *Analysis and Intervention in Developmental Disabilities*, **5**, 373–387.

Mackay, H.A. and Ratti, C. (1990) Position/numeral equivalences and delayed position recognition span. *American Journal on Mental Retardation*.

Mackay, H.A. and Sidman, M. (1984) Teaching new behavior via equivalence relations. In B. Sperber and C. MacCauley (eds), *Learning and Cognition in the Mentally Retarded* (pp. 493–513), Erlbaum, Hillsdale, New Jersey.

McCuller, W.R. and Salzberg, C.L. (1984) Generalized action-object instruction-following by profoundly retarded mentally retarded adults. *American Journal of Mental Deficiency*, **88**, 442–445.

McIntire, K.D., Cleary, J. and Thompson, T. (1987) Conditional relations by monkeys: Reflexivity, symmetry, and transitivity. *Journal of the Experimental Analysis of Behavior*, **47**, 279–285.

Osborne, J.G. and Gatch, M.B. (1989) Stimulus equivalence and receptive reading by hearing-impaired children. *Language, Speech, and Hearing Services in Schools*, **20**, 63–75.

Remington, B. and Clarke, S. (1983) Acquisition of expressive signing by autistic children: An evaluation of the relative effect of simultaneous communication and sign-alone training. *Journal of Applied Behavior Analysis*, **16**, 315–328.

Remington, B., Watson, J. and Light, P. (1990) Beyond the single sign: A matrix-based approach to teaching productive sign combinations. *Mental Handicap Research*, **3**, 33–50.

Saunders, K.J. (1989) Naming in conditional discrimination and stimulus equivalence. *Journal of The Experimental Analysis of Behavior*, **5–1**, 379–384.

Saunders, R.R., Wachter, J. and Spradlin, J.E. (1988) Establishing auditory stimulus control over an eight-member equivalence class via conditional discrimination procedures. *Journal of the Experimental Analysis of Behavior*, **49**, 95–115.

Saunders, R.R., Saunders, K.J., Kirby, K.C. and Spradlin, J.E. (1988) The merger and development of equivalence classes by unreinforced conditional selection of comparison stimuli. *Journal of the Experimental Analysis of Behavior*, **50**, 145–162.

Sidman, M. (1971) Reading and auditory–visual equivalences. *Journal of Speech and Reading Research*, **14**, 5–13.

Sidman, M. (1986) Functional analysis of emergent verbal classes. In T. Thompson and M.D. Zeiler (eds), *Analysis and Integration of Behavioral Units*, pp. 213–245, Erlbaum, Hillsdale, New Jersey.

Sidman, M. and Cresson, O. (1973) Reading and crossmodal transfer of stimulus equivalences in severe mental retardation. *American Journal of Mental Deficiency*, **77**, 515–523.

Sidman, M., Cresson, O., Jr and Willson-Morris, M. (1974) Acquisition of matching to sample via mediated transfer. *Journal of the Experimental Analysis of Behavior*, **22**, 261–273.

Sidman, M., Kirk, B. and Willson-Morris, M. (1985) Six-member stimulus classes generated by conditional discrimination procedures. *Journal of the Experimental Analysis of Behavior*, **43**, 21–42.

Sidman, M. and Tailby, W. (1982) Conditional discrimination vs. matching-to-sample: An expansion of the testing paradigm. *Journal of the Experimental Analysis of Behavior*, **37**, 5–22.

Sidman, M., Willson-Morris, M. and Kirk, B. (1986) Matching-to-sample procedures and the development of equivalence relations: The role of naming. *Analysis and Intervention in Developmental Disabilities*, **6**, 1–19.

Sidman, M., Rauzin, R., Lazar, R., Cunningham, S., Tailby, W. and Carrigan, P. (1982) A search for symmetry in the conditional discriminations of rhesus monkeys, baboons, and children. *Journal of the Experimental Analysis of Behavior*, **37**, 23–44.

Sidman, M., Wynne, C.K., Maguire, R.W. and Barnes, T. (1989) Functional classes and equivalence relations. *Journal of the Experimental Analysis of Behavior*, **52**, 261–274.

Sigurdardottir, Z.G., Green, G. and Saunders, R.R. (1990) Equivalence classes generated by sequence training. *Journal of the Experimental Analysis of Behavior*, **53**, 47–63.

Silverman, K., Anderson, S.R., Marshall, A.M. and Baer, D.M. (1986) Establishing and generalizing audience control of new language repertoires. *Analysis and Intervention in Developmental Disabilities*, **6**, 21–40.

Spradlin, J.E., Cotter, V.W. and Baxley, N. (1973) Establishing a conditional discrimination without direct training: A study of transfer with retarded adolescents. *American Journal of Mental Deficiency*, **77**, 556–566.

Spradlin, J.E. and Dixon, M. (1976) Establishing conditional discriminations without direct training: Stimulus classes and labels. *American Journal of Mental Deficiency*, **80**, 555–561.

Spradlin, J.E. and Saunders, R.R. (1984) Behaving appropriately in new situations: A stimulus class analysis. *American Journal of Mental Deficiency*, **88**, 574–579.

Spradlin, J.E. and Saunders, R.R. (1986) The development of stimulus classes using match to sample procedures: Sample classification versus comparison classification. *Analysis and Intervention in Developmental Disabilities*, **6**, 41–58.

Stoddard, L.T. and McIlvane, W.J. (1986) Stimulus control research and developmentally disabled individuals. *Analysis and Intervention in Developmental Disabilities*, **6**, 155–178.

Stoddard, L.T., Brown, J., Hurlbert, B., Manoli, C. and McIlvane, W.J. (1989) Teaching money skills through stimulus class formation, exclusion, and component matching methods: Three case studies. *Research in Developmental Disabilities*, **10**, 413–439.

Stromer, R. (in press) Stimulus equivalence. In W. Ishaq (ed.), *Human Behavior in Today's World: A Handbook*, Praeger, New York.

Stromer, R. and Mackay, H.A. (1990) A note on the study of transitive relations in stimulus sequences. *Experimental and Analytical Human Behavior Bulletin*, **8**, 2–5.

Stromer, R. and Osborne, J.G. (1982) Control of adolescents' arbitrary matching-to-sample by positive and negative stimulus relations. *Journal of the Experimental Analysis of Behavior*, **37**, 329–348.

Stromer, R. and Stromer, J.B. (1989) Children's identity matching and oddity: Assessing control by specific and general sample-comparison relations. *Journal of the Experimental Analysis of Behavior*, **51**, 47–64.

Stromer, R. and Stromer, J.B. (1990a) The formation of arbitrary stimulus classes in matching to complex samples. *The Psychological Record*, **40**, 51–66.

Stromer, R. and Stromer, J.B. (1990b) Matching to complex samples: Further study of arbitrary stimulus classes. *The Psychological Record*, **40**, 505–516.

VanBiervleit, A. (1977) Establishing words and objects as functionally equivalent through manual sign training. *American Journal of Mental Deficiency*, **82**, 178–186.

Wetherby, B., Karlan, G.R. and Spradlin, J.E. (1983) The development of derived stimulus relations through training in arbitrary-matching sequences. *Journal of the Experimental Analysis of Behavior*, **40**, 69–78.

Wetherby, B. and Striefel, S. (1978) Application of miniature linguistic system of matrix training. In R.L. Schiefelbusch (ed.), *Language Intervention Strategies* (pp. 317–356), University Park Press, Baltimore.

Wulfert, E. and Hayes, S.C. (1988) Transfer of a conditional ordering response through conditional equivalence classes. *Journal of the Experimental Analysis of Behavior*, **50**, 125–144.

Section 3

Behaviour Analysis and Service Delivery

Chapter 12

The Task Demonstration Model: A Program for Teaching Persons with Severe Disabilities

ALAN C. REPP AND KATHRYN G. KARSH

INTRODUCTION

The American Association on Mental Retardation's definition of mental handicap refers to 'significantly subaverage general intellectual functioning existing concurrently with deficits in adaptive behavior and manifested during the developmental period' (Grossman, 1983). While this may be a useful definition for many purposes, we find a less elegant one more useful: people are labeled mentally handicapped when they require an inordinate number of trials to learn a broad range of tasks.

Our purpose, of course, is not to argue definitions; rather, it is to underscore what is the pragmatic problem for these people—they require longer to learn something than we do. With this as a working definition, our task if we are interested in combating the problem is to learn how we can reduce the number of trials required to learn tasks.

In this chapter, we will describe a program we have developed to meet this objective. Called the task demonstration model (TDM), it is based upon research, teaching experience, and common sense. The chapter is divided into three sections: the first presents background research; the second, the TDM; the third, research with TDM.

BACKGROUND RESEARCH

Much of what we do depends upon discriminations we make. For example, we cut our meat with a knife instead of a spoon because we

The Challenge of Severe Mental Handicap. Edited by Bob Remington
© 1991 John Wiley & Sons Ltd

can discriminate one from the other; we walk into a proper restroom because we can discriminate signs for men and women; we pay for soda correctly because we can discriminate one coin from another. Discriminations are very important in what we do daily, but, in addition, they serve as prerequisites for other skills that are more complex.

In many cases, discriminations are easy and require few trials for us to learn. But these same discriminations may be very difficult for persons with severe handicaps. Fortunately, there has been considerable research on learning either in, or directly applicable to, teaching situations. Operant discriminations are learned through differential reinforcement, a procedure in which a correct response is reinforced and an incorrect one is not. In most cases, that which is being discriminated remains unchanged. For example, if we were to teach a child a conditional discrimination (Mackay, this volume), we might draw the numbers 1 and 2 on two cards, tell the child which was the 1, model a few responses, ask the child to make a few responses, and provide differential reinforcement. Because this procedure (called *trial and error*) works so well with nonhandicapped persons, we generally use it when teaching persons with severe handicaps; and, as we all know, it works sometimes but not all the time.

When it does fail, several approaches can be tried. The most common one is to provide prompts for the learner. We may provide cues such as highlighting the correct stimulus (e.g., the 1) by increasing its size, or by colouring it, and so forth. Or, we might use a hierarchy of prompts such as verbal cues, demonstration, pointing, or physical guidance. Many teachers and indeed researchers (Brown *et al.*, 1972; Cuvo, Leaf and Borakove, 1978; Gold, 1972, 1976; Koop *et al.*, 1980) have found this approach to be successful; others, however, have not (e.g., Koegel and Rincover, 1976; Schreibman, 1975; Schreibman, Charlop and Koegel, 1982).

The reasons for disparate findings can, of course, be many. But as we sought to develop a procedure that would fail less frequently, we were impressed by several lines of research. The first was Terrace's research on stimulus fading with laboratory animals (1963a, 1963b, 1966), which showed how discrimination between colors, and even between two angles of a line, could be learned virtually without errors. Terrace's work was based on a procedure in which the discrimination was initially very easy and became progressively more difficult. The important procedural point of this research to us was that the stimuli themselves were manipulated (faded) in a way that produced few errors during learning. Prompts such as verbal cues, demonstration, etc., could not be used, yet we saw animals learning discriminations that many severely handicapped clients were not learning.

Another series of papers provided a possible explanation of the high occurrence of errors we often found while teaching these individuals. Sidman and Stoddard (1966, 1967) used fading techniques with persons who were severely handicapped, and obtained virtually errorless discrimination learning when fading was used, but either many errors, or even a failure to learn, when the stimuli were not faded (as in the traditional trial-and-error teaching). Finally, the authors used the fading procedure, already shown to be effective with some participants, to teach the same discriminations to those who had not learned by trial and error. One finding, remarkable to us, was that some of these individuals did not learn the task even when fading was used. They had learned error patterns under trial and error that they were unable to break even when the fading procedure was used.

Our interpretation of error patterns was that some individuals might treat a cue as relevant when indeed it was not, or they might randomly attend to different elements of a stimulus, first one (e.g., color) then another (e.g., size), and so forth, eventually hitting the right element (e.g., form). However, reinforcement might strengthen a *chain* of incorrect responses (to color and to size) ending in a correct response (to form) rather than *just* the last (correct) response. If so, the clients might learn either a specific chain which included incorrect responses, or a strategy of 'choosing randomly'. In addition, occasional intermittent reinforcement of an error pattern of responding would tend to make errors more resistant to extinction. Therefore, we tried to design a procedure that would eliminate this problem—a procedure based upon fading.

PRINCIPLES OF THE TASK DEMONSTRATION MODEL

Using the research we have just described as a foundation, we devised a general-purpose procedure for teaching discriminations to people with learning difficulties. We thought two elements were essential. First, we needed to identify—and then to teach—what were and what were not the critical features of any discrimination. Second, we wanted to use fading procedures in which the child moved systematically from easier to more difficult discriminations.

In order to teach in this manner, we must first identify what features *are* critical for the task, and what features *are not*. For example, if we wanted to teach a child to discriminate the color *red* as part of a program to enable him to cross the street at a traffic light, we would first specify the critical dimension (color) and some noncritical dimensions (size, form, etc.) of the stimulus objects. Following a traditional trial-and-error procedure, one might use only two cards, one of which showed a *large red square* and the other a *small white triangle*. However, such an approach could produce problems. A child might correctly follow the instruction to 'touch red' by attending to the critical feature of color (*red*), or to a noncritical feature such as size (or four-sidedness or right-angularity). Alternatively, the child might have chosen the red object by exclusion, i.e., because it was the one that was *not* white or *not* triangular or *not* small. To avoid both these possibilities, we would have to present multiple examples which included the critical element but did not contain the same noncritical elements across trials (e.g., a small red triangle). We would also have to present incorrect stimuli that did contain some of the noncritical elements of the correct stimulus (e.g., a large white square as well as the small white triangle). By presenting two small triangles, one red and one white, we could force the discrimination to be made on the critical feature of color rather than the noncritical features of size or form. Further, by later presenting two large squares, one red and one white, we could show that red itself rather than red when also small and/or a triangle was the critical feature. Then, by presenting a red and a green object, we could show that the critical feature was not 'anything other than white'; it was, in fact, redness. Our procedure selects stimuli for teaching in the light of these considerations, and then applies the principle of stimulus fading in order to move gradually from less to more difficult discriminations.

While the program manipulates stimuli through fading and the use of multiple examples to teach conditional discriminations, it also establishes a hierarchy of skills for the learner from matching to sample, to identification of stimuli from spoken names, to naming the stimuli. Our reasoning was that if expected to *name* a stimulus such as a coin, a student should already be able to *identify* that coin when the instructor named it and presented it along with several distractors. Furthermore, if expected to identify the coin, the student should already be able to *match* it to an identical sample which was presented with several distractors. Thus we would assess each person at these three levels and teach those skills not in the repertoire in the following order: matching, identification, and naming.

The elements of the program have developed over perhaps ten years (Repp, 1983), and have met with regular success. Recently, it was revised (Deitz, Rose and Repp, 1986) and formalized, a prerequisite was added, a group teaching component was added, and it was given a name—the task demonstration model (TDM). In the next section, we will describe the TDM as it is presently used.

PROCEDURES USED IN THE TASK DEMONSTRATION MODEL

The TDM is based upon the reasoning and the research presented in the previous section. However, the previously described procedure has been broadened in several important ways so that we now train students to follow instructions, teach groups in which all students responded simultaneously, and systematically fade the stimuli presented in the discriminations. In this section, we will briefly describe these components.

Goal

Our working definition of mental handicap was that it described individuals who required many more trials to learn a task than did nonhandicapped people. From this definition, we developed two goals. The first was to present stimuli in a systematic manner that would make discrimination learning easier. The second was to develop a procedure for presenting learning tasks to groups of students with severe or moderate retardation who would then respond simultaneously. Our reasoning was that most teachers instructed only one student at a time whether they were in a one-to-one or a group situation, that handicapped people required more trials to learn, and that to combat retardation we needed a procedure in which many (rather than a few) trials would be presented in a day to all students. Because we could not have one teacher per student, we had to teach the students to respond simultaneously in a group.

Instruction following

The importance of teaching students to follow instructions cannot be overemphasized. This is a skill that should be considered a prerequisite to any learning task, and some comparative data have shown it to be a critical one. If we expect all members of a group to respond quickly and in unison, we must first teach each student to respond to instruction quickly and very reliably. To reach this objective, we developed a simple program of three steps. In the first, about 15 instructions are selected for teaching students individually. The instructions include, but are not limited to, the prerequisite skills for TDM (e.g., 'touch___', 'hand me___'). Throughout the day, many trials are presented until each student responds consistently, correctly, and quickly. In many cases, no formal sessions are set aside. Rather, during the general course of the day, an instruction is given; a few minutes later, another is given, and so forth. Correct responses are reinforced immediately while incorrect responses are followed by a prompting hierarchy (repeated instruction, demonstration, physical prompt, full physical guidance).

Once students meet criterion, they move to the second step and are put in a formal one-to-one teaching situation, first with tasks for which they have previously exhibited mastery (i.e., easier tasks), and then with tasks which are in the acquisition stage (i.e., more difficult tasks). When instruction following has been established across many tasks, it is more likely to generalize to the group teaching situations which will be presented later. Next, in the third step, a group of two or three students is taught to respond to an instruction in unison. Importantly, the same 15 instructions used in the informal one-to-one teaching situation are used here, so the prerequisites are in place. The teacher selects a group cue (e.g., 'everybody', 'students'), presents the cue and then follows it with the instruction (e.g., 'students, pass the card to your left'). Correct responses are individually reinforced with either social or tangible reinforcers, and errors, which should be few, are corrected. Finally, students learn to follow the instruction in groups of the size in which teaching will occur; then, discrimination tasks are introduced.

Stimulus materials

Stimuli to be discriminated are categorized as correct (S+) or incorrect (S−), and multiple examples of each are gathered before teaching. The first step is to determine the critical and noncritical features of the S+. This is done systematically along various dimensions or properties of the stimulus. For example, if we are trying to teach a client to identify the number 1 given the spoken name, the critical dimension of the number 1 is form; noncritical dimensions include size, color of the number or the background, thickness, script, texture, and location. We then select 15 or so examples of a 1 which differ across the noncritical dimensions (e.g., five colors, six sizes, three scripts). These are the S+ examples and are randomly presented throughout the teaching trials.

The S− examples, though, are not randomly chosen. Rather, they match each example of S+ on all but the critical dimension. Three sets of S− are created according to the degree to which they differ from the S+. In general, we select 15 very different, 15 moderately different, and 15 slightly different examples of S−. The S− stimuli are faded from very to slightly different on the critical dimension so that the discrimination becomes increasingly more difficult (Terrace 1963a, 1963b, 1966). Each of the S− examples, however, possesses the same irrelevant dimensions as its corresponding S+ example.

If, as in the example shown in Table 12.1, we are teaching a client to identify the number 1, an S+ example and the corresponding very different S− example will share the same noncritical dimensions (i.e., size, color of the number, color of the background, thickness, script, texture, and location). However, the critical dimension of the S− (i.e., form) will be very different from the S+ example. For the number 1, a very different S− example could be the number 0 because it has no straight lines. A moderately different S− for the number 1 could be the number 2 because it has both straight and curved lines. A slightly different S− could be the number 7 because it is comprised of a short horizontal and a long vertical line. We have found that the difficulty of the initial discrimination between the S+ example and the very different S− example depends on the developmental level of the client, i.e., the difficulty level necessary for the client. The S− examples in the slightly different category, however, are always the most difficult discriminations the person would find in the natural environment.

In addition, discriminations of three-dimensional functional objects (e.g., eating and cooking utensils, clothing and grooming items) are also taught with TDM. In these cases we are able to fade the critical dimension for the S− (e.g., form), but we are not always able to match the irrelevant dimensions for the S+ and S− examples in each trial.

Once the S− examples have been chosen for each S+ example, they are placed into categories of very, moderately, and slightly different. After the teaching stimuli have been grouped, the instructor teaches the discrimination for each S+ example and its corresponding, very different S− example (see Table 12.1). If we were teaching the student to identify the number 1, a trial at this level might include a 1 written in black ink in the middle of a 3 × 5 inch notecard. The S− for this trial could be a 0 written in the same size as the 1, also in black ink in the middle of a 3 × 5 inch notecard. After the very different S− stimuli have been presented, the instructor teaches the discrimination for each S+ example and its corresponding, moderately different S− example, and finally, the discrimination for each S+ example and its corresponding, slightly different S− example. After the first discrimination (e.g., 1) is taught,

Table 12.1 Examples of stimuli in TDM

Trial	S+	S− (very different)	S− (moderately different)	S− (slightly different)
1.	1	0	9	5
2.	1	8	6	4
3.	1	3	2	7

the instructor moves to another discrimination (e.g., 5) and so forth. However, a critical component of the TDM is the requirement that maintenance trials be provided for a previously taught discrimination (e.g., 1) when a new one (e.g., 5) is being taught.

Activity analysis

The discriminations we teach should be functional ones, i.e., those the client would be expected to make in the normal context of the day (e.g., eating, selecting foods to buy, setting a table). They are selected by analyzing the requirements of the individual's *present environment* in the home, school, workplace, and community (Albin, McDonnell and Wilcox, 1987). In addition, the same analysis is made of the person's *future environment*, the one into which the client is expected to move within a year or so (e.g., a transfer of residences). After these environments are identified, we visit them and identify the following:

- The generic discrimination to be made (e.g., numbers necessary for functioning in the community).
- The S+ stimuli (e.g., bus numbers, addresses, date, amount of sale).
- The *relevant* S− for each S+ identified (e.g., numbers found in the environment but not necessary to the client's functioning).
- The variations that each S+ may evidence (e.g., color, size, background, texture, script, location).
- Variations the generic response may require (e.g., walking to the correct bus, entering the correct building, keeping an appointment for the correct date).
- Anticipated problems.

This information is then used to identify the relevant and irrelevant dimension of each S+ stimulus, the three categories of S− stimuli for each S+, and the type of response the person should be taught.

Assessment

As previously mentioned, we teach three types of skills that are successively more difficult: matching to sample, identification, and naming. In general, students are given ten trials with ten examples of S+ and the corresponding slightly different S− for the naming pretest. If the criterion is not passed, they are given ten identification trials with the same S+ and S− examples. If this assessment is passed, naming is taught; if failed, matching to sample performance is assessed in the same way. If this test is passed, identification is taught; if not, matching to sample is taught.

One-to-one teaching

In general, students are taught one or more tasks in a one-to-one setting before moving to group teaching. This format is followed so that we can be sure that the student has the prerequisite skills of following instructions, attending to stimuli, and responding rapidly before moving to group settings. In both cases, however, matching to sample, identification, and naming can be taught.

In matching to sample, an example of the S+ (the sample) is placed in front of the client and a matching example, in front of the instructor. In a few trials, the client is taught to follow the appropriate instruction (e.g., 'Touch the other____', or 'Touch the one like it') with only the two examples of S+ present. Then, a very different S− is placed close to the matching S+, but further from the student than the sample S+. After a few trials, the S+ and S− are moved equally distant from the client. After each trial, all stimuli are brought back to the instructor, at least one stimulus (the sample, the match, or the S−) is exchanged for another example, and the stimuli are returned to a position different from that which they occupied on the previous trial. When criterion is met with the very different S−, moderately different ones are used, followed by slightly different ones. All correct responses are reinforced in a manner suitable for the individual, while errors are followed with an error correction procedure: the instruction is repeated, a new trial is given with the materials removed but returned to the same place, and another trial is given with the materials removed and returned to different positions on the table. When correct responses occur in all three trials, a new set of stimuli is presented.

Following matching to sample, identification is taught. The general procedures remain the same; however, no sample S+ is presented (instead, an S+ example and the corresponding S− example are presented), and the instruction is changed to 'Touch the____.' Following identification, naming is taught. Again, the general procedures remain the same, but two changes are made. Only one stimulus is presented at a time (S+ or S−), and the instruction is changed. When the S+ is presented, the teacher gives the instruction (e.g., 'This is ____', or 'What is this?'), and the student supplies its name; when an S− is presented, the student is taught to say 'Not____', or its name. During the initial stages of naming, we supply the verbal prompts but fade them in the following fashion. Using 'pen' as the S+:

1. For a few trials the instructor says, 'Pen; John, this is a pen. Now you say it. This is a ___(x)___ '.
   At point (x), the instructor says 'pen' once or twice until the student says it.

2. Then, the first prompt is dropped and the instruction becomes 'This is a __(x)__.' Again the prompt 'pen' is given at (x). However, the prompt is successively delayed across trials.
3. Finally, the last prompt is faded over a few trials from 'pen' to 'pe' to no prompt. The teacher than says 'This is a ____', and with no prompt the student says 'pen'.

Group teaching

After succeeding on a few one-to-one tasks, the student is brought to a group setting in which one to seven other students are taught. The objective in this situation is to increase significantly each class member's rate of contact with the learning environment. Obviously, one-to-one teaching is extremely inefficient because the other members of the group are generally not being taught. In general, group teaching is also inefficient because it becomes in effect a series of one-to-one exercises. That is, the instructor usually asks one or two students a question, and ignores the other students who are expected to await their turn quietly and perhaps to learn through observation. Our goal is for an instruction to be presented every 20 seconds or so, and for all students in the group to answer in unison. In this way, each student is learning almost as quickly as when being taught in a one-to-one situation, but the teacher is being extremely efficient in that several students are being taught simultaneously. As emphasized earlier, the prerequisite for this task is good instruction-following behavior. Note that by this stage each student would have learned to follow familiar instructions, to generalize across many new instructions, and to respond rapidly.

The major components to group teaching are pacing, signaling students to respond, and presenting materials in the TDM manner previously explained. As noted before, we believe that teachers should present materials, and ask questions, quickly. If the teacher can provide more trials in a unit of time, students will learn more. Also, faster pacing increases student engagement and often reduces problem behaviors (data on the latter will be shown in the next section).

Because students in groups respond in unison, there must be a signal to which they know they should respond. Our general rule for instructors is that they should provide the instruction first and then the signal, and that the interval between the two should be 1 second. Three types of signals are used during group instruction, the type depending upon the task. An audible signal (e.g., 'everybody', or a hand-clap) is given when students are looking at materials and not at the teacher. A hand-drop signal is used when materials are presented orally and the students are looking at the teacher (e.g., the instructor, says 'What is this?', holds up an object, and drops his hand). A third signal, the point-touch, is used when the teacher points to materials on the blackboard or table, and the students are to respond only when the teacher touches the materials (Cowart, Carnine and Becker, 1976). Students must follow the instruction rapidly and in unison; otherwise, instead of responding to the materials, an individual could be imitating the response another person produced a second or two earlier.

A third component of group teaching involves the presentation of materials. In many cases, the teacher simply holds the stimuli, or names them, or puts them on a board, etc. In other cases, the materials are placed in front of the students. In the latter, we follow a simple procedure that again relies on good instruction-following skills. For the first trial, a different set of S+ and S− examples is put in front of each student (e.g., numbers). The task instruction and signal are given, the students respond, and the teacher reinforces correct responding. Then, the group instruction 'Pass to your left' is given. Each student passes the materials to the left, and one of them passes materials to the teacher who in turn provides a new set of examples to the student to her left. In this way, multiple examples are provided for each student in an orderly fashion within a few seconds.

Generalization and maintenance

When tasks involve words, coins, numbers, etc., and they are taught in classrooms or other settings in which the behavior does not naturally occur, we cannot be sure whether the response will generalize or whether we have taught a setting-specific skill. All skills should, therefore, be assessed in the natural environment where they are expected to occur after training. However, generalization is seldom a problem because we survey this environment before teaching the task, use materials from it or like those in it while teaching, and use multiple examples of both S+ and S−. In addition, maintenance probes are scheduled for tasks the student has already learned.

RESEARCH ON THE TASK DEMONSTRATION MODEL

We believe that instruction can be more effective when it is based upon research from the learning literature. Much of the TDM is based upon the findings of others, but to be consistent with our belief we are compelled to conduct research on TDM ourselves. Currently, six studies are in progress using stimulus materials in the ways previously discussed. In this section, we will present data from four completed studies—two in one-to-one settings and two in group settings.

Study 1: One-to-one teaching—identifying numbers

Our first formal study of TDM (Repp, Karsh and Lenz, 1990) involved teaching eight mentally handicapped students to identify two- and three-digit numbers while in a one-to-one setting. Although the goal of TDM is ultimately to teach in groups, one-to-one teaching provided a more controlled situation in which to conduct our first experiment. In this study, two procedures were compared: the TDM and the standard prompting hierarchy (SPH). The latter involves a least-to-most intrusive prompting hierarchy and is described as a standard procedure for teaching discriminations (Mosk and Bucher, 1984; Schreibman, Charlop and Koegel, 1982; Snell, 1987; Steege, Wacker and McMahon, 1987; Sternberg, 1988; Wolery, Bailey and Sugai, 1988).

An alternating treatments design was used in which each of the eight students learned two numbers (S+[1] and S+[2]) by TDM and two (S+[3] and S+[4]) by SPH with the numbers counterbalanced across procedures. As previously explained, TDM is a fading procedure which uses multiple examples of both S+ and S− stimuli. In this condition, each two- or three-digit S+ number appeared in various combinations of 7 colors, 15 sizes, 5 scripts, 3 textures, 6 background colors, 3 background sizes, and 3 locations on the table used for teaching. In addition, the S− stimuli were faded, first appearing as very different, then moderately different, and finally as slightly different examples. The very different S− examples matched the irrelevant dimensions of the S+ examples and differed on the critical dimensions by including single letters or digits and four-letter nonsense words or digits that were very different in form from the S+. The moderately different set included two- or three-letter nonsense words or two- or three-digit numbers (e.g., when S+ was 74, moderately different S− examples were H7, HI, 7W). Slightly different S− examples were minimally different from the S+ examples on the relevant dimensions of form (e.g., when S+ was 74, slightly different examples included 41, 17, and so on).

In contrast, the SPH is a non-fading procedure in which S+ and S− are presented in their terminal state (which are equivalent to our examples in the set of slightly different S−) generally with one example of each, without any effort to vary the irrelevant features of the S+. SPH relies on a prompting hierarchy which is presented in a least-to-most intrusive fashion in the following sequence: (a) repeated instruction, (b) instruction plus pointing to the S+, (c) instruction plus modeling (the instructor touches the S+), (d) instruction plus physical prompt (the instructor touches the back of the student's hand), and, finally, (e) instruction plus full physical guidance.

Three sets of data were collected six months after training: acquisition, generalization with untrained S+ and S− examples, and maintenance. Results showed that *all* eight students had more *unprompted* correct responses in TDM (76%) than in SPH (51%); *all* made fewer errors in TDM (14%) than in SPH (25%); *all* made more correct responses in the generalization test in the training room in TDM (70%) than in SPH (54%), and seven of the eight students had more correct responding in a six-month maintenance test in TDM (74%) than in SPH (58%). Thus TDM proved to be superior in 31 of the 32 comparisons.

In addition, data on trials to criterion provided a measure of efficiency. In SPH, the study ended when a student was correct on five consecutive trials as well as nine of the last ten. In TDM, each of the three components (i.e., with very different, moderately different, and slightly different S−) ended when the same criterion was met. Thus, because the student was forced to cycle through three successive criteria in TDM and only one in SPH, the latter could be expected to be more efficient. The results, however, proved otherwise with TDM requiring an average of 102 trials and SPH 137.

Thus this study showed a clear superiority for TDM in all measures (unprompted correct responses, errors, and trials to criterion) as well as in all conditions (acquisition, generalization, and maintenance). Given these results, we were prepared to conduct a second study to determine whether the findings could be replicated.

Study 2: One-to-one teaching—identifying words

The first study compared TDM with SPH, with the latter being used in the manner in which it is described in textbooks and journal articles. In the second study (Karsh, Repp and Lenz, 1990), we sought to improve SPH by adding a component from TDM—the prerequisite that matching to sample be taught before identification.

We again used an alternating treatments design to teach six persons with severe or moderate retardation to identify three words by TDM ($S+^1$, $S+^2$, $S+^3$) and three words by SPH ($S+^4$, $S+^5$, $S+^6$) with the words counterbalanced across procedures. Words that related to grocery shopping were selected as S+ to meet objectives in each student's individualized educational program. In TDM there were approximately 12 examples of each S+ word varying in script, in size and color of letters, and in size and color of background. The S− examples for each S+ were taken from a list of grocery shopping words and were again in the three categories represented as follows: *very different* S− examples, which differed from the S+ on the relevant dimension of form in both

the number and shapes of letters (e.g., when S+ was *produce*, an S−
could be *nuts*); *moderately different* S− examples, which had a similar
number of letters and a few of the same letters (e.g., an S− example for
produce could be *pickle*); and *slightly different* S− examples, which had
the same number of letters and similar letters (e.g., *produce* and *product*).
The SPH was again presented as a nonfading procedure in which the
S+ and S− examples remained the same throughout training (0.5 cm
high, handwritten in black ink on a 5 × 7 inch white card). The S−
examples were four words taken from the set of slightly different words
used in TDM. The prompting hierarchy used in study 1 was again used,
as were all procedures except one: all subjects were taught to match each
SPH word to an identical sample before being taught to identify the
words.

Three sets of data that were again collected were acquisition, generalization with untrained S+ and S− examples, and maintenance. The
acquisition data showed that *unprompted* correct responding was better
in TDM (94%) than in SPH (76%) and that error responding was less in
TDM (4%) than in SPH (14%). Moreover, correct responding in
generalization was slightly better in TDM (91%) than in SPH (86%), and
correct responding during maintenance one week and one month later
was slightly better in TDM (92%) than in SPH (86%).

Taken together, the data from studies 1 and 2 suggest that TDM is
superior to SPH even when training on matching to sample is also
incorporated into the SPH procedure. The acquisition data clearly show
that the TDM procedure is more effective than SPH when teaching
persons who often fail to acquire various skills. The generalization and,
to a lesser extent, the maintenance data also favor TDM, presumably
because multiple examples of the S+ are used during training. In both
studies, the same criterion for stopping training was used for SPH and
TDM, so the students might be expected to do equally well on the
maintenance tests. Because the number of trials to criterion had been
less for TDM, the total number (but not percentage) of correct responses
to each S+ had been approximately the same for both procedures, so
total correct trials was probably not a factor.

Study 3: Group teaching—task demonstration model versus standard prompting hierarchy

The results of the previous studies led us to move to group teaching
situations in which TDM could be studied. As we have already noted,
one goal of TDM is to increase the contacts each person has with
the learning environment. This objective is reached by teaching the

prerequisite skills while moving from training persons to follow instructions, through teaching them in one-to-one situations, to teaching them in groups. After the first two studies were conducted, we trained teachers and aides to use TDM in these group settings. In our first comparison of group TDM and SPH, we wanted to determine whether the different effects of these two procedures were specific to settings in which students were taught in one-to-one fashion. In this study (Karsh and Repp, 1990), three groups of students were taught three discriminations by each procedure. One group was taught six 'safety' words; a second, six 'shopping' words; a third, six times on a clock. The six members of a set were rated equally difficult by the teachers, and were randomly assigned to the TDM and SPH conditions. Four assessment probes were conducted to compare the students' correct and error performance on the two procedures in four conditions: baseline (i.e., being taught in a group the way teachers did before being trained in SPH and TDM), acquisition, generalization, and maintenance. In addition, data were collected on other student behaviors (task engagement and inappropriate behavior) and on teacher behaviors (instructions, prompts, and praise).

Probe data on acquisition, generalization, and maintenance again showed TDM was superior to SPH in eight of the nine measures (three conditions × three groups of students). The results, then, addressed a major purpose of the research and showed the superiority of TDM in group teaching as well as in one-to-one teaching.

For illustrative purposes in this chapter, however, we would like to focus on two other sets of data. Three measures of student responding were made: task engagement, percentage unprompted correct responses, and rate of unprompted correct responses. We find the relationship among these three measures interesting for what it says about this study and many other studies. Task engagement has become a popular method for assessing the effects of various instructional interventions in classrooms. Our engagement data showed quite similar results across baseline, TDM, and SPH for group 1 (76%, 72% and 79%), group 2 (81%, 80%, and 84%), and group 3 (74%, 88%, and 76%). From these data, one might conclude that there was no significant difference among these three conditions. When we examine the data on the *percentage* of unprompted correct responses, however, a different—albeit tentative—conclusion emerges. The figures for this measure under TDM and SPH were 94% and 90% for group 1, 86% and 71% for group 2, and 96% and 83% for group 3. Although not compelling, these data suggest that TDM is a little better than SPH. When we look at the *rate* of unprompted correct responses, however, a firmer conclusion emerges. The rates under baseline (B), TDM and SPH were 0.26 (B), 1.93 (TDM) and 0.66 (SPH) responses per minute (rpm) for group 1; 0.39, 1.50 and 0.74 for group 2;

and 0.39, 3.45 and 1.70 rpm for group 3. Methodologically, these data show that task engagement may not be an appropriate measure for some experimental questions. In the present study, TDM clearly meets our objective of increasing a learner's rate of contact with the environment. This effect is particularly evident when the difference between baseline and TDM is compared. The increase for the three groups was by a factor of 7.4, 3.8, and 8.8 respectively.

Two other measures are relevant to this discussion: the rate of teacher prompts and praise. The prompt data showed that prompts were two to three times more frequent in SPH than in baseline for two of the three teachers, but that in TDM the rates decreased significantly. The prompts for TDM and SPH for the three groups were 0 (TDM) and 1.66 (SPH) rpm, 0.38 and 2.70 rpm, and 0.07 and 1.45 rpm. Since prompts are a direct function of errors, these data support the difference in error rates found under these two conditions. The praise data showed no significant difference between the two conditions but a significant difference between both conditions and baseline. Taken together, the results suggest that neither of these teacher behaviors can account for the differences between TDM and SPH in the student data. The inference is that the differences are due to variables of the TDM package such as fading.

The results of this study and the first two showed a systematic replication of the differential effects of TDM and SPH. In the fourth study, we moved from procedural comparison to a more careful analysis of the effects of TDM compared with baseline responding.

Study 4: Group teaching—task demonstration model

Study 4 used a multiple-baseline design across four teachers, each of whom taught a group of four students. In the baseline phase, teachers instructed their groups in the manner which they had used all year; in the second phase, they used TDM; and in the third phase, measures were taken after training.

Data were collected on the following categories: percentage and rate of correct responding, rate of teacher praises and prompts, rate of questions received by students, passive and active engagement, and stereotypy. The results replicated study 3 in that rates of correct responses increased 416%, percentage of correct responses increased 258%, percentage of prompts decreased to 4% of baseline, and praise increased 251%.

In addition, data were collected on engagement—but for a different reason than in study 3. In a previous paper (Repp et al., in press), we assessed the stereotypic responding of 12 persons with severe handicaps and found that some, but not all, would substitute other motor movements for stereotypy (essentially, an unplanned program of the differential reinforcement of incompatible or alternative behaviors). Because the TDM can be viewed as a procedure which differentially reinforces alternative behavior (e.g., correct responding), we thought that measuring the effects on stereotypy would be interesting. To do this, we measured the rate of questions each person received, active engagement (e.g., answering questions verbally, passing materials), passive engagement (e.g., looking at materials), and stereotypy. Although these data are best presented as single-subject data, we will summarize them here to make the major point. Questions received, active engagement, and passive engagement increased over 400%, 230%, and 115%, while stereotypy decreased to 60% of baseline levels. Further, as in a prior study, some individuals showed quite different patterns of responding than others (Repp *et al.*, in press). Results showed that seven subjects actually increased stereotypy slightly (from 65% to 71% of the time on average), while the other nine subjects decreased responding (from 50% to 5% of the time). Our supposition, which is now under study, is that stereotypy can be viewed as either environmentally independent or dependent. In the latter case, behavior is under the control of either self-stimulation (i.e., an effort to maintain a homeostatic level of overall motoric responding), positive reinforcement (attention, in this case), or negative reinforcement (usually in the form of task avoidance or escape). Our supposition is that for those subjects who decreased stereotypy during TDM, this behavior served a self-stimulatory function; that is, the more stimulating the environment, the less stereotypic self-stimulation. Those who were not affected maintained the behavior either because it was environmentally independent or because it was maintained by the presentation or removal of a specific stimulus which was still functional during TDM. A study currently being conducted attempts to determine from baseline data which students will be affected by procedures such as TDM.

CONCLUSION

In the previous section, we have described some of the components of the TDM. There are other components, however, based upon research, that are important to implementation of TDM in the classroom. Each of these components is incorporated in the workshops given to teachers and direct care staff trained to use this procedure.

There are five major components and 15 subcomponents; major components are task dimensions, stimulus modality, teacher presentation, environmental arrangements, and generalization. These along with their subcomponents are summarized in Table 12.2.

Table 12.2 Components of the TDM

Component

1. *Task Dimensions*

A. The *activity analysis* determines the learner demands placed on the student
    by the environment. Analysis allows the instructor to design interventions
    that will bring student responding under the control of relevant stimuli

B. *Stimulus* presentations are based on errorless discrimination training. The
    teacher arranges a sequence of stimuli to increase the probability that only
    correct responses occur

C. *Task variation* involves interspersing items that have already been taught
    with new items during instruction

D. *Within-stimulus prompting* consists of exaggerating the relevant component of
    the critical dimension of the positive stimulus

2. *Stimulus modality*

E. *Stimulus modality* (i.e., real objects, photos, pictures), when assessed and
    correctly used for instruction, lead to better generalization to the natural
    environment. When two modes are to be used (e.g., student is to locate in
    a grocery store cereal when given a picture of a certain brand), teach picture-
    to-picture and item-to-item MTS[a] and ID[b] before teaching student to match
    the picture to the real item

3. *Teacher presentation*

F. Presentations with short intertrial intervals produce higher levels of correct
    responding and increased learning rate

G. *Stimulus delay* requires the teacher to provide increasingly long delays
    between the discriminative stimulus and the artificial prompt

H. In *response delay*, the teacher does not allow the student to make a response
    until after some designated period of time has elapsed, increasing attention
    to the discriminative stimulus. Used for students who respond too quickly,
    often without looking at stimuli

I. *Differential reinforcement* increases the likelihood that the response will occur
    again in the presence of the antecedent stimulus. Reinforcement can be
    selected on the basis of a functional relationship between response and
    reinforcer (e.g., correct discrimination of a cup is reinforced with a drink of
    water from a cup)

4. *Environmental arrangements*

J. *Environmental arrangements* including schedules for instruction, management
    of transition times, and organization of work areas can increase student-
    engaged time

K. *Group instruction* provides teacher direction, prompts, reinforcement, correc-
    tion, and repeated practice

Table 12.2 Continued

Component

L. *Incidental teaching* uses time not allocated for direct instruction of the target skill to provide a greater number of examples for 'loose training' and maintenance

M. *Trans-environmental programming* requires the teacher to bring natural, relevant cues from the environment systematically into the classroom and then to assess (and teach if needed) the student in the natural setting

5. *Generalization*

N. *Delayed reinforcement* provides gradual delays between the response and the delivery of the reinforcer to increase maintenance of the skill in the natural environment

O. *Generalization across instructional settings* is accomplished by systematically varying teachers and the location of instruction, by using multiple settings for instruction, and by providing instruction at various times of the day

[a]MTS = matching to sample
[b]ID = identification

We believe that TDM is methodology that offers several advantages for teaching persons with severe handicaps. One is that it produces fewer errors, a result that becomes more dramatic as the difficulty of the task increases. For tasks of a simpler nature, though, TDM would not be necessary.

A second advantage is that it can be used to teach groups of students, thereby increasing substantially the rate at which they are going to learn *across* tasks. Although we have not gathered data directly on this point, it is an obvious one. Student's responses increase by 400–1000% when TDM is introduced; this increase in sheer behavioral output means they are going to learn many more skills.

A final, and perhaps unexpected, advantage is that for some students TDM decreases stereotypies substantially. Given that we are seeking alternatives to punitive means of controlling maladaptive responding (Repp and Singh, 1990), TDM offers a method that is both non-aversive and academically appropriate. We believe the important point here is to develop an assessment protocol that will tell us which students will benefit from TDM before it is implemented.

There are many things to learn about TDM, from training to implementation to tasks for which it is suitable. We would hope that others would also be encouraged by the results of its use and join us in this line of research.

Address for correspondence

Alan C. Repp, Educational Research and Services Center, 425 Fisk Avenue, DeKalb, Illinois 60115, USA.

REFERENCES

Albin, R.W., McDonnell, J.J. and Wilcox, B. (1987) Designing interventions to meet activity goals. In B. Wilcox and G.T. Bellamy (eds), *A Comprehensive Guide to the Activities Catalogue: An Alternative Curriculum for Youth and Adults with Severe Disabilities*, Brookes, Baltimore.

Brown, L., Bellamy, T., Perlmutter, L., Sackowitz, P. and Sontag, E. (1972) The development of quality, quantity, and durability in the work performance of retarded students in a public school prevocation workshop. *Training School Bulletin*, **68**, 58–69.

Cuvo, A.J., Leaf, R.B. and Borakove, L.S. (1978) Teaching janitorial skills to the mentally retarded: Acquisition, generalization, and maintenance. *Journal of Applied Behavior Analysis*, **11**, 345–355.

Deitz, D.E.D., Rose, E. and Repp, A. (1986) *The Task Demonstration Model for Teaching Severely Handicapped Persons*, Educational Research and Services Center, DeKalb, Illinois.

Gold, M.W. (1972) Stimulus factors in skill training of the retarded on a complex assembly task: Acquisition, transfer, and retention. *American Journal of Mental Deficiency*, **76**, 517–526.

Gold, M.W. (1976) Task analysis of a complex assembly task by the retarded blind. *Exceptional Children*, **43**, 78–84.

Grossman, H.J. (ed.) (1983) *Manual on Terminology and Classification in Mental Retardation*, American Association on Mental Retardation, Washington, DC.

Karsh, K.G. and Repp, A.C. (in press) The Task Demonstration Model: A Concurrent Model for Teaching Groups of Persons with Severe Handicaps. *Exceptional Children*.

Karsh, K.G., Repp, A.C. and Lenz, M.W. (1990) A comparison of the Task Demonstration Model and the Standard Prompting Hierarchy in teaching word identification to persons with moderate retardation. *Research in Developmental Disabilities*, **11**, 395–410.

Koegel, R.L. and Rincover, A. (1976) Some detrimental effects of using extra stimuli to guide learning in normal and autistic children. *Journal of Abnormal Child Psychology*, **4**, 59–71.

Koop, S., Martin, G., Yu, D. and Suthons, E. (1980) Comparison of two reinforcement strategies in vocational-skill training of mentally retarded persons. *American Journal of Mental Deficiency*, **84**, 616–626.

Mosk, M.D. and Bucher, B. (1984) Prompting and stimulus shaping procedures for teaching visual-motor skills to retarded children. *Journal of Applied Behavior Analysis*, **17**, 23–34.

Repp, A.C. (1983) *Teaching the Mentally Retarded*. Prentice-Hall, Englewood Cliffs, New Jersey.

Repp, A.C., Karsh, K.G. and Lenz, M.W. (1990) Discrimination training for persons with developmental disabilities: A comparison of the Task Demonstration Model and the Standard Prompting Hierarchy. *Journal of Applied Behavior Analysis*, **23**, 43–52.

Repp, A.C. and Singh, N.N. (eds) (1990) *Perspectives on the Use of Nonaversive and Aversive Interventions for Persons with Developmental Disabilities*, Sycamore Publishing, Sycamore, Illinois.

Repp, A.C., Karsh, K.G., Deitz, D.E.D. and Singh, N.N. (in press) A Study of Stereotypic and Other Motor Movements of Persons with Moderate Mental Retardation. *Journal of Mental Deficiency Research*.

Schreibman, L. (1975) Effects of within-stimulus and extra-stimulus prompting on discrimination learning in autistic children. *Journal of Applied Behavior Analysis*, **8**, 91–112.

Schreibman, L., Charlop, M.H. and Koegel, R.L. (1982) Teaching autistic children to use extra-stimulus prompts. *Journal of Experimental Child Psychology*, **33**, 475–491.

Sidman, M. and Stoddard, L.I. (1966) Programming, perception, and learning for retarded children. In N.R. Ellis (ed.), *International Review of Research in Mental Retardation II*, Academic Press, New York.

Sidman, M. and Stoddard, L.I. (1967) The effectiveness of fading in programming a simultaneous form discrimination for retarded children. *Journal of the Experimental Analysis of Behavior*, **10**, 3–15.

Snell, M.E. (ed.) (1987) *Systematic Instruction of Persons with Severe Handicaps* (3rd edn), Merrill, Columbus.

Steege, M.W., Wacker, D.P. and McMahon, C.M. (1987) Evaluation of the effectiveness and efficiency of two stimulus prompt strategies with severely handicapped students. *Journal of Applied Behavior Analysis*, **20**, 293–299.

Sternberg, L. (ed.) (1988) *Educating Students with Severe or Profound Handicaps*, Aspen, Rockville, Maryland.

Terrace, H. (1963a) Discrimination learning with and without errors. *Journal of the Experimental Analysis of Behavior*, **6**, 1–27.

Terrace, H. (1963b) Errorless transfer of a discrimination across two continua. *Journal of the Experimental Analysis of Behavior*, **6**, 223–232.

Terrace, H.S. (1966) Stimulus control. In W.K. Honig (ed.), *Operant Behavior: Areas of Research and Application*, Appleton–Century–Crofts, New York.

Wolery, M., Bailey, D.B. and Sugai, G.M. (1988) *Effective Teaching: Principles and Procedures of Applied Behavior Analysis with Exceptional Students*, Allyn & Bacon, Boston.

Chapter 13

Using Behavioural Principles in the Development of Effective Housing Services for Adults with Severe or Profound Mental Handicap

DAVID FELCE

INTRODUCTION

The last twenty-five years have seen a radical change in our ideas of how people with severe or profound mental handicap should live. Institutional care has been criticized for its inadequate standards, excessive restrictiveness and absence of therapeutic treatment. New philosophies now emphasize the individuals' right to live in the community, to enjoy the least restrictive environment possible and to receive habilitative treatment. The elaboration of the principle of normalization (Wolfensberger, 1972; Wolfensberger and Glenn, 1975) has underpinned a new examination of service design. The growing demonstration of the potential for learning and behavioural development shown by people with severe or profound mental handicap has also been significant. The process of deinstitutionalization has been fuelled not only by a desire to rectify the negative characteristics of traditional institutional provision but also by the belief that alternative services will allow individuals to develop more fully and lead a more productive and stimulating life. The deinstitutionalization movement has therefore created an imperative need to redesign residential services for people with severe or profound mental handicap and to assess the consequences of such changes on development and lifestyle. This chapter will describe one body of work, carried out in the Wessex Region of southern England, which used an applied behavioural analytic framework to achieve these ends.

The Challenge of Severe Mental Handicap. Edited by Bob Remington
© 1991 John Wiley & Sons Ltd

Twenty years ago in Wessex, an attempt was made to provide a comprehensive, community-based service for all people with severe or profound mental handicap requiring residential care (Kushlick, 1970). The evaluation of that scheme (Felce, Kushlick and Smith, 1980; Felce, 1987) yielded two principal conclusions. First, community residential care *was* feasible for people with severe or profound disabilities and other associated difficulties, but, second, the scale of improvement was disappointing given such a major restructuring of service design. Many rhetorical claims were made for the benefits of a move away from institutional features such as 'block treatment', 'rigidity of routine', 'depersonalization' and 'social distance' (King, Raynes and Tizard, 1971) to more domestic arrangements with a family ethos. However, the hope that such changes would generate a radically changed quality of life and consequent positive development over time has been hard to sustain. Although beneficial change was discernible (e.g., Felce, Kushlick and Mansell, 1980; Smith, Glossop and Kushlick, 1980), it was on a scale that left considerable room for further improvement.

One explanation for the failure of change to match rhetoric was that initial attempts to create domestic conditions did not go far enough. The Wessex units were still large group residences with many differences to the way family households operate. When the results of their evaluation appeared, mental handicap policy was moving forward. The use of ordinary housing of a genuinely domestic scale, which had until then only been provided to people with moderate disabilities, was being advocated for people with much greater levels of impairment (Mathieson and Blunden, 1980). However, a second explanation for the limited success of the scheme was that even the new community-based services had not been designed explicitly to achieve the outcomes upon which the services were being evaluated. A specific technology for achieving particular behavioural outcomes seemed required to complement the more general analysis of desirable environmental characteristics.

Over the same period of time during which services for people with mental handicap developed rapidly, the field of applied behaviour analysis has also grown. Its remit has been to apply the understanding of behaviour developed in the operant laboratory to the solution of socially important problems in the real world (Baer, Wolf and Risley, 1968). To date, the most effective techniques for ameliorating skill deficits and developing prosocial behaviours in people with mental handicap have been derived from applied behaviour analysis. Inherent in the behavioural approach is the premise that behaviour is responsive to the environmental context in which it occurs. It follows that behaviour can be changed by the adjustment of environmental events.

Numerous books have been written specifically on the application of behavioural principles to the development of people with mental handicap (e.g., Gardener, 1971; Matson and McCartney, 1981; Repp, 1983; Yule and Carr, 1987).

In recent years, however, behavioural psychology has broadened its scope from a concentration on discrete behaviour change to include a wider ecological perspective. A growing number of examples show how behaviour analytic methods have been brought to bear on the design of service systems structured to achieve complex behavioural outcomes involving the performance of service users, staff and managers. Successful examples of such systems include services for delinquent adolescents (Phillips *et al.*, 1974), pre-schoolers (O'Brien *et al.*, 1979), and adults with severe mental handicap in productive work settings (Bellamy, Horner and Inman, 1979; McLouglin, Garner and Callahan, 1987).

The aim in the research described here was to bring together the emphasis in emerging policy on ordinary housing and community integration with a behaviour analytic perspective on how to organize environments and structure staff performance. The work set out to find out how good a service could become if it developed specific ways of working which matched its aims and objectives. An opportunity to do this work became available in 1979, when a Wessex-based Health Authority (Winchester) began to develop a comprehensive housing service in the town of Andover for adults with the most severe or profound mental handicap requiring residential care.

BEHAVIOUR ANALYSIS APPLIED TO SERVICE DESIGN

How should the applied behaviour analysis paradigm be applied to the design of service systems? In principle, the problem is no different from its application to the management of individual problems. For example, Schwartz and Goldiamond (1975) described a constructional approach to working with individual clients which involved stating goals in terms of behavioural repertoires, identifying current relevant repertoires, assessing resources for change, and developing and evaluating self-sustaining change procedures. In a similar description of procedures for producing service change, Blunden (1984) has described a four-stage process, involving: identification of target behaviours; behavioural analysis of the environment; design of new contingencies; and implementation and evaluation. The remainder of this chapter will describe these stages in the context of the small homes project.

Stage 1: Identification of target outcomes

Clarification of objectives is widely held to be important in organizational theory. For example, the mental handicap policy document *An Ordinary Life* (King's Fund, 1980) argues that, too often, insufficient attention is paid to analysing objectives clearly, particularly with regard to the ways in which they relate to service philosophy. Defining objectives in behavioural terms is, of course, the starting point for a behavioural analysis.

Much has been written on the quality of residential services for people with mental handicap. Approaches to its assessment (see Raynes, 1986) include the use of detailed checklists of standards informed by expert opinion (e.g., NDG, 1980; ACMRDD, 1978); scales concerning the physical or social environment (e.g., Gunzburg, 1973; Moos, 1974; Wolfensberger and Glenn, 1975); and observational studies of the impact on the lifestyle or development of service users (e.g., Hemming, Lavender and Pill, 1981; Landesman, 1987). Unfortunately, while clarity of objectives is seen almost universally as a prerequisite for sound planning and evaluation of outcome, a clear definition of quality which carries universal agreement does not yet exist.

The principle of normalization (Wolfensberger, 1972) or social role valorization (Wolfensberger, 1983) has been articulated in great detail and is perhaps now the most widely accepted basis for framing the objectives of services for people with mental handicap. It defines both the desired outcomes for clients and the methods used to obtain these outcomes in terms of 'the utilization of means which are as culturally normative as possible, in order to establish and/or maintain personal behaviour and characteristics which are as culturally normative as possible' (Wolfensberger, 1972, p. 28). Thus, in terms of outcomes, the emphasis is on individuals participating as much as possible as full members of a valued social culture. It is generally acknowledged that the normalization principle seeks to represent the interests of service users by comparing their circumstances and experiences with those of typical citizens in the wider community.

The major failing of the principle of normalization from the point of view of a behavioural analysis is its openness to varied interpretation. Clarification is required to reach a set of service objectives that can provide the basis for a behavioural analysis of service characteristics. Recently, O'Brien (1987) has offered a framework of five essential accomplishments which define the principle of normalization. The concept of accomplishment as the foundation for organizational design stems from the application of a behavioural analysis described by Gilbert (1978). O'Brien specifies the five accomplishments in terms of community presence, choice and autonomy of action, competence to perform valued activities, respect from other members of the community, and participation in community life including sustaining friendships and other personal relationships.

Although this framework was not available at the time objectives were specified for the housing project, O'Brien's suggestions overlap very closely with the behavioural definitions that were developed. These were that service users would:

- Engage in a wide range of activities typical of ordinary *home* life for people of their age (e.g., participate in their own self-care, housework, food preparation, gardening, hobbies and social activity).
- Engage in a wide range of activities typical of ordinary *community* living for people of their age (e.g., shopping, use of community leisure amenities, socializing, attendance at clubs and societies, gaining services such as a dentist or hairdresser).
- Engage in a *social* life typical of citizens of their age, maintaining family, friendship and acquaintanceship ties; visiting, going out with, and inviting home their family and friends; and frequently going out within the community.
- Develop competence in home and community settings over time by acquiring new skills relevant to an ordinary home and community life, losing disruptive and inappropriate behaviours that limit or deny access to ordinary places or activities, and using all existing skills so as to maintain their repertoire.

What appears at first sight to be an overriding concern with everyday behaviour in fact specifies the wider and longer-term notions embodied in O'Brien's framework. The approach operationalizes the enduring quality of 'accomplishment' in terms of the regular occurrence of ordinary activities. Ensuring engagement in such activities formed the cornerstone of our service objectives.

Having identified target outcomes, the next stage of a behaviour analytic approach to service development focuses on the factors which maintain client behaviour at baseline levels.

Stage 2: Behavioural analysis of existing environments

A central theme of client experience in a traditional institution is one of a dependent lifestyle with little opportunity for experiences of ordinary life. Institutions are custodial cultures in which 'care' is the defining characteristic of the staff role. As a consequence, support to enable participation in normal daily activities and social relationships is absent, and clients pass time in inactivity, engagement in inappropriate behaviours, or trivial occupation. A number of research studies have graphically illustrated the lack of purposeful activity and the unstimulating nature of the life which people with severe disabilities lead (e.g., Beail, 1985; Bratt and Johnston, 1988; DHSS, 1978; Felce, Kushlick and Mansell, 1980; Hemming, Lavender and Pill, 1981; Morris, 1969; Oswin, 1971, 1978; Rawlings, 1985; Landesman-Dwyer, Sackett and Kleinman, 1980; Landesman, 1987; Thomas et al., 1986). Often, institutionalized clients spent less than 20% of the waking day occupied in any meaningful activity. Developmental progress was barely discernible (e.g., Conroy, Efthimiou and Lemanowicz, 1982; Smith, Glossop and Kushlick, 1982) and evidence of regression has been documented (Mitchell and Smeriglio, 1970). Residents have little contact with the outside world either in terms of community visits or family and friendship contacts (e.g., Felce, Lunt and Kushlick, 1980; Firth and Short, 1987).

The analysis of what accounts for this poor state of affairs is not a simple one. Single provision variables such as facility size, location or staffing level have not proved powerful determinants of outcome (e.g., Balla, 1976; Birenbaum and Re, 1979; Dalgleish and Matthews, 1981; Harris et al., 1974; King, Raynes and Tizard, 1971; Landesman-Dwyer, Sackett and Kleinman, 1980; Landesman, 1987). Butler and Bjaanes (1977) have discussed the need to develop a typology for community settings to distinguish custodial, therapeutic and maintaining environments. Janicki (1981) has emphasised the *habilitative intent* of the setting as an independent factor which cannot be derived from other setting characteristics.

In analysing how existing environments produce their effects, and in considering the design of new contingencies, I will consider three dimensions of service provision. First, the degree of habilitative intent will be examined by addressing factors concerned with the *orientation of the service*. Second, *service structure* will be considered to understand how organization can either create obstacles to the achievement of stated objectives, or facilitate their accomplishment. Third, the way in which *service procedures* work will be analysed to assess how directly they relate to client objectives.

Service orientation: Degree of habilitative intent

Rosynko et al. (1973) have pointed to the importance of verbal stimuli in the determination of social behaviour. The verbal communities (Skinner, 1957) within which staff operate are likely to be key influences on their behaviour. A central problem for many services is that they fail to provide staff with a clear specification of their objectives for clients. In the absence of a definition of service philosophy, staff may assume alternative orientations which fit existing practice. These include principles inherited from the past (e.g., the custodial model), those which reflect commonly held low expectations for client achievement (e.g., by specifying life-long care as the primary aim), and those which reflect current service arrangements (e.g., the medical model, with its emphasis on medical and nursing care).

Even where an up-to-date philosophy is stated it can be vague and qualified. Such terms as 'maximizing potential' and 'encouraging independence' are used and couched with a liberal sprinkling of the phrase 'as much as possible'. Against more dominant traditional orientations, radical aims may become marginalized. Thus, while the new philosophy may be adopted in how staff speak (to demonstrate correct attitudes), little change in performance may occur.

Service orientation can also be judged in terms of managerial concern. Staff performance may be influenced by definition of the staff role, the content of job descriptions or by implied or explicit managerial feedback. Staff may be seen as 'carers', 'nurses', or 'attendants' with the definition of expertise and function rooted in nursing or custodial care. Job descriptions may be inconsistent with perceived role, and may be imprecise in defining the performances expected of staff. Management attention to budgeting, hygiene standards, or the proportion of trained nurses within staff establishments may imply that targets of clinical efficiency and nursing care are paramount.

Woods and Cullen (1983) contend that client achievement is often insufficiently reinforcing, i.e. that improvement alone does not maintain staff performance in the absence of managerial intervention. Since the absence of clear statements of client objectives and associated managerial monitoring is typical of most existing settings, it is hardly surprising that staff behaviour rarely matches that which, in the applied treatment literature, has been shown to produce client gains. If there is also a specification of objectives counter to those which are habilitative, and if managers monitor indicators largely unconnected with client welfare, the poor outcomes found in much of the research cited above are to be expected.

To summarize, orientation and management focus within existing services can fail to reflect contemporary philosophies. As a result, the staff performances which promote client participation and development remain a low priority. Staff skills inevitably remain underdeveloped.

Service structure: Obstacles in the environmental context

If clients are to engage in and develop skills relevant to a broad range of normal activities, they must be exposed to a corresponding range of normal contingencies. A major deficit of many existing residential service settings is the absence of environmental arrangements typical of ordinary houses. Lack of access to kitchens, utility rooms, household equipment, and the low level of material enrichment in areas such as living, dining, and bedrooms which clients can enter, removes the opportunity for the regular practice of such activities as cooking, cleaning, laundry, shopping and the naturally occurring social behaviours attendant on them. The location of settings away from town centres or city precincts used by the rest of the population creates obstacles to such activities as shopping, eating out and using community leisure facilities, clubs and associations. When physical proximity is achieved, the size of facility may still attenuate the real opportunities available to each client.

Even where the physical environment resembles an ordinary home, residents do not necessarily have opportunities to engage in the activities of ordinary home life. They may be denied access to the functional areas of the environment, where they may be considered a nuisance or a risk to their own safety through being exposed to sources of danger such as the cooker, sharp kitchen utensils, electrical equipment or hot water. Obstacles to clients engaging in daily living activities are also created by implicit or explicit definitions of the staff role. The role of caring or nursing is likely to be fulfilled by doing things for clients without their participation. Further, domestic and catering staff are often employed with the explicit task of doing all necessary household tasks, thus removing from clients many opportunities for cleaning, tidying, household upkeep, food preparation, cooking, and shopping.

The 'hotel' model of provision is extended by service agencies making centralized arrangements for such things as supply of food, laundry, furnishings, and property maintenance. These mechanisms remove yet more natural opportunities for engagement in ordinary activities while transferring the service budget allocated to residents to other service departments. The amount of disposable revenue that staff and residents have to transact their relationship with the community is thus diminished and integration is bound to suffer. Residents have few natural opportunities left to use community amenities and little income to do it with. This promotes a focus on activity within the residence, but, with no opportunities for household and domestic activity, an overriding emphasis on personal care and leisure pursuits results. The severity of some handicaps means that leisure activities need to be organized at a very simple, and often repetitious, level, suggestive of very young children.

In the absence of a function, such activity, even when achieved successfully (e.g., Mansell *et al.*, 1982a; Porterfield, Blunden and Blewitt, 1980), can seem trivial and meaningless.

To summarize, existing service structures can often prevent the arrangement of setting conditions in which important components of an effective domestic behavioural repertoire can achieve reinforcement.

Service procedures: Deficiencies in staff performance

Staffing is clearly an important resource for people with severe or profound mental handicap. What staff do and how they do it must be central to an analysis of quality in service environments. Evidence from the behavioural intervention literature unquestionably shows that staff interactions which are deliberate and conscious in both nature and occurrence can have a direct effect on the behaviour of clients (e.g., Berkson and Landesman-Dwyer, 1977). Typically, however, staff behaviour in natural service settings shows little similarity with that of demonstration projects. Many observational studies have shown disappointingly low rates of interaction between staff and residents (e.g., Burg, Reid and Lattimore, 1979; Cullen *et al.*, 1983; Hemming, Lavender and Pill, 1981; Landesman-Dwyer, Sackett and Kleinman, 1980; Montegar *et al.*, 1977; Moores and Grant, 1976; Oswin, 1978; Rawlings, 1985; Wright, Abbas and Meredith, 1974). Individuals can typically expect interaction with staff for around 3–7% of the time (e.g., Hemming, Lavender and Pill, 1981; Rawlings, 1985; Wright, Abbas and Meredith, 1974). They may wait 20–30 minutes between interactions (e.g., Cullen *et al.*, 1983; Moores and Grant, 1976), which are typically less than 30 seconds in duration (Cullen *et al.*, 1983; Moores and Grant, 1976). Such levels of interaction are clearly insufficient to support people with severe or profound mental handicap in any reasonable quality of existence.

The distribution of staff interaction reveals further problems. Clients with higher levels of maladaptive behaviour, and lower levels of independence and adaptive behaviour, receive fewer positive interactions from staff (Grant and Moores, 1977). Similarly, more severely mentally handicapped clients receive less informative speech (Pratt, Bumstead and Raynes, 1976), and both older and longer institutionalized persons receive fewer verbal interactions (Paton and Stirling, 1974). Clients perceived by aides as attractive, likeable, and intellectually more competent receive relatively high levels of attention (Dailey *et al.*, 1974), but those who are depressed are more likely to receive directives ('do . . . ') than potentially educative or therapeutic conversational speech (Schloss, 1982). These studies show quite clearly that there are client characteristics which affect the number and nature of their interactions with staff who, like most of us, tend to interact more with people they like than with those they do not. Clients competent enough to provide social reinforcement are thus advantaged. From an habilitative perspective, however, these results suggest that those who are less competent will receive fewer learning opportunities and hence become even less competent relative to peers— a situation summed up well by Raynes (1980): 'The less you've got, the less you get.' Opportunities for development and a good quality of life are unlikely to occur naturally for people with the most severe disabilities.

The content of interaction, its relationship to client behaviour, and its impact on client behaviour cause further concern. Oswin (1978) studied 223 profoundly multiply handicapped children in eight mental handicap hospitals, and found that a child might typically receive an average of one hour of physical care, but only 5 minutes of 'mothering' attention (cuddling, play, talking) in a 10-hour period. Other research has shown that staff do not frequently use the type of speech that occasions verbal responses (Prior et al., 1979) or the type of instruction associated with correct responses (Repp, Barton and Brulle, 1981, 1982). Further, Warren and Mondy (1971) monitored staff attention as a consequence of the appropriate and inappropriate behaviours of children with mental handicap. They found that behaviour in both categories was ignored for more than three quarters of the time. However, inappropriate behaviours were attended to on what could amount to a lean and variable reinforcement schedule, which could build behaviour with high resistance to extinction. Clearly, there is a need to train staff how to interact with residents in ways which are most likely to achieve desirable objectives.

Staff training has been recognized as a means of generating therapeutic performance, and there is a modest literature concerning the teaching of programming skills (e.g., Gardener, 1972; Page, Iwata and Reid, 1982; Watson and Uzzell, 1980). But even if staff are successfully trained to work with clients on individualized programmes, this may not change the overall nature of their performance if the setting is not organized for one-to-one work. In any case, many staff receive little in-service training specific to their job, and the main process for the development of expertise in practice falls on a system of qualifying training. Qualified staff are then expected to pass on principles and working methods to untrained workers whom they supervise. This approach produces three kinds of problems. First, qualifying training by definition occurs some time in the past; thus only a minority of qualified staff have been trained on an up-to-date curriculum. Secondly, qualifying training relates to professional identities (e.g., nurse, social worker) and, because its content is not purpose-built for the particular client group, it may be relatively incomplete or even irrelevant. Finally, training may be conducted in a pedagogic form that teaches academic knowledge but not practical skills (cf. Adams, Tallon and Rimell, 1980; Watson and Uzzell, 1980). Subsequent practical placements may fail to produce effective skills because the traditional services in which they occur provide the trainee professional with a less than exemplary model of staff performance.

Allocation of staff to duties presents a common problem in many services. A lack of specific definition of staff duties, and a lack of planning of staff and client activities, mean that there is no specific method of ensuring that staff are deployed effectively. Experimental studies have shown the benefits of activity planning, clear staff roles and specific deployment of staff (e.g., Doke and Risley, 1972; LeLaurin and Risley, 1972; Mansell et al., 1982a; Porterfield, Blunden and Blewitt, 1980). Mansell et al. (1982b) and Cataldo and Risley (1972) have shown that increasing numbers of staff results in decreasing marginal, and even absolute, returns in terms of interaction with clients. Both studies showed, however, that this problem was eased when staff were given clear and separate assignments. Further, Harris et al. (1974) observed improved interaction rates with better staff : client ratios only when the number of residents with one member of staff was decreased. Improvement did not follow the allocation of more staff to large client groups. Dalgleish and Matthews (1981) have also argued that small groupings with only one or two staff present are associated with the most efficient use of staff time. Groupings and the design and organization of settings are clearly related. A greater level of staff-initiated communication has been found in smaller enclosed areas than in larger open areas (Dalgleish and Matthews, 1980) and staff produced more comments, instructions and questions in structured rather than in unstructured settinga (Prior et al., 1979).

The work reviewed above implies that many existing services are too large, provide rooms that allow the congregation of too many clients and staff, and lack adequate mechanisms for activity planning or assigning staff responsibility. In addition, inadequate staff training or an absence of monitoring can contribute to poor staff performance. In 1976, Patterson, Griffin and Panyan commented that 'Training alone does not insure that skills will be utilized on the job, and a consistent program of reinforcement appears to be necessary to maintain the applications of these skills' (p. 249). Since then, many studies have addressed this problem using various means of giving feedback on performance (see Anderson, 1987). In practice, however, little has changed. As Mittler (1987) recently wrote, 'Neglect of organizational and managerial variables could largely nullify many current approaches to training' (p. 34).

In conclusion, a behaviourally oriented analysis of existing environments reveals a number of severe deficits. Most services fail to define client-centred objectives adequately, fail to define how staff must behave to meet those objectives, fail to implement ways of working needed to produce appropriate staff performances, and fail to establish the managerial contingencies needed to generate such performances. The scope for redesigning the parameters of an effective residential service is thus considerable.

Stage 3: Design of new contingencies

The task of redesigning the parameters of a residential service is seen as remedying the deficiencies in *orientation, structure* and *procedures* described above. This will be illustrated in this section by describing the arrangements made in the small homes project. The description will be taken in three parts, relating to the following clusters of service objectives: promoting client engagement in daily living at home; promoting engagement in the community, and with family and friends; and promoting skill development and the corresponding loss of inappropriate behaviours.

A number of behaviourally based principles were followed in generating the new service specification. The orientation of the service was stated behaviourally, communicated to staff, and reflected in managerial contingencies. Service structure was judged in terms of its ability to facilitate required staff and thus client behaviour, and procedures were developed to provide a structure for staff performance in relation to each key service objective. These included the use of written routines, pro forma, checklists, job aids and practical training in specific modes of interaction. The staff procedures provided a link to management by each, including a built-in recording method to produce data for monitoring and review purposes.

Design for engagement in activities of adult homelife

Service orientation, structure and procedures were specified so as to maximize clients' opportunities, support and reinforcement for participating in the major spheres of their own existence at home, despite their very limited skills for independent functioning.

Service operation was underpinned by an unequivocal statement that it had an obligation to ensure its users had wide-ranging experiences and high levels of involvement in day-to-day activity. The operational policy stated:

Staff will provide each person living in the home with access to at least one activity at any time of the waking day. Activities will be carefully planned and sequenced to avoid time spent by clients passively waiting for the next event. Each activity will be organized to ensure that: materials are arranged so that the client can get to them and use them; developmentally appropriate help and encouragement is readily available from staff; the activity is appropriate to the chronological age of the client; a range of activity is available for every single client each week (including activities outside the home which bring people living in the house into contact with other citizens and integrate them into the local community); priority is given to organizing housework activities in which clients can participate (rather than providing 'occupational' activities with pre-school toys).

The job description for the person in charge of each house contained a very detailed section on the 'Organization of client participation' which included a wide range of responsibilities. For example, the person in charge was responsible for:

- Planning the organization of the residential day to promote the active participation of all clients, including the most intellectually impaired or behaviourally disturbed. The ultimate aim was for all clients to have the opportunity for engaging in some form of meaningful occupation at all times.
- Allocating staff to duties, and teaching them how to encourage client participation effectively (through instruction, prompting, physical guidance, and reinforcement), without fostering undue dependence.
- Determining household organization and standards, and arranging activities outside the home in which clients could participate, in ways that were age-appropriate for them.
- Implementing a system of monitoring client participation in activity within the house and in the community to allow review of working methods and to safeguard the opportunities made available to clients.

The front-line staff also had similarly specific job descriptions which highlighted their role to support client participation. For example, it was emphasized that 'The staff role is one of supporting and teaching clients rather than of doing things for them or to them or as efficiently as possible without them.'

Performance monitoring also emphasized service orientation in recording the number of opportunities for household activity given to each person during each shift. What was important enough to record was important enough to do. Finally, staff's verbal behaviour was 'shaped' in ways designed to internalize the orientation. Being engaged in activity was viewed as 'a learning opportunity'. The role of staff to support client participation was encapsulated in the following 'slogan': 'If the materials are in your hands, you have probably got it wrong. Think of a way of getting them into the clients' hands and of you helping them to do it for themselves.'

The service structure was made to support this orientation through the use of ordinary housing. Two residential houses offered a number of small rooms, each designed for different functional activities. This naturally encouraged spatial separation of staff and residents into the kind of subgroups found beneficial for effective staff performance (see Stage 2). The houses were furnished and equipped to a high domestic standard, and a rule of unrestricted client access throughout the house was observed. People, particularly those with extensive disabilities and little language, need many objects to pursue their lives. In addition to affording physical opportunities for engagement, the 'richness' of the environment formed a setting for the normal social interactions that such engagement engendered.

The homes had been designed for eight residents (with one place reserved for short-term care). They were well staffed, although their revenue costs were in line with those of larger facilities. Nine day staff and four half-time night staff provided two to three people on daytime duty and one at night. Savings from domestic and catering staff costs were used to enlarge the number of care staff. Senior staff were given considerable managerial autonomy, including control over the consumable budget and staff recruitment. They ran the houses like private households with all domestic maintenance activity carried out by clients and staff. There were no centralized services to fall back on: no supplies of provisions or equipment, no linen or laundry service, and no property maintenance services.

Many service procedures were developed to ensure that staff used appropriate working methods. Because staff do not intuitively interact apppropriately with clients with severe disability (cf. Repp, Felce and de Kock, 1987; Warren and Mondy, 1971), they were taught how to do so. Role-play was used during in-service training; subsequently, in the workplace, training continued through supervision and feedback from the person in charge. Methods taught included graduated guidance to support correct responding by clients (using an instruct/show/prompt/ guide hierarchy); task analysis to simplify and sequence activity, and contingent attention to motivate appropriately engaged clients (cf. Mansell et al., 1982a; Porterfield, Blunden and Blewitt, 1980). The graduated guidance hierarchy and task analysis techniques ensured that support could be matched to differing individual abilities, allowing clients to participate to the limit of their independent abilities.

Staff deployment, client activity and staff : client groupings were not left to chance, but planned daily by each shift. The system combined a weekly routine of major household tasks and individual appointments with a means by which staff could communicate changes and additions to the routine (see Brown and Brown, 1987; Felce and de Kock, 1983; Mansell et al., 1987). This latter mechanism helped to keep routines flexible and varied. Each oncoming staff shift decided who would be responsible for each resident, what activities they would do, and how individual programmes would be arranged. A form of individual programming called opportunity plans (Toogood *et al.* 1983) was used to pinpoint and monitor specific engagement opportunities which would allow new experiences and develop new skills for each person. Opportunities, categorized and summed under 12 headings, were reviewed on a weekly basis for each person to ensure that participation levels were maintained or improved. This review was conducted by constructing staff rotas to ensure that all day staff and some night staff could attend a 2½-hour staff meeting on the same day each week. This forum provided staff with an essential opportunity to express views, recognize successes, discuss anxieties and address deficiencies. It was thus a mechanism through which staff gained 'ownership' of their working methods and, because they monitored their own effectiveness, it acted as a quality circle or quality action group (see Blunden and Beyer, 1987).

Design for client engagement in community activities and with family and friends

A similar analysis was made of the orientation, structure and procedures needed to promote successful community integration. In this area, operational policy statements focused on activities outside the house and on relationships with other citizens. They also emphasized the importance of both continued family involvement and the use of generally available customer services (e.g., opticians, hairdressers, dentists). Community integration was covered in the senior staff job description relating to client participation and in an emphasis on 'fostering existing family and friendship ties, and helping to initiate new friendships with members of community for individuals who need a greater range of social relationships'. Monitoring procedures, designed to track each person's community activities and social contacts, underscored the importance of these objectives.

In terms of service structure, the size and location of the houses were viewed as influential in two separate ways. Because each house was within the small local catchment area which it served, residents lived near their immediate family and any existing wider friendship networks. Secondly, because the houses were located as near as possible to the town centre, any obstacles to frequent use of community amenities imposed by distance and isolation were avoided. Once problems arising from sheer physical distance had been removed, the frequency of community use and family/friendship contact was open to influence by many other factors. The small size of the residences allowed individual and small group trips to the community, in order to maximize personal integration and acceptance. The use of well-furnished ordinary housing gave residents the opportunity to receive visitors and offer reasonable comfort, privacy and hospitality. Because centrally organized supply and works department services were not used, the local shops and services available in the community could be used as other households use them. A fully devolved budget to conduct this daily business allowed the staff to be flexible in the use of community amenities rather than always needing to be self-sufficient (e.g., using restaurants and launderettes rather than always eating and washing at home).

It was important to good community relationships for residents to be actively engaged and behave appropriately outside the houses, and this depended on effective staff performance. The procedures used by staff within the houses to support activity were equally relevant to community-based engagement. In addition, both community use and family/friendship relationships were encouraged by positive goal planning. Individual programme plan reviews (Jenkins *et al.*, 1988) were held for every resident on a six-monthly basis. Preparation for each meeting focused on constructing a prospective *needs list*, two sections of which related to social relationships and opportunities for community participation. Each review produced a wide range of forward-looking goals stated in behavioural terms. Staff recorded community activities and social contacts on a daily basis, and produced weekly summaries. These data were fed back so that individual programme planning goals could be reviewed routinely in staff meetings.

Design for client development: Learning skills relevant to adult home and community living and losing inappropriate behaviours

Developmental progress as a goal of services for people with mental handicap has assumed central importance in recent years. To this end, emphasis has been placed on the need for individual, structured programmes which develop new and change existing patterns of behaviour. There has been a tendency, however, to divorce, or at least fail to relate, individual programming to what happens at other times of the person's day. Ferguson and Cullari (1983) have described problems of implementing individual programmes by care staff in real settings rather than for the purposes of research. We assumed that the relevance of individual teaching aimed at producing behaviour change would be evident to staff only against a background of well-organized activity and high levels of engagement. Thus, a basic engaging environment was seen as a prerequisite for individual programming. Moreover, we felt skill teaching must be part of everyday life, not a marginal addition concentrated into short 'sessions' during the day. The reasons for this are practical as well as philosophical. Skills will not be maintained if they are unused, and long-term suppression of difficult behaviour cannot be achieved unless alternative, acceptable behaviours are developed to take their place. It is necessary, therefore, to create a milieu which supports and encourages a wide range of constructive, meaningful activity.

Individual programming was established in service objectives, as reflected by the following extract from the operational policy:

Every person living in the home will have a written individual programme plan which will set long-term and/or medium-term goals for: teaching new skills; arranging participation in particular activities (including family contact); weakening and replacing disruptive behaviours; and remedying or ameliorating health problems (including problems of disfigurement or stigmatizing appearance).

The responsibilities of the person in charge for programming care of individual clients was directly specified in the job description. He or she had responsibility for maintaining individual programme planning, setting up individual teaching, behaviour change and other treatment programmes and monitoring outcomes. The analysis of patterns of client–staff interaction in relation to inappropriate behaviour by residents was also included. Job descriptions for front-line staff specified their responsibility for implementing and monitoring individual programmes and treatments as directed by senior staff.

The *needs list* used in the six-monthly individual programme plan reviews (Jenkins *et al.*, 1988) prompted attention to teaching priorities as well as other goal areas such as health/hygiene, physical appearance and opportunities for increased or more varied occupation. Agreed goals, phrased as behavioural objectives, were assigned to a person who took responsibility for programme development. Skill teaching was organized at two levels of intensity. Opportunity planning (Toogood *et al.*, 1983) provided a simple mechanism through which between six and ten behavioural goals were set fortnightly and reviewed weekly for each resident. The system provided a way of focusing staff attention on a few skills to develop, among the many that existed, using the natural opportunities offered by the domestic and community environment. At a more intense level (Mansell *et al.*, 1986), formal teaching programmes were written, based upon a thorough task analysis of the goals to be taught. Teaching charts included a precise specification of the teaching objective, necessary preparations for the teaching sessions, instructions and help levels, reinforcement and correction procedures, and monitoring procedures.

The implementation and effectiveness of teaching were monitored using the records produced, summarized to give a weekly check on the status of programming for the household as a whole. Residents' individual programme plan achievements were reviewed at each six-monthly meeting and checked periodically at intervening staff meetings. Behaviour reduction programmes were drawn up as required with the assistance of a consultant psychologist. But the major approach to inappropriate behaviour came in the emphasis on establishing appropriate engagement. Staff knew how to support alternative activity, and they understood the power of their attention both to cue and to reinforce behaviour. Thus, they realized the dangers of attending to incipient, inappropriate behaviours rather than ignoring them or responding as neutrally as possible until the situation could be discussed and a programmed response agreed. The routine interactional model comprised a combination of graduated guidance and contingent attention for appropriate be-haviours. Graduated guidance is an appropriate procedure for responding to escape-motivated behaviour such as non-compliance. Contingent attention approximates a differential reinforcement of incompatible behaviour contingency for attention-seeking inappropriate behaviours. Therefore, reduction in some challenging behaviours could be expected to result from the way staff routinely interacted.

Stage 4: Implementation and evaluation

The two houses used in the course of the research each served a similar defined catchment area. The *two* demographically selected resident groups were found to be similar to each other and representative of the most handicapped adults in residential care (Felce *et al.* 1985). These groups included people who had been characterised as severely behaviour disordered for most of their lives, some of whom had been living in specially restricted institutional environments for many years immediately prior to their transfer to the houses. The evaluation assessed all of the features discussed in the descriptions of the preceding stages. Thus, the nature and incidence of staff interactions with individuals was monitored. Similarly, resident dependent variables included the extent of their active engagement in daily living, household and community activities; their involvement in the social and community life of the town; and their skill development over time. The efficacy of the small homes scheme was assessed by comparing it with both large institutions and with 25-place community-based units. Matched group designs provided the primary comparisons, but a number of within-group comparisons were made by exploiting the fact that the opening of the two houses was temporally staggered (e.g., Felce, de Kock and Repp, 1986; Felce *et al.*, 1986). The main findings of the research will be summarized very briefly in the remainder of this section. Further procedural details are available in the research cited below.

Nature and incidence of staff interaction with residents

Two studies addressed the success of the system in achieving high levels of interaction between residents and staff. Felce, de Kock and Repp (1986) demonstrated that each resident received instruction from staff, on average, for 19.8% and 11.3% of his or her time in the two houses respectively, and physical guidance for 5.2% and 3.2% of time. This compared very favourably with pre-transfer levels in residents' previous institutional placements which averaged 1.0% for instruction and 0.0% for physical guidance. Staff support for residents varied in inverse relationship to the latters' mental age and adaptive behaviour. A second study (Thomas et al., 1986) confirmed that levels of interaction in the two homes were, on average, at least five times greater than for comparative groups in two different institutions and two large community units.

A third study addressed the relationship between staff interaction and client engagement in appropriate activity (Felce et al., 1987). The density of attention given to residents when appropriately engaged was almost double in the houses compared to the other settings. Staff attention occurred in 57.3% of the 15-second intervals during which residents were recorded as appropriately engaged in the houses, compared to only 32.6% and 33.5% of intervals in institutions and large community units respectively. Overall, more than three-quarters of the attention staff gave to residents in the houses occurred when clients were appropriately engaged. In contrast, staff working with comparable individuals in community units and institutions provided only two-thirds and half of their attention (respectively) for appropriate engagement.

The extent of active resident participation

The results of three studies (Felce, de Kock and Repp, 1986; Mansell et al., 1984; Thomas et al., 1986) which compared levels of engagement in domestic, personal (self-help), leisure and social activities in the houses, institutions and large community units are presented in Figure 13.1. Adults living in the houses were meaningfully occupied in domestic, leisure, personal care, or social pursuits, for about half of their time—an exceptional result given their level of disability. The comparison with institutional or large community unit care confirmed the contrast. Like most of the published research concerning people with similar disabilities living in non-domestic settings, it showed institutional and community

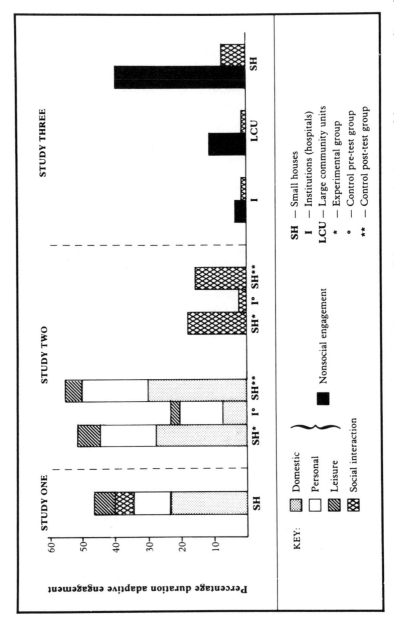

Figure 13.1 Appropriate adult engagement in three studies in small houses, institutions, and large community units

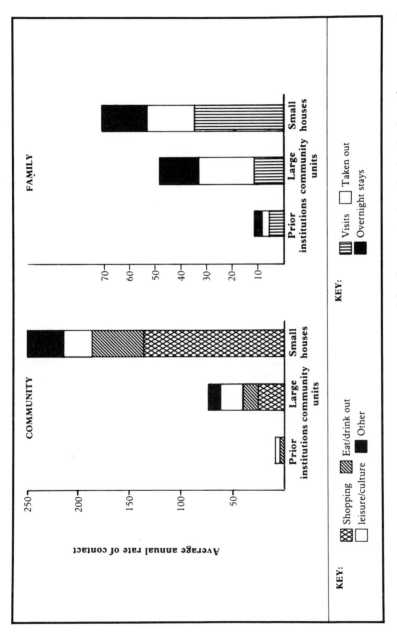

Figure 13.2 Average annual rates of adults' community and family contacts in prior institutions, large community units, and small houses.

unit residents spent between 75% and 95% of their time either doing nothing or behaving inappropriately. For them, time passed with little meaningful interaction with the material or social world.[1]

Participation in domestic activity, which took up about one-third of the residents' time, provided a successful and fitting source of age-appropriate activity in the houses. The importance of residents' access to the different activity areas of the houses and of material enrichment in general was demonstrated in Felce et al. (1985). They showed that engagement depended largely on materials and equipment which were not present in institutional settings. Residents thus had a greater variety of activity on transfer to the small houses, and a significant proportion of it occurred in the functional areas of the houses, such as the kitchen and utility room. These were areas to which people in other settings typically did not have access.

An analysis using repeated measures across individuals showed a high correlation (Speaman rank order = 0.97) between the level of staff support that residents received and their level of appropriate engagement. Thus, the higher levels of support given to more handicapped individuals could be seen as helping them to participate at levels approaching those of the more able residents (Felce, de Kock and Repp 1986).

Involvement in a social and community life

The rates of family contact (i.e., with family and friends) and community contact (involvement in community activities) for residents of the two houses were compared to their prior institutional experience and to those of similar residents living in large community units (de Kock et al., 1988). Figure 13.2 shows that, in terms of average annual rates, residents had massively higher community and family contact after transfer to the houses. In comparison with matched groups living in large community units, their community contact was also 'significantly greater (Kruskal-Wallis, $p<0.001$). However, the difference in family contact was not significant, possibly reflecting the fact that these community units also served local catchment areas.

A direct observational study of house residents' actions in shops, pubs, cafes and restaurants (Saxby et al., 1986) assessed whether they were actively engaged in activities appropriate to the setting or whether they

---

[1] Figures 13.1 and 13.2 are reprinted by permission of BIMH Publications, Stourport House, Stourport Road, Kidderminster, Worcs., DY11 7QG and Paul H. Brookes Publishing Co. They originally appeared in Felce, D. (1988) Behavoural and social climate in community group residences. In M.P. Janicki, M.W. Krauss and M.M. Seltzer (eds), *Community Residences for persons with developmental disabilities: Here to Stay* (pp. 133–148). Paul H. Brookes Publishing Co., Baltimore.

were accompanying staff passively. Engagement occupied about one-third of residents' time on average, confirming that, with appropriate support, community contacts legitimately extended the range of ordinary occupation available to them.

Skill development

Assessments of the 28 adults with mental ages under 48 months from the two catchment areas served by the houses were carried out using the Adaptive Behavior Scale (Nihira *et al.*, 1974). Mental ages (Griffiths, 1954, 1971) and equivalent language ages (Reynell, 1977) were also assessed. This gave comparable measures of progress for matched groups living in the houses, other residential institutions and parental homes (Felce *et al.*, 1986). The data showed that adults living in the houses made significantly more progress than the institutional control group who made no progress, and people living in parental homes, who made only moderate progress. Progress was mainly found in the domains of independent functioning, domestic activity and self-direction as defined by the Adaptive Behavior Scale.

CONCLUSIONS

The evaluation demonstrated that the housing model was superior to the other settings investigated in areas of adaptive functioning, range of environmental opportunity, appropriateness of staff interaction, development and integration. As in many other service evaluations, it is not possible to demonstrate the relationships between particular components of the model and the dependent outcomes empirically. A case has been made above for the central mediating role of staff performance in supporting and motivating appropriate resident activity patterns. The research has demonstrated that staff performance in the houses was radically different to that generally reported. Taking the available literature into account, it is probable that the improvements found can be attributed to the structure for planning activity and the deployment of staff to work with individuals or small groups, to the access to and enriched opportunities of the domestic and community environments, and to the job specifications, training and operational procedures followed by staff (including in-house monitoring of outcome). If one were to think in terms of necessary and sufficient conditions, it is likely that very few, if any, single components of the housing model are sufficient for quality, but the majority may be necessary. It is likely that interaction effects are more powerful than the impact of single variables.

This conclusion may appear unsatisfactory to exponents of applied behaviour analysis, with its explicit remit to isolate the determinants of behaviour. In fact applied behaviour analysis is not alone in this endeavour; multivariate statistical inference too has been developed to estimate the separate contributions of different independent variables. However, the systems or model-building approach taken here can be defended in that it more closely resembles the task of service providers. Whereas the goal of much research may be to isolate relationships between independent and dependent variables, service providers seek to arrange as many factors as possible that are conducive to resident welfare. It is important that the effort to do so should be based on a logical consideration of factors open to manipulation, and should take account of empirical evidence, as I hope I have shown in my analysis. But the task of empirically validating the resulting service design may best be achieved by comparative evaluation against representative examples of existing services rather than by attempting to demonstrate that each component of the package produces some functional effect. There are costs to this strategy. One is that superstitious elements within the overall package go undetected. The second is that one can only generalize the results to service models which are similar with respect to every salient variable. In response to the first point, I would argue that a little superstition may be tolerable. With regard to the second, I would emphasize that careful replication and detailed planning is not an optional extra but a routine requirement. Certainly, it appears desirable that service planners pay explicit attention to the many issues of service orientation, structure and procedures that I have outlined and determine arrangements consciously rather than allowing them to occur by default.

The definition of the housing model as providing permanent homes was central. It produced an orientation to support the residents' involvement in as many spheres of adult domestic and community life as possible. The homes were not 'half-way houses' implying a through-put model and a narrow emphasis on training. Nor were they 'caring' environments implying a custodial or maintaining model where staff perform many activities for, but independently of, residents. It was assumed that people with the most severe and profound mental handicap would require support and training for most of their lives at a level which could only be phased out gradually.

A second assumption was that support and training are best given in the actual environment that the terminal behaviour is to occur in, rather than in a pre-placement training environment (cf. Ager, this volume). Thus individuals were not required to reach some criterion level before they could transfer to live in the community. The people coming back from institutional settings were moved without prior training and the community environment was designed to deliver the level of support and subsequent training suitable to their needs. In conception, a direct parallel can be drawn to the supported employment approach to vocational habilitation (e.g., McLoughlin, Garner and Callahan, 1987). Individuals with severe disabilities are placed in jobs with support and on-the-job training, which can then be designed specifically for the particular job and work environment (cf. Gaylord-Ross *et al.*, this volume). Support and training, which may have to be intensive and sustained, is withdrawn only as the person builds the relevant skills. The implementation of this model is resulting in people gaining access to competitive employment who have not done so in the past due to their level of mental handicap (see Rusch, 1986). Similarly, models of staffed housing are enabling people with the greatest disabilities to access ordinary patterns of living directly.

This analysis of *in situ* versus prior training can also be extended to the training of staff. Our emphasis was on training a particularly well-defined set of staff behaviours in the workplace rather than emphasizing possession of formal qualifications (a form of pre-placement prior training). Key elements of the staff job were defined procedurally and trained in the actual environment. Following a short period of induction (two weeks), training continued on the job backed up by procedural handbooks and job aids and guidance from the senior staff. In terms of the triadic model set out by Tharp and Wetzel (1969) of a consultant disseminating skills to mediators who work with target individuals, the previously untrained staff were able to assume the role of behavioural mediators given the 'prosthetic environment' (Lindsley, 1964) established by the procedural guides and supervision system. As a result, genuine consultants such as clinical psychologists could channel their input into a receptive system. For example, a clinical psychologist monitored and gave constructive input into skill-teaching programmes and contributed to the design of behaviour modification programmes. However, all programmes were implemented by the front-line staff.

Maintenance of quality is clearly an important issue for services designed to have a lifelong relationship with individuals. A two-year follow-up study was conducted to examine resident engagement and staff–resident interaction, repeating the methodology of one of the earlier studies (Saxby *et al.*, 1988). This showed a gratifying maintenance of behavioural levels despite an intervening period which had seen the withdrawal of research involvement (except to collect data) and a sizeable level of staff turnover. Sustainability of the system may be enhanced by its clarity, by the self-monitoring devices built into each procedural system and by the fact that, designed as a whole, procedures were complementary and did mesh together in a way which was feasible within the time constraints imposed by staff availability. The formulation of clear procedures and the description of how they should operate in practical handbooks also provided a mechanism for in-service training of new staff following turnover. Detailed job descriptions and written procedures provided an unchanging reference point by which to judge standards and, in particular, the training of new staff over time. Without these, job content and methods can only be passed on by word of mouth with the greater potential for decay at transition.

The concern for maintenance arises from the fact that contingencies which maintain particular desired behaviours may not be embedded in natural communities of reinforcement. Behaviour change decays with the passage of time as the contingencies instigated during the setting up of a project or experimental condition weaken and alternate behaviours recur in response to the return to pre-existing or traditional contingencies. Experience of the housing model gives some promise that the model was robust and self-sustaining. However, adequate testing of this proposition would require more than has been achieved. All of the research has been undertaken in a period of continuous and close collaboration between the researchers and the service which initially extended beyond evaluation to the setting up of the service model. Secondly, key actors, such as the senior staff in the houses and their most senior line manager within the health authority who sponsored the research development, were yet to leave and be replaced by newcomers. Maintenance of systems under new managerial conditions has to be tested, particularly when, as is generally the case, people in middle to senior managerial conditions have gained the bulk of their experience in traditional services. A real possibility exists that change may be reversed not by decay at the front line, but by positive managerial action as innovative managers are replaced by more traditional colleagues.

In conclusion, I think it is useful to return to O'Brien's (1987) framework of five accomplishments as a means of defining the objectives of long-stay services. A theme of participation in activity, similar to the emphasis on appropriate engagement described here, runs through the definitions of all five of O'Brien's accomplishments. His and our sets of objectives have similarities in breadth of scope. It is important that the technology of behaviour change and ideologically derived statements such as O'Brien's should complement each other in this way. Both are enhanced; ideology by its association with a means by which the stated values can be achieved and behavioural technology by its application to socially important outcomes.

Address for correspondence

David Felce, Mental Handicap in Wales, Applied Research Unit, 55 Park Place, Cardiff CF1 3AT, UK.

REFERENCES

Accreditation Council for Services for Mentally Retarded and other Developmentally Disabled Persons (ACMRDD) (1978) *Standards for Services for Developmentally Disabled Individuals*, Joint Commission on the Accreditation of Hospitals, Chicago.

Adams, G.L., Tallon, R.J. and Rimell, P. (1980) A comparison of lecture versus role-playing in the training of the use of positive reinforcement. *Journal of Organizational Behavior Management*, **2**, 205–212.

Anderson, S.R. (1987) The management of staff behaviour in residential treatment facilities: A review of training techniques. In J. Hogg and P. Mittler (eds), *Staff Training in Mental Handicap*, Croom Helm, London.

Baer, D.M., Wolf, M.M. and Risley, T.R. (1968) Some current dimensions of applied behavior analysis. *Journal of Applied Behavior Analysis*, **1**, 91–97.

Balla, D. (1976) Relationship of institution size to quality of care: A review of the literature. *American Journal of Mental Deficiency*, **81**, 117–124.

Beail, N. (1985) The nature of interactions between nursing staff and profoundly multiply handicapped children. *Child Care, Health and Development*, **11**, 113–129.

Bellamy, G.T., Horner, R.H. and Inman, D.P. (1979) *Vocational Habilitation of Severely Retarded Adults*, University Park Press, Baltimore.

Berkson, G. and Landesman-Dwyer, S. (1977) Behavioral research on severe and profound mental retardation (1955–1974). *American Journal of Mental Deficiency*, **81**, 428–454.

Birenbaum, A. and Re, M.A. (1979) Resettling mentally retarded adults in the community: Almost 4 years later. *American Journal of Mental Deficiency*, **83**, 323–329.

Blunden, R. (1984) Behavior analysis and the design and evaluation of services for mentally handicapped people. In S.E. Breuning, J.L. Matson and R.P. Barrett (eds), *Advances in Mental Retardation and Developmental Disabilities*, JAI Press, Greenwich.

Blunden, R. and Beyer, S. (1987) Pursuing quality: A practical approach. In L. Ward (ed.), *Getting Better All The Time? Issues and Strategies for Ensuring Quality in Community Services for People with Mental Handicap*, King's Fund Centre, London.

Bratt, A. and Johnston, R. (1988) Changes in lifestyle for young adults with profound handicaps following discharge from hospital care into a 'second generation' housing project. *Mental Handicap Research*, **1**, 49–74.

Brown, H. and Brown, V. (1987) *Bringing People Back Home: Participation in Everyday Activities*, Pavilion Publishing, Brighton.

Burg, M.M., Reid, D.H. and Lattimore, J. (1979) Use of a self-recording and supervision program to change institutional staff behavior. *Journal of Applied Behavior Analysis*, **12**, 363–375.

Butler, E.W. and Bjaanes, A.T. (1977) A typology of community care facilities and differential normalization outcomes. In P. Mittler (ed.), *Research to Practice in Mental Retardation. Vol. 1, Care and Intervention,* University Park Press, Baltimore.

Cataldo, M.F. and Risley, T.R. (1972) *The Organisation of Group Care Environments: The Infant Day Care Center.* Paper presented at American Psychological Association, Honolulu.

Conroy, J., Efthimiou, J. and Lemanowicz, J. (1982) A matched comparison of the developmental growth of institutionalized and deinstitutionalized mentally retarded clients. *American Journal of Mental Deficiency,* **86,** 581–587.

Cullen, C., Burton, M., Watts, S. and Thomas, M. (1983) A preliminary report of interactions in a mental handicap institution. *Behaviour Research and Therapy,* **21,** 579–583.

Dailey, W.F., Allen, G.J., Chinsky, J.M. and Veit, S.W. (1974) Attendant behavior and attitudes toward institutionalized retarded children. *American Journal of Mental Deficiency,* **78,** 586–591.

Dalgleish, M. and Matthews, R. (1980) Some effects of environmental design on the quality of day care for severely mentally handicapped adults. *British Journal of Mental Subnormality,* **26,** 94–102.

Dalgleish, M. and Matthews, R. (1981) Some effects of staffing levels and group size on the quality of day care for severely mentally handicapped adults. *British Journal of Mental Subnormality,* **27,** 30–35.

de Kock, U., Saxby, H., Thomas, M. and Felce, D. (1988) Community and family contact: An evaluation of small community homes for adults. *Mental Handicap Research,* **1,** 127–140.

Department of Health and Social Security (DHSS) (1978) *Report of the Committee of Inquiry into Normansfield Hospital, Cmnd 7357,* HMSO, London.

Doke, L.A. and Risley, T.R. (1972) The organisation of day-care environments: Required vs. optional activities. *Journal of Applied Behavior Analysis,* **5,** 405–420.

Felce, D. (1987) The planning and evaluation of community-based residences for individuals with severe and profound mental retardation. In S. Landesman and P. Vietze (eds), *Living Environments and Mental Retardation,* American Association on Mental Deficiency, Washington, DC.

Felce, D. and de Kock, U. (1983) *Planning Client Activity: A Handbook,* Health Care Evaluation Research Team, University of Southampton.

Felce, D., de Kock, U. and Repp, A. (1986) An eco-behavioural analysis of small community-based houses and traditional large hospitals for severely and profoundly mentally handicapped adults. *Applied Research in Mental Retardation,* **7,** 393–408.

Felce, D., Kushlick, S. and Mansell, J. (1980) Evaluation of alternative residential facilities for the severely mentally handicapped in Wessex: Client engagement. *Advances in Behavior Research and Therapy,* **3,** 13–18.

Felce, D., Kushlick, A. and Smith, J. (1980) An overview of the research on alternative residential facilities for the severely mentally handicapped in Wessex. *Advances in Behavior Research and Therapy,* **3,** 1–4.

Felce, D., Lunt, B. and Kushlick, A. (1980) Evaluation of alternative residential facilities for the severely mentally handicapped in Wessex: Family contact. *Advances in Behavior Research and Therapy,* **3,** 19–23.

Felce, D., Thomas, M., de Kock, U., Saxby, H. and Repp, A. (1985) An ecological comparison of small community-based houses and traditional institutions for severely and profoundly mentally handicapped adults: II: Physical settings and the use of opportunities. *Behavior Research and Therapy*, **23**, 337–348.

Felce, D., de Kock, U., Thomas, M. and Saxby, H. (1986) Change in adaptive behaviour of severely and profoundly mentally handicapped adults in different residential settings. *British Journal of Psychology*, **77**, 489–501.

Felce, D., Saxby, H., de Kock, U., Repp, A., Ager, A. and Blunden, R. (1987) To what behaviors do attending adults respond? A replication. *American Journal of Mental Deficiency*, **91**, 496–504.

Ferguson, D.G. and Cullari, S. (1983) Behavior modification in facilities for the mentally retarded: Problems with the development and implementation of training programs. In S.E. Breuning, J.L. Matson and R.P. Barrett (eds), *Advances in Mental Retardation and Developmental Disabilities* (Vol. 1), JAI Press, Greenwich.

Firth, H. and Short, D. (1987) A move from hospital to community: Evaluation of community contacts. *Child Care, Health and Development.*, **13**, 341–354.

Gardener, J.M. (1972) Teaching behavior modification to nonprofessionals. *Journal of Applied Behavior Analysis*, **5**, 517–521.

Gardener, W.I. (1971) *Behavior Modification in Mental Retardation*, Aldine-Atherton, Chigaco.

Gilbert, T.F. (1978) *Human Competence: Engineering Worthy Performance*. McGraw Hill, New York.

Grant, G.W.B. and Moores, B. (1977) Resident characteristics and staff behavior in two hospitals for mentally retarded adults. *American Journal of Mental Deficiency*, **82**, 259–265.

Griffiths, R. (1954) *The Abilities of Babies*, University of London Press, London.

Griffiths, R. (1971) *The Abilities of Young Children*, Association for Research in Infant and Child Development, Amersham.

Gunzburg, H.C. (1973) The physical environment of the mentally handicapped. *British Journal of Mental Subnormality*, **19**, 91–99.

Harris, J.M., Veit, S.W., Allen, G.J. and Chinsky, J.M. (1974) Aide–resident ratio and ward population density as mediators of social interaction. *American Journal of Mental Deficiency*, **79**, 320–326.

Hemming, H., Lavender, T. and Pill, R. (1981) Quality of life of mentally retarded adults transferred from large institutions to new small units. *American Journal of Mental Deficiency*, **86**, 157–169.

Janicki, M.P. (1981) Personal growth and community residence environments: A review. In H.C. Haywood and J.R. Newbrough (eds), *Living Environments for Developmentally Retarded Persons*, University Park Press, Baltimore.

Jenkins, J., Felce, D., Toogood, S., Mansell, J. and de Kock, U. (1988) *Individual Programme Planning*, BIMH Publications, Kidderminster.

King, R., Raynes, N. and Tizard, J. (1971) *Patterns of Residential Care*, Routledge and Kegan-Paul, London.

King's Fund (1980) *An Ordinary Life: Comprehensive Locally-based Residential Services for Mentally Handicapped People*, King's Fund Centre, London.

Kushlick, A. (1970) Residential care for the mentally subnormal. *Royal Society of Health Journal*, **90**, 255–261.

Landesman, S. (1987) The changing structure and function of institutions: A search for optimal group care environments. In S. Landesman and P. Vietze (eds), *Living Environments and Mental Retardation*, American Association on Mental Deficiency, Washington, DC.

Landesman-Dwyer, S., Sackett, G.P. and Kleinman, J.S. (1980) Relationship of size to resident and staff behaviour in small community residences. *American Journal of Mental Deficiency*, **85**, 6–17.

LeLaurin, K. and Risley, T.R. (1972) The organisation of day-care environments: 'Zone' vs 'Man-to-Man' Staff Assignments. *Journal of Applied Behavior Analysis*, **5**, 225–232.

Lindsley, O.R. (1964) Geriatric behavioral prosthetics. In R. Kastenbaum (ed.), *New Thoughts on Old Age*, Springer, New York.

Mansell, J., Felce, D., de Kock, U. and Jenkins, J. (1982a) Increasing purposeful activity of severely and profoundly mentally handicapped adults. *Behaviour Research and Therapy*, **20**, 593–604.

Mansell, J., Felce, D., Jenkins, J. and de Kock, U. (1982b) Increasing staff ratios in an activity with severely mentally handicapped people. *British Journal of Mental Subnormality*, **28**, 97–99.

Mansell, J., Jenkins, J., Felce, D. and de Kock, U. (1984) Measuring the activity of severely and profoundly mentally handicapped adults in ordinary housing. *Behaviour Research and Therapy*, **22**, 23–29.

Mansell, J., Felce, D., Jenkins, J., Flight, C. and Dell, D. (1986) *The Bereweeke Skill-teaching System: Handbook* (2nd edn), NFER–Nelson, Windsor.

Mansell, J., Felce, D., Jenkins, J., de Kock, U. and Toogood, S. (1987) *Developing Staffed Housing for People with Mental Handicaps*, Costello, Tunbridge Wells.

Mathieson, S. and Blunden, R. (1980) NIMROD is piloting a course towards a community life. *Health and Social Services Journal*, **90**, 122–124.

Matson, J.L. and McCartney, J.R. (1981) *Handbook of Behavior Modification with the Mentally Retarded*, Plenum Press, New York.

McLoughlin, C.S., Garner, J.B. and Callahan, M. (1987) *Getting Employed, Staying Employed: Job Development and Training for Persons with Severe Handicaps*, Brookes, Baltimore.

Mitchell, A.C. and Smeriglio, V. (1970) Growth in social competence in institutionalised retarded children. *American Journal of Mental Deficiency*, **74**, 666–673.

Mittler, P.J. (1987) Staff development: Changing needs and service contexts in Britain. In J. Hogg and P. Mittler (eds), *Staff Training in Mental Handicap*, Croom Helm, London.

Montegar, C.A., Reid, D.H., Madsen, C.H. and Ewell, M.D. (1977) Increasing institutional staff-to-resident interactions through in-service training and supervisor approval. *Behavior Therapy*, **8**, 533–540.

Moores, B. and Grant, G.W.B. (1976) On the nature and incidence of staff–patient interactions in hospitals for the mentally handicapped. *International Journal of Nursing Studies*, **13**, 69–81.

Moos, R. (1974) *The Social Climate Scales: An Overview*, Community Psychologists Press, Palo Alto.

Morris, P. (1969) *Put Away*, Routledge and Kegan-Paul, London.

National Development Group (NDG) (1980) *Improving the Quality of Services for Mentally Handicapped People: A Checklist of Standards*, Department of Health and Social Security, London.

Nihira, K., Foster, R., Shellhaus, M. and Leland, H. (1974) *AAMD Adaptive Behavior Scale*, American Association on Mental Deficiency, Washington, DC.

O'Brien, J. (1987) A guide to life-style planning. In B. Wilcox and G.T. Bellamy (eds), *The Activities Catalog: An Alternative Curriculum for Youth and Adults with Severe Disabilities*, Brookes, Baltimore.

O'Brien, M., Porterfield, J., Herbert-Jackson, E. and Risley, T.R. (1979) *The Toddler Center*, University Park Press, Baltimore.

Oswin, M. (1971) *The Empty Hours*, Penguin, Harmondsworth.

Oswin, M. (1978) *Children Living in Long-stay Hospitals*, Heinemann, London.

Page, T.J., Iwata, B.A. and Reid, D.H. (1982) Pyramidal training: A large-scale application with institutional staff. *Journal of Applied Behavior Analysis*, **15**, 335–351.

Paton, X. and Stirling, E. (1974) Frequency and type of dyadic nurse–patient verbal interactions in the mentally subnormal. *International Journal of Nursing Studies*, **11**, 135–145.

Patterson, E.T., Griffin, J.C. and Panyan, M.C. (1976) Incentive maintenance of self-help skill training programmes for non-professional personnel. *Journal of Behavior Therapy and Experimental Psychiatry*, **7**, 249–253.

Phillips, E.L., Phillips, E.A., Fixsen, D.L. and Wolf, M.M. (1974) *The Teaching Family Handbook* (rev. edn), University of Kansas, Lawrence.

Porterfield, J., Blunden, R. and Blewitt, E. (1980) Improving environments for profoundly handicapped adults: Using prompts and social attention to maintain high group engagement. *Behavior Modification*, **4**, 225–241.

Pratt, M.W., Bumstead, D.C. and Raynes, N.V. (1976) Attendant staff speech to the institutionalized retarded: Language as a measure of the quality of care. *Child Psychology and Psychiatry*, **17** , 133–143.

Prior, M., Minnes, P., Coyne, T., Golding, B., Hendy, J. and McGillivary, J. (1979) Verbal interactions between staff and residents in an institution for the young mentally retarded. *Mental Retardation*, **17**, 65–69.

Rawlings, S. (1985) Behaviour and skills of severely retarded adults in hospitals and small residential homes. *British Journal of Psychiatry*, **146**, 358–366.

Raynes, N. (1980) The less you've got the less you get: Functional grouping, a cause for concern. *Mental Retardation*, **18**, 217–220.

Raynes, N. (1986) Approaches to the measurement of care. In J. Beswick, T. Zadik and D. Felce (eds), *Evaluating Quality of Care*, BIMH Conference Series, Kidderminster.

Repp, A.C. (1983) *Teaching the Mentally Retarded*, Prentice-Hall, Englewood Cliffs, New Jersey.

Repp, A.C., Barton, L.E. and Brulle, A.R. (1981) Correspondence between effectiveness and staff use of instructions for severely retarded persons. *Applied Research in Mental Retardation*, **2**, 237–245.

Repp, A.C., Barton, L.E. and Brulle, A.R. (1982) Naturalistic studies of mentally retarded persons V: The effects of staff instructions on student responding. *Applied Research in Mental Retardation*, **3**, 55–65.

Repp, A.C., Felce, D. and de Kock, U. (1987) Observational studies of staff working with mentally retarded persons: A review. *Research in Developmental Disabilities*, **8**, 331–350.

Reynell, J.K. (1977) *Reynell Developmental Language Scales*, NFER–Nelson, Windsor.

Rozynko, V., Swift, K., Swift, J. and Boggs, L.J. (1973) Controlled environments for social change. In H. Wheeler (ed.) *Beyond the Punitive Society: Operant Conditioning: Social and Political Aspects*, Wildwood House, London.

Rusch, F.R. (1986) *Competitive Employment Issues and Strategies*, Brookes, Baltimore.

Saxby, H., Thomas, M., Felce, D. and de Kock, U. (1986) The use of shops, cafes and public houses by severely and profoundly mentally handicapped adults. *British Journal of Mental Subnormality*, **32**, 69–81.

Saxby, H., Felce, D., Harman, M. and Repp, A. (1988) The maintenance of client activity and staff–client interaction in small community houses for severely and profoundly mentally handicapped adults: A two-year follow-up. *Behavioural Psychotherapy*, **16**, 189–206.

Schloss, P.J. (1982) Verbal interaction of depressed and nondepressed institutionalised mentally retarded adults. *Applied Research in Mental Retardation*, **3**, 1–12.

Schwartz, A. and Goldiamond, I. (1975) *Social Casework: A Behavioral Approach*, Colombia University Press, New York.

Skinner, B.F. (1957) *Verbal Behavior*, Appleton–Century–Crofts, New York.

Smith, J., Glossop, C. and Kushlick, A. (1980) Evaluation of alternative residential facilities for the severely mentally handicapped in Wessex: Client progress. *Advances in Behavior Research and Therapy*, **3**, 5–11.

Tharp, R.G. and Wetzel, R.J. (1969) *Behavior Modification in the Natural Environment*, Academic Press, New York.

Thomas, M., Felce, D., de Kock, U., Saxby, H. and Repp, A. (1986) The activity of staff and of severely and profoundly mentally handicapped adults in residential settings of different sizes. *British Journal of Mental Subnormality*, **32**, 82–92.

Toogood, S., Jenkins, J., Felce, D. and de Kock, U. (1983) *Opportunity Plans*, Health Care Evaluation Research Team, University of Southampton.

Warren, S.A. and Mondy, L.W. (1971) To what behaviors do attending adults respond? *American Journal of Mental Deficiency*, **75**, 449–455.

Watson, L.S. and Uzzell, R. (1980) A program for teaching behavior modification skills to institutional staff. *Applied Research in Mental Retardation*, **1**, 41–53.

Wolfensberger, W. (1972) *Normalization: The Principle of Normalization in Human Services*, National Institute of Mental Retardation, Toronto.

Wolfensberger, W. (1983) Social role valorization: A proposed new term for the principle of normalization. *Mental Retardation*, **21**, 234–239.

Wolfensberger, W. and Glenn, L. (1975) *Program Analysis of Service Systems: Handbook and Manual* (3rd edn), National Institute on Mental Retardation, Toronto.

Woods, P.A. and Cullen, C. (1983) Determinants of staff behaviour in long-term care. *Behavioural Psychotherapy*, **11**, 4–17.

Wright, E.C. Abbas, K.A. and Meredith, C. (1974) A study of the interactions between nursing staff and profoundly retarded children. *British Journal of Mental Subnormality*, **20**, 38.

Yule, W. and Carr, J. (1987) *Behaviour Modification for People with Mental Handicap*, Croom-Helm, London.

Chapter 14

Social and Vocational Factors in the Employment of Persons with Developmental Disabilities

Robert Gaylord-Ross, Chuck Salzberg,
Rita Curl and Keith Storey

INTRODUCTION

There have been many notable changes of late in vocational education for disabled people. Until recently, most developmentally disabled individuals were not considered capable of substantive employment in real work settings. Rather, they were trained for likely employment in sheltered workshops. The training, in fact, took place in special education classrooms, often located in all-handicapped schools. Near-revolutionary changes in service delivery for this population have occurred in the last decade. The 'least restrictive environment' movement in the US (and in some European countries like Italy) has placed an increasing number of disabled students in regular public school (Gaylord-Ross, 1987). In addition, a 'functional curriculum' approach has emerged which prepares the individual for survival in real adult environments, rather than focusing on academic and developmental tasks. Functional curriculum has also led to attention to the setting where instruction takes place under the assumptions that disabled students have limited transfer of learning skills, and that maximal generalization will occur when there is a relative correspondence between the training and criterion environments. In practice, the reasoning was that if people were to work on an assembly line in a factory, then they should be trained in a similar assembly line or factory. School-based, simulated environments could not approximate the stimuli of real work settings (Horner, McDonnell and Bellamy, 1986). Thus, a 'community-based' training approach emerged

The Challenge of Severe Mental Handicap. Edited by Bob Remington
© 1991 John Wiley & Sons Ltd

whereby students were trained in real work environments—factories, restaurants, and shopping malls—in order to guarantee that they could perform functional skills in these criterion settings.

Community-based school integration also expressed a concern about what would happen to disabled adults upon leaving school. The prospects were quite dismal. Adults worked in sheltered workshops, at best; and at worst remained on waiting lists for enrollment in segregated day programs (i.e., stayed at home). Attention began to focus on the transition of school-leavers from integrated school and community training environments to similar adult nonsheltered work and community living arrangements. While we are still in the infancy of this transition initiative, a substantial number of projects have demonstrated that disabled adults, even those with the most severe disabilities, can be successfully employed in nonsheltered work settings. If further empirically documented successes create a database which could be unambiguously supported by policy makers and funding agencies (Gaylord-Ross, 1990), integrated employment services for adults are likely to catch up with these school-based advances.

Integrated employment may therefore be viewed within the broader context of community integration. The chapters by Ager and Felce in this volume nicely demonstrate how a behavioral science and technology is emerging in the residential sphere. Parallel developments have transpired in the school and work domains. The present chapter sequentially asks:

- How best can developmentally disabled persons be trained to work in community employment settings?
- When developmentally disabled persons are working successfully in such settings, do they fully integrate with nondisabled co-workers?
- When integration does not occur naturally, how can it best be brought about?

Research issues

In spite of (or perhaps because of) these program and policy advances and challenges, there exist a number of research issues related to integrated vocational education. These issues may be construed from an 'ecosocial' framework (Bullis and Gaylord-Ross, 1990). That is, some issues focus primarily on the individual, in terms of learning and social interaction. Others weigh more heavily on the surrounding environment of the workplace. In almost all cases, though, there is some interaction between the individual and the environment. Thus, an ecosocial framework may elegantly account for the multiple factors affecting behavior in the workplace. Chadsey-Rusch and Rusch (1988) reviewed the assessment literature of person and environment variables in employment settings. They then described how interventions may be individually designed based on assessment findings. Fortunately, intervention technology for job training and social integration is now gradually emerging in the vccational arena.

In the remainder of the chapter three topics are addressed. First, we examine the questicn of which is the best way to train developmentally disabled persons on the job. Next, we delineate the methods of measuring social behavior in the workplace. Third, we illustrate and evaluate a number of ways to enhance socialization at work. Clearly, research on vocational and social behavior in the workplace is a relatively unaddressed topic. Earlier work relied mostly on surveys and questionnaires to assess the nature of social life in the workplace. While valuable, we are biased toward direct behavioral observation as being the most useful way to assess the social environment and to evaluate effective interventions in the workplace (cf. Felce, this volume).

JOB SKILLS TRAINING

Supported employment: Current state of affairs

Employment has long been the focus of habilitation services (Salzberg, Lignugaris-Kraft and McCuller, 1988). However, for the first time, individuals with severe disabilities are being placed in jobs and professionals are asking what supports are needed for long-term employment success. The supported employment movement is gaining momentum as more individuals with disabilities obtain employment, and the benefits become increasingly evident. While there are several supported employment models (Kregel, Wehman and Banks, 1989; Mank, Rhodes and Bellamy, 1986), individualized employment is emerging as the preferred model when it is possible. In individualized employment, workers with disabilities work as employees of community businesses where, ideally, they interact primarily with nondisabled workers and are accountable for their assigned responsibilities. Compared to other supported employment models, workers in individualized employment enjoy better wages, active integration, and fringe benefits (Kregel, Wehman and Banks, 1989). In this approach, specialists, often referred to as job coaches, orchestrate the job placement and training process.

Job coach systems have been described elsewhere (Wehman and Kregel,

1989). Thus, their essential functions will only be summarized here. A coach first finds a job that matches an individual with disabilities. Then, the coach learns the job, analyzing the tasks and performance criteria needed for success. Next, the worker receives on-site training from the coach, who uses a variety of methods to teach the necessary skills. The job coach may also help the worker with other problems that affect employability (e.g., transportation, dress) and encourage positive social interaction between the disabled worker and co-workers, especially during breaks and lunch periods. After the worker learns the job, the coach gradually withdraws from the work site except for occasional visits and/or telephone follow-up calls.

Job coaches versus co-worker/trainers

Supported employment models that depend on a job coach have enabled a large number of individuals with disabilities to experience community-based employment (Kregel, Wehman and Banks, 1989). However, job coaches have limitations, some of which may be ameliorated by using co-workers as trainers and advocates (Nisbet and Hagner, 1988; Rusch and Minch, 1988; Shafer, 1986). First, there is a question of efficiency. Every time a worker is placed in a new job, the coach must learn the job. In contrast, co-workers already know the job. Second, as newcomers, job coaches may be in a weaker position than co-workers to give disabled workers social entrées. Further, since disabled workers interact primarily with their coaches during work time, opportunity for interaction with nondisabled co-workers may be limited to breaks and lunch. Third, as outsiders, the job coaches' presence may cause co-workers to alter their normal work routines and interaction patterns. If that occurs, the patterns learned by a disabled co-worker during training may differ from the patterns that emerge after the coach leaves. This problem is less likely with co-worker/trainers (CTs). Next, our research (McConaughy, Curl and Salzberg, 1987) indicates that many employers would rather train new workers themselves. A CT is clearly preferable for their businesses. Fifth, disabled workers may become dependent on the job coach and fading the presence of the job coach is difficult and time consuming (Nisbet and Hagner, 1988; French and Bell, 1984). Problems of dependency are more likely with job coaches than with CTs because job coaches devote all their attention to the disabled worker. In contrast, CTs have job responsibilities apart from training, and thus are more likely to be avalable when needed and occupied with their usual work tasks at other times.

Sixth, and finally, work settings are dynamic; co-workers turn over, managers leave, new equipment and procedures are introduced as businesses shift activities to meet changing demands of the market place. With these shifts, workers' responsibilities change, as do organizational structures and interaction patterns. Workers with severe disabilities often need help adapting to these changes, but when this support is needed job coaches may long since have moved on to other sites. Co-workers can provide on-site assistance over long periods of time.

It appears that CTs can provide critical supports to workers with disabilities. However, there are challenging issues in developing a CT transition model. First, most co-workers do not automatically become trainers. They must be assigned those responsibilities, taught to perform those functions, and receive ongoing supervision and assistance to fulfill mentor, coach, and advocate roles. Further, as Nisbet and Hagner (1988) point out, monetary or other incentives may be needed to encourage co-workers to assume major responsibilities over a long period of time.

A study of co-worker-implemented training procedures for workers with developmental disabilities

While the practical advantages of using a CT seem clear, research has not delineated specific training procedures that CTs might use. A recent study by Likens et al. (1989) focused on this issue. The trainees were three 24- to 32-year-old women with full-scale IQs of 54–67 who had been in a sheltered workshop from 2–25 years. The CTs were nondisabled individuals who had worked part-time in restaurants on campus, but who had no prior experience with individuals with mental handicap. These CTs, like other workers in the restaurant, were university students, had specific tasks to complete apart from training, worked part-time, received instructions and some supervision from the restaurant manager, and received compensation slightly above the prevailing minimum wage. However, they were employed by the research project, not by the restaurant.

The study took place in a university-operated restaurant. The task to be learned by trainees was preparation of a 19-step chef salad. Daily data were collected on the accuracy of trainees' performance and the time required to prepare the salad. These measures were taken during a daily probe in which trainees received no help or feedback from their CTs. During training sessions, a CT and trainee worked side by side; the CT prepared simple lettuce salads while the trainee prepared chef salads. On the first day of baseline, CTs demonstrated and described each step in making the chef salad. After the demonstration, they left the completed salad as a model and worked on their own task. When the trainee completed her salad, the CT praised the steps performed correctly and suggested how to improve incorrect steps. For each succeeding baseline session, CTs gave trainees a model salad and then worked on their task. Following completion of the chef salad, CTs provided feedback on the trainee's performance.

In the first coincidental training condition, CTs praised correctly performed steps and trained incorrectly performed steps. Training tactics included verbal instructions, models, practicing the step, and providing corrective feedback and praise as appropriate. Trainees learned to make the chef salad, but progress was slow. Consequently, a second intervention was begun in which trainees were taught to do a quality-control check for each step of the salad. This quality-control checking appeared to improve the rate of learning. However, a second study was needed for verification.

The second study used an alternating treatments design to compare the training procedure with and without the quality-control checking component. The results are presented in Figure 14.1.

During baseline, performance of all trainees stabilized at a low level. In the second condition, the basic training procedure was used for half of the salad steps, and the same procedure plus the quality-control checking component was used for the other half. In every case, trainees learned faster and reached a higher plateau with the quality-control checking component. The use of the multiple baseline across trainees design showed that improvements were a function of the training procedures. In the third condition, all steps were trained with the quality-control checking component and performance accuracy rapidly increased to 90–100%.

This study provided a foundation for a CT model. First, simple coincidental teaching tactics such as verbal instructions, modeling, practice and feedback enabled workers with mild and moderate disabilities to learn a complex task, preparing a 19-step chef salad. Second, the quality-control checking made training more effective and efficient which, given employers' preference for short training periods, is of practical significance. Third, CTs readily learned these procedures and were able to carry them out with only temporary, minor reductions in their own work output.

Although these studies provided a base for a CT model, some serious limitations remained. One was that in these studies the CTs were college students. In contrast, many restaurant workers have not even completed high school. Typical workers might not learn the training procedures as readily or as well as college-level CTs in these studies. Furthermore, CTs had been trained by a doctoral level professional using an individualized tutorial process. However, the successful operation of a CT model would

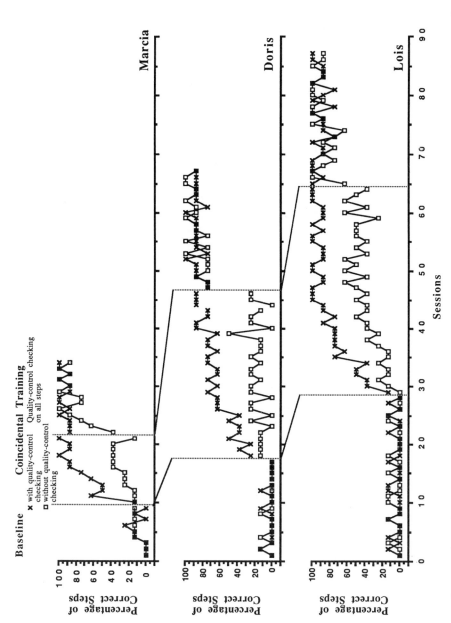

Figure 14.1 The use of an alternating treatments design to examine the effects of a job training procedure with and without a quality-control checking component.

require standardized training for CTs which could be carried out by typical employment specialists. Finally, the study was limited to three trainees with mental handicap, three CTs for one task, and one type of job in a university restaurant. Systematic replication was needed to explore the applicability of the findings to other trainees and jobs.

Continuing research

Continuing research was directed toward two goals. First, we wanted to establish a standard set of procedures which CTs could use to train job tasks to workers with disabilities. Second, our aim was to identify how to train CTs and discover what continuing guidance they would need.

A standard co-worker/trainer curriculum

Continuing research led to the development of a set of training procedures which seemed to have broad applicability across jobs and trainees. Figure 14.2 shows the basic teaching sequence used by trainers to teach new job tasks plus five supplementary procedures to improve performance, consistency, and rate of work.

   The basic training sequence was derived in part from the Likens *et al.* (1989) study described earlier. The key to its successful application is that CTs must integrate the tactics as they use them. That is, CTs should give verbal instruction along with models, then observe and evaluate trainee performance, and coach as appropriate. Prior to training, CTs commonly present long strings of instructions and explanations without models or practice. They also frequently model a job task (e.g., loading and running a dishwasher) but then fail to watch the trainee work and provide coaching. Further, it became clear that, even when trainees initially learned a job task, there were often deficits remaining, including slow rates of work, inconsistent performance, inaccuracies on particular components of tasks, and difficulty remembering task sequences. The supplementary procedures described in Figure 14.2 were developed to address these deficits. The 1-minute reminder was always applied first. Then other procedures were added as needed. The last four supplementary procedures were always applied in combination with the 1-minute reminder, but never simultaneously with each other.

The basic training sequence: Instruct, model, observe, and coach

Give an instruction with a model, observe the trainee perform the task and coach as needed. To coach, praise correct responses and give feedback and practice for incorrect responses.

Supplementary procedures

1. *One-minute reminder.* Used to improve performance. Reminders are given at the beginning of the work day. CT *succinctly* tells worker the tasks he did well the previous day and the ones that he needs to improve. For example, 'John, yesterday you did a great job on the beds, wastebaskets, and vacuuming. But today you need to do better getting spots off the mirrors and shining the bathtub and sink faucets.'

2. *Timer.* Used to help trainees improve their rate of work. CT sets a timer to the criteria for the task. Worker tries to 'beat the clock'.

3. *Picture checklist.* Used if trainee cannot remember a sequence of required tasks or steps. CT prepares a picture sequence and teaches trainee to check off each task as it is completed.

4. *Quality-control check.* Used if trainee continues to make minor errors performing tasks or needs to sharpen accuracy. CT presents tasks with some components incorrect (e.g., bed corners not correctly tucked in). Trainee has to discriminate errors and correct them.

5. *Bonus-warning.* Used when trainee knows how to do tasks but does them inconsistently. CT first explains that worker will earn an extra 50 cents if his performance meets a certain specified level, but that he will lose 50 cents if it falls below another level. Further, if after a warning trainee's performance continues below a specified level, he will not be allowed to work for one day.

Figure 14.2 A standard set of procedures with which co-workers/trainers can teach job tasks to workers with disabilities.

Applying the co-worker/trainer model

One application of the CT model is illustrated below with two workers with moderate and severe mental handicap (IQs from 23 to 46) and limited speech who were placed in two restaurants as food preparers. The CTs were a man and a woman, 19 and 26 years old, who had been at their jobs for at least 18 months. Both were high school graduates; one had completed one year of college.

The workers' tasks included preparing salads and washing dishes. Figure 14.3 shows the training behavior of both CTs and the work performance of their trainees. The top two graphs display the percentage of steps of the basic teaching sequence that CTs performed correctly. Correct performance required that CTs observe and evaluate their trainee's performance, and coach using instruction, modeling, practice, and feedback. During baseline, before CTs received training, they never performed the teaching sequence correctly. They did use various tactics, including instructions, models, and feedback, but these tactics were not integrated in the prescribed sequence. To standardize training for CTs, a written and video curriculum was developed in which the training procedures summarized in Figure 14.2 were presented and illustrated (Curl *et al.*, 1987). In the first intervention, CTs studied the manual and watched the videotape. In each lesson, they had to respond to questions about the critical aspects of each training procedure. The pertinent material was reviewed as needed and CTs were retested before proceeding to the next lesson. Figure 14.3 shows that studying the manual and the videotape did not improve the CTs' use of the prescribed teaching sequence. On the first day of the final condition, CTs were exposed to a brief (15-minute) training session prior to their scheduled work day in which training procedures were role played and CTs practiced giving concise instructions using scripts provided in the manual. Each CT also received one retraining session later in the condition. These pre-work rehearsals resulted in dramatic improvement in CTs' ability to apply the teaching sequence. The bottom two graphs in Figure 14.3 display the percentage of job task steps performed correctly by the trainees. During the baseline, their performance ranged between approximately 58% and 80%, and when the CTs studied the manual and videotape their skills did not improve. However, when the CTs use of the training sequence improved in the third condition, their trainees' performance of job tasks also improved.

This study affirmed the effectiveness of the basic training sequence with severely disabled workers who were not otherwise learning to adequately perform required job tasks. Further, it verified that, without training, co-workers do not effectively teach job tasks to workers with severe disabilities. It was also evident that, while the written manual and videotape were important training tools, they were not sufficient. However, with brief (15-minute) pre-work rehearsals, CTs readily learned to apply the basic training sequence.

While the basic training sequence enabled workers with severe disabilities to learn job tasks, deficits in rate consistency remained. Two supplementary procedures designed for these problems are illustrated below. Figure 14.4 shows how Jan, a laundry worker with a mild mental handicap, learned to increase her accuracy and speed sorting clothes and linens into ten categories based on type of garment, color, material, and type of soil. Jan's CT was an experienced worker who had never previously trained other workers before. During baseline, the CT used instructions, models and coaching tactics, but her use of these tactics was uncoordinated and unsystematic. Jan's performance during baseline

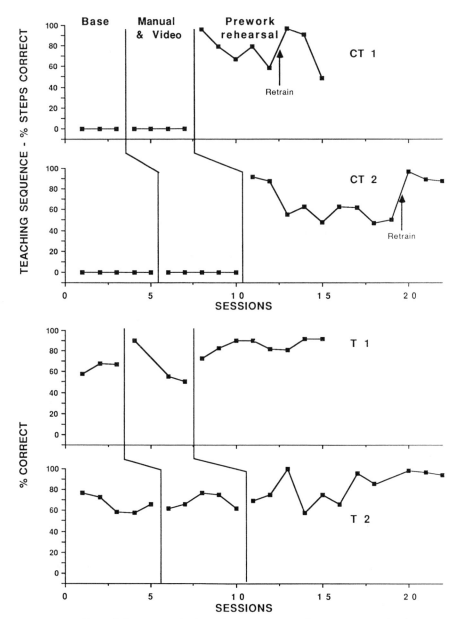

Figure 14.3 Use of the prescribed teaching sequence by two co-worker/trainers as they proceed through three experimental conditions (top two graphs) and the performance accuracy of their trainees (lower two graphs).

averaged about 70% correct but varied from day to day. Further, Jan
worked very slowly. Consequently, the employment specialist asked the
co-worker to teach Jan to use a timer, which improved her speed and
accuracy dramatically. However, Jan's performance was still inconsistent
from day to day. Therefore, the CT was advised to use a bonus/warning
procedure in which Jan earned or lost an extra 50 cents a day, depending
upon her accuracy and speed over several days. This procedure further
improved accuracy and speed and both remained consistent thereafter,
even after the bonus/warning process was ended.

Figure 14.5 presents data for Pam (another trainee with mild mental

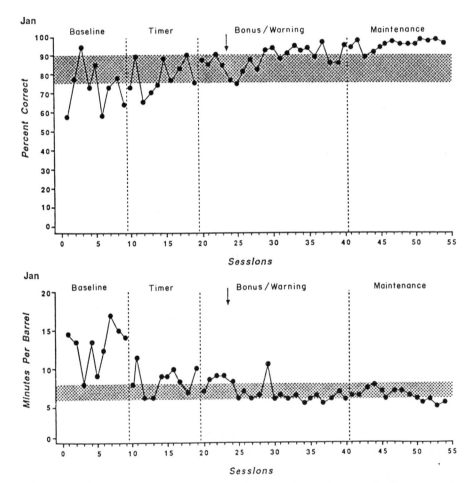

Figure 14.4 Jan's performance accuracy (top graph) and speed (bottom graph)
sorting garments in a nursing home laundry across four training conditions.

handicap) who had not previously been successful in community employment. This case is particularly notable because the CT was the worker (Jan) in the previous example. Although Jan had only recently learned her job, her performance was quite adequate. Thus, she was asked to be a CT for a new employee. It is notable that Jan's use of the basic teaching sequence during baseline was excellent. An observer noted that her instructions sounded like the script her CT had followed when she was trained. The accuracy of Pam's work improved to an exemplary level during baseline and was maintained during the following non-training phase. However, Pam's speed was slow compared to other non-handicapped workers. Therefore, the employment specialist suggested that Jan use 1-minute reminders to help focus on speed and also teach Pam to use a timer. The reminder and timer improved Pam's speed to a very acceptable level, where it was maintained.

As of this writing, many individuals with disabilities ranging from severe mental handicaps to mild learning disabilities and from ages 16 to 50 have been placed in community jobs using the CT model. It is premature to present an analysis of employment outcomes at this time. However, most workers are successfully employed and earning wages that average above the US minimum wage. Many have advanced from entry levels to positions with greater responsibility and compensation.

THE MEASUREMENT OF SOCIAL BEHAVIOR IN WORK SETTINGS

Social integration

If supported employment is to have a positive effect on the lives of persons with severe disabilities, it is critical that the services delivered are of high quality and that they produce measurable outcomes that are important and socially valid (Sandow et al., in press; Schalock et al., 1989). Workers with disabilities should receive the outcomes of wages, support, and integration when in supported employment (Bellamy et al., 1988; Wehman and Moon, 1987). Perhaps the most important and the most elusive of those outcomes is social integration.

Integration in supported employment settings has been difficult and enigmatic to define and measure. Several definitions of integration have been suggested. Mank and Buckley (1989) see integration 'in its simplest and most elegant form as a degree of community presence and participation for persons with disabilities that is no different from that enjoyed by persons without a disability label' (p. 320). In relation to employment, Mank and Buckley (1989) describe integration as 'adherence

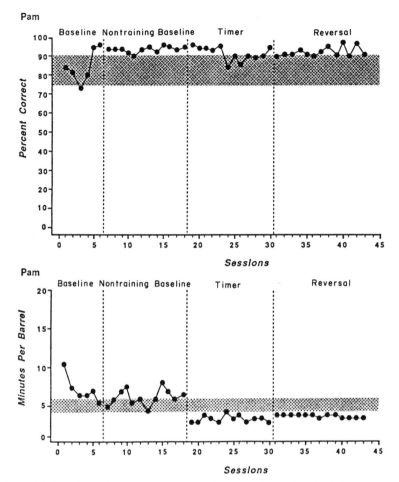

Figure 14.5 Pam's performance accuracy (top graph) and speed (bottom graph) sorting garments in a nursing home across four training conditions.

to regular and ordinary patterns of minute-to-minute and day-to-day working life' (p. 320). Four different components of integration have been considered. These are physical integration, social integration, relationships, and social networks (Mank and Buckley, 1989).

Review of research assessing integration in supported employment

Social integration in supported employment settings has been assessed using direct observation procedures (Storey and Horner, in press; Storey and Knutson, 1989; Storey *et al.*, 1989), clique analysis (Yan *et al.*, 1989), narrative recording (Chadsey-Rusch, 1990; Chadsey-Rusch and Gonzalez, 1988; Chadsey-Rusch *et al.*, 1989), and questionnaires/surveys (McDonnell *et al.*, 1989; Rusch, Hughes and Johnson, 1990; Rusch *et al.*, in press; Schalock, McGaughey and Kiernan, 1989; Shafer *et al.*, 1989).

If supported employment is to be successful it will be necessary to enhance interactions and integration. For instance, Rusch *et al.* (in press) reported that only 34.5% of workers with severe/profound mental handicap in Illinois had involvement with co-workers and that only 1% involved befriending and 7% advocating. In a related study, Rusch, Hughes and Johnson (1990) found that supported employees in individual job placements and enclaves (more than two workers with disabilities) had more co-worker involvement than employees in mobile work crews. However, the employees with severe or profound disabilities experienced lower levels of associating with, and befriending by, co-workers than those with borderline, mild, or moderate disabilities. These data must be viewed with caution, however, because they are reported by job coaches and only indicated the occurrence or non-occurrence of co-worker involvement. There was no reliability assessment, no concurrent use of direct observation or other assessment procedures, and no indication of how often the co-worker involvement occurred.

Chadsey-Rusch (1990) used narrative recording procedures to compare the social interaction patterns of ten high school students with severe disabilities in school and community-based vocational training experiences to those of eight nondisabled workers described by Chadsey-Rusch and Gonzalez (1988). The results indicated that the students were involved in more interactions, interacted almost exclusively with teachers (99% of interactions), and hardly at all with peers with or without disabilities (1% of interactions). Chadsey-Rusch *et al.* (1989) compared the social interaction patterns of workers with mild disabilities and those without disabilities in seven competitive employment sites using the narrative recording procedures from Chadsey-Rusch and Gonzalez (1988). A social network questionnaire, a debriefing questionnaire, and a work performance evaluation form were also used. The results of this study indicate that there was no difference between the two groups concerning the rate of social interactions at work, but that there were differences in their quality, particularly with respect to non-work or non-task related interactions. The workers without disabilities were also more likely to do things outside of work with the co-workers than the workers with disabilities. The two groups did not differ in the evaluation of their work performance.

McDonnell *et al.* (1989) used the six point behaviorally anchored rating scale developed by the Berkeley Planning Associates (1986) to assess integration. They found the levels of integration in supported employment sites in the state of Utah were positively correlated with procedural components of individualized program planning, design of training programs, development of a formal marketing plan, formal services contracts, and specific job descriptions.

Storey and Knutson (1989) used direct observation procedures to compare the social interaction patterns of six workers with, and six workers without, mental handicap. The workers were matched according to their having similar job responsibilities. They found that, generally, the workers without disabilities tended to interact more with co-workers and customers while the workers with disabilities tended to interact more with their school or agency supervisor. They also received more instruction than did the workers without disabilities. Another difference observed in this study was that the workers without disabilities tended to spend more time in work and personal conversation than did the workers with disabilities.

Storey *et al.* (in press) used the observation system developed by Storey and Knutson (1989) to study the social interaction patterns of eight workers with and seven without severe disabilities in an enclave-supported employment setting. The results of this study are consistent with those of Storey and Knutson (1989). The employees with disabilities tended to interact more with the enclave supervisors and their interactions involved receiving instruction and compliments more often than those of the employees without disabilities. The latter group tended to engage more in work and personal conversation with co-workers and they generally had interactions with a greater number of different people than the employees with disabilities. However, the interaction patterns varied widely for each of the individual employees, with considerable overlap between the interaction patterns of the two groups.

Yan *et al.* (1990) analyzed the social structure of an employment setting using a clique analysis of the social interaction data from Storey *et al.* (in press). It was found that most employees without disabilities cliqued with each other while the employees with disabilities cliqued among themselves. Storey and Horner (in press) used the observation system developed by Storey and Knutson (1989) to compare social interaction patterns across three different supported employment options (individual sites, enclaves, and work crews). They found that workers with severe disabilities in individual and enclave sites interacted more with persons without disabilities than workers in work crews. However, there was a wide variation in the amount of social interactions across the different individual and enclave sites. Some workers in both sites had frequent interactions with persons without disabilities and other workers rarely did.

Schalock *et al.* (1989) used survey questionnaires and found that 98% of the competitive employment sites and 90% of the supported employment sites indicated that breaks and lunch afforded natural opportunities to interact with nondisabled persons. A survey of nondisabled co-workers' attitudes towards employees with disabilities was conducted by Shafer *et al.* (1989). They found that over 72% of the workers indicated that they had contact at least once a day with a co-worker with disabilities but that the context of these interactions was primarily work related. Only a minority of the workers indicated that they interacted with the co-workers during breaks or after work.

In summary, an array of measurement procedures are evolving to assess social behavior in work settings. Such a multi-method assessment technology is likely to enhance our ability to design and evaluate effective interventions. While we are biased in favor of a behavioral approach toward measurement, attitudinal and related social validation measures are likely to contribute substantively to the successful evaluation of this assessment intervention process.

ENHANCING SOCIALIZATION AT WORK

So far, supported employment programs have been primarily concerned with elevating the job task performance of disabled workers so they can meet the employer's criteria and are retained. Good programs have successfully attempted to embed the disabled worker into the social network of the workplace. At present our data on these efforts is largely anecdotal and unsystematic, and this remains an area which awaits further systematic research.

Social skills training

The main approach to enhancing social behaviors in the workplace has used some variant of social skills training. For example, Breen *et al.* (1985) applied a sufficient exemplar strategy (Stokes and Baer, 1977) to induce social interactions between four autistic youths and their nondisabled co-workers. Training consisted of role-plays or behavioral rehearsals of a script of conversational interactions that were practiced between autistic and nondisabled students. The autistic youth successfully generalized these scripted routines from the role-plays to actual interactions with co-workers. The critical number of exemplars (role-play confederates) needed to induce generalization varied across trainees: rehearsals with between one and four confederates were necessary before generalization occurred. Most importantly, the trainees' approaches were well received, and led to appropriate interactions with their co-workers.

Self-monitoring is another treatment approach that may foster social interactions in work settings. For example, Storey and Gaylord-Ross (1987) increased positive, and decreased negative, verbalizations during a breaktime pool game at work. They used a combined treatment package of role-play, model, positive reinforcement, and self-monitoring. Ultimately, self-monitoring alone maintained these behaviors. Yet, self-monitoring in the criterion setting does not represent completely successful generalization, for when self-monitoring was discontinued the treatment gains regressed. Still, self-monitoring may be viewed as a useful vocational prosthetic to induce job task acquisition (cf. Sowers, Jenkins and Powers, 1988).

Self-mediation is another technique to promote generalization (Stokes and Baer, 1977). While self-mediation has been avidly embraced in the cognitive behavior modification of some clinical problems (e.g., anxiety, depression), it has been largely overlooked in work with developmentally disabled persons. Recently, Park and Gaylord-Ross (1989) have drawn on the 'cognitive process' work of McFall (1982) to promote social interactions in vocational settings. They developed a treatment package in which youths with mental handicap learned to decode a social situation, generate alternative social behaviors appropriate to it, and select the best behavioral solution. They then rehearsed the behaviors with the instructor, while self-monitoring their performance.

In a two-part experiment, three participants successfully generalized these skills to real social interactions with co-workers and customers. Social validity data confirmed the value of training; co-workers viewed the participants to be more interactive on a number of conversational measures. In the second experiment, the effectiveness of cognitive process training was compared to purely behavioral rehearsal (role-play) training. In both cases the process approach produced significant generalization, while the rehearsal procedure had negligible effects. Interpretation of relative treatment efficacy must be guarded for two reasons. First, the trainees experienced role-play before process training, which in itself included a rehearsal component. Thus, the effects may have been due to treatment order. Second, the role-play included only one training exemplar person, which may not be a sufficient number to induce generalization with this treatment.

Although more research is clearly needed, cognitive process approaches to social skill training offer real promise for some individuals with mental handicap. Future work may demonstrate their further potential in employment settings.

Relationship interventions

Rather than focusing on discrete behaviors in social interactions, it may be possible to directly engender relationships between disabled and nondisabled co-workers. This would parallel 'special friend' efforts in schools where friendships have been successfully formed (Voeltz, 1982). In the workplace, a disabled worker could be intentionally 'bonded' with one or more co-workers. This nondisabled co-worker/benefactor might provide instruction, leisure exchanges, advocacy, and emotional support (cf. Shafer, 1986). Most importantly, the benefactor could mediate the integration of the disabled worker intc the social network at the workplace.

There are essentially no studies reporting such relationship interventions, although it should be remembered that co-worker/advocate training designed to teach job tasks also undoubtedly led to the development of social relationships. There is a study in progress that is evaluating the efficacy of relationship interventions. Park et al. (1990b) have arranged relationship and social skills interventions in work settings for mildly disabled youths. Participants were referred to the project because of their relative isolation at the workplace. After baseline data were collected, co-worker advocate training began. Here, a designated co-worker met for six weeks with a staff person in order to generate integration-fostering activities which could be carried out with the disabled employee. A wide range of activities, e.g. meeting co-workers at breaks, going bowling off-hours, were carried out with the youths. Yet, except for one case, there were few changes in the targeted behavioral measures of social interaction at the workplace. A process-based social skills training procedure was subsequently implemented, and this produced modest increases in social interaction. Behavior change was interpreted from an ecosocial perspective. That is, where the individuals had many opportunities to interact with willing companions, the social skills training program produced substantial results.

Finally, a systematic replication of the relationship programs was conducted with a more severely disabled, deaf–blind individual (Gaylord-Ross et al., in press). Again, few behavior changes resulted from the co-worker advocate procedure, but substantive gains followed social skills training. Thus, it appears that while relationship interventions lead to integration activities which are intuitively appealing, their effects have not so far been detected in outcome measures. In contrast, more familiar and validated social skills training procedures have continued to produce success in work settings.

Interestingly, a literature is emerging which examines the quality of work life and social support for developmentally disabled persons. Horner and his colleagues (Kennedy, Horner and Newton, 1989, 1990) have reported that persons with severe disabilities receive much more social support than they give. This is understandable since they must be supervised by caretakers at school, work, or home. However, Park *et al.* (1990a) extended these findings to mildly disabled persons. They found that this group also gave less support than they received; in a ratio of 4 : 5, which contrasted to the 1 : 2 ratio reported by the Horner group for severely disabled persons. Nondisabled persons gave about as much social support as they received. Park *et al.* speculated that perhaps there is a continuum of giving support from severely, to mildly, to nondisabled persons. In this same study, Park *et al.* found that young adults with mild learning disabilities had a relatively good quality of work life, particularly with respect to the satisfactoriness of their job tasks. At the same time, they did not become more independent in making decisions in their life as they moved from school-age to adulthood.

AN ECOSOCIAL VIEW

This chapter began by pointing out that the considerations of generalization have created a rationale for community-based vocational training. That is, training *in situ* at real work sites should advantageously promote the development of general work skills and facilitate their generalization to future employment sites. Interestingly, there has as yet been little direct confirmation of this principle. Certainly, community training benefits job development, parents' expectations, vocational assessment, and socially valid goals. Yet, it is still not clear that *in situ* training leads to better generalization than simulated in-school training. Recently, Horner, McDonnell and Bellamy (1986) reported a superior effect of the former procedure in terms of trials to learn new tasks. Yet, this difference may not offset the cost sometimes accrued by lost instructional time moving students around the community (Horner, McDonnell and Bellamy, 1986). There is a clear need for research focusing on the interaction between aptitude and treatment procedure to uncover who benefits most from community vocational training. There is some evidence (Close and Keating, 1988; Horner, McDonnell and Bellamy, 1986) that more severely disabled students require proportionately more community training to promote generalization. Conversely, mildly disabled students appear to benefit from a greater proportion of simulated versus *in situ* training.

In summary, vocational education has shown many recent advances in successfully placing disabled persons in nonsheltered employment. Although community-based training serves a number of functions, its efficacy has yet to be shown in terms of generalization to other and future work environments. For job tasks, it may be that a null hypothesis, 'sequential programming' strategy (Stokes and Baer, 1977) toward generalization, may have to be taken. That is, we should not expect the transfer of a learning set (i.e., learning to learn) to new tasks from previous job task training. Thus, each new job task must be taught anew, *in situ*.

In contrast to work-related activity, social behaviors and relationships have developed throughout a person's life. It is therefore more likely that interaction and relationship skills may carry over from other experiences. Yet, we need to further demonstrate the utility of social skill and relationship formation interventions. There is a small but growing database showing that social skills training is effective in work settings.

At present, it might be useful to interpret the social standing of a disabled employee from an 'ecosocial perspective'. Figure 14.6 displays the four levels of social reality outlined by Bullis and Gaylord-Ross (1990). The graphic is useful in defining such levels and suggesting corresponding interventions. For example, a macro-setting level defines global situational events like sheltered workship, business office, etc. Different employment settings produce different work climates, and social rules. Macro interventions typically move an individual from one context to another, e.g. sheltered to nonsheltered settings. A second level of social reality identifies the social networks and relationships which may develop at work. Unfortunately, almost all of our work in this area has been anecdotal. A descriptive database is emerging, though, which is characterizing the nature of social support and the quality of work life for disabled employees. Preliminary research on relationship interventions has not been promising. The most studied level of social reality has been with direct social interactions between individuals. A social skills training literature has been rich in other domains (Strain and Odom, 1987) and is beginning to emerge in this difficult to control work setting. The intra-individual level of social reality offers possibilities for cognitive-behavioral interventions. While positive results have appeared with mildly disabled individuals, it is questionable whether persons with more severe disabilities are capable of mastering the process steps of this method.

As has been stated many times, social skills are very important at work for job performance and enjoyment. A technology is emerging for the multiple measurement of social behavior in this challenging setting. A co-worker advocate approach to teaching job skills has been validated and shows interesting parallels with peer tutoring approaches in schools. Similarly, a social skills training technology is presently being developed to better integrate the disabled employee in the workplace through relationship and friendship formation.

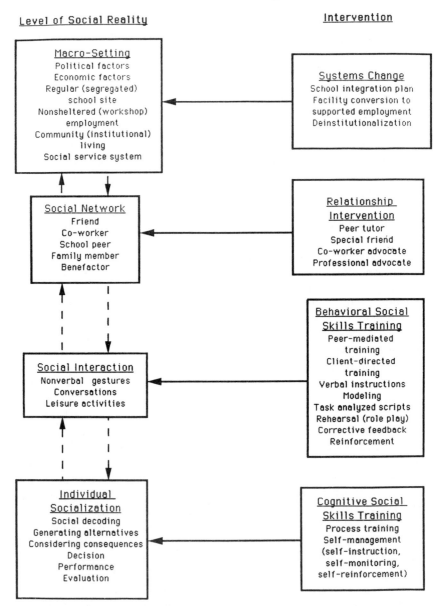

Figure 14.6 An ecosocial model of assessment and intervention.

CONCLUSIONS

The chapter has attempted to overview the emerging assessment and intervention literature on integrated employment. The job task training research is showing that both professional educators (e.g., job coaches) as well as nondisabled co-workers can successfully train developmentally disabled employees in their required job tasks. The success of co-worker trainers bodes well as both a more natural and cost-effective procedure. Such co-worker participation may enhance the maintenance of acquired job skills, due to the availability of co-workers for quality control, retraining, and crisis intervention.

It is essential to measure and evaluate the job tasks and social performance of disabled workers. It is easy for such workers to become isolated at work, with a resulting reduction in their quality of worklife. The behavioral measurement of social interactions in the workplace offers a powerful index of social integration. Social validation measures of vocational and social competence also can provide a sensitive and efficient method of measurement and evaluation. Future developments may further establish the differential weighting and importance of behavioral, social validation, and related measures.

It is evident that a small but expanding literature of effective procedures for social intervention is emerging. The traditional social skills training programs have entailed the use of behavioral rehearsals of targeted responses. More recently, problem-solving training methods have enabled young adults with mild and sometimes moderate mental handicap to think about, and thus modify, their social behavior in vocational contexts. Finally, socialization intervention may focus on the relationship as a means of facilitating integration. Rather than targeting molecular behaviors or cognitive processes for specific interventions, disabled and nondisabled employees participate in broadly defined friendship-building activities.

As the reader may sense, a number of assessment and intervention procedures are developing to promote the vocational integration of persons with developmental disabilities. Given the parallel progress in the school and residential spheres (cf. Ager, and Felce, this volume) we may be guardedly optimistic about the ability of an applied behavioral approach to deliver meaningful improvements in the general quality of life and specific quality of worklife for people with mental handicap.

Address for correspondence

The senior author of this chapter, Robert Gaylord-Ross, died while the book was in the process of publication. Any correspondence should, therefore, be addressed to Keith Storey, Allegheny-Singer Research Institute, 320 East North Avenue, Pittsburgh, Pennsylvania 15212-9986, USA.

REFERENCES

Bellamy, G.T., Rhodes, L.E., Mank, D.M. and Albin, J.M. (1988) *Supported Employment: A Community Implementation Guide*, Brookes, Baltimore.

Berkeley Planning Associates (1986) *Development of Performance Measures for Supported Employment Programs. Tasks 4 and 5* (Contract No. 300-85-0138). Department of Education, Washington, DC.

Breen, C., Haring, T., Pitts-Conway, V. and Gaylord-Ross, R. (1985) The training and generalization of social interaction at two job sites in the natural environment. *Journal of the Association for Persons with Severe Handicaps,* **10,** 41–50.

Bullis, M. and Gaylord-Ross, R. (1990) The transition of behaviorally disordered youth. In R. Rutherford and L. Bullock (eds), *Monograph Series Published by the Council for Children with Behavior Disorders*, CEC, Reston, Virginia.

Chadsey-Rusch, J. (1990) Social interaction of secondary aged students with severe handicaps: Implications for facilitating the transition from school to work. *Journal of the Association for Persons with Severe Handicaps,* **15,** 69–78.

Chadsey-Rusch, J. and Gonzalez, P. (1988) Social ecology of the workplace: Employers' perceptions versus direct observation. *Research in Developmental Disabilities,* **9,** 229–245.

Chadsey-Rusch, J. and Rusch, F.R. (1988) Ecology of the workplace. In R. Gaylord-Ross (ed.), *Vocational Education for Persons with Handicaps*, Mayfield, Mountain View, California.

Chadsey-Rusch, J., Gonzalez, P., Tines, J. and Johnson, J.R. (1989) Social ecology of the workplace: Contextual variables affecting social interactions among employees with and without mental retardation. *American Journal on Mental Retardation,* **94,** 141–151.

Close, D.W. and Keating, T.J. (1988) Community living and work. In R. Gaylord-Ross (ed.), *Vocational Education for Persons with Handicaps*, Mayfield, Mountain View, California.

Curl, R.M., McConaughy, E.K., Pawley, J.M. and Salzberg, C.L. (1987) *Put That Person to Work! A Co-Worker Training Manual for the Co-Worker Transition Model*, Development Center for Handicapped Persons, Utah State University, Logan.

French, W. and Bell, C. (1984) *Organizational Development: Behavioral Science Interventions for Organizational Improvement*, Prentice-Hall, Englewood Cliffs, New Jersey.

Gaylord-Ross, R. (1987) School integration for students with mental handicaps: A cross-cultural perspective. *European Journal of Special Needs in Education,* **2,** 117–129.

Gaylord-Ross, R. (1990) Issues in supported employment. In F.R. Rusch (ed.), *Supported Employment: Models, Methods, and Issues*, Sycamore, DeKalb, Illinois.

Gaylord-Ross, R., Lee, M., Johnston, S. and Goetz, L. (in press) Social-communication and co-worker training for deaf–blind youth in supported employment settings. *Behavior Modification.*

Horner, R.H., McDonnell, J.J. and Bellamy, G.T. (1986) Teaching generalized skills: General case instruction in simulation and community settings. In R.H. Horner, L.H. Meyer and H.D.B. Fredericks (eds), *Education of Learners with Severe Handicaps*, Brookes, Baltimore.

Kennedy, C.H., Horner, R.H. and Newton, J.S. (1989) Social contacts of adults with severe disabilities living in the community. *Journal of the Association for Persons with Severe Handicaps*, **14**, 190–196.

Kennedy, C.H., Horner, R.H. and Newton, J.S. (1990) The social networks and activity patterns of adults with severe disabilities: A correlational analysis. *Journal of the Association for the Severely Handicapped*, **15**, 86–90.

Kregel, J., Wehman, P. and Banks, P.P. (1989) The effects of consumer characteristics and type of employment model on individual outcomes in supported employment. *Journal of Applied Behavior Analysis*, **22**, 407–415.

Likens, M., Salzberg, C.L., Stowitschek, J.J., Lignugaris-Kraft, B. and Curl, R. (1989) Co-worker implemented job training: The use of coincidental training and quality-control checking procedures on the food preparation skills or employees with mental retardation. *Journal of Applied Behavior Analysis*, **22**, 381–393.

Mank, D.M. and Buckley, J. (1989) Strategies for integrating employment environments. In W. Kiernan and R. Schalock (eds), *Economics, Industry, and Disability: A Look Ahead*, Brookes, Baltimore.

Mank, D.M., Rhodes, L.E. and Bellamy, G.T. (1986) Four supported employment alternatives. In W.E. Kiernan and J.A. Stark (eds), *Pathways to Employment for Adults with Developmental Disabilities*, Brookes, Baltimore.

McCcnaughy, E.K., Curl, R.M. and Salzberg, C.L. (1987, May) *Ecological Assessment of Business Environments*. Paper presented at the 13th Annual Convention of the Association for Behavior Analysis, Nashville.

McDonnell, J., Nofs, D., Hardman, M. and Chambless, C. (1989) An analysis of the procedural components of supported employment programs associated with worker outcomes. *Journal of Applied Behavior Analysis*, **22**, 417–428.

McFall, R.M. (1982) A review and reformulation of the concept of social skills. *Behavior Assessment*, **4**, 1–33.

Nisbet, J. and Hagner, D. (1988) Natural supports in the workplace: A re-examination of supported employment. *Journal of the Association for Persons with Severe Handicaps*, **13**, 260–267.

Park, H.S. and Gaylord-Ross, R. (1989) Problem solving social skills training in employment settings with mentally retarded youth. *Journal of Applied Behavior Analysis*, **22**, 373–380.

Park, H.S., Tappe, P., Cameto, R. and Gaylord-Ross, R. (1990a) Social support and quality of life for learning disabled and mildly retarded youth in transition. In R. Gaylord-Ross, S. Siegel, H.S. Park, S. Sacks and L. Goetz (eds), *Readings in Ecosocial Development*, Department of Special Education, San Francisco State University.

Park, H.S. Johnson, B., Tappe, P., Simon, M., Wozniak, T. and Gaylord-Ross, R. (1990b) Relationship and social skills interventions for disabled youth in work settings. Manuscript submitted for publication.

Rusch, F.R., Hughes, C. and Johnson, J.R. (1990). Analysis of co-worker involvement in relation to level of disability versus placement approach among supported employees. *Journal of the Association for Persons with Severe Handicaps*.

Rusch, F.R. and Minch, K.E. (1988) Identification of co-worker involvement in supported employment. *Research in Developmental Disabilities*, **9**, 247–254.

Rusch, F.R., Hughes, C., Johnson, J.R. and Minch, K.E. (in press) A descriptive analysis of interactions of co-workers and supported employees. *Mental Retardation.*

Salzberg, C.L., Lignugaris-Kraft, B. and McCuller, G.L. (1988) Reasons for job loss: A review of employment termination studies of mentally retarded workers. *Research in Developmental Disabilities,* **9**, 153–170.

Sandow, D., Rhodes, L., Mank, D.M., Ramsing, K.D. and Lynch, W.F. (1990) Assuring quality in supported employment. *Rehabilitation Administration Quarterly,* **14**, 20–25.

Schalock, R.L., McGaughey, M.J. and Kiernan, W.E. (1989) Placement into nonsheltered employment: Findings from national employment surveys. *American Journal on Mental Retardation,* **94**, 80–87.

Schalock, R.G., Keith, K.D., Hoffman, K. and Karan, O.C. (1989) Quality of life: Its measurement and use. *Mental Retardation,* **27**, 25–31.

Shafer, M.S. (1986) Utilizing co-workers as charge agents. In F.R. Rusch (ed.), *Competitive Employment Issues and Strategies,* Brookes, Baltimore.

Shafer, M.S., Rice, M.L., Metzler, H.M.D. and Haring, M. (1989) A survey of nondisabled employees' attitudes towards supported employees with mental retardation. *Journal of the Association for Persons with Severe Handicaps,* **14**, 137–146.

Sowers, J., Jenkins, C. and Powers, L. (1988) Vocational education for persons with physical handicaps. In R. Gaylord-Ross (ed.), *Vocational Education for Persons with Handicaps,* Mayfield, Mountain View, California.

Stokes, T.F. and Baer, D.M. (1977) An implicit technology of generalization. *Journal of Applied Behavior Analysis,* **10**, 349–367.

Storey, K. and Horner, R.H. (in press) Social interactions in three supported employment options: A comparative analysis. *Journal of Applied Behaviour Analysis.*

Storey, K. and Horner, R.H. (in press) An evaluative review of social validation research involving persons with handicaps. *Journal of Special Education.*

Storey, K. and Gaylord-Ross, R. (1987) Increasing positive social interactions by handicapped individuals during a recreational activity using a multicomponent treatment package. *Research in Developmental Disabilities,* **8**, 627–649.

Storey, K. and Knutson, N. (1989) A comparative analysis of social interactions of handicapped and nonhandicapped workers in integrated work sites: A pilot study. *Education and Training in Mental Retardation,* **24**, 265–273.

Storey, K., Rhodes, L., Sandow, D., Loewinger, H. and Petherbridge, R. (in press) Direct observation of social interactions in a supported employment setting. *Education and Training in Mental Retardation.*

Strain, P.S. and Odom, S.L. (1986) Innovations in the education of preschool children with severe handicaps. In R.H. Horner, L.H. Meyer and H.D.B. Fredericks (eds), *Education of Learners with Severe Handicaps,* Brookes, Baltimore.

Voeltz, L.M. (1982) Effects of structured interactions with severely handicapped peers on children's attitudes. *American Journal of Mental Deficiency,* **86**, 380–390.

Wehman, P. and Kregel, J. (1989) *Supported Employment for Persons With Disability,* Human Sciences, New York.

Wehman, P. and Moon, M.S. (1987) Critical values in employment programs for persons with developmental disabilities. *Journal of Applied Rehabilitation Counselling,* **18**, 12–16.

Yan, X., Storey, K., Rhodes, L., Sandow, D., Petherbridge, R. and Loewinger, H. (1990) Clique analysis of interpersonal interactions: Grouping patterns in a supported employment work setting. *Behavioral Assessment,* **12**, 337–354.

Chapter 15

Effecting Sustainable Change in Client Behaviour: The Role of the Behavioural Analysis of Service Environments

ALASTAIR AGER

INTRODUCTION

The last three decades have seen the development of a broad range of habilitative programmes and procedures of demonstrable effectiveness in establishing therapeutic gains with people with severe mental handicap. Such developments have contributed to a transformation in the nature of mental handicap services, with custodial concerns having increasingly given way to an emphasis on the acquisition of functional skills and the opportunity to practise them in the natural environment (Evans, *et al.*, 1987; Saxby *et al.* 1988). In contrast to previous times (Clarke and Clarke, 1980), change in client behaviour is now an anticipated—and achieved—goal in most service settings.

The durability of therapeutic change with this client group, however, has remained a persistent focus of concern (Rincover, 1981; Stokes and Osnes, 1988). In the scientific literature, convincing evidence for the long-term maintenance of behaviour change remains elusive (Ager, 1987; Favell and Reid, 1988). Forehand and Atkeson (1978) note that there appears to be a clear negative correlation between the rigour with which researchers investigate maintenance issues and the durability they claim for training effects. Neither is such scepticism concerning long-term influence on the behaviour of people with mental handicap limited to the research community. Clinical reports frequently document the failure of a successful intervention to produce lasting change in clients' behaviour (Hall, 1979; Partridge, Chisholm and Levy, 1985).

The Challenge of Severe Mental Handicap. Edited by Bob Remington
© 1991 John Wiley & Sons Ltd

Means of encouraging the maintenance of adaptive change in the behaviour of clients form the central focus of the current chapter. It is argued that the failure of much therapeutic change to be maintained over time is due less to deficiencies in specific intervention techniques than to a common neglect of analysis of the behavioural environment in which such intervention is implemented.

More attention needs to be paid to determining those factors operating in a service environment which act to encourage or, alternatively, discourage the maintenance of change. Adopting the framework of the functional analysis of behaviour to identify those features of the environment that may serve to sustain change beyond the termination of intervention may prove of particular value when seeking means to engineer lasting change.

THE PROBLEM OF CREATING LASTING CHANGE

Effective education and behavioral intervention should change the way people live their lives ... Hard won changes in behavior should be functional across the full range of situations encountered in school, work, and community settings ... and should be maintained for months and years

(Horner, Dunlap and Koegel, 1988, p. 1).

The concept of intervention implicitly assumes the goal of functional and lasting change (Ager, 1987). Through the use of individual programme planning systems and the like, interventions are increasingly planned with respect to the long-term needs of clients. Training is frequently aimed at establishing a level of competence required for functioning in some future environment (e.g., group home or staffed house).

Many clients of services, however, do not experience the steady attainment of adaptive change. Clearly, some of these clients may be in services where there is little emphasis on habilitative intervention, often as a result of a lack of crucial resources (such as staffing) which renders adequate physical care of clients the only attainable service goal (see Felce et al., 1987). But for others adaptive change will have been won— and subsequently lost.

Failure to effect lasting change

The following accounts are each instances of the failure to effect lasting change, and will serve as a basis for subsequent discussion. Each is based on fact, though identifying information has been amended.

Newtown Day Care and Home Visiting Service

The Newtown Association for the Parents of the Mentally Handicapped was formed by parents dissatisfied with the level of service provided for the families of people with mental handicaps in the Newtown area. One of its first achievements was the establishment of a day care unit at a local community centre, where instructors were employed to work on habilitation programmes with clients. The unit also acted as a base for volunteer workers who visited families with a handicapped child, and advised them on child care and management.

The association subsequently approached the local psychology service about providing a training workshop for parents, instructors and volunteers. The two psychologists to lead the workshop drew up a programme which included principles of curriculum planning, assessment, teaching methods and intervention with problem behaviour. The five-day workshop was hailed a great success by all. Visiting the unit the following week, the psychologists assisted instructors in goal-setting and teaching exercises. Sessions with the volunteer home visitors were also arranged. One month after the workshop—with all instructors and most volunteers now devising and implementing their own teaching plans—the psychologists began to reduce their involvement. The association was grateful that they had had assistance in 'getting themselves on their own feet', and asked that the psychologists continue to call in on the project on a monthly basis.

Six months later, however, the day care unit was closed and the home visiting service suspended. Turnover in both instructors and volunteers had been high, and those that remained from the commencement of the project had abandoned individual programme work some time ago. The atmosphere of the unit had grown increasingly chaotic, with children roaming around the centre freely. A group 'music-and-movement' session latterly represented the only structured activity provided.

Shirley Jones

Aged 14, Shirley Jones had been resident at a service facility for people with severe mental handicap for the past 11 years. For much of this time she had displayed severe self-injurious behaviour. Pharmacological treatment had been the main previous form of intervention, but had seen little benefit. Control of behaviours such as eye-gouging and hand-biting was now principally through the use of arm-splints for restraint, which were worn for up to 12 hours each day.

Shirley attended the school attached to the residential facility. The school was functioning as a placement for a PhD student from the local college researching into the applications of behavioural analysis.

Distressed by the limited opportunities afforded Shirley as a result of the use of prolonged restraint, the student—with the full cooperation of Shirley's teacher—conducted observations of Shirley's behaviour in the classroom during the brief periods where her arm-splints were removed. The resulting functional analysis strongly suggested that attending behaviours of staff were reinforcing self-injury.

A structured intervention programme was introduced whereby the teacher initiated brief individual teaching sessions with Shirley. These sessions were to be conducted without the use of restraint, but were to be terminated on the first instance of self-injurious behaviour. Within three weeks of the programme's introduction, Shirley's rate of self-injurious behaviour was less than 10% of baseline levels.

The student initially took responsibility for collating all behavioural records regarding the intervention but, after six weeks, passed this responsibility to the teacher. After the end of the placement, some ten weeks after programme initiation, the student retained periodic contact with the school and arranged for comprehensive follow-up observations after three months. These data showed that Shirley's rate of self-injury was still below 10% of baseline levels. The teacher reported being very pleased with progress, and whilst residential staff at the facility still made frequent use of restraint, it was now seldom required at school.

After a gap of some two months the student visited the school to find Shirley once more wearing arm-splints for most of the day. No behavioural records had been kept for the past six weeks. Staff reported having reluctantly reintroduced restraint as 'the only means of curbing self-injury'.

Woodlands Social Education Centre

Woodlands SEC was selected as a centre for an evaluation of the impact of room management procedures (see Cullen, 1985) on client engagement. Managers and staff discussed the proposals with the research team who would implement the study, and fully supported the project.

Following baseline observations of client engagement and staff–client interactions, intensive training was provided in room management procedures. Competence in the required skills was established through use of a positive monitoring procedure, whereby direct feedback on staff performance was initially given by researchers and subsequently the centre manager.

Prior to implementation of the room management procedure, clients at the centre were actively engaged in appropriate activity less than 15% of the time. Two weeks after implementation this figure was in excess of 80%, and engagement levels of between 70% and 80% were retained throughout the remaining ten weeks of the project. Follow-up observations at three, six and twelve months indicated engagement in appropriate activity at a similar level. Researchers concluded that room management was a potent intervention procedure for increasing levels of engagement in such settings.

Twelve months later, the principal researcher of the project team visited Woodlands with local government officials to discuss with the centre manager the lessons that could be applied to other SECs in the region. From observing activity in the teaching areas it was clear that staff were not following room management procedures in their work with clients. On enquiring about this, the researcher was told by the centre manager that she had not been aware that they had wished to carry out more follow-up observations, but that staff could be asked to 'do room management' if they wanted. Despite its potent influence on client behaviour, this pattern of working had clearly not become an integral part of the work of the centre. 'Room management' was a discrete repertoire, engaged in by staff only in special circumstances.

Programming for generalization and maintenance

Avoiding the problems illustrated by the above examples has long been acknowledged as an important challenge to workers in the field of mental handicap. Those of a behavioural orientation, in particular, have been urged to address the issues of generalization and maintenance for many years (e.g., Stokes and Baer, 1977; Tennant, Cullen and Hattersley, 1981).

The classic paper of Stokes and Baer (1977) is perhaps the most widely acknowledged treatise on this subject in the behavioural literature. Stokes and Baer (1977) reviewed the extant literature on generalization and maintenance and suggested a number of tactics to maximize the generalization of change across behaviours, settings and time. The resulting concept of 'generalization programming' has come to describe the practice of adopting such strategies explicitly within intervention programmes. Generalization and maintenance of change are now firmly acknowledged as active processes, rather than passive 'by-products' of an intervention (Ager, 1987).

Interventions now commonly adopt some form of generalization programming strategy, particularly during the latter stages of a programme where the durability of established therapeutic gains becomes an obvious concern. In many cases such strategies are effective, but the mere adoption of some such training tactic is no guarantee of success. In each of the instances outlined above, explicit attempts were made to foster maintenance of change. With the Newtown project, staff training was extended into the physical and social environment in which people would subsequently function, giving the workshop leaders the opportunity to reinforce appropriate generalization and maintenance of newly acquired skills. With Shirley Jones and the Woodlands SEC, similar attempts to programme generalization across personnel and time were established.

What is clear is that the adoption of generalization tactics *per se* is of little consequence. It is not the structural qualities of an intervention that matter but rather its functional qualities. In other words, successful generalization programming (like successful intervention itself) involves not the slavish application of techniques but a careful functional analysis of the situation in which intervention is planned.

Although practice may not always reflect this, the stated principles of generalization programming suggest just this kind of sensitive analysis of the prevailing environment (see Stokes and Osnes, 1986). Capitalizing upon natural sources of reinforcement and training across an appropriate range of natural settings, for example, clearly both require environmental analysis prior to intervention. The complexity of this task is daunting. Yet the logic of generalization programming forces us towards acknowledging its importance. To plan a successful intervention, knowledge of the contingencies operating in the pre- and post-intervention environments is crucial.

Behavioural ecology

The importance of understanding the complexity of behavioural systems is essentially a central tenet of behaviour analysis (Skinner, 1953), but has perhaps found its clearest expression through Willems (1974). Behavioural ecology has been the term used to emphasize the interdependence of behavioural repertoires in any given environment. The effects of intervention in behavioural systems may often be different from those predicted (Cullen, 1988). Changes may not be maintained because of competition from incompatible behavioural repertoires. When changes do occur they may be the result of contingencies other than those manipulated by an intervention procedure (Woods and Cullen, 1983).

Ecological analysis (Willems, 1974) has been proposed as a means of clarifying the complexity of behavioural systems, and thereby rendering the effects of intervention more predictable. While such analysis would undoubtedly be of real value, there have been conspicuously few successes in comprehensively mapping an environment in the required manner (Cullen, 1988). Recent work on the functional equivalence of behaviours (Carr, 1988) and competing behaviour analysis (Horner and Billingsley, 1988) are notable exceptions to this trend. In general, however, environments appear to have been inaccessible to the required rigour of analysis (Baer, 1974).

Discouraged by such failure, yet eager to formulate some form of analysis, a number of behavioural workers have presented quasi-functional accounts of behavioural environments. Praill and Baldwin (1988), for example, propose an analysis of the behavioural systems which may operate in institutional and community-orientated services. The tactics recommended for maintaining change in such service environments, which include choosing visible goals, creating subsystems to support change, taking responsibility for mistakes and so on, have clear face validity. The status of such formulations, however, is hard to evaluate. To demand direct, unequivocal empirical support for such analysis may be unrealistic given our current level of ignorance. Yet the intuitive nature of such arguments, devoid of any coherent theoretical structure, renders them almost impossible to adequately operationalize.

To illustrate, 'supportive management', suggested by Praill and Baldwin (1988) as a valuable catalyst of change, is indeed most likely to be a key factor in encouraging innovation. But what is 'supportive management'? How should it be defined, specified, and operationalized? Without such precision in defining key variables—a problem which has consistently troubled researchers in the staff training and management field (Cullen, 1988)—it is impossible to advance the sophistication of our analysis of service environments (Stolz, 1981).

A number of analyses of service environments (e.g., Reppucci, 1973; Hall, 1979; Fawcett, Mathews and Fletcher, 1980) offer a similar degree of plausible, and potentially valuable, insight. Without clear theoretical coherence, however, such accounts are unable to generate testable hypotheses and thereby provide a means for their own potential falsifiability. There is a real danger that the analysis of behavioural environments may be considered so complex a task that it is believed inaccessible to serious scientific enquiry.

Work in the areas of both generalization programming and behavioural ecology thus emphasize the need to consider factors operating in an environment which will influence the outcome of intervention programmes. But whilst the need for analysis of contingencies operating in service environments may be apparent, the means of effecting such analysis remains elusive. Quasi-functional analyses have suggested a number of plausible principles for understanding the behavioural dynamics of systems and the establishment and maintenance of change within them. What seems to be lacking is some conceptual scheme which integrates such insights and ties them to some theoretical structure—preferably a rigorous, behavioural one.

SUSTAINABLE CHANGE

The probability of establishing lasting change is not reliably associated with the characteristics of an intervention *per se*. Rather, it is the interaction or, perhaps better, the coherence between intervention and environment that is crucial. In no meaningful way are interventions, or environments, in themselves 'bad' for achieving maintenance of change. Interventions that are successful in some environments will fail in others. An ineffective procedure in one environment may facilitate lasting change in another. The coherence of intervention and environment is what is important, with such coherence reflected in what may be termed the sustainability of change.

The concept of sustainability

The concept of sustainability has won wide currency in recent years with respect to the planning of intervention programmes, particularly in the fields of economic and agricultural development (Baum and Tolbert, 1985; Commonwealth Heads of Government, 1989; Grant, 1989). This follows an earlier period during which the unsustainability of many such programmes had become painfully obvious. Individuals trained in handicraft skills for self-sufficient production returned to the fields with no markets for their products. Tractors imported to Third World countries with the aim of improving agricultural productivity lay dormant for want of spares and the technical expertise to maintain them (Batchelor, 1981; Derham, 1988).

In response to this situation, development agencies have steadily turned from a preoccupation with their programmes to an analysis of the resources within developing nations that might foster change. The complex ecology of human societies was acknowledged, but not with overwhelming despair. Agencies began the task of constructing an audit of environmental resources within the cultures where they were seeking to create lasting change. The concept of sustainability cements this concern:

A sustainable society is one that can live indefinitely within its means—its natural as well as human and financial resources
                                                                (Baum and Tolbert, 1985, p. 538).

With sustainability as a concern, there is a natural focus on appraisal of environmental resources. Plans for specific schemes of intervention are secondary to a more global analysis of those factors which will act to assist change and those which will act to obstruct it.

To date economic, physical and biological resources have dominated the analysis of development agencies (Grant, 1989). It should be apparent, however, that the logic of the sustainability of change applies equally well—and perhaps even more crucially—to behavioural environments (Ager, 1990).

Principles of behavioural sustainability

In behavioural terms the 'resources' of an environment are the behavioural repertoires exhibited there and the contingencies which operate to maintain them. In any given environment, the sustainability of behaviour change is thus determined by the extent to which the contingencies present there foster such newly acquired behaviour.

Baer and Wolf (1970) are essentially addressing the issue of sustainability, therefore, when they urge that 'newly learned social behavior should mesh with, and be trapped by, the reinforcement contingencies provided by the maintenance environment'. Kiernan (1978) shows similar sensitivity to available environmental resources in arguing for an awareness that 'generalization to non-training conditions must take into account the contingencies in that environment'. The work of Wahler (e.g., Wahler, 1980; Wahler and Fox, 1981) remains perhaps the clearest example of sustainable behavioural intervention being formulated with respect to a thorough analysis of existing environmental contingencies.

The behavioural model posits the development of an operant as defined by a 'three-term' contingency: antecedents, behaviour and consequences. Skinner (1969) has commonly stressed changes in behaviour brought about by the manipulation of consequences, and the emphasis of much applied behaviour analysis has followed this lead. Tennant, Cullen and Hattersley (1981) have cogently argued, however, that manipulations in antecedent conditions may often provide a valuable alternative means of influencing behaviour. Sidman (1978, 1979) has given a careful analysis of the value of understanding antecedent–behaviour relationships, and suggests that the concept of stimulus control (which describes such relationships) has a crucial, yet neglected, role in our understanding of human behaviour (cf. Mackay, this volume).

The analysis of contingencies required when evaluating the sustainability of change in a given environment should not, therefore, be narrowly identified with the appraisal of the consequences which shape behaviour. Mapping 'natural communities of reinforcement' (Baer and Wolf, 1970) in this manner is important. But tracing the discriminative control of behaviour exerted by antecedent events adds a powerful additional dimension to such analysis.

This is most clearly illustrated with respect to recent developments in our understanding of the processes involved in skills training. When an individual learns some new behaviour, those antecedent conditions used to prompt this response during training will often form a part of the resulting functional operant. As Tennant, Cullen and Hattersley (1981) emphasize, such conditions are far more than merely stimuli in the presence of which responses are reinforced. They are an integral and crucial part of the contingency sustaining the behaviour.

The vast literature on stimulus-fading and stimulus-shaping procedures (see Schoen, 1986) clearly commends the identification of such controlling relationships and, where necessary, suggests attempting to withdraw or amend such conditions before the termination of training. If responses under stimulus control are to successfully generalize to a post-training, maintenance environment, it is crucial to ascertain what antecedent conditions are operative there.

It is most satisfactory for this appraisal to be completed before intervention, such that the prompting stimuli used in acquisition can be chosen by virtue of their presence in the maintenance environment. For discrimination learning, there is a good deal of evidence supporting the use of 'criterion-related cues' (Ager, 1991); that is, providing prompts in the same stimulus dimension with respect to which the required discrimination must be made. Such cues are, by definition, a reliable feature of the post-intervention environment.

In many circumstances, prior engineering of intervention methods to fit in with a prospective maintenance environment may not be possible. The skills training literature here points to a strategy of explicitly scheduling the required stimuli in the maintenance environment or, alternatively, creating a shift in stimulus control to cues that are already present there (Ager, 1991). Either way, a clear appreciation of the antecedent conditions operative in the environment is vital if maintenance of performance to the post-training environment is to be achieved.

Little attention has so far been paid to the application of such principles outside the narrow confines of discrimination learning, but there are sound theoretical grounds for considering their relevance to the more general concern of maintaining adaptive change within services. A comprehensive analysis of the environmental contingencies influencing the sustainability of change must consider the role of antecedent events, as well as the consequences of behaviour.

THE BEHAVIOURAL ANALYSIS OF SERVICE ENVIRONMENTS

In some environments, as a result of powerful and/or coercive contingencies maintaining behavioural stability, change may be virtually impossible to establish (see Partridge, Chisholm and Levy, 1985). In other environments, contingencies exist which readily foster innovation and lead to constant development and elaboration of behavioural repertoires (see Praill and Baldwin, 1988).

Most behavioural environments fall somewhere between these two extremes. Change is possible, but invariably some forms of change will be more readily established and maintained than others. Pre-existing contingencies give a functional 'grain' to an environment. Interventions which 'follow the grain' will generally be more successful than those that cross it (Ray and Sidman, 1970). Determining the 'grain' of an environment is essentially what functional analysis achieves, thereby assisting in the identification of intervention strategies of plausible effectiveness. The behavioural analysis of a service environment cannot of itself prevent failure to achieve lasting change. Behavioural environments remain too complex, and contingencies too enmeshed, to allow perfect prediction. But such prior analysis can suggest an approach to engineering change which maximizes the probability of its proving sustainable.

The analysis of behavioural systems

The functional analysis of behaviour has generally been pursued with respect to the analysis of the behaviour of individuals. In rebelling against the practice in much of psychology of determining general laws of behaviour by averaging across groups of subjects, the experimental analysis of behaviour has strongly allied itself to the single-case experimental design (Hersen and Barlow, 1976). Skinner himself, however, has seldom fought shy of emphasizing the essentially social dimension of behaviour analysis (Skinner, 1974). There are commonalities in the contingencies experienced by individuals in any behavioural environment, and the behavioural repertoires of such individuals inevitably interact and shape one another. Through the use of concepts such as control and counter-control (see Blackman, 1980) behavioural analysis can readily address itself to the dynamics of behavioural systems.

In proposing principles for the behavioural analysis of service environments there need, therefore, be no suggestion of a theoretical discontinuity with the established principles of the experimental analysis of behaviour. It is important to understand that the fundamental unit of analysis remains the operant—an act by an individual on his or her environment.

The analysis of a system proceeds by aggregating the effects of individuals' behaviour on the environment and on the behaviour of others.

Described in this manner, the behaviour analysis of service systems may appear theoretically sound, yet practically unattainable. Functional analysis of the behaviour of a single individual is often a complex and time-consuming operation, with repeated empirical tests required to support or disconfirm the analysis. How much more complex does the analysis become when more than one individual is involved, and interaction effects must also be considered?

In practice, the empiricism at the heart of the experimental analysis of behaviour renders the analysis of systems such as service environments more attainable than one might suppose. It is indeed only empiricism that renders behavioural analysis of individual behaviour attainable. Sidman (1978, 1979) has pointed out the phenomenal range of stimuli and associations which may plausibly control the occurrence of a response in an individual. When attempting functional analysis with regard to such a response, one makes a 'best guess' of the key stimuli involved, and then tests this hypothesis by empirical means. It would be impossible to test the functional control over a response exerted by all stimuli impinging on an individual. Assumptions and generalizations are inevitably made concerning the likelihood of certain stimuli proving salient (Sidman, 1978).

An exhaustive catalogue of all environmental events impinging upon persons operating in some service environment is thus clearly unattainable. But by sensitive application of the principles which are known to govern human operant behaviour, certain hypotheses concerning functional relationships between environmental conditions and human behaviour may be proposed and then tested.

When attempting to produce a genuinely functional picture of a behavioural system such as a service environment, it is obviously important to define the boundaries of the environment functionally rather than structurally. The behaviour of many different participants within the service may be of relevance. Client behaviour will often be the ultimate focus of concern. In most service environments, however, the behaviour of staff will be such an important determinant of the behaviour of clients (see Felce, this volume; Felce *et al.*, 1987) as to render its analysis essential. In other service systems, incorporating the behaviour of clients' families may be functionally justified; the behaviour of managers will be of functional relevance in many services also. Few service systems will have a clear and absolute boundary. Again, it is likely that empirical investigation will ultimately be the only reliable means of determining where the boundary of analysis may be most usefully drawn.

Table 15.1 A checklist of environmental prerequisites for the sustainability of change

---

CONSEQUENT CONDITIONS

Functional reinforcement
- Will reinforcers of established functional potency be available in the environment for *all* participants?
- Will some such reinforcers be directly contingent upon the maintenance of behaviour change by participants?

Appropriately scheduled reinforcement
- Will adherence to the desired changes be promptly reinforced?
- Will adherence to such changes be consistently reinforced, especially on their initial introduction?
- Is there a reliable mechanism for ensuring at least periodic reinforcement of such behaviour for the indefinite future?

Natural reinforcement
- Will benefits to participants flow naturally from adherence to change?
- If key reinforcers are to be contrived, is their long-term availability guaranteed?

Limited response cost
- What will be the response cost(s) to participants of adherence to change?
- Are such costs likely to be outweighed by benefits?

ANTECEDENT CONDITIONS

Environmental reliability
- Will major setting events (such as involved personnel, service location, financial resourcing) remain constant for a suitably long period after implementation of change?

Appropriate functional control of behaviour
- Will the focus of functional control of behaviour change be identifiable for all participants?
- Will such functional control generally be associated with permanent features of the environment?
- If not, will shifts in control to such permanent features be attainable?

Minimal sources of competing control
- Will any continuing features of the environment have strong association with behaviour incompatible with adherence to change?

With respect to previous discussion, the following analysis of service environments considers in turn the consequent and antecedent conditions necessary to sustain change. These environmental prerequisites for the sustainability of change—derived from the application of basic behavioural principles—are listed in Table 15.1. This checklist may usefully provide a basis for considering issues of sustainability for those involved in creating service change. The subsequent section examines these prerequisites in some detail, and notes their implications for the service environments previously discussed.

Consequent conditions required to sustain change

Functional reinforcement

The law of effect is the keystone of behavioural theory, as relevant to understanding complex behavioural systems as to the actions of a single individual. For behaviour change to be maintained over time it must be reinforced. To maintain service change, functional reinforcers need to be established for the relevant behaviours of all participants in the service system—be they clients, staff, managers or family members.

To determine whether an environment will plausibly sustain established change, there are therefore essentially two questions to be answered concerning functional reinforcement. The first asks about the availability in the service environment of reinforcers of proven functional potency for all service participants. These must not be 'presumed' reinforcers, but proven ones. Perhaps the most common cause for poor sustainability of change is a failure to appreciate this simple principle. In each of the case examples given earlier there was a failure to secure a functional source of reinforcement for the changed behaviour of at least one group of service participants—commonly staff. Assumptions were often made— for example, that staff inevitably find client behaviour change reinforcing—that have been demonstrated to be unreliable (Woods and Cullen, 1983).

The second question of importance is whether such reinforcers—if available—are appropriately contingent upon the maintenance of change. Their presence alone is insufficient. In the case of Woodlands SEC, for example, external interest in the room management project appears to have been a functional reinforcer for the behaviour of staff and manager alike. The contingency operated, however, to maintain research programme objectives rather than reliable daily staff performance. For change to be sustainable, functional rewards need to be directly related to the maintenance of the targetted change.

Appropriately scheduled reinforcement

Developing the above analysis, behavioural theory suggests other aspects of the scheduling of reinforcement that are likely to be crucial in attempts to maintain change. Prerequisites of an environment in which change can be maintained include such behaviour being reinforced both promptly and reliably.

From considering the early history of the Newtown project, it is plausible to conclude that the supervision by psychologists was a functional reinforcer of appropriate staff behaviour. With supervision cut to once-monthly visits, however, this source of reinforcement was not available to promptly reward staff's adherence to specified project goals. Given that supervision appeared to be the only reinforcer of appropriate staff behaviour, the delay and paucity of reinforcement probably allowed a number of inappropriate, but more immediately reinforced, staff repertoires to develop, leading to the eventual collapse of the project.

Reinforcers need to be available promptly on the completion of appropriate behaviour if the maintenance of change is to be a viable goal within services. Although this principle is commonly accepted for clients, perhaps, its applicability to all participants in a service is arguably less appreciated. Events such as supervisor's praise and monetary incentives have proved effective reinforcers of staff behaviour (Cullen, 1988), but there is little probability of their functioning thus if they are not promptly contingent upon appropriate behaviour. Again, families' and managers' adherence to programme objectives will be severely disrupted if there is lengthy delay before they receive potentially reinforcing feedback, encouragement, reports or whatever.

The reliability of reinforcement is important too. Programme adherence by Shirley Jones' teacher appeared to be reinforced by the feedback and concern of the student placed in her school. With termination of the programme coming during a lapse in the student's attendance at the school, this unreliability of contact (in the context of an apparent lack of alternative sources of reinforcement) appears to have been critical. There can be no theoretical surprise at the extinction of behaviours in such circumstances.

This is not to say that reinforcement needs to be continuous. A continuous schedule of reinforcement may be of value in the early stages of an intervention, but the subsequent thinning of reinforcement will usually act to strengthen rather than weaken responding (Bandura, 1969). In any service environment, the ultimate concern must be for a reliable source of periodic reinforcement. The exact frequency of reinforcement is perhaps less crucial than its being perceived as fundamentally reliable.

Unless participants receive signals that reinforcement is still available behaviour will extinguish.

Natural reinforcement

The requirement for the benefits to participants to flow naturally from adherence to change (rather than involving contrived contingencies) is part theoretically, and part pragmatically, based. Theoretical analysis supports the use of natural contingencies particularly for improving the acquisition of behaviours (Williams, Koegel and Egel, 1981), although there is some support for benefits in maintenance too (Favell and Reid, 1988). Most critically, though, the use of natural contingencies is, pragmatically, often the best way of ensuring the reliability of reinforcement. All contrived systems of reinforcement require, in their turn, some means of maintenance. Capitalizing upon 'natural contingencies of reinforcement' (Baer and Wolf, 1970) remains a crucial tactic for ensuring the sustainability of change.

Degree of response cost

Not only is it important that adherence to change brings functional benefits to service participants, it is also of value to ascertain the extent to which change activates punishing contingencies. In other words, change will often bring costs to participants as well as (hopefully) benefits. The relative impact of these costs and benefits is obviously crucial for the ultimate sustainability of change.

The response cost(s) to participants of adherence to change are seldom enumerated, but this can be an important step in deciding between alternative intervention strategies in an environment. In the case of Woodlands SEC, for instance, it is likely that the room management procedure introduced would have had considerable costs for the staff. Given data which suggest that staff in facilities for those with mental handicap often spend little time in staff–client contact, and rather more in staff–staff interaction (see Felce, this volume, Felce et al., 1987), increased physical and mental effort, loss of autonomy, decreased contact with other staff, etc., were all likely to have been salient costs for staff adherence to the procedure. It is apparent that external interest in the work of the unit was a sufficient positive reinforcer to outweigh these costs during the running of the project. With the absence of such reinforcement, however, the punishing consequences of the procedure were sufficient to bring about its abandonment.

Antecedent conditions required to sustain change

Environmental reliability

If, as was argued previously, antecedent conditions form an integral part of an acquired operant, it follows that disruption to such conditions will lead to the disruption of behaviour. Details of staff behaviour and service location can easily become part of the antecedent conditions exerting control over behaviour (Redd and Birnbrauer, 1969). Tactics such as training across a range of settings with a range of personnel may be useful in diminishing the problem of narrow control of behaviour by such specific antecedent stimuli (Stokes and Osnes, 1988). But environmental stimuli will nearly always retain some degree of discriminative control of behaviour. Reasonable reliability of environmental conditions is thus vital if newly acquired behaviour is not to be put at risk.

In the Newtown project, a high degree of staff turnover in the weeks following the training workshop precluded such environmental reliability. Adaptive repertoires of behaviour that had been previously established were vulnerable to disruption, as the rhythm and structure of the service in which they had been developed began to change. Staff turnover is just one of several factors which render many service environments for persons with mental handicap unsuitably unreliable (Favell and Reid, 1988). Ager (1989) reported a series of case studies regarding the introduction of computer aids into the living environments of handicapped clients. In all cases the aids were initially well received and established tangible benefits for clients. Subsequently, however, circumstances ranging from staffing shortages, through withdrawal of key personnel to the transfer of the client to another facility, rendered all environments insufficiently stable for the maintance of computer use.

When environments are in a state of flux, maintenance of change will inevitably be difficult to secure. In such situations sustainable change is only likely to be produced by identifying those features of the environment that are most liable to remain fairly constant (e.g., a regular staff member, the pattern of daily routine) and attempting to establish stimulus control of behaviour by such features.

Appropriate functional control of behaviour

Identifying which aspects of the environment exert functional control over behaviour is a valuable step in engineering lasting change. The locus of such control may often be other than that assumed or intended (Ray and Sidman, 1970). When this is the case, even small changes in the environment can have unexpected consequences for behaviour change. As noted previously, this is a well-documented phenomenon within the skills training literature, but it has wider relevance.

Functional control can often be exerted by specific personnel within an environment, with the result that behaviour change is at risk from their eventual withdrawal. Georgiades and Phillimore (1975) document the dangers of change brought about by such 'hero innovators'. Woodlands SEC provides a subtle variation to this theme. The abandonment of room management after a successful research demonstration of its efficacy appears initially to be a classic example of the Hawthorne effect. External interest rather than perceived therapeutic gain maintained adherence to the procedure. However, the failure of staff to engage in room management when researchers visited for some other purpose suggests that factors controlling behaviour were more complex than this. Rather, the requirements of completing the research evaluation appear to have been what exerted control over staff behaviour. External interest outside the framework of research evaluation was insufficient to prompt engagement in room management.

Whenever functional control is exerted by the behaviour of external personnel or other impermanent features of the environment, it is important to attempt a shift in control to more permanent features. Again the skills teaching literature is likely to prove instructive here in suggesting methods of stimulus fading and shaping (see Ager, 1991) which may help establish such shifts. Most methods will involve incremental adjustment to the environment, usually related to increases in the saliency of targeted stimuli and gradual withdrawal of those features of the environment which initially controlled responding. If behaviour change is, for example, under the functional control of the behaviour of some external consultant to a unit, a shift in control to that of a regular staff member may be achieved by repeated imitation of the behaviour of the consultant whilst the latter gradually withdraws his or her involvement.

Minimal sources of competing control

Behaviour change is really behaviour exchange. As new repertoires develop, other are displaced. Such displaced repertoires will have previously been under the control of some features of the environment, and there is always the danger that such repertoires will re-emerge if environmental control over the new repertoire weakens.

Shirley Jones' eye-gouging or hand-biting had long been the prompt for school staff to attend to her in an attempt to avoid serious harm. The behavioural programme initiated by the visiting student established an alternative and incompatible repertoire of staff behaviour with respect to her self-injury. When this alternative repertoire weakened as a result of a lack of reinforcement, environmental control of the previous repertoire was sufficiently intact for it to become readily re-established.

Change is likely to be more sustainable, therefore, when continuing features of the environment do not have strong associations with previous repertoires incompatible with the change. Although there is a need for continuity in the environment with respect to those features which control newly established adaptive behaviour, there is also a case for deliberate disruption of features which may encourage the re-emergence of maladaptive behaviour. Changes in personnel, service policy, daily routine, physical features of the environment, etc., may all in some circumstances be warranted if there is evidence that these have exerted strong control over repertoires which may compete with newly established change.

ENGINEERING LASTING CHANGE

The above analysis may clearly be used as a basis for *post hoc* discussion regarding the failure to secure lasting change in an environment. Such *post hoc* analyses may be comforting, but they are of little utility unless they suggest means in which future interventions may be more sensibly framed. What is of real value is not so much being told why a previous intervention proved unsustainable, but rather learning how the probability of a subsequent intervention proving sustainable might be increased.

Equally, the suggested framework for understanding the sustainability of change within environments will be of limited value if it simply asserts the difficulty of establishing lasting change in certain environments. Often there is no choice regarding the environment in which we must intervene. Choice is only available concerning the intervention procedure adopted. To be of utility, the framework must suggest strategies for intervention in the most unpromising of environments, the analysis helping to identify the (perhaps few) features of the environment that might be used to sustain change.

It is clear that in each of the case examples discussed the environments were unsuitable to sustain change of the form established by the intervention procedures described. Can the proposed framework suggest by what means more sustainable change might have been achieved?

Applying the principle of sustainability

Newtown Day Care and Home Visiting Service

The failure of innovation in this service seems largely attributable to the workshop leaders who initiated completely novel work practices for instructors and volunteers but failed to secure reliable reinforcement for adherence to such repertoires. With the new repertoires extinguishing, environmental disruption led to the development of a range of competing repertoires of lower response cost and, presumably, capable of recruiting some form of naturally occurring reinforcement.

Here we have a picture of intervention proceeding largely in ignorance of the environment. It was not known, for instance, what were salient reinforcers for those involved in the project. What were the motives of the volunteers? What did instructors see as their role? An awareness of such matters should assist in identifying what are the outcomes which will reinforce staff behaviour.

A knowledge of the existing structure and routine of the service—even though of fairly recent origin—would have given insight into the environmental features currently exerting control over behaviour. Some of these structures and routines may have formed a valuable foundation for planning change.

Prospects for establishing more lasting change would, therefore, have generally been improved if the workshop leaders had shown greater sensitivity to existing repertoires that could be shaped, and been less preoccupied with the superimposition of a predetermined pattern of working.

Shirley Jones

The intervention programme devised for Shirley Jones involved running a teaching session outside the usual timetabled routine of the class. Such a strategy meant that, from the outset, a large number of sources of competing control would prompt alternative staff behaviours (e.g., toileting, drinks, staff tea-break) which would compete with individual work with Shirley. The fact that the programme continued in operation as long as it did suggests that staff must have found the reduction in Shirley's self-injury produced by the intervention powerfully reinforcing.

The repertoire of recording and monitoring Shirley's behaviour was developed solely by the visiting student. Although the teacher took over this task after several weeks, it remained an isolated repertoire—out of context with the routine of the class and the rest of the teacher's activities. Despite nominal attempts to shift responsibility to the teacher, functional control of the intervention was always likely to remain invested in the behaviour of the student. When the student's involvement began to reduce and become unpredictable, pre-existing repertoires for dealing with Shirley's self-injury (under the control of continuing features of the environment) consequently re-emerged.

The likelihood of sustainable change in the manner of dealing with Shirley's self-injury would have been increased if the repertoire involved was clearly under the functional control of permanent features of the environment. An individual teaching session—which is often difficult to sustain regularly within service environments—was not the ideal medium for providing Shirley with attention contingent on desisting from self-injury. Taking the class register, serving drinks or food, preparing children for return home or any other aspect of classroom routine could have been used instead as a reliable basis for spending extra time with Shirley in the required manner.

Attempts could also have been made to identify more precisely what aspects of Shirley's behaviour the teacher, and other classroom staff, found rewarding. If interaction with Shirley was a potent reinforcer, for example, the intervention could have taken advantage of this by encouraging frequent, incidental interaction with Shirley whenever she was not engaged in self-injurious behaviour. Such an informal—less programmatic—approach would have a far greater likelihood of remaining a quasi-permanent feature of class routine, with little grounds for supposing diminished efficacy in terms of control of self-injury.

Woodlands Social Education Centre

It is apparent that at Woodlands SEC it was participation in a research evaluation which exerted control over the room management repertoire. What was needed was some means of shifting control onto permanent features of the environment—essentially 'institutionalizing' the procedure. As external interest proved a powerful reinforcer for staff, there is the possibility that some similar contingency already operating within the environment could have been made use of. If the Day Services Manager of the Local Authority had paid regular visits to the centre for other purposes, for example, such visits could perhaps have been used successfully as a time for reviewing progress in the levels of engagement attained with clients. However, reliance on external personnel in the above manner—even if their involvement is long term—is not an ideal strategy. Ultimately, if room management is to become a regular feature of the centre's work, those who engage in it must find it reinforcing. It would perhaps have been appropriate, therefore, for the centre manager to look into such issues as incentive payments, promotion, etc., for staff taking on more demanding responsibilities. Once the benefits of adherence to room management clearly outweighed the costs it would become a far more sustainable repertoire.

The design of service systems

In circumstances where a new service is to be developed, the prerequisites of sustainable change identified in Table 15.1 could be used as a set of design criteria for ensuring the encouragement of innovation and adaptive change. Adopting such principles would influence not only client care and treatment practices but also the design of work practices, conditions of service, methods of staff supervision, managerial structure, etc.

In such an ideal service, staff would receive tangible rewards for appropriate behaviour. This might include financial benefits, as discussed in the example above, but supervisor praise and feedback also constitute potentially effective reinforcers (Cullen, 1988). Work practices would allow for such reinforcement to be scheduled with appropriate reliability and frequency. The availability of such reinforcers would be an integral part of the service structure, such that benefits accrue naturally to staff attaining desired work goals.

Such a service would be stable, allowing for the development of staff competence without perpetual disruption. Structures and practices which encourage inappropriate behaviour (perhaps dehumanization of clients or low levels of staff–client interaction) would be abandoned. Change and innovation would be encouraged to grow out of existing repertoires, and not be externally imposed. Functional control of change would then be focused within the service environment itself.

Seldom, however, does service planning proceed with such a 'clean slate', and few services have the resources at their disposal to create the sort of service environment described above. Nonetheless, an awareness of the sort of service structure commended by the above analysis may be of value in attempts to facilitate organizational change within services, particularly to the extent that it can set an agenda for service development.

Participation

'Participation' is frequently commended as a means of establishing sustainable change (Batchelor, 1981; Askew, 1989). Along with other terms such as 'needs-led planning' and 'bottom-up decision-making' (Praill and Baldwin, 1988), it has come to be used as a touchstone for effecting lasting change within behavioural systems. Relating such concepts to a behavioural framework, it is interesting briefly to reflect on their congruence with the identified prerequisites for sustainable change.

Involving those directly influenced by a service in its development has several consequences. Service users are put in a position to articulate their needs and this maximizes the probability that service outcomes will be functional reinforcers for them. The scheduling of such reinforcers is likely to be adaptive to the extent that users are given effective means of control over the behaviour of service providers. Service users can then exert pressure on the service if expected benefits are not forthcoming. It is worth noting that such a sophisticated counter-control mechanism (see Blackman, 1980) will only operate if 'participation' is genuine, that is, it involves real accountability of the service to users.

Participation also increases the probability that developments will involve the elaboration of existing repertoires rather than establishment of novel ones. This, in turn, maximizes the likelihood of the functional control of behaviour change being exerted by permanent features of (or personnel in) the environment. Participation thus creates both consequent and antecedent conditions conducive to the sustainability of change.

CONCLUSION

Clients are poorly served by services which fail to create lasting change in behaviour. Effective intervention requires that changes brought about should have a durable influence on a client's lifestyle. Work in the fields of generalization programming and ecological analysis points to the value of a better understanding of the manner in which environments act to encourage or discourage the maintenance of change. The concept of sustainability draws attention to the fact that certain resources are necessary in an environment if changes in behaviour are to continue. Behavioural analysis of service environments, in terms of operating antecedent and consequent conditions, promises to be a particularly useful approach in this regard. Such analysis may assist the development of intervention strategies which increase the probability of delivering sustainable change. These strategies will often involve less programmatic intervention methods, attempting to build upon existing repertoires rather than to instate novel ones. Although such methods may be less potent in the short term, in the longer term they are likely to prove more effective in establishing truly lasting change.

The principles developed from such an analysis may also be of value in the more general task of service design. Work practices, conditions of service, methods of staff supervision, etc., all influence the extent to which a service encourages innovation and change, and may be designed to foster explicitly such a service environment. Finally, the present analysis gives insight into the value of 'participation' and related concepts in encouraging appropriate service developments.

Acknowledgements

I gratefully acknowledge the comments of Derek Blackman, Chris Cullen and Gerry Evans on a draft version of this chapter.

Address for correspondence

Alastair Ager, Department of Psychology, Chancellor College, University of Malawi, Box 280, Zomba, Malawi.

REFERENCES

Ager, A.K. (1987) Minimal intervention: A strategy for generalized behaviour change with mentally handicapped individuals. *Behavioural Psychotherapy*, **15**, 16–30.

Ager, A.K. (1989) *The Use of the Psion Organiser as an Intellectual Prosthesis for People with Severe Mental Handicaps*. Mental Handicap Research Group Report, Department of Psychology, University of Leicester, Leicester.

Ager, A.K. (1990) Planning Sustainable Services: Principles for the Effective Targetting of Resources in Developed and Developing Nations. In W.I. Fraser (ed.), *Key Issues in Mental Retardation Research* (pp. 385–394), Routledge, London.

Ager, A.K. (1991) Mental handicap. In W. Dryden and R. Rentoul (eds), *Adult Clinical Problems: A Cognitive-Behavioural Approach* (pp. 232–254), Routledge, London.

Askew, I. (1989) Organizing community participation in family planning projects in South Asia. *Studies in Family Planning*, **20**, 185–202.

Baer, D.M. (1974) A note on the absence of Santa Claus in any known ecosystem: A rejoinder to Willems. *Journal of Applied Behavior Analysis*, **7**, 167–170.

Baer, D.M. and Wolf, M.M. (1970) The entry into natural communities of reinforcement. In R. Ulrich, T. Stachnik and J. Mabry (eds), *Control of Human Behavior, Volume Two: From Care to Prevention* (pp. 319–324), Scott Foresman, Glenview, Illinois.

Bandura, A. (1969) *Principles of Behavior Modification*, Holt, New York.

Batchelor, P. (1981) *People in Rural Development*, Paternoster, Exeter.

Baum, W.C. and Tolbert, S.M. (1985) *Investing in Development: Lessons of World Bank Experience*, Oxford University Press/World Bank, New York.

Blackman, D.E. (1980) Images of man in contemporary behaviourism. In A.J. Chapman and D.M. Jones (eds), *Models of Man* (pp. 99–112), BPS, Leicester.

Carr, E.G. (1988) Functional equivalence as a mechanism of response generaliz-
ation. In R.H. Horner, G. Dunlap and R.L. Koegel (eds), *Generalization and
Maintenance: Life-style Changes in Applied Settings* (pp. 221–242), Brookes,
Baltimore.

Clarke, A.M. and Clarke, A.D.B. (1980) Jack Tizard 1919–1979. *Journal of Child
Psychology and Psychiatry*, **21**, 1–4.

Commonwealth Heads of Government (1989) *The Langkawi Declaration on
Environment*, Commonwealth Secretariat, London.

Cullen, C. (1985) Working with groups of mentally handicapped adults. In F.N.
Watts (ed.), *New Developments in Clinical Psychology* (pp. 84–95), BPS/Wiley,
Chichester.

Cullen, C. (1988) A review of staff training: the emperor's old clothes. *Irish Journal
of Psychology*, **9**, 309–323.

Derham, M. (1988) The right kind of development. *TEAR Times*, **39**, 4–6.

Evans, G., Todd, S., Blunden, R., Porterfield, J. and Ager, A. (1987) Evaluating
the impact of a move to ordinary housing. *British Journal of Mental Subnormality*,
33, 10–18.

Favell, J.H. and Reid, D.H. (1988) Generalizing and maintaining improvement in
problem behavior. In R.H. Horner, G. Dunlap and R.L. Koegel (eds),
Generalization and Maintenance: Life-style Changes in Applied Settings
(pp. 171–196), Brookes, Baltimore.

Fawcett, S.B., Mathews, R.M. and Fletcher, R.K. (1980) Some promising dimensions
for behavioral community technology. *Journal of Applied Behavior Analysis*, **13**,
505–518.

Felce, D., Saxby, H., de Kock, U., Repp, A., Ager, A. and Blunden, R. (1987) To
what behaviors do attending adults respond? A replication. *American Journal
of Mental Deficiency*, **91**, 496–504.

Forehand, R. and Atkeson, T.M. (1978) Generalization of treatment effects with
parents as therapists: A review of assessment and implementation procedures.
Behavior Therapy, **3**, 575–598.

Georgiades, N.J. and Phillimore, L. (1975) The myth of the hero-innovator and
alternative strategies for organizational change. In C.C. Kiernan and F.P.
Woodford (eds), *Behavior Modification with the Severely Retarded*. Associated
Scientific Publishers, Amsterdam.

Grant, J.P. (1989) *The State of the World's Children 1989*, Oxford University
Press/UNICEF, Oxford.

Hall, J.N. (1979) Maintaining change in long-stay wards. *Apex: Journal of the
British Institute of Mental Handicap*, **7**, 4–6.

Hersen, M. and Barlow, D.H. (1976) *Single Case Experimental Designs: Strategies
for Studying Behavior Change*, Pergamon, New York.

Horner, R.H. and Billingsley, F.F. (1988) The effect of competing behavior on the
generalization and maintenance of adaptive behavior in applied settings. In
R.H. Horner, G. Dunlap and R.L. Koegel (eds), *Generalization and Maintenance:
Life-style Changes in Applied Settings* (pp. 197–220), Brookes, Baltimore.

Horner, R.H., Dunlap, G. and Koegel, R.L. (1988) *Generalization and Maintenance:
Life-style Changes in Applied Settings*, Brookes, Baltimore.

Kiernan, C.C. (1978) Behaviour modification. In A.M. Clarke and A.D.B. Clarke
(eds), *Readings from Mental Deficiency: The Changing Outlook* (3rd edn,
pp. 382–456), Methuen, London.

Partridge, K., Chisholm, N. and Levy, B. (1985) Generalization and maintenance
of ward programmes. *Mental Handicap*, **13**, 26–29.

Praill, T. and Baldwin, S. (1988) Beyond hero innovation: Real change in unreal
systems. *Behavioural Psychotherapy*, **16**, 1–14.

Ray, B.A. and Sidman, M. (1970) Reinforcement schedules and stimulus control. In W.N. Schoenfield (ed.), *The Theory of Reinforcement Schedules* (pp. 187–214), Appleton–Century–Crofts, New York.

Redd, W.H. and Birnbrauer, J.S. (1969) Adults as discriminative stimuli for different reinforcement contingencies with retarded children. *Journal of Experimental Child Psychology*, **7**, 440–447.

Reppucci, N.D. (1973) Social psychology of institutional change: General principles for intervention. *American Journal of Community Psychology*, **1**, 330–341.

Rincover, A. (1981) Some directions for analysis and intervention in developmental disabilities: An editorial. *Analysis and Intervention in Developmental Disabilities*, **1**, 109–115.

Saxby, H., Felce, D., Harman, M. and Repp, A. (1988) The maintenance of client activity and staff–client interaction in small community houses for severely handicapped adults: A two-year follow-up. *Behavioural Psychotherapy*, **16**, 189–206.

Schoen, S.F. (1986) Assistance procedures to facilitate the transfer of stimulus control: Review and anlaysis. *Education and Training of the Mentally Retarded*, **21**, 62–74.

Sidman, M. (1978) Remarks. *Behaviorism*, **6**, 265–268.

Sidman, M. (1979) Remarks. *Behaviorism*, **7**, 123–126.

Skinner, B.F. (1953) *Science and Human Behavior*, Macmillan, New York.

Skinner, B.F. (1969) *Contingencies of Reinforcement*, Appleton–Century–Crofts, New York.

Skinner, B.F. (1974) *About Behaviorism*, Knopf, New York.

Stokes, T.F. and Baer, D.M. (1977) An implicit technology of generalization. *Journal of Applied Behavior Analysis*, **10**, 349–367.

Stokes, T.F. and Osnes, R.G. (1986) Programming the generalization of children's social behavior. In P.S. Strain, M. Guralnick and H. Walker (eds), *Children's Social Behavior: Development, Assessment and Modification* (pp. 407–443), Academic Press, Orlando.

Stokes, T.F. and Osnes, P.G. (1988) The developing applied technology of generalization and maintenance. In R.H. Horner, G. Dunlap and R.L. Koegel (eds), *Generalization and Maintenance: Life-style Changes in Applied Settings* (pp. 5–20), Brookes, Baltimore.

Stolz, S.B. (1981) Adoption of innovations from applied behavioral research: 'Does anybody care?' *Journal of Applied Behavior Analysis*, **19**, 125–135.

Tennant, L., Cullen, C. and Hattersley, J. (1981) Applied behavioural analysis: Intervention with retarded people. In G.C.L. Davey (ed.), *Applications of Conditioning Theory*, Methuen, London.

Wahler, R.G. (1980) The insular mother: Her problems in parent–child treatment. *Journal of Applied Behavior Analysis*, **13**, 207–220.

Wahler, R.G. and Fox, J.J. (1981) Setting events in applied behavior analysis: Toward a conceptual and methodological expansion. *Journal of Applied Behavior Analysis*, **14**, 327–338.

Willems, E.P. (1974) Behavioral technology and behavioral ecology. *Journal of Applied Behavior Analysis*, **3**, 131–160.

Williams, J., Koegel, R. and Egel, A. (1981) Response–reinforcer relationships and improved learning in autistic children. *Journal of Applied Behavior Analysis*, **14**, 53–60.

Woods, P.A. and Cullen, C. (1983) Determinants of staff behaviour in long-term care. *Behavioural Psychotherapy*, **11**, 4–17.

Chapter 16

Professional Ethics: Behaviour Analysis and Normalization

CHRIS KIERNAN

INTRODUCTION

The last quarter of a century has seen massive changes in attitudes toward people with severe and profound mental handicap. These changes have been significantly fostered by the development of techniques based on applied behaviour analysis. In both the UK and USA the move was begun by liberal humanists concerned with, and sometimes appalled by, prevailing institutional conditions. In the UK pioneers like Tizard and the Clarkes were able to demonstrate that changing living conditions, and offering humane care and teaching, could lead to significant behavioural development. The Brooklands project showed that children with mental handicap responded well to normal child care practices. The Clarkes showed that institutionalized adults could learn useful work skills. These, and other, demonstration projects quite literally inspired parents and carers working with people with mental handicap.

Why was such inspiration necessary? The explanation lay in the incredible pessimism of professionals concerning the developmental potential of people with mental handicap. The general attitude was that those with severe and profound disabilities could not learn. The implication of this was that there was no point in wasting valuable resources in trying to teach them, and that all that could be offered was 'care'. The fact that such care was typically provided in impoverished institutional environments meant, however, that it was often not possible to deliver it humanely. Setting aside deliberate cruelty, the best that could be expected was benign neglect.

These conditions and attitudes provided the backdrop for the reception of techniques derived from applied behaviour analysis. Professionals

The Challenge of Severe Mental Handicap. Edited by Bob Remington
© 1991 John Wiley & Sons Ltd

prepared to work with people with severe and profound disabilities were rare; those who could teach meaningful skills were even rarer. They were usually welcomed and given a free hand to do what they could. Until then, any question of children or adults with mental handicap having rights to education or to effective treatment of problem behaviour had been irrelevant; with 'behaviour modification' came the promise that both goals could be achieved.

BEHAVIOURAL INTERVENTION AS A CONTENTLESS TECHNOLOGY

In a seminal article on the application of applied behaviour analysis to mental handicap, Bijou (1966) argued that the central problem in mental handicap was failure to learn or anomalous learning. Biological, sociological and other factors could affect the form which this failure might take, but learning was prime. However, functional analyses could identify factors currently controlling behaviour, task analysis could provide the structure for new behaviours to be taught, and the techniques of operant conditioning could facilitate learning. The optimistic promise of behavioural work was that, with the earliest possible intervention, and the specification of appropriate goals, the child who was potentially mentally handicapped could be 'cured'.

Most behavioural interventionists viewed their procedures as tools with which behaviour could be changed. In essence, they saw their approach as contentless in terms of specifying which behaviours should be modified. Programmes were therefore based on a variety of foundations. Researchers working with children often turned to literature on child development to provide a structure for intervention, (e.g., Bricker, 1972), or to early academic skills (O'Leary, 1972). Self-help and vocational skills, (e.g, Budde and Menolascino, 1971) were also early goals for intervention.

There is no doubt that, directly and indirectly, the use of behavioural techniques has brought considerable benefit to people with mental handicap. Successive reviews of the literature have shown increases in the range and effectiveness of application (e.g., Kiernan, 1985). Less directly, the influence of behavioural methods can be seen in the professional practice and more positive general orientation of teachers, nurses and others working in the field, none of whom would now agree with the once dominant belief that people with mental handicap cannot learn.

But the power of behavioural techniques also led to less desirable applications. Behavioural interventionists working in institutions felt pressured to 'help the staff do their jobs more effectively'. If, in large overcrowded, understaffed, institutions those jobs were essentially defined as keeping order, the technology could be turned to this end. At the extreme, in North America, this approach led to the introduction of the infamous cattle-prod. The development of token economies can be seen similarly. On a ward with a large number of residents and high staff turnover, tracking of individual programmes and contingencies is virtually impossible. The token system promised an ideal solution. Once the principle of agreed 'payments' for specified performances was grasped, any new member of staff could operate the system. However, token economies not infrequently became settings in which behaviour was simply controlled and in which human contact was effectively lacking. Tizard (1975, p. 258) describes 'bored and cynical behaviour technicians ... giving tokens to bored and cynical patients'. Earlier, Winnett and Winkler (1972) had similarly criticized token economies in schools for doing no more than keeping children seated, quiet, and compliant. Risley (1975) also reported finding applications of behavioural techniques which he saw as inappropriate and unethical.

There are several reasons why behaviour modification was 'misapplied'. The central proposition of applied behaviour analysis, that behaviours are occasioned by antecedents and supported by reinforcers, places the burden for changing behaviour on the people with whom a client interacts throughout his or her waking life—relatives, educators, residential and day-care workers. It proved to be a relatively easy task to teach the fundamentals of behaviour modification to these 'front-line' personnel, and techniques were 'given away' with what seems with hindsight to have been incautious enthusiasm. Moreover, the essentially technological orientation of many early behavioural interventionists led them to make naive assumptions about the belief and value systems of those to whom they were disseminating their techniques, a minority of whom clearly believed that the competence of people with mental handicap could not be expanded, or was not worth expanding. Some carers saw their primary job as controlling the injurious or self-injurious behaviour sometimes exhibited by institutional residents, since such problem behaviour might reduce the quality of the life of others, and create stressful working conditions. This was a sure recipe for the use of behavioural techniques in ways which the vast majority of their originators would have rejected on ethical grounds. However, having effectively disseminated the techniques, they were powerless to intervene.

THE RISE OF NORMALIZATION

It is probably fair to say that, until the development of the philosophy of normalization, service providers in the mental handicap field lacked a clear positive philosophy. Care and compassion, informed by liberal humanism, said a great deal about attitudes and general action, but little about where people with severe and profound mental handicap should live and what they should be able to do with their lives. Early Scandinavian formulations of normalization argued that the living conditions should be brought close to what was 'normal' in terms of their housing, education, work, and leisure, and that people with mental handicap should be given the same legal and human rights as other citizens (Bank-Mikkelson, 1980; Nirje, 1969). The philosophy envisaged a lifestyle with a normal rhythm to the day, week, and year; self-determination, the development of heterosexual relations and equal economic and environmental standards. However, as Emerson (1990) points out, these early formulations did not propose an approach to service design incompatible with segregation. The 'standards for physical facilities like schools, work settings, group homes and boarding houses [were to] be modelled on those available in society for ordinary citizens' (Nirje, 1980, p. 44). The approach, when realized in the UK, was largely reflected in the design of segregated services (Gunzberg, 1970; Gunzberg and Gunzberg, 1987).

Wolfensberger's initial definition of normalization emphasized the need to establish and maintain 'personal behaviours and characteristics which are as culturally normative as possible', using means as 'culturally normative as possible' (Wolfensberger, 1972, p. 28). On the face of it, there is no conflict between Wolfensberger's proposed goals and the use of behaviour intervention, in that the technology was a refinement and systematic application of ways in which people taught and learned. Later formulations added two further considerations. The first was an essentially sociological construction of deviancy. People with mental handicap were so defined because impairments or disabilities led them to be seen as unable to fill the roles that are normal, depending on age, sex, and social and cultural values. Wolfensberger's second consideration involved replacing the term 'normalization' with 'social role valorization', which he saw as the central element of normalization. People with mental handicap are 'devalued citizens' who should be given 'valued social roles'. The first job of services is to prevent such devalued roles as 'subhuman organism', 'holy innocent' or 'eternal child', being ascribed in the first instance. Ascribing these roles, he argued, encouraged people to live up to them. Service providers and the public also need to learn what 'gifts' people with mental handicap can give (Wolfensberger, 1983). The notion of a 'gift system' has a substantial history (e.g., Hamblin *et al.*, 1971) and is a crucial element in the working of the French L'Arche community. Shearer (1974), writing about L'Arche, suggested that finding 'ways of accepting what receivers of care have to offer is one of our most urgent tasks'. Rather than seeing people with mental handicap as 'deviant' and thereby devaluing them, their particular qualities need to be recognized and rejoiced.

In the UK, Wolfensberger's views have been interpreted mainly through the work of the Community and Mental Handicap Education and Research Association (CMHERA). O'Brien's formulation of normalization has become particularly influential (O'Brien, 1987; O'Brien and Tyne, 1981). As Emerson (1990) notes, O'Brien's interpretation differs from Wolfensberger's in emphasis and style rather than in the practical interpretation of theory. Reflecting Wolfensberger's social role valorization, O'Brien (1987) lists five major service accomplishments: presence and participation in the community, developing competence and supporting people with mental handicap in making choices, and enhancing respect for people with mental handicap as full citizens. The formulation places individual choice in a central position in normalization theory.

Overall, within the UK, training within the normalization framework has increasingly included an emphasis on value and respect for people with mental handicap. Training experiences are now designed to encourage professionals to see and feel what it is like to be a person with mental handicap. Techniques such as 'gentle teaching' (McGee, Menousek and Hobbs, 1987) which promote the values of 'gentleness, respect and solidarity with the person with mental handicap' appear to be gaining increasing support, despite lack of clear empirical backing (see below). Their attraction lies, at least in part, in a perceived consistency with normalization philosophy.

These developments, signalled by Wolfensberger's formulation of social role valorization, appear to have crystallized 'differences' between normalization and behavioural intervention. An increasing volume of comment rejects the use of behavioural techniques as inherently controlling and inhumane. This rejection is in some cases total, and in others restricted to 'aversive techniques'. In subsequent sections of this Chapter I will suggest that these differences are complex and are often based on confusions and misperceptions. In order to set the stage for this analysis a useful starting point seems to be a general consideration of the ethics of professional practice.

A FRAMEWORK OF PROFESSIONAL ETHICS

Beneficence and autonomy

It is important to consider two central principles in medical ethics: beneficence and autonomy. Beneficence requires that 'one should help others further important and legitimate interests and abstain from injuring them' (Beauchamp and McCullogh, 1984, p. 27). The principle demands that, for any course of action that is proposed, the resulting 'goods' and 'harms' should be assessed, and the chosen course should be the one which results in the maximum good and minimum harm to the individual. Short-term harms, such as injuring a person by operating on them, can be outweighed by the long-term good of removing a diseased organ that will cause early death. A different principle, that of autonomy, argues that other people should be regarded as rightly self-governing, and therefore that their best interests should be interpreted exclusively from their perspective. Although derived in the context of medicine, principles of beneficence and autonomy are clearly applicable in the context of any service framework. However, the two concepts are not necessarily in harmony. If a person refuses an operation, beneficence would lead a physician to do everything possible to persuade the patient. It might, at the (ethically unacceptable) extreme, lead to the physician coercing a patient into surgery. Autonomy, with its central respect for self-determination, would dictate that—once the consequences of each action were explained—the physician would accept the person's right to choose.

The principles of beneficence and autonomy also apply to third parties. In deciding on the advice to give parents of a severely impaired newborn, a paediatrician would need to take into account the goods and harms which may result for the family, as well as those accruing to the child. In the case of decisions regarding treatment of people with mental handicap and problem behaviour, similar issues arise for service providers. The harms and goods for other people with mental handicap who live with them would need to be taken into account. A person who screams continuously is clearly creating harm by reducing the quality of life of others: removing the person who is screaming to a less desirable setting may harm that person but bring relief to others. Similarly, other third parties, such as relatives and care staff, have to be included in the equation. Contemporary 'good practice' suggests that parents of people with mental handicap living in the family home should be encouraged to 'let go'. It is argued that the short-term goods which parents may experience in terms of enjoyment of the company of their son or daughter, and their peace of mind in knowing that he or she is safe and well looked after, have to be balanced by long-term harms. These include restriction of their son or daughter's independence, even if he or she does not see it that way, and avoidance of the trauma of bereavement and separation when parents die and their son or daughter has to leave the family home. In the case of people with mental handicap and problem behaviour, direct harms to parents in the form of physical injury, anxiety, and restriction of opportunities may be more dramatic (Qureshi, 1990). Similar considerations apply to care staff, whose work with problem behaviour can result in stress and physical injury. The psychiatrist faced with requests for medication to control such behaviour has to balance the needs of staff, and their duty to protect other residents, against the needs of the person showing the behaviour.

Beneficence, autonomy and competence

Beauchamp and McCullough argue that a decision is autonomous if it 'derives from the person's own values and beliefs', is 'based on adequate information and understanding' and if it is 'not determined by internal or external constraints that compel the decision' (1984, p. 44). Clearly, people with severe or profound mental handicap would not be considered able to make autonomous decisions about critical aspects of their lives. In technical parlance they would be deemed 'incompetent'. Tests of competence include (1) the ability to indicate a choice, (2) the ability to give a reason for that choice, (3) evidence that the reason given is rational, and that if so (4) it is based on analysis of risks and benefits. Other tests refer to the individual's understanding in making the decision, in relation (5) to the situation and (6) to the information given. A final test (7) concerns whether the decision is reasonable, as judged by a 'reasonable person' (Beauchamp and McCullough, 1984). Although these tests are offered in relation to competence to judge medical interventions, they can equally well be applied in the context of decisions about personal lifestyles and particular interventions to manage problem behaviour.

Judgements about the competence in decision-making by people with mental handicap on these criteria are clearly fraught with problems. Those with mild disability, especially if they have been institutionalized, may display the sort of compliance described by Balla and Zigler (1979). People with limited language may be restricted in their ability to indicate limited choices in immediate situations. In many cases preference for alternatives, such as different residential locations, will have to be inferred from behaviour. However, here, the implication that acting on such an inference reflects autonomous decision-making stretches the concept too far, rendering it almost meaningless.

Paternalism and problem behaviour

Problems of assessing competence are never more clearly apparent than in dealing with problem behaviour. Given a 'free choice' it is not uncommon to find people with severe or profound mental handicap spending their days pacing or rocking, and, in general, avoiding all social contact. Such behaviours are not simply confined to people who have been raised, or are resident in, segregated facilities. In terms of beneficence, these activities are likely to adversely affect general development, and diminish interaction with others, frustrating the development of natural relationships. Normal professional practice would lead service providers to try to reduce stereotyped behaviour, to encourage engagement with 'meaningful' tasks, and to encourage social interaction. Similarly, if an individual aggresses against others and is thereby rejected by them, intervention to reduce this behaviour would be justified on the grounds that his or her life would be improved if positive relationships with others could be developed. Under these circumstances, service providers would be operating at least to some degree 'paternalistically'. Paternalism, in Beauchamp and McCullough's terms, is the intentional limitation of autonomy, where the person who limits autonomy appeals exclusively to grounds of beneficence for the person whose autonomy is limited.

But there are degrees of paternalism. 'Weak' paternalism would involve the argument that the person cannot make an autonomous decision and that it is therefore justifiable to override any apparent wishes. In the two instances just described, service providers might argue that the people concerned cannot understand (are not competent to judge) that their long-term good would be better served by engaging in meaningful activities and developing positive social relationships. In contrast, 'strong' paternalism involves overriding both the non-autonomous and autonomous decisions of people with mental handicap. For example, the service provider who insists that a young woman should not be allowed to travel on public transport, despite her wish to do so, on the grounds that she might be assaulted, would be overriding an autonomous choice. This would hold even if there had been instances of assault, provided that the young woman knew this and knew what it meant. In the example of the person who attacks others, it may be that he can 'justify' his attacks on the basis that he does not like other people, and that he does not care if other people reject him. Given this evidence of autonomous choice, persisting with an intervention designed to 'show him that other people are really OK' may involve strong paternalism.

As already noted, the needs of third parties have to be balanced with the needs of the particular individual. Stereotypy and social withdrawal may be distressing to parents and other professionals. Decisions on interventions with a person who attacks others will need to take into account the effect of aggression on them. An intervention that involves removing the 'aggressor' to a less desirable setting may be justified on the grounds that, in taking others' safety into account, the overall balance of goods and harms favours that course of action. Likewise, parents might find self-injury extremely disturbing and sanction or encourage any measures, however much they appear to limit autonomy.

Professional ethics and virtues

The system of professional ethics described requires certain personal qualities of practitioners. Beauchamp and McCullough (1984) argue that these include truthfulness, compassion, and sympathy. Sympathy is seen as allowing practitioners to put themselves in the place of others, to feel what they feel, and thus become sensitive to their circumstances. Sympathy helps to ensure that practitioners act in other people's best interests. Clearly, truthfulness and sympathy are essential qualities, but special problems again arise in work with people with severe and profound mental handicap. In particular, there are difficulties in 'feeling what the other person is feeling'. I will suggest later that concerns about behavioural intervention arise from differing interpretations of what it means to act with sympathy in this context.

Ethical considerations: A summary

The general arguments presented in the previous section can be summarized as follows. The professional ethics governing the behaviour of people working with those with mental handicap should further their legitimate interests and not cause them harm (beneficence). Beneficence is ensured at least in part by the virtue of sympathy. On the other hand, the best interests of people should be viewed from their perspective as assessed from what they say (autonomy). However, restrictions in the competence of people with mental handicap to make autonomous decisions could justify ignoring their perspective, and extending benefi- cence at risk of being paternalistic. In the case of people with mental handicap and problem behaviour, paternalism, at some level, appears to be inevitable. In addition, in determining courses of action, professionals have to take into account the interests and perspectives of third parties, relatives and other caregivers, as well as clients themselves. Especially in the case of problem behaviour, taking account of third parties may lead professionals to behave in ways that limit their ability to operate the principles of beneficence and autonomy with the person whose behaviour is problematic. The overall balance of goods and harms may weigh against the person with problem behaviour.

ETHICS AND NORMALIZATION

How well does the framework of ethics just described mesh with normalization philosophy? Clearly, some of the 'service accomplishments' outlined by O'Brien (1987) are compatible with the analysis. In particular, developing the overall competence of people with mental handicap is an aspect of beneficence. At a simple level, supporting people with mental handicap in making choices appears to fit well with the principle of autonomy. Here, however, conflict arises because normalization philosophy appears to contain neither clear statements concerning the assessment of competence to make autonomous decisions, nor a discussion of ways in which to balance autonomy with the requirement to develop general competence. As argued above, judging the competence of people with severe and profound disability to make autonomous decisions is difficult and, given this, it is not clear how service providers should behave when a person takes an 'autonomous' decision to stay in bed all day and avoid activities which would enhance general competence. In line with the duty of supporting choices, exponents of normalization would explain the importance of the decision for future well-being, and ensure that other possible alternatives are offered. However, if the person holds adamantly to the original decision, would staff conclude that he or she was not competent (possibly on the grounds that the decision was not reasonable as judged by a 'reasonable person')? Should they override the decision by some means and behave in a paternalistic way? This issue of competence to make autonomous decisions is by no means easily resolved. It is certainly not uncommon to find service providers who argue, on the basis of their interpretation of normalization, that stereotyped or self-injurious behaviours should go unchecked since the people concerned have 'chosen' to behave in this way.

The service accomplishments of presence and participation in the community emerge in normalization as absolute rights. The philosophy states that the harms of segregation outweigh the harms of integration (and vice versa for goods). However, those propositions relate only in the loosest way to empirical evidence. It would seem that if, in individual cases, it was demonstrated that segregation was less harmful and more beneficial, such evidence would be dismissed as reflecting poor integrated provision. Paradoxically, it thus seems likely that there will be instances of 'strong' paternalism in, for example, relocating from segregated to integrated settings, despite the autonomously expressed wishes of individuals. Normalization philosophy may generate its own internal contradictions.

The remaining service accomplishment, enhancing respect, implies clear professional duties. These would include, at a personal level, honesty, the willingness to listen and to emphasize the person's strengths, as well as the duty to encourage others to behave similarly. Wolfensberger (1983) has emphasized these points in arguing that people with mental handicap have 'common assets' such as 'heart qualities' (the ability to 'give life and warmth' and to 'recognize another person and his or her needs'), natural spontaneity, responsiveness to kindly human contact, and the ability to relate to other people as people.

Respect is surely related to the virtue of sympathy, and this leads us back to the issue of assessment of competence for autonomous decision-making. It has been argued that, through cultural conditioning, we do not listen to people with mental handicap and consequently underestimate their abilities. In Williams' (1975) terms, non-handicapped people show widespread incompetence in relation to handicapped people—it is the former, not the latter, who require social training to enhance their competence. Perhaps, if we were better listeners, we would realize that people with mental handicap were more competent decision-makers than we initially believed. This emphasis on our incompetence may explain, in part at least, the failure clearly to articulate issues surrounding competence. However, the emphasis on respecting competence can overbalance if the focus shifts from eliciting and understanding the views of people with mental handicap to imagining 'how it must feel' to be a person with profound and multiple disabilities. The danger of slipping into fantasy concerning thoughts and feelings which are essentially unknowable is here substantial.

PROFESSIONAL ETHICS AND BEHAVIOURAL TREATMENT

I argued earlier that one of the 'mistakes' which behavioural intervention-ists made in the 1970s was to be over-enthusiastic in disseminating behavioural methods. They failed to ensure that the people to whom they disseminated techniques were operating an acceptable framework of professional ethics. However, it would be naive to assume that all interventionists were ethical in their use of techniques within the ethical model described here. Aside from all other factors, the model does contain the element of weighing the goods and harms to the individual and those created for third parties. It seems very likely that, in making treatment decisions, a lack of clear emphasis on the rights and worth of people with mental handicap and problem behaviour led to the over-use of time out, over-correction, or punishment.

Controversies about the use of behavioural methods since the 1970s have led to a plethora of reports and sets of prescriptive guidelines. Most recently, a group of eminent workers in the field (Van Houten *et al.*, 1988) has drafted a position statement under the title 'The right to effective behavioural treatment'. This summarizes what may be seen as the current ethic of behavioural treatment. In the context of the ethical model described in the previous section, it is worth examining Van Houten *et al.*'s statement in some detail to identify the important similarities and differences between it and normalization philosophy.

Van Houten and his colleagues argue that an individual has a right to a therapeutic environment; a physical and social environment which is safe, humane, and responsive to human needs is a prerequisite to effective treatment. Activities and materials should be responsive to client preferences and mediated by parents, teachers, and staff who are competent, sensitive, and caring. The environment should impose the fewest restrictions possible whilst ensuring individual safety and development. However, Van Houten *et al.* emphasize that 'freedom of individual movement and access to preferred activities, rather than type or location of placements, are the defining characteristics of a least restrictive environment' (1988, p. 382).

The statement thus envisages conflict between ideologically based decisions on living environments, and the right to choice within environments designed to promote development. However, this argument certainly does not amount to a rejection of the goal of integration. Van Houten *et al.* later emphasize that 'unless clear evidence exists to the contrary, an individual is assumed capable of full participation in all aspects of community life and to have a right to such participation' (1988, p. 383). They argue that the primary purpose of behavioural treatment is to assist in the acquisition of functional skills and personal independence, and that 'the ultimate goal of all services is to increase the ability of individuals to function effectively in both their immediate environment and the larger society' (1988, p. 382). It seems clear that the position statement is arguing for the right of individuals to live, obtain education, and receive behavioural treatment where this goal can be achieved most effectively. Sometimes this may involve segregation from community settings, and if so, the statement places the rights of individuals at any given time above the rights of the group of people with mental handicap as a whole. The individual's right to treatment should not be jeopardized by principles of presence and participation. At a particular time, treatment within segregated provision may provide greater freedom of movement and access to preferred activities for some individuals than treatment within facilities located to ensure presence and participation.

The position statement emphasizes the necessity for treatment programmes to be planned, delivered, and evaluated by appropriately trained and experienced professionals. Behaviour analytic training should produce, amongst other things, a thorough knowledge of professional ethics. Van Houten *et al.* argue that where 'a problem or treatment is complex or may pose risk, individuals have a right to direct involvement by a doctoral-level behaviour analyst' to plan, direct, evaluate and follow up interventions. This recommendation has a particularly hollow ring in the UK, where the training of specialist behaviour analysts to work with people with mental handicap has never been pursued on an adequate scale, despite the fact that it was recognized as a high priority by a Department of Health Working Party over a decade ago (HMSO, 1980).

Van Houten *et al.* emphasize the entitlement of the individual to 'effective and scientifically validated treatment' (1988, p. 383). Programmes should be based on complete diagnostic evaluation. This may reveal pre-existing physiological or environmental determinants, manipulation of which may diminish the need to rely on changes in behavioural contingencies. Where behavioural intervention is necessary, Van Houten *et al.* state the 'obligation to use only those techniques that have been demonstrated by research to be effective' and 'to search continuously for the most optimal means of changing behaviour' (1988, p. 383). Treatment should be based firmly on researched procedures; 'selection of a specific treatment technique is not based on personal conviction' (1988, p. 384). Selection of techniques is, however, a matter of judging goods in terms of goal achievement, and harms in terms of restrictiveness, for each individual case. The statement argues that 'exposure of an individual to restrictive procedures is unacceptable unless it can be shown that such procedures are necessary to produce safe and clinically significant behaviour change'. However, on the other hand it is 'equally unacceptable to expose an individual to a non-restrictive intervention . . . if assessment results or available research indicate that other procedures would be more effective' (1988, p. 383). Indeed, the statement argues that a slow-acting, non-restrictive procedure could be seen as highly restrictive if it delays achievement of goals such as entering more optimal social environments.

These arguments represent a clear embodiment of the principle of beneficence. They stress the need for staff who are 'competent, responsive, and caring'; and lay emphasis on the role of committees of 'consumers, advocates, and other interested citizens' to determine the degree to which a programme ensures an individual's basic rights to dignity, privacy and humane care. In contrast to this stress on beneficence, there is no clear articulation of the principle of autonomy. Client preferences are emphasized, but only in relation to selection of materials. Access to personal possessions, social interaction and physical exercise are seen as rights, but there is no mention of the client's role in negotiating a treatment programme.

Behavioural treatments and sympathy

Although Van Houten *et al.*'s (1988) position statement fails to make clear the client's role in programme formulation, this cannot be used to suggest that the authors lack regard for client feelings. However, one of the commonest and most persistent arguments about behavioural treatments is that they are dehumanizing to staff and people with mental handicap. For example, Sumarah (1989) argues that the behavioural approach encourages or imposes a 'mechanical metaphor' in which people are seen as machines, whose interrelated parts are understandable and adjustable. Thus, Sumarah claims that staff relationships to people with mental handicap may become *I–It* relationships, in which individuals are treated as objects, rather than recognized as people, as in *I–Thou* relationships (Buber, 1958). Similarly, Lovett (1985) proposes that the use of behavioural techniques can prevent people from being seen as operating within the framework of normal human social motivation. He remarks 'when I read about "treatment programs" that do not take a person's emotional and social needs and responses into account, I feel the sense of lost opportunity' (Lovett, 1985, p. 31). Lovett does not question the empirical validity of a behavioural approach, but he stresses the necessity of 'translating and incorporating its findings into non-empirical social reality' (Lovett, 1985, p. 29).

In summary, while neither Sumarah nor Lovett see a necessary connection between adherence to behavioural principles and a lack of sympathy, both see the need for deliberate attempts to counter what they see as serious dangers in the approach.

'Agency' and functionality

Sumarah (1989) argues that two elements are necessary in what he terms a more appropriate 'personal metaphor' for working with people with mental handicap. The first is 'agency'—the tendency of human beings to engage their physical and social world (the latter principally through communication) and thereby to affect it. According to Sumarah, a sense of agency is dependent on others who promote, restrict or deny its development. Consequently, the second element of the metaphor is 'relationship'. Unlike impersonal relationships which limit the sense of agency, staff–client relationships should encourage it.

The concept of agency is at least akin to the behavioural concept of functionality. In everyday terms, functional analysis is designed to reveal the 'reasons' for particular behaviours. Skinner's (1957) analysis of verbal behaviour stressed the centrality of social aspects of language, and Guess et al. (1976) argued that programmes must 'rapidly bring children into contact with the potential of (their) speech as an effective means of controlling the environment' (p. 305). Carr (e.g., 1977) has demonstrated that problem behaviours can have a communicative function. In these and other approaches, the centrality of encouraging social effectiveness and examining 'motivation' is stressed.

These considerations suggest that the differences between behaviour analysts and their critics may be one of emphasis. Although there is no reason why behaviour analysts should not place greater emphasis on the development of relationships as a tool of therapy, by and large they have not done so. While they might well argue that the development of I–Thou relationships is a necessary condition for effective therapy, few would argue that it would be sufficient. No matter how sympathetic staff may be, they still have to act, and these actions should sensibly be guided by the use of well-developed behavioural principles. Furthermore, in dealing with problem behaviour, decisions may have to be informed by beneficence, in which case a degree of restriction of agency, or autonomy, is inevitable.

PROBLEM BEHAVIOUR AND THE AVERSIVES DEBATE

The use of aversive stimuli has, above all other aspects of behavioural work with people with mental handicap, produced the greatest controversy. This controversy has raged at several levels: technical disputes about concepts and evidence, moral disputes about human rights, and personal disputes about the moral character of people who use aversives. I will review these disputes as they surround the treatment of problem behaviour through the use of behavioural techniques.

Problem behaviour and behaviour modification

Save for the use of common-sense solutions (which may well have worked) and sedative drugs, little effective treatment for problem behaviour appears to have been offered prior to the development of behavioural techniques. With their introduction, a range of approaches including extinction, exclusionary and non-exclusionary time out, negative reinforcement and punishment, and differential reinforcement procedures (Kiernan, 1985; see also Jones, this volume) became available. More complex techniques, notably over-correction procedures, were rapidly added.

Reviews of the use of behavioural methods in modifying problem behaviour have consistently emphasized the interplay of positive and negative consequences. Kiernan (1974, p. 760) suggested that 'unless the environment or activity from which the individual is withdrawn is heavily rewarding, time out does not lead to elimination of undesirable behaviour'. Birnbrauer *et al.* (1965) suggested that 'removing a child from a classroom is effective to the extent that it is, in fact, timeout from positive reinforcement'. In the case of punishment training, Azrin and Holz (1966) concluded that lasting elimination occurred only if other, competing responses were positively reinforced. Vukelich and Hake (1971) reported a study where dangerous aggressive behaviour in a woman with severe mental handicap was reduced by time out for aggressive behaviour, and continuous positive social reinforcement for non-aggressive behaviour. Whenever this additional attention was phased out, however, aggression recurred. The authors concluded that, for people with severe mental handicap, 'positive reinforcers are frequently scarce, and they may have to be increased by staff to increase the likelihood of success of treatment programmes ... that are based on positive reinforcement'.

This body of work illustrates the clear, early awareness, at least amongst applied researchers, of the limitations on the use of 'decelerative' procedures based on time out or punishment. They led directly to the exploration of complementary or alternative methods of managing problem behaviour and to attempts to enhance the quality of environments (e.g., Horner, 1980). Analysis of the limitations of the use of aversives has continued within technical literature (Axelrod and Apsche, 1983; Hollis and Meyers, 1982; Kiernan, 1985). However, the rejection of their use has grown for several reasons. They can be summarized as relating to the confusion of common-sense and technical terminology, over-generalization of arguments based on inadequate data and, within these arguments, a failure to respect the professional integrity of others. I will consider each of these in turn.

'Aversives': Confusion of traditional and technical use of terminology

Mulick (1990) sees one powerful element in the current controversy as a confusion between ideological and scientific perspectives on the concept of punishment. He points out that ideological positions which exclude the use of aversives assume traditional concepts of punishment. Within this framework, depriving individuals of something that they want or acting in such a way as to 'hurt' them, are based, in Mulick's thesis, on the practice of reasoning from introspection about the just balance between the harm caused by the offence and the effects of punishment on the offender. He points out that these concepts relate to social ideologies and only historically and tangentially to the technical usage of the terms punishment and reinforcement.

Mulick argues that there is a critical distinction between the ideological and current scientific use of the terms. In scientific use, within behavioural theory, whether a particular stimulus acts to suppress behaviour or increase its probability depends on the individual's history. Premack (1971) demonstrated that, within an individual's repertoire, more probable acts reinforce less probable acts, and less probable acts serve to punish more probable acts when they are made contingent on them. Across time, deprivation of the opportunity to perform acts can enhance their probability. Consequently, punishment and reinforcement can only be understood relationally (see Remington, this volume). Mulick points out that, for the professional, 'the question is not whether to sanction deprivation in planning for the needs of people with handicaps, but what sort of behaviour will be supported by the inevitable transitions between deprivation and satiation'. Mulick also points out that stimuli can be reinforcers or punishers depending on context, time out may be a reward if time in is a punisher; and that, for all stimuli, there is an intensity range from reinforcing to aversive. He further draws attention to the critical issue that, although it may be possible to rank stimuli in terms of aversiveness, restrictiveness, or effectiveness as a suppressive consequence, such listings are based on introspection—personal feelings— possibly inferred from other people's feelings. Such listings are distinct from the functional reality of these events which is the proper context for scientific analysis.

'Aversives': Over-generalization of arguments based on inadequate data

Even given Mulick's strictures, the debate on the use of punishment and other techniques utilizing aversive contingencies is hampered by lack of published evidence. One central thread in this argument is that research has tended to concentrate on the use of aversives as a means of controlling problem behaviour, and neglected the development of non-aversive techniques (LaVigna and Donnellan, 1986). Removing the judgemental element from this argument, it is certainly the case that such techniques have not led to a substantial volume of published work. Lancioni and Hoogeven (1990) reviewed studies using non-aversive and mildly aversive procedures. The review covered databased reports for the previous 15 years. In all, the studies covered 164 individuals for whom, in 68 of the reported instances, (42%), target behaviour was reduced to zero or near zero, in 81 instances to 50% or less, with 15 reported failures. The failure rate was highest with differential reinforcement of other behaviour (DRO) (11 of 30 reported cases) as opposed, for example, to a zero failure rate for the next most frequently reported procedure, DRO combined with response interruption, brief restraint and/or verbal reprimand. While reinforcing the point that more research is necessary, Lancioni and Hoogeven's analysis suggests that pleas for a complete abandonment of the use of any aversive contingencies is premature on scientific grounds. As Mulick (1988) points out, the major review by proponents of non-aversive methods (LaVigna and Donnellan, 1986) relies heavily on examples based on minor problem behaviours in fairly able people.

Similar patterns exist in the other area of literature commonly cited in the controversy. Guess *et al.* (1987) reviewed data concerned with the effects of the negative reinforcement, over-correction and punishment on problem behaviour. Although claiming that studies showed these procedures to be generally effective, no comparison was made with non-aversive procedures, and the generalizability of gains was poor. Guess *et al.* also argue that the side effects of the procedures, although rarely well documented, were negative as well as positive. In practice, relatively little is known about the positive and negative side effects of positive or aversive techniques (Kiernan, 1985: see also Remington, and Scotti *et al.*, this volume). However, without a comparison with the side effects of non-aversive techniques (cf. Balsam and Bondy, 1983) little can really be concluded. This is likely to be a highly complex area. For example, a programme successful in teaching mobility may well lead to the person interacting more successfully with his physical environment but also allow him to be more effectively aggressive toward peers. As elsewhere, balancing 'goods' and 'harms' is a complex issue, with time as a critical dimension.

Lack of sound empirical evidence also hampers evaluation of particularly controversial techniques. For example, the proponents of gentle teaching (McGee, Menousek and Hobbs, 1987) have made broad statements concerning its effectiveness, but presented few interpretable data. Jordan,

Singh and Repp (1989) evaluated the claims of gentle teaching by comparing it with (aversive) facial screening in terms of its effectiveness, in terms of reducing stereotypy and developing 'bonding'. The study showed that, for the three participants, visual screening coupled with task training suppressed stereotypy more successfully than gentle teaching. Furthermore, 'bonding' occurred at the same (low) level under both treatments.

The key to much of the data-based debate lies in the question of whether, for the thankfully few people who show life-threatening behaviour, or behaviours which are chronic in character and seriously limiting, non-aversive procedures alone can be effective. There is no disagreement on the necessity to use such procedures, but will they work without additional aversive procedures? This question may be unanswerable—certainly the answer is at present unclear.

'Aversives': Failure to respect the professional integrity of others

Possibly the most disturbing aspect of the aversives debate is the questioning of the motives or moral values of people who use, or have used, aversive procedures. Matson (1988) has commented on 'a McCarthy style approach to philosophy and service': being in favour of using non-aversives is something none would disagree with, therefore to use them—for whatever reason—must be wrong. He claims the blacklisting of people and topics and distortions concerning his professional conduct. Mulick (1990) cites guilt by association in the Guess et al.'s (1987) 'gratuitous comparison' of the use of aversive stimuli in research studies with reprehensible political repression. He points out that this 'torture analogy' deliberately obscures the moral and practical distinctions between political crime and the actions of professionals motivated by a desire to ameliorate suffering and enhance independent functioning. Iwata (1988) describes his involvement in the development of an automated device to reduce extreme self-injury which both delivers aversive, and cues positively reinforcing, stimuli. He reports that the debate over his involvement has been conducted largely indirectly; most of his critics have refused to reply to communications or meet him. Instead, portions of his communications to them, selected out of context, led to further allegations.

This situation is nothing short of tragic. In an area of service delivery where the people to be served are amongst the most vulnerable in society, attacks on the morals of others, rather than urgent debate based on principles and on clearly presented data, surely have no place at all. However, it would be vain to enter the plea that people should get together to sort things out. The degree to which ideology has consumed reason appears to be so great that no immediate solutions offer themselves.

CONCLUSION

This chapter has tried to present an account of some of the controversies surrounding normalization and its relation to behavioural intervention within the context of the ethics of treatment of people with mental handicap. Several major issues emerged. It seems clear that, in their attempts to ensure the wide dissemination of applied behaviour analytic methods, interventionists achieved substantial successes. They may, however, also have inadvertently created the conditions for misuse of techniques and possibly for 'mechanistic' staff perceptions of client groups. They naively assumed that the professional ethics of people using behavioural techniques would always be appropriate. In fact, the problems which behavioural interventionists met may be inherent in any 'package' approach to staff training. Certainly the packaging of normalization into short courses can be seen as at least in part responsible for distortions of the concept of choice described earlier in the chapter.

Normalization and applied behaviour analysis conflict because the former contains some absolute principles—for example the right to presence and participation—which are of a different order from any statement arising out of applied behaviour analysis. These are ethical absolutes, and if they are to influence treatment decisions they must be recognized as such. There is simply not enough evidence to justify the argument that the balance of goods and harms will clearly indicate that community presence and participation for all people with mental handicap will inevitably come down in favour of integrated as opposed to segregated provision. An applied behaviour analyst, operating with the framework outlined above, could quite well recommend segregated provision for a particular individual, given present evidence for and against integrated provision.

In practice, this conflict seems to be resolvable in two ways. Where there is an equal balance of goods and harms between a treatment plan in the community and one in a segregated facility, the practitioner operating within normalization philosophy could choose the community alternative. The other strategy for resolution involves prioritizing amongst the 'service accomplishments' and arguing, for example, that for an individual personal choice and development of competence are more important than presence and participation. This solution then becomes indistinguishable from the position adopted by Van Houten *et al.*, in that 'freedom of individual movement and access to preferred activities, rather than type of location of placements, are the defining characteristics of a least restrictive environment' (1988, p. 382). This type of solution is clearly embodied in Wolfensberger's (1983) endorsement of L'Arche communities which, although essentially segregated, emphasize enhanced acceptance and respect for people with mental handicap. Prioritization amongst service accomplishments clearly makes normalization philosophy more flexible and realistic. The strategy also brings it more in line with the formulation of behaviour analytically focused treatment plans. However, in rejecting absolute solutions, it must place the burden of judging individual cases on the professionals involved, and has the potential for generating conflict amongst professionals if there is no consensus on the weighting of accomplishments.

Normalization philosophy reflects elements of a social constructionalist viewpoint. However, it is not the explicit opposition of applied behaviour analysis and social constructionalist elements which have created conflict. Conflict has arisen because people working within a normalization tradition have identified misuse of techniques as attributable to the techniques themselves rather than the ethics of those using them. In addition, there have been attacks arising from the argument that behaviour analysts lack sympathy. The argument has two levels. At one level, it is clearly presumptuous to conclude that, because someone adopts a particular approach, they inevitably have inadequate feelings for and on behalf of the people they treat. The other level is more subtle and relates, in the end, to empirical evidence. Social constructionalists would argue that mental handicap can best be understood from their viewpoint and that, because applied behaviour analysis approaches the phenomenon of mental handicap from a different perspective, it cannot yield the same understandings. However, the crucial question here is whether social constructionalists can show that their theoretical perspective leads to more effective treatment of, for example, severe problem behaviour. As yet, there appears to be no clear evidence bearing on this issue.

Many of these issues are central to the aversives debate, and here positions have become so entrenched that it seems likely that people with mental handicap run the risk of being the ultimate losers. There are some lessons to be learned from this account. It indicates the dangers of too rapid dissemination of new concepts and technologies. It also proposes that differing theoretical viewpoints be clearly distinguished from professional ethics. The account leads to the suggestion that the relative utility of different theories needs to be more clearly assessed. This comparison needs to be made against clear criteria about which different professionals can agree or disagree. These strategies need to be adopted unless the field is to descend into further misunderstandings and personal acrimony.

Address for correspondence

Chris Kiernan, Hester Adrian Research Centre, University of Manchester, Manchester M13 9PL, UK.

REFERENCES

Axelrod, S. and Apsche, J. (1983) *The Effects of Punishment on Human Behavior*, Academic Press, New York.

Azrin, N.H. and Holz, W.C. (1966) Punishment. In W.K. Honig (ed.), *Operant Behavior: Areas of Research and Application*, Appleton–Century–Crofts, New York.

Balla, D. and Zigler, E. (1979) Personality development in retarded persons. In N.R. Ellis (ed.), *Handbook of Mental Deficiency, Psychological Theory and Research*, Erlbaum, Hillsdale, New Jersey.

Balsam, P.D. and Bondy, A.S. (1983) The negative side effects of reward. *Journal of Applied Behavior Analysis*, **16**, 283–296.

Bank-Mikkelson, N. (1980) Denmark. In R.J. Flynn and K.E. Nitsch (eds), *Normalization, Social Integration and Community Services*, Pro-Ed, Austin, Texas.

Beauchamp, T.L. and McCullough, L.B. (1984) *Medical Ethics*, Prentice-Hall, Englewood Cliffs, New Jersey.

Bijou, S. (1966) A functional analysis of retarded development. In N.R. Ellis (ed.), *International Review of Research in Mental Retardation* (Vol. 7), Academic Press, London.

Birnbrauer, J.S., Wolf, M.M., Kidder, J.D. and Tague, C.E. (1965) Classroom behavior of retarded pupils with token reinforcement. In H.N. Sloane and B.D. MacAulay (eds), *Operant Procedures in Remedial Speech and Language Training*, Houghton Mifflin, Boston.

Bricker, W.A. (1972) A systematic approach to language training. In R.L. Schiefelbusch (ed.), *Language and the Mentally Retarded*, University Park Press, Baltimore.

Buber, M. (1958) *I–Thou*, Scribner, New York.

Budde, J.F. and Menolascino, F.J. (1971) Systems technology and retardation: Application to vocational habilitation. *Mental Retardation*, **9**, 11–16.

Carr, E.G. (1977) The motivation of self-injurious behavior: A review of some hypotheses. *Psychological Bulletin*, **84**, 800–816.

Emerson, E. (1990) What is normalisation? In H. Brown and H. Smith (eds), *Normalisation: A Reader for the 1990s*, Routledge, London.

Guess, D., Sailor, W., Keogh, W. and Baer, D. (1976) Language development programs for severely handicapped children. In N. Haring and L. Brown (eds), *Teaching The Severely Handicapped: A Yearly Publication* (Vol. 1), Grune & Stratton, New York.

Guess, D., Helmstatter, E., Turnbull, H.R. and Knowlton, S. (1987) *Use of Aversives with People who are Disabled: An Historical Review and Critical Analysis*, Association for Persons with Severe Handicaps, Seattle.

Gunzberg, H.C. (1970) The hospital as a normalising training environment. *Journal of Mental Subnormality*, **16**, 71–83.

Gunzberg, H.C. and Gunzberg, A.L. (1987) *Mental Handicap and Physical Environment*, Ballière Tindall, London.

Hamblin, R.L., Buckholdt, D., Ferritor, D., Kozloff, M. and Blackwell, L. (1971) *The Humanization Processes: A Social, Behavioral Analysis of Children's Problems*, Wiley, New York.

HMSO (1980) *Report of a Working Party on Behaviour Modification*, London.

Hollis, J.H. and Meyers, C.E. (1982) *Life-Threatening Behavior*, American Association on Mental Deficiency, Washington, DC.

Horner, R.D. (1980) The effect of an environmental 'enrichment' program on the behaviour of institutionalized profoundly retarded children. *Journal of Applied Behavior Analysis*, **13**, 473–491.

Iwata, B.A. (1988) The development and adoption of controversial default technologies. *Behavior Analyst.*, **11**, 149–157.

Jordan, J., Singh, N.N. and Repp, A.C. (1989) An evaluation of gentle teaching and visual screening in the reduction of stereotypy. *Journal of Applied Behavior Analysis*, **22**, 9–22.

Kiernan, C.C. (1974) Behaviour modification. In A.M. Clarke and A.D.B. Clarke (eds), *Mental Deficiency: The Changing Outlook* (3rd edn), Methuen, London.

Kiernan, C.C. (1985) Behaviour modification. In A.M. Clarke, A.D.B. Clarke and J.M. Berg (eds), *Mental Deficiency: The Changing Outlook* (4th edn), Methuen, London.

Lancioni, G.E. and Hoogeven, F.R. (1990) Non-aversive and mildly aversive procedures for reducing problem behaviours in people with developmental disorders. *Mental Handicap Research*, **3**, 137–160.

LaVigna, G. and Donnellan, A.M. (1986) *Alternatives to Punishment: Solving Behavior Problems with Non-Aversive Strategies*, Irvington, New York.

Lovett, H. (1985) *Cognitive Counselling and Persons with Special Needs*, Praeger, New York.

Matson, J.L. (1988) Setting the record straight, *AAMR News and Notes*, **1**, 3.

McGee, J.J., Menousek, P.E. and Hobbs, D.C. (1987) Gentle teaching: An alternative to punishment with people with challenging behaviors. In S.J. Taylor, D. Biklen and J. Knoll (eds), *Community Integration for People with Severe Disabilities*, Teachers College Press, New York.

McGee, J.J., Menolascino, F.J., Hobbs, D.C. and Menousek, P.E. (1987) *Gentle Teaching: A Non-Aversive Approach to Helping Persons with Mental Retardation*, Human Sciences Press, New York.

Mulick, J.A. (1988) Book review. *Research in Developmental Disabilities*, **9**, 317–327.

Mulick, J.A. (1990) The ideology and science of punishment in mental retardation. *American Journal on Mental Retardation*, **95**, 142–156.

Nirje, B. (1969) The normalization principle and its human management implications. In R.B. Kugel and W. Wolfensberger (eds), *Changing Patterns in Residential Services for the Mentally Retarded*, Presidential Committee on Mental Retardation, Washington, DC.

Nirje, B. (1980) The normalization principle. In R.J. Flynn and K.E. Nitsch (eds), *Normalization, Social Integration and Community Services*, University Park Press, Baltimore.

O'Brien, J. (1987) A guide to life style planning: Using the activities catalogue to integrate services and natural support systems. In B.W. Wilcox and G.T. Bellamy (eds), *The Activities Catalogue: An Alternative Curriculum for Youth and Adults with Severe Disabilities*, Brookes, Baltimore.

O'Brien, J. and Tyne, A. (1981) *The Principle of Normalization: A Foundation for Effective Services*, Campaign for Mentally Handicapped People, London.

O'Leary, K.D. (1972) Behavior modification in the classroom: A rejoinder to Winnett and Winkler. *Journal of Applied Behavior Analysis*, 5, 505–511.

Premack, D. (1971) Catching up with common sense or two sides of a generalization: Reinforcement and punishment. In R. Glaser (ed.), *The Nature of Reinforcement*, Academic Press, New York.

Qureshi, H. (1990) *Parents Caring for Young Adults with Mental Handicap and Behaviour Problems*. Final report to Department of Health, Hester Adrian Research Centre.

Risley, T.R. (1975) Certify people not procedures. In W.W. Wood (ed.), *Issues in Evaluating Behavior Modification*, Research Press, Champaign.

Shearer, A. (1974) Making the most of scarce resources: Sharing-consumer participation. *Residential Social Work*, 14, 354–357.

Skinner, B.F. (1957) *Verbal Behavior*, Appleton–Century–Crofts, New York.

Sumarah, J. (1989) Metaphors as means of understanding staff–resident relationships. *Mental Retardation*, 27, 19–23.

Tizard, J. (1975) Comment. In C.C. Kiernan and F.P. Woodward (eds), *Behaviour Modification with the Severely Retarded*, Elsevier, Amsterdam.

Van Houten, R., Axelrod, S., Bailey, J.S., Favell, J.E., Foxx, R.M., Iwata, B.A. and Lovaas, O.I. (1988) The right to effective behavioral treatment. *Journal of Applied Behavior Analysis*, 21, 381–384.

Vukelich, R. and Hake, D.F. (1971) Reduction of dangerously aggressive behaviour in a severely retarded resident through a combination of positive reinforcement procedures. *Journal of Applied Behavior Analysis*, 4, 215–225.

Williams, P. (1975) The development of social competence. In C.C. Kiernan and F.P. Woodward (eds), *Behaviour Modification with the Severely Retarded*, Elsevier, Amsterdam.

Winnett, R.A. and Winkler, R.C. (1972) Current behavior modification in the classroom: Be still, be quiet, be docile. *Journal of Applied Behavior Analysis*, 5, 499–504.

Wolfensberger, W. (1972) *The Principle of Normalization in Human Services*, National Institute on Mental Retardation, Toronto.

Wolfensberger, W. (1983) Social role valorization: A proposed new term for the principle of normalization. *Mental Retardation*, 21, 234–239.

Index